the ULTIMATE book of words STUDENTS SHOULD KNOW

the ULTIMATE book of words STUDENTS SHOULD KNOW

ROBERT W. BLY & BURTON JAY NADLER

AVON, MASSACHUSETTS

Published by
Adams Media, a division of F+W Media, Inc.
57 Littlefield Street, Avon, MA 02322. U.S.A.
www.adamsmedia.com

Contains material adapted and abridged from *Words You Should Know in High School* by Burton Jay Nadler, Jordan Nadler, and Justin Nadler, copyright © 2005 by Burton Jay Nadler, ISBN 10: 1-59337-294-9, ISBN 13: 978-1-59337-294-1; *The Words You Should Know to Sound Smart* by Robert W. Bly, copyright © 2009 by Robert W. Bly, ISBN 10: 1-59869-886-9, ISBN 13: 978-1-59869-886-2; *Test Words You Should Know* by P.T. Shank, copyright © 2006 by F+W Media, Inc., ISBN 10: 1-59337-521-2, ISBN 13: 978-1-59337-521-8.

ISBN 10: 1-4405-1057-1
ISBN 13: 978-1-4405-1057-1

Printed in the United States of America.

10 9 8 7 6 5 4 3 2 1

Library of Congress Cataloging-in-Publication Data
is available from the publisher.

CONTENTS

INTRODUCTION

IN THIS DAY AND AGE, words are perhaps more important than ever before. We are no longer just communicating with our neighbors, friends, and coworkers. Today, with Internet, e-mail, and even global businesses, we are communicating with people from all over the country, all over the world. One thing hasn't changed, however. The words we choose to express ourselves continue to be the strongest representation of who we are as individuals. Being able to express ourselves articulately continues to be one of the best ways we can present ourselves as intelligent, well-educated people.

Okay. Great. But how will this book help you? If you are studying for the SAT or the GRE standardized tests, the answer is relatively obvious. Every word in this book has been identified as one that you might encounter in the verbal sections of one, if not both, of those tests. Even if you are not studying for a standardized test, these words will increase your vocabulary and assist you in presenting yourself well.

The body of the text includes over 2,000 words that have a strong possibility of appearing on a standardized test. These words are defined in easy-to-understand language that won't leave you more confused than when you started. A pronunciation guide that actually makes sense and a sentence using the word correctly accompanies each entry. Along with the words, within the main body of the text, you will find helpful hints about word usage, definitions, and common mistakes.

So what makes this book different from other words books? The words in this book range from those that are probably refreshers for high school students to words that a professional who's been out of school for over a decade might never have run across. If you are in high school and want to increase your SAT scores or if you have been out of high school longer than you want to admit and simply want to learn a new word or two, I believe you will find words that challenge you and, hopefully, enjoy this book.

Yes, I said enjoy this book. Because words should be and can be fun. That's one of the hardest concepts for some people to grasp, and yet it is true. The more fun you can have with words, the easier it becomes to remember them and use them correctly. The goal of this book, as with its predecessors, is to help make words—even words for a standardized test—fun and easy to use. So, whether you are studying for a test or just reading for yourself, we hope you come to enjoy both the book and the words inside.

A NOTE ON THE PRONUNCIATION

Pronunciation keys given in this book are rendered phonetically, without using special symbols or systems.

Many of the words in this book have meanings and pronunciations—in addition to those listed here—that are entirely correct.

Regional influences can affect pronunciation of certain words. In this book, we use the most commonly accepted pronunciation or pronunciations for each word, recognizing that they are by no means the only acceptable pronunciations.

A NOTE ON THE SOURCES

In his book *The Meaning of Everything: The Story of the Oxford English Dictionary*, Simon Winchester observes that there are essentially three sources for the words in any dictionary: (1) words found in existing dictionaries; (2) words overheard in conversation; and (3) words found "by a concerted trawl through the text of literature."

This book is our attempt at a listing of all three sources.

doctrinaire
levity abstemious
hubris panacea
veracity cerebellum
criterion labyrinth
nonagenarian
meticulous zither

A

erbiage
colloquial quondam
vok palpable paginatio
incipient salutary
evity redact fervent
beleaguered yawnful
elixir beneficent

abash *(uh-BASH), verb*
To make another feel ashamed, embarrassed, uncomfortable, or humiliated. To make someone feel uncomfortable, including yourself, or to cause someone to lose composure.

Traditionally, high school athletes ABASH new team members; some call it rookie or freshmen hazing.

abate *(uh-BATE), verb*
To put an end to, diminish, or reduce something in intensity. To lessen or weaken another thing.

With a zit on your face, you may fear that your potential to date will rapidly ABATE.

abatement *(ah-BAIT-ment), noun*
The reduction or elimination of a tax, claim, fine, or debt.

By having her daddy pull strings in the mayor's office, Sylvia received a quick ABATEMENT of her traffic ticket.

abbreviate *(a-BREE-vee-ate), verb*
To shorten or condense by omitting letters or words

These days, not many people realize R.S.V.P. was originally used to ABBREVIATE the French phrase "répondez s'il vous plait," meaning "please reply."

abdicate *(AB-di-kate), verb*
To formally give up a position or responsibility; commonly, refers to royalty renouncing the throne. To step down from a high government office or other powerful position.

King Edward VIII, as you may know, ABDICATED the throne rather than give up the woman he loved.

aberrant *(aa-BER-ant), adjective*
Unusual from accepted or expected norms; unexpected in light of past behaviors

The girl knew her brother wanted something because of his ABERRANT friendly behavior.

abet *(AH-bet), verb*
To assist or urge another person, usually to do something illegal; to help commit a crime

She was shocked to learn that by simply driving him to the airport, she had ABETTED in the commission of a crime.

You often hear the phrase "aid and ABET" on crime shows like Law and Order.

Which Word?

Often, words look and/or sound almost identical, especially if you are unfamiliar with them. *Abet* (AH-bet) and *abut* (uh-BUT) can easily be confused, especially when you are reading quickly. Abet means to aid someone in a criminal act, and abut means to border or be on the edge. Remember to read carefully to catch words like these!

abeyance *(uh-BAY-ens), noun*

A temporary halt to an activity; a short suspension

The presentation was in ABEYANCE until the technical problems could be resolved.

abhor *(ab-HORE), verb*

To find something or someone loathsome, contemptible, reprehensible, or repulsive. While it rhymes with *adore,* this word means quite the opposite.

Many ABHOR reality shows that feature plastic surgery because they find the visual images detestable and the topic contemptible.

abide (*uh-BIDE), verb*

To patiently wait or tolerate. To abide is to endure; to bear or accept a person or condition; to withstand or persevere. In the old days, it meant to live or reside in a place; one would "abide" in an "abode." While you may abide someone or something, you really don't want that person or thing by your side.

Sitters can only ABIDE the constant whining of misbehaving children for so long before they threaten to call their parents.

abject *(AB-jekt), adjective*

Allowing no hope of improvement or relief. In a state of hopelessness, destitution, or resignation. Describes the most miserable kind of situation; the most wretched or degraded person or thing. Can also mean extremely humble, as in an apology or request. Rather than feeling pity, some might object to an abject thing or person.

Many spring break partiers are not aware that in many Caribbean countries, ABJECT poverty is often found side-by-side with luxury hotels, spas, and resort properties.

abjure *(ab-JOOR), verb*

To recant, take back, or publicly give up previously held thoughts, opinions, or beliefs

Thomas More's refusal to ABJURE his Catholic beliefs eventually cost him his life.

When taking the U.S. oath of citizenship, one must ABJURE allegiance to any other nation.

ablution *(ab-LOO-shun), noun*
The act of washing oneself usually for a ritual or as part of a religious rite

The surgeon considered scrubbing up not only hygienic but an act of ABLUTION that helped prepare her mentally for her work.

Getting pushed into the gym pool and yelling "Holy cow, that's cold!" doesn't count as an ABLUTION.

abnegate *(AB-ne-gate), verb*
To renounce something or deny it to yourself, in particular something considered vital or important, such as food in the case of a hunger strike. To give up, as in rights or claims.

Stephanie ABNEGATED fried food and soda before the prom, hoping to fit into her newly purchased dress.

abominate *(Uh-BOM-in-ate), verb*
When you *abominate* something, you really, really hate and dislike it—and view it with considerable loathing.

Mary ABOMINATED Brussels sprouts and refused to eat them, despite her mother's pleas.

Know This Quote
"For my part, I ABOMINATE all honorable respectable toils, trials, and tribulations of every kind whatsoever." —Herman Melville, American author

aboriginal *(a-buh-RIDGE-ih-nul), adjective*
Indigenous or native; something that existed first, or an area's first inhabitants. Used in reference to the Aborigines of Australia. The root "original" is part of this word and communicates much of the meaning of "aboriginal."

In most cases, ABORIGINAL people sadly have little or no say in issues related to their original homeland.

abortive *(uh-BOR-tive), adjective*
Failing to reach completion; unsuccessful or fruitless.

Apollo 13 was the most famous ABORTIVE mission of the U.S. space program.

abrade *(uh-BRADE), verb*
To wear away, rub off, or erode through friction. For example, over time, a wood post will abrade a braided rope. Also, to break or wear down in a spiritual sense.

In the past, revelations about infidelity ABRADED voter support for candidates, but now such character traits don't seem that important.

abridge *(uh-BRIJ), verb*

To shorten a text without changing the meaning of the document

Over the years, many students have appreciated others' ability to ABRIDGE some of the longer literary works required in English classes.

abrogate (*AB-ruh-gayt), verb*

To cancel or remove by a person of authority

So many officers had abused the power of the position, it was finally ABROGATED and the authority for decisions split up among several different departments.

The two business partners agreed to ABROGATE their contract after they discovered their venture was no longer profitable.

abscond *(ab-SKOND), verb*

To run away; to leave in a hurry and in secret to avoid detection or arrest

The plan was to ABSCOND with the money and to retire, drinking margaritas on the beach.

The plan was to rob the jewelry store, ABSCOND to a safe location, and later fence the goods.

absolve *(ab-ZOLV), verb*

To publicly or formally pronounce someone guiltless and blameless. To release someone from any responsibility for an alleged misdeed or, for a priest, to forgive them of sins. When a crime is solved, some are absolved, while the guilty parties are arrested or jailed.

Over the objections of the district attorney, the judge ABSOLVED the accused of all charges.

abstemious *(ab-STEE-mee-us), adjective*

To actively avoid being self-indulgent, especially when eating or drinking

After a particularly wild night, he decided to be more ABSTEMIOUS in the future when it came to alcohol.

In these days of conspicuous consumption, it is harder to find individuals following an ABSTEMIOUS lifestyle.

abstinence *(AB-sti-nans), noun*

The practice of avoiding certain specific behaviors

Some health professionals believe that encouraging ABSTINENCE from sex while teaching about condoms is a legitimate and effective way to reduce the spread of STDs.

abstract *(AB-strakt), adjective*

Not based in fact or absolute existence; based in thought, idea, or theory

He prided himself on the fact that his students not only learned names and dates but could also grasp more ABSTRACT concepts by the end of the term.

abstruse *(ab-TROOS), adjective*

Confusing; not easy to understand; muddled and unclear

The dean thought the professor's teaching style was intentionally and unnecessarily ABSTRUSE.

After the first few classes, Jack thought calculus was an ABSTRUSE collection of abstract ideas, and at the end of the semester, he realized his initial impressions were correct.

abut *(uh-BUT), verb*

To be next to; to share a border; to come to the edge of something else

They were pleased their new property would ABUT a national park, so no one could build too close to them.

a capella *(ah kuh-PEH-la), adjective*

Without accompaniment from musical instruments, usually in reference to singing, often in a rhythmic and inventive vocal style. Don't try out to be the pianist for an a capella group, because you won't get the job.

Singing groups are so popular at that college that every weekend brings at least one A CAPELLA concert.

accede *(ak-SEED), verb*

To take or rise to office or position of authority; or to agree to a demand

Gerald Ford never dreamed that he would ACCEDE to the office of President of the United States.

The police recommended the family ACCEDE to the ransom demands.

It is the policy of the U.S. government to never ACCEDE to the demands of terrorists.

accentuate *(ak-SEN-shoo-ate), verb*

To make a feature of something more noticeable. To put emphasis on a syllable, word, or phrase. To strengthen or heighten the effect of something. Comedians sometimes accentuate accents to get laughs.

The architects determined that large bay windows would ACCENTUATE the colonial style of the new home.

accessible *(ak-SESS-uh-bul), adjective*

Easily approached, reached, or entered

The developers knew the plaza had to be interesting, fun, and ACCESSIBLE for the project to succeed.

acclaim *(uh-KLAYM), verb or noun*

To praise loudly (verb) or loud and public praise (noun)

The critical ACCLAIM for her work made her hopeful for an award nomination.

Even other scientists ACCLAIMED his work as the breakthrough that would change the way doctors treated illnesses.

Which Word?

Many words are virtually synonymous—their definitions seem identical. However, they cannot always be used in exactly the same way. Just because they are similar doesn't mean they are interchangeable. *Acclaim* (uh-KLAYM) and *accolade* (AA-koh-layd) are two of these words. Use the word acclaim when you are referring to words of praise. An accolade, on the other hand, may be words of praise or something more tangible, such as a prize or an award. Be aware of the subtle differences between words that seem the same and you'll be sure to choose the right one.

accolade *(AA-koh-layd), noun*

Any word, token, or prize given in appreciation, usually formal

As nice as the official ACCOLADE from the school was, his father's look of pride meant more.

Students who enroll in Ivy League schools usually have a history of ACCOLADES and academic achievements.

Where'd That Word Come From?

Accolade—In medieval times, men were knighted in a ceremony called the *accolata* (from the Latin *ac,* "at," and *collum,* "neck"), named for the hug around the neck received during the ritual, which also included a kiss and tap of a sword on the shoulder. From *accolata,* we get the English word *accolade* for an award or honor.

accrue *(uh-CRUE), verb*

To gather over a period of time; accumulate or grow. To realize an increase or accumulation by gradual means. A crew can accrue possessions in a week, or maybe two.

Money held in a bank will ACCRUE interest over time.

acculturation *(ah-kul-cherr-AYE-shin), noun*

The process of adapting to a different culture.

Just because sushi makes me queasy, that doesn't mean I'm opposed to ACCULTURATION.

acerbic *(AA-ser-bik), adjective*
Blunt, bitter, and sarcastic, usually regarding a personal attitude or way of speaking

She knew underneath her grandfather's ACERBIC persona beat the heart of a teddy bear.

acquiesce *(ak-wee-ESS), verb*
To accept reluctantly but without complaint; to give in

He decided to ACQUIESCE to his girlfriend's request that he wear a suit rather than face her hurt silence.

acrid *(AK-rid), adjective*
Sharp, bitter, unpleasant; generally describing a taste or smell

The ACRID smell throughout the science wing was a telltale sign something had burned in the lab.

Her anger was released in the ACRID remarks she hurled at her father.

acrimonious *(ah-kri-MOAN-ee-us), adjective*
Angry; bitter; disputed. "Acrid" and "acrimonious" have the same first four letters as well as similar meanings.

Billy and Mary's argument over where they should go for dinner was more ACRIMONIOUS than their friends expected.

ACRIMONIOUS marriages cause stress and anxiety for all involved and inevitably end in divorce.

Know This Quote

"There is something about the literary life that repels me, all this desperate building of castles on cobwebs, the long-drawn ACRIMONIOUS struggle to make something important which we all know will be gone forever in a few years . . . ." —Raymond Chandler, American author

acrimony *(AK-rhi-mo-nee), noun*
Bitterness, anger, bad feelings, usually mutually held

The bride's parents agreed to set aside their feelings of ACRIMONY in order to keep the wedding day peaceful.

acronym *(a-kroh-NIM), noun*
A word that is formed from the initials or other parts of several words, such as NATO (for "North Atlantic Treaty Organization").

GIGO is an ACRONYM that computer programmers created to stand for the phrase "garbage in, garbage out."

acrophobia *(a-croh-FO-bee-a), noun*
An irrational fear of high places, characterized by feelings of dread, danger, and helplessness.

It's almost impossible to find a roofer with ACROPHOBIA, at least one who isn't unemployed.

acumen *(AA-kyoo-men), noun*
The ability to make wise decisions in a particular area or profession

He was well-respected, even early in his career, for his obvious business ACUMEN.

Laurie was said to have great business ACUMEN because every venture she became involved in quickly turned a profit.

acute *(a-CUTE), adjective*
Extremely serious, painful, sharp, shrewd, perceptive, or severe. Keenly perceptive, intellectual, and sensitive to details. Also used in reference to a disease that is severe and quick to crisis.

Most teenage girls have ACUTE skills when it comes to identifying a cute boy; it's like a form of radar.

ad hoc *(ad HOK), adjective*
Set up in response to a particular situation or problem; not focused on general issues. Formed for immediate or specific need. From the Latin meaning "for this purpose."

As a response to student concerns, an AD HOC committee was formed to investigate the current dress code.

ad infinitum (*ad in-fi-NEYE-tum), adjective*
Forever, or for so long as to seem endless. This Latin phrase translates as "to infinity." Can be used to describe some lectures given by parents or teachers.

After reading an initial draft of the speech, the candidate's aide commented that the speech rambled on AD INFINITUM, and so it was thoroughly edited.

ad nauseam *(ad NAW-zee-um), adverb*
Something that goes on and on, or is done over and over again, to a ridiculous, even sickening degree.

At first we were all impressed that Steve could recite the entire Gettysburg Address, but we all got kind of sickened when he repeated the feat AD NAUSEAM.

adage *(AD-ij), noun*
A short saying or old phrase that states an accepted truth. Examples of these brief, commonly accepted expressions include "A stitch in time saves nine" and "Actions speak louder than words."

Many ADAGES currently in use were originally penned by Benjamin Franklin.

Though it is a cliché, athletes are fond of quoting the ADAGE, "We'll take one game at a time."

adamant *(AD-uh-ment), adjective*
Insistent; refusing to change one's mind; determined

Even though the actress was sick, she was ADAMANT about going on with the performance.

Despite the concerns of his parents, Steve was ADAMANT about not attending college after graduating from high school.

addendum *(a-DEN-duhm), noun*
Something added, or a supplement to a book or magazine. If you are addin' 'em, it's an addendum.

No matter how thorough the committee's report was, someone always wanted to suggest an ADDENDUM.

adept *(a-DEPT), adjective*
Highly proficient, skilled, or expert.

The league's most valuable player was ADEPT at hitting home runs, particularly with men on base late in the game.

adjudicate (*a-DJOO-di-cate), verb*
To reach a judicial decision. To use an official procedure to hear and settle a case, usually within a legal setting. A judge tried the case, so he could adjudicate.

Those on the Supreme Court ADJUDICATE only the most difficult cases and only those with constitutional implications.

admonition *(ad-MON-ish-shun), noun*
An official warning; a scolding, usually followed by the threat of greater punishment for another offense

The vice principal let the vandal go with detention and an ADMONITION not to do it again or she would be expelled.

adroit *(a-DROIT), adjective*
Endowed with physical or mental skills. Ingenious, nimble, expert, or skillful; adept at accomplishing a goal.

Michael Jordan, a supremely ADROIT basketball player, wasn't nearly as skilled when he played minor league baseball.

adulation *(ad-dyoo-LAY-shun), noun*
Excessive flattery; deep love and affection

Some public figures become so accustomed to the ADULATION of their fans that retirement is difficult.

adulatory *(ad-JYOO-lah-tore-ee), adjective*
Complimentary; giving of effusive praise.

The way Susan spoke about her friend's wedding dress was amazingly ADULATORY.

Know This Quote

"He includes in his final chapter a passage of ADULATORY prose from Henry James." —Joyce Carol Oates, American author

adulterate *(uh-DUL-ter-ayt), verb*
To lower the quality of something by adding another substance

Her father could never understand why she chose to ADULTERATE her coffee by adding cream and sugar.

adumbrate *(AAD-um-brayt), verb*
To explain very briefly; to outline the high points

The outline was supposed to ADUMBRATE the research paper.

adversary *(AAD-ver-sayr-ree), noun*
Opponent; someone on the other side of an argument or competition

History teaches us that even ADVERSARIES can come to respect one another's skills on the battlefield.

adversity *(AAD-vers-ih-tee), noun*
Trouble; misfortune; difficulty; a time of personal trials and challenges

She considered herself lucky to have had a relatively easy childhood instead of one filled with ADVERSITY and hardship.

advocate *(AAD-vuh-kut), noun or (AAD-voh-kayt), verb*
A person who publicly speaks for or on behalf of another (noun) or to speak for or on behalf of another; to argue or speak in favor of something (verb)

As a mother, she knew she must act as an ADVOCATE for all children, not just her own.

The panel was moved listening to the doctor ADVOCATE for patients' rights.

Which Word?

Many words can be used as either a noun or a verb. Advocate is one of them. The verb to advocate is pronounced (AAD-voh-kayt) and means to speak for and help another person. The non advocate is pronounced (AAD-vuh-kut) and is the person doing the speaking for and helping of another person. Therefore, an advocate's job is to advocate for his clients. Be sure to pay attention to the context of the word so you don't get the verb confused with the noun!

aegis *(AYE-jis), noun*
The protection, support, and help rendered by a guardian, supporter, backer, or mentor.

Jill thinks she's above reproach because she's under the AEGIS of that marketing vice-president with a penchant for younger women.

aesthetic (*ahs-THEH-tik), adjective*
Regarding beauty and/or enjoyable appearance; pleasing to the senses

For AESTHETIC reasons, the girls enjoyed having the football team warm up outside their dorm.

affable *(AAF-uh-bul), adjective*
Friendly; likeable; easy to get along with

His AFFABLE nature meant he made friends all over campus even though he was only a freshman.

affectation *(ah-fek-TAY-shun) noun*
Behaviors or mannerisms that are exaggerated, extreme, eccentric, and deliberately showy, often an effort to attract attention.

When her boyfriend started to pay attention to the other girls at the roller skating rink, Maria's behavior started to show signs of AFFECTATION.

Know This Quote
"AFFECTATION is awkward and forces imitation of what should be genuine and easy." —John Locke, British philosopher

affinity *(uh-FI-nih-tee), noun*
A natural attraction or inherent similarity between two people or things. To be similar in structure or closely connected, as with ideas or concepts.

Dr. Seuss's AFFINITY for rhyming words resulted in much happiness for several generations of children.

affirmation *(AA-fur-may-shun), noun*
A statement or declaration of support or acceptance; a statement of agreement

The student body president's AFFIRMATION of the school's new homework policy was necessary for it to pass through the student government.

afflatus *(uh-FLAY-tuss), noun*
Inspiration that seems to come from divine origin.

The Nobel Prize-winning novelist attributed her abilities to AFFLATUS, rather than to her own abilities.

aficionado *(uh-fish-ee-uh-NAH-doe), noun*
A devotee, someone who is enthralled with and supports a particular activity.

Dwight often refers to himself as an AFICIONADO of American-made microbrews.

aggrandize *(uh-GRAN-dize), verb*

To increase the size, scope, power, wealth, status, or influence of someone or something. To make someone or something appear bigger or better, often through exaggerated praise. You can *aggrandize* a guy's ego to a grand size.

The boxer Muhammad Ali was known to AGGRANDIZE his own abilities, just before pulverizing his opponents.

aggravate *(AAG-gruh-vayt), verb*

To make something worse; to exacerbate a situation; to annoy or frustrate

Picking at a scab will only AGGRAVATE it, not make it heal faster.

aggregate *(AAG-gruh-gut), noun*

A whole or total, usually made up of unexpected or disparate parts

Individually, the team members were a motley crew of different personalities and temperaments, but taken in AGGREGATE, they were talented and effective.

agile *(AA-jyl), adjective*

Being able to move quickly and easily; light on one's feet; having quick reflexes

She learned quickly that being AGILE was her most important asset when babysitting the rambunctious child.

agog *(AH-gog), adjective*

Eager, excited, in anticipation of

The young woman was AGOG at the thought of seeing New York City for the first time.

akimbo *(ah-KIM-bo), adverb*

With hands on hips and elbows turned outward.

When my father gets really mad, he stands stock-still, arms AKIMBO, and slowly turns red in the face.

akin *(uh-KIN), adjective*

Related by blood. Similar or closely related to someone or something; related by common features or qualities. A "kin" is "akin" to a family member.

Jodi's constant exaggerations were AKIN to lies, but she believed they were just embellishments.

alacrity *(uh-LA-krih-tee), noun*

Promptness; eager and speedy readiness. Action characterized by speed and politeness.

Mark's ALACRITY when a call came for help was always appreciated.

albeit *(al-BEE-it), conjunction*
Though.

Vickie thought Charles was dim-witted, ALBEIT cute, in a childlike way.

alchemy *(AL-khem-ee), noun*
The ancient, scientific study of trying to turn one substance into another, specifically metal into gold

The practice of ALCHEMY seems foolish today but it was once considered a legitimate science.

alcove *(AL-kohv), noun*
A small cut-out or deeper area, usually in a room

The small studio seemed larger than it was due to the ALCOVE for the bed and the large windows that let in light.

aleatory *(AIL-ee-ah-tore-ee), adjective*
An action that is unplanned, spontaneous, or spur of the moment rather than deliberately though out and carefully considered; an outcome that is anything but certain and depends on luck, randomness, or chance.

"Of course you lost the election!" Miranda yelled. "An ALEATORY, fly-by-the-seat-of-your-pants campaign is never going to be a recipe for success!"

allay *(uh-LAY), verb*
To calm a strong emotion like anger, fear, or suspicion. To relieve, ease, or reduce pain or painful feelings.

The CEO met with the entire staff to ALLAY their fears regarding possible layoffs and firings.

allegory *(AL-eh-gor-ee), noun*
A story told to communicate a hidden meaning or deeper theme.

Many of the Grimm Brothers' fairy tales are clear ALLEGORIES of the consequences of children's rotten behavior.

alleviate (*uh-LEE-vee-ayt), verb*
To reduce, lessen, or make less severe

He took yoga classes in order to ALLEVIATE stress and improve his overall physical as well as mental health.

alliteration *(ah-lit-ter-AYE-shun), noun*
The repetition of similar sounds, especially at the beginnings of words, in written speech or the spoken word.

I'd forgotten how much Alicia likes to use ALLITERATION in her insults, but I was reminded quickly when she called me a cruel, callous cretin.

allude *(uh-LOOD), verb*
To refer to someone or something without using a name or identification, while still making clear who or what is being referenced. To make passing reference. Sometimes it's best to allude to a dude, but not use his name, for it would be crude.

Politicians often ALLUDE to their "esteemed opponent," and everyone knows exactly who they mean.

aloof *(uh-LOOF), adjective*
Emotionally cold, distant, or withdrawn

Most people thought he was stuck-up and ALOOF when really he was just very shy.

altruistic *(al-TROO-is-tik), adjective*
Selfless; concerned for the greater good

The family refused to take their ALTRUISTIC donations off their taxes because they felt it would demean the gift.

amalgamate *(uh-MAL-guh-mate), verb*
To combine two or more groups into a whole, or to join multiple things together to form a unified unit. In technical terms, to alloy or unite a metal with mercury.

Anticipating that the two departments would soon AMALGAMATE, the members held several strategic planning meetings.

amatory *(AM-uh-tore-ee), adjective*
Having to do with sexual love.

Pete hasn't stopped sulking since Alice spurned his AMATORY advances at the office Christmas party.

ambiance *(AWM-bee-awnce), noun*
The typical atmosphere, feeling, or mood of a place.

The new restaurant became popular for its AMBIANCE as well as for its food and drink.

ambidextrous *(am-BEE-deks-truss), adjective*
Able to use either the right or the left hand equally well

Although I can write my name with my left hand, I am in no way AMBIDEXTROUS.

Where'd That Word Come From?

Ambidextrous—This word combines two Latin roots: *ambi-*, meaning "both," and *dexter*, meaning "right." The word therefore implies that being ambidextrous gives you two right hands, as the right hand has long been thought to be superior to the left. You might think of this word as the complete opposite of saying someone has two left feet, an expression for clumsiness.

ambiguity *(am-bih-GYOO-ih-tee), noun*
Uncertainty; lacking clear definition.

Poets who revel in AMBIGUITY are one of the reasons many people hate poetry.

ambiguous *(am-BIG-yoo-us), adjective*
Having more than one possible meaning or interpretation; unclear and undecided

The rules on how to handle an abusive client were AMBIGUOUS so the staff members often had to use their own judgment and hope for the best.

ambivalence *(am-BIV-uh-lenss), noun*
The state of having strong yet conflicting feelings about the same situation or person

Breaking up with him should have been easy but she couldn't get past her own AMBIVALENCE about doing so.

amble *(AM-bul), verb*
To walk leisurely and slowly in a relaxed manner; to saunter or stroll.

Some tourists AMBLE up and down the boardwalk in Atlantic City, while others remain firmly in one seat, playing blackjack.

ameliorate *(uh-MEEL-yoh-rate), verb*
To improve or upgrade. To make better or put right. When an unacceptable state of affairs is changed for the better, it is said to have been ameliorated.

The marriage counselor's attempts to AMELIORATE conflicts between the Smiths were welcomed, but, unfortunately, they were not successful.

amenable *(uh-MEEN-ah-bul), adjective*
Responsive to suggestion; able to be swayed to do something

The class hoped the teacher would be AMENABLE to giving them another day to work on their research papers.

Students were AMENABLE to a new dress code if they were asked to give input when it was being decided.

amend *(uh-MEND), verb*
To formally change a document in order to improve or correct. To rectify or improve upon. To alter in face of new circumstances or information. If I amend, I mend the broken and make it better.

Representative Smith's expertise surfaced when she was asked to AMEND the appropriations bill in ways amenable to members of both parties.

amenity *(uh-ME-nih-tee), noun*
A useful, attractive, or pleasant feature. A service, manner, or feature that gives pleasure or satisfaction.

No longer satisfied with a minor AMENITY like a mint on the pillow, frequent guests at five-star hotels demand much more.

amiable *(AY-me-uh-bul), adjective*
Pleasant and friendly; cordial, with a happy disposition, and easy to get along with.

My friend Amy is able to get along with everyone because she is AMIABLE.

amicable *(AM-ik-ah-bul), adjective*
Friendly, nice; without serious disagreement

The landlord hoped to fill the apartments with people who were AMICABLE, relatively quiet, and tidy.

amorphous *(UH-mor-fus), adjective*
Without clear shape or form; undefined

Everyone involved was thrilled to see a thriving business grow from what started as an AMORPHOUS idea.

Know This Quote
"Of course the illusion of art is to make one believe that great literature is very close to life, but exactly the opposite is true. Life is AMORPHOUS, literature is formal." —Françoise Sagan, French novelist and playwright

anachronism *(ah-NAK-ruh-niz-em), noun*
A person, place, thing, or idea whose time has past, and that seems to belong to an earlier age.

His three record players—and the fact that he doesn't even know what an mp3 is—make Jim something of an ANACHRONISM.

anachronistic (*uh-NAK-kron-is-tik), adjective*
Based on another, earlier period in history; out of place in the present time

The idea of being a gentleman may seem ANACHRONISTIC but many women still appreciate the effort.

anagram *(A-nuh-GRAM), noun*
A word or phrase spelled from the rearranged letters of another word or phrase: "no more stars" is an *anagram* of "*astronomers.*"

ANAGRAMS can be used as memory devices and can also be enjoyed as fascinating word puzzles.

analogous (*uh-NAL-uh-gus), adjective*
Similar to; easily comparable; alike in core ways

Although their backgrounds were ANALOGOUS, they discovered they didn't agree on many issues.

anarchist *(AN-ar-kist), noun*
One who believes in, wants, and may work toward a society without government where the individuals are free from societal laws

Many teens consider themselves ANARCHISTS but it is usually because they don't understand the ramifications of a lawless society.

anathema *(uh-NA-theh-muh), noun*
Someone or something that is greatly disliked, detested, or shunned. Someone or something cursed, denounced, or excommunicated by a religious authority.

The events of the Holocaust are ANATHEMA to all moral and civilized human beings.

ancillary *(ANT-sih-luhr-ee), adjective*
In a position of secondary or lesser importance; subordinate. Responsible for providing support or performing support duties. For example, my Aunt Hillary is ancillary to my mom, but I still listen to her.

Those who serve in ANCILLARY roles are often unsung heroes and deserving of more kudos than they regularly receive.

androcentrism *(an-druh-SEN-tri-zum), noun*
An outlook that emphasizes a masculine point of view.

"Larry," Joan warned, "that ANDROCENTRISM may be all the rage in the locker room, but you'd better leave it out of our bedroom if you know what's good for you."

androgynous *(Ann-DRAH-gen-us), adjective*
Something or someone who is neuter—sexless; of indeterminate sex; or hermaphrodite (having characteristics of both a male and a female).

The models at fashion week were so ANDROGYNOUS that Katherine couldn't tell if the clothes were designed for men or women.

anecdote *(AN-ek-doht), noun*
A short, sometimes amusing retelling of an event

Some of my favorite memories involve sitting listening to my grandfather tell ANECDOTES about my father's childhood.

Which Word?

Words that look or sound almost identical can cause confusion, especially if they are unfamiliar. Anecdote (AN-ek-doht) and antidote (AN-tee-doht) are two commonly confused words. An anecdote is a humorous story, and an antidote is a medicinal cure. Just remember to read carefully!

anfractuous *(an-FRACK-chuh-wuss), adjective*
Full of windings and intricacies, like a good mystery novel.

The novel's ANFRACTUOUS plot worked on paper, but it became stupefyingly confusing—actually, just plain stupid—onscreen.

animadversion *(an-uh-mad-VER-zhun), noun*
Very harsh criticism that suggests disapproval of what is being criticized.

My boss's frequent ANIMADVERSIONS have led to high staff turnover.

animosity *(a-nih-MAW-sih-tee), noun*
Intense hostility toward a person or thing, usually taking the form of action. A bitter dislike directed at something or someone.

Clyde's first few months on the job were fine, but after he was transferred to a new department he came to harbor real ANIMOSITY toward his supervisor.

anomaly *(ah-NOM-ah-lee), noun*
Something unusual or out of the norm; unexpected based on previous actions or occurrences

Her poor grade on the test was an ANOMALY considering she was usually the professor's best student.

Know This Quote

"After a thousand meters of this broken-field walking, Mitsuno came upon an ANOMALY: a patch of sand perhaps ten meters square." —Fred Pohl and Thomas Thomas, American science fiction authors

anonymous (*uh-NON-uh-mus), adjective*
Unnamed; by an unknown person

Many authors use pseudonyms because they want to remain ANONYMOUS.

antagonist *(an-TAG-ohn-ist), noun*
One who is openly adversarial or hostile; an enemy

The substitute teacher was easily able to identify both the ANTAGONISTS and the studious kids in the class.

antebellum *(an-tih-BEH-luhm), adjective*
Pertaining to the period preceding a war, in particular the American Civil War. From the Latin for "before the war."

For those once held in slavery, the ANTEBELLUM period was not to be remembered with fond or romantic thoughts of Southern traditions.

antecedent *(AN-tih-SEE-dent), noun*
The thing that happened or existed before the thing or idea in question. A preceding trend, idea, fashion, or event.

The military Humvee all-terrain vehicle was the ANTECEDENT of the consumer vehicle so popular today.

antediluvian *(an-tee-deh-LOO-vee-ahn), adjective*
Old-fashioned to the point of being humorous; traditionally, during the time before the biblical flood

The senior partner decided it was time to retire when he realized the younger partners considered his ideas ANTEDILUVIAN.

antidisestablishmentarianism *(ant-eye-dis-es-STAB-lish-men-tarry-an-izm), noun*
A movement or protest against an established institution or authority.

No, Walter, bringing your own coffee to Starbuck's is not an example of ANTIDISESTABLISHMENTARIANISM. It's just foolish.

antidote *(AN-tee-doht), noun*
Cure for poison; anything that makes a person feel better

Her friends took her out dancing in the hopes a night out would be an ANTIDOTE for the funk she had been in all month.

antipathy *(an-TI-puh-thee), noun*
Anger, hostility, and aversion directed toward a particular person or thing. The object of someone's anger, hostility, or disgust.

His ANTIPATHY toward animals originated from an attack he experienced as a youth.

antiquated *(AN-tee-kway-ted), adjective*
Old-fashioned, often to the point of being obsolete

The plumbing in the old building was ANTIQUATED and needed to be replaced before the couple could move in.

antiquity *(an-TI-kwih-tee), noun*
Ancient history, especially ancient Greek or Roman civilization. *Antiquities* are decorative, valuable, or interesting objects that dates from ancient times.

Museums display the treasures of ANTIQUITY for all to enjoy.

antithesis *(an-TIH-theh-sus), noun*
Something that is in direct opposition to something else

The run-down motel was the ANTITHESIS of the luxury hotel they had hoped for on their honeymoon.

apartheid *(Ah-PAR-thide), noun*
South Africa's government-sanctioned policy of segregation and racial discrimination.

Since APARTHEID ended in 1994, South Africa has elected three native African presidents.

apathy *(AA-puth-ee), noun*
A notable lack of interest, emotional connection, or passion; indifference

Many people believe it is voter APATHY that causes election turnout to be so low.

aphorism *(A-fuh-rih-zum), noun*
A succinct saying that expresses an opinion or a general truth. A concise summation of opinion or wisdom, such as "People who live in glass houses should not throw stones, nor should they get dressed in their living rooms."

APHORISMS may seem oversimplified to some, but when you think about it, their basic wisdom is often quite striking.

aplomb *(uh-PLUM), noun*
Self-assurance and grace, especially when under pressure; the ability to handle oneself well in stressful situations

Her friends were impressed with her APLOMB when her ex-boyfriend brought a new girl to the party.

apocryphal *(uh-PO-krih-fuhl), adjective*
Probably not true, but widely believed to be so. Generally accepted or repeated as fact, though excluded from the official version of events. A story that is fabricated long after the fact is considered apocryphal. Did George Washington really have "a pocket full" after chopping down the cherry tree?

It is hard to believe that some still think that the Apollo missions, with men landing on the moon, are APOCRYPHAL.

apogee *(AA-poh-gee), noun*
The point in the moon's or a satellite's orbit at which it is furthest from the earth; the climax or culmination of a project or event

He knew presenting his dissertation would be the APOGEE in his quest to receive a Ph.D.

apoplectic *(ap-up-PLECK-tic), adjective*
An extremely agitated state of rage.

Emily's careless event planning make me so APOPLECTIC that I just want to step in and plan the luncheon myself.

apostasy *(A-PA-stah-see), noun*
The act of abandoning, ignoring, or openly flaunting an accepted principle or belief.

Walter's distrust of democracy was seem by some as APOSTASY.

Know This Quote

"It was his idea of grand APOSTASY to drive to the reform synagogue on the high holidays and park his pink-eye nag among the luxurious, whirl-wired touring cars of the rich." —Saul Bellow, American author

apostate *(ah-PAH-stayt), noun*
A person who rejects a religious or political belief

In countries without religious freedom, APOSTATES are usually outcasts.

apotheosis *(uh-PAH-thee-oh-sis), noun*
The raising of someone to divine status

Even many non-Catholics believe that the APOTHEOSIS of Mother Teresa from nun to saint is appropriate.

apparition *(aa-puh-RIH-shun), noun*
A phantom or ghostlike image

The girls thought they were being visited by an APPARITION but it was just their brother making shadows on the wall.

appease *(uh-PEEZ), verb*
To placate, calm, or satisfy a person by meeting his or her demands

He always wore his seatbelt when driving in order to APPEASE his mother.

appeasement *(ah-PEEZ-meant), noun*
The act of making others happy by agreeing to their demands.

Charlene realized too late that her policy of APPEASEMENT would not cause Warren to treat her with more respect.

appelation *(ah-pull-AYE-shun), noun*
A formal name, label, or title.

Even though he has only an honorary degree, he insists on being called by the APPELLATION of "doctor" everywhere he goes.

apposite *(AA-puh-zit), adjective*
Appropriate for the situation; completely suitable

The woman was relieved she had worn a dress instead of pants as it was APPOSITE for the garden lunch she decided to attend.

apprehension *(app-ree-HEN-shun), noun*
Fear, concern, or anxiety that something bad will occur; nerves or jitters

New mothers often have a difficult time letting go of their APPREHENSION over having a new baby.

apprise *(uh-PRYZ), verb*
To inform, tell, or fill in; to bring up to date

When his parents got to the hospital, they could not find a doctor who could APPRISE them of their son's situation.

The teacher promised she would APPRISE all class members of their semester grades as soon as possible.

approbation *(aa-pro-BAY-shun), noun*
Great praise; rave reviews; high compliments and honors, generally formal or public

Everyone expected great things from the young writer after she had received such APPROBATION for her first book.

Know This Quote

"In a virtuous and free state, no rewards can be so pleasing to sensible minds, as those which include the APPROBATION of our fellow citizens. My great pain is, lest my poor endeavours should fall short of the kind expectations of my country." —Thomas Jefferson

apropos *(a-pruh-POE), adjective*
Appropriate in a particular situation; relevant and fitting. From the French for "to the purpose."

Stan's parents did not think jeans APROPOS for his sister's wedding ceremony.

arable *(AYR-uh-bul), adjective*
Suitable or ready for planning and growing plants or crops

As a city girl, she had no idea if the farmland was ARABLE or not.

arbiter *(AR-bih-ter), noun*
Someone with the authority to settle a dispute or decide an issue. Someone with great influence over what others think, say, or do.

If arguments between two persons cannot be resolved, an ARBITER is sometimes called in to solve them.

arbitrary *(AHR-buh-trayr-ree), adjective*
Left to personal interpretation; vague and undefined; without strict guidelines

Due to the ARBITRARY nature of the coach's instructions, none of the players understood what was expected of them.

arboreal *(uh-BOR-ee-uhl), adjective*
Living in trees; describing animals living in trees; regarding or having to do with trees

The rainforest is a good place to see gibbons, sloths, and other ARBOREAL creatures.

arcane *(Are-CAYNE), adjective*
Strange and mysterious; understood by only a few.

Bill's ARCANE knowledge of all Lexus models and their accessories is just a waste of grey matter.

archaic *(ar-KAY-ik), adjective*
Very old-fashioned; from an earlier point in history and no longer in use

Before judging the past, we must remember that in 1,000 years what we now consider normal will be considered ARCHAIC and out of date.

archetype *(ARE-ke-type), noun*
A prototypical example; a recurrent theme or pattern; an original model that is widely imitated.

Boys never played with dolls until G.I. Joe became the ARCHETYPE of the "action figure."

argosy *(are-guh-SEE), noun*
A rich, seemingly endless, supply.

The deceased hermit's home turned out to be an ARGOSY of Cuban cigars, Swiss timepieces, and historical erotica.

ardor *(AR-dor), noun*
Emotional heat or passion; passionate, often overwhelming love

I admit I was amazed by the ARDOR in my grandfather's old letters to my grandmother.

arduous *(AR-joo-wus), adjective*
Difficult, requiring continuous effort and hard work. Challenging to travel, endure, or overcome.

Exam period was ARDUOUS, to say the least, even for the most dedicated students.

argot *(AR-go), noun*
The language or slang used by a specific group

Her most difficult adjustment in college was no longer using the ARGOT of the streets where she had grown up.

arid *(AYR-id), adjective*
Very dry; desert-like, often used to describe climate

It is important to stay hydrated when visiting ARID climates, or you risk a number of unpleasant physical problems.

arrant *(AYR-unt), adjective*
Complete and total; unarguable; plainly obvious

She couldn't understand why her son missed the ARRANT logic in finishing his report early instead of putting it off until the last minute.

arrogance *(AYR-uh-ganz), noun*
A sense of being better than others; exaggerated pride

Underdogs are often inspired to play better by the ARROGANCE of higher ranked teams.

articulate *(ar-TIH-kyu-lut), adjective*
Able to speak clearly and express one's thoughts well; well spoken

He resented people's surprise that he was ARTICULATE when they learned he had grown up in the inner city.

artifact *(AR-tih-fakt), noun*
Something made by humans that has historical or archeological importance

The museum hosted a display of priceless ARTIFACTS from the early third century.

artifice *(ARE-ti-fis), noun*
The use of clever strategies and cunning methods to fool or best others and tip an outcome in your favor.

Carla was upset that Martha's use of ARTIFICE won Martha the concert tickets Carla so desperately wanted.

Know This Quote

"Every art and ARTIFICE has been practiced and perpetrated to destroy the rights of man."
—Robert Ingersoll, American orator

artisan *(AR-tih-zen), noun*
Someone skilled in making crafts by hand

Although I had heard his mother was talented, I didn't realize she was such an ARTISAN until I saw her woven baskets.

ascendancy *(AH-sen-den-see), noun*
Position of power; superiority, or dominance

Many sociologists believe Japan's ASCENDANCY in the global arena is inevitable.

ascetic *(EH-set-tik), noun or adjective*
A person who rejects nearly all physical comforts and lives a bare, Spartan life, usually for spiritual development or devotion (noun) or living a life of self-denial, usually for spiritual development or devotion (adjective)

Not many people can handle the sacrifices required to become an ASCETIC.

The monks' lives were ASCETIC but happy.

ascribe *(uh-SKRYBE), verb*
To assign cause to a person or thing; to give responsibility to a particular person for creation of something. To identify someone or something as belonging to a particular group.

While there was no name on the paper, the teacher was able to ASCRIBE it to Mark, for his writing style was quite distinctive.

asperity *(ah-SPEHR-i-tee), noun*
Harshness, roughness, or nastiness of manner; irritability

No one was shocked by the ASPERITY in her voice when she talked about the teacher who had given her a failing grade.

aspersion *(uh-SPUR-zhun), noun*
False accusation; slander; a statement that attacks someone's character or reputation.

Angry individuals are likely to cast ASPERSIONS on the targets of their hostility.

aspire *(ah-SPYR), verb*
To dream; to hope to achieve; to set as a goal

He ASPIRED to be a great hockey player from the first day he put on skates as a five-year-old boy.

assiduous *(ah-SIH-joo-us), adjective*
Having great attention to detail; consistent and diligent; overly aware of details

A research assistant must be ASSIDUOUS in weeding out fact from fiction, finding missing details, and meeting all deadlines.

assiduously *(ah-SID-you-us-lee), adverb*
Diligent and persistent, especially in an effort to help others, achieve a goal, or deliver on one's promises.

David worked ASSIDUOUSLY to complete his first novel, writing for three hours a night after work and dinner.

assuage *(ah-SWAYJ), verb*
To ease; to make something less painful or severe; to relieve a desperate need or desire

Even apologizing was not enough to ASSUAGE her guilt over making such a stupid, insensitive comment to her friend.

Know This Quote

"But history must not yet tell the tragedies enacted here; let time intervene in some measure to ASSUAGE and lend an azure tint to them." —Henry David Thoreau, American author and transcendentalist

asunder *(ah-SUN-derr), adjective*
A whole that has been split into parts; a union that has been eliminated, leaving the people or things once joined now separate.

His marriage torn ASUNDER, Mike decided to quit his job, move to Tangiers, and become a year-round beach bum.

astringent *(uh-STRIN-jent), noun*
A solution that causes skin or other tissue to tighten or contract

A good ASTRINGENT may help clean pores and keep skin healthy.

astute *(uh-STOOT), adjective*
Being able to read a situation and figure it out accurately; being able to read between the lines

An ASTUTE therapist will read a client's body language and not just listen to what is said.

asylum *(ah-SIY-lem), noun*
Protection and safety offered by a government, church, or other ruling body

Many refugees from war-torn countries seek ASYLUM in the United States.

asynchronous *(aye-SINK-crow-nuss), adjective*
Acting or functioning with no regularity or discernible time schedule.

Maggie's ASYNCHRONOUS habits drive her friends crazy because they can never make advance plans with her.

attest *(uh-TEST), verb*
To state that something exists or is true or valid, especially in a formal written statement. To make a firm assertion regarding the validity of a statement, idea, or claim.

The prosecutor ATTESTED over and over that the defendant was guilty of murder.

atonement *(uh-TOHN-ment), noun*
Payment, through action, for an injury or harming another; an action that repays a debt

The principal required the students who spit on the floor to stay late and scrub the floors for both punishment and ATONEMENT.

atrophy *(AA-tro-fee), noun*
To weaken and deteriorate though lack of use

The new mother was afraid her intellect would ATROPHY after spending the first year at home with her children.

attribute *(uh-TRI-byoot), verb or (AA-tri-byoot), noun*
To credit a particular source or cause; to cite the source (verb) or a specific characteristic or trait (noun)

The young man preferred to take credit himself rather than correctly ATTRIBUTE his jokes to his grandfather.

A sense of humor is the best ATTRIBUTE one can have in a stressful situation.

audacious *(aw-DAY-shus), adjective*
Bold and adventurous, sometimes recklessly so; without concern for the normal or expected

The comedian's AUDACIOUS jokes shocked people as often as they made people laugh.

augment *(AWG-ment), verb*
To increase in growth, size, strength, loudness, or scope.

To finish the remodeling job, the foreman said he would AUGMENT his crew as well as the pool of bulldozers on site.

augur *(AW-ger), verb*
To predict or foretell the future.

The three witches of Shakespeare's Macbeth *AUGUR the cataclysmic fate of the play's titular character.*

augury *(AW-gur-ree), noun*
An omen or sign of things to come; a foretelling of future events

In the theater, a bad final rehearsal is seen as an AUGURY for a good opening night.

auspices *(AWS-pih-suhs), noun*
The support, encouragement, permission, or patronage of a person or organization. Not to be confused or misused with the next word, *auspicious.*

Doctors and nurses were able to travel safely throughout the war zone under the AUSPICES of the Red Cross.

auspicious *(aw-SPIH-shus), adjective*
Marked by lucky signs or good omens, with the promise of success. Full of encouragement, hope, or reason for optimism, often describing the beginning of an activity or event.

Everyone in attendance agreed that it was an AUSPICIOUS sign that the clouds parted and the sun shone just fifteen minutes before the commencement ceremony was scheduled to begin.

austere *(aw-STEER), adjective*
Severe and strict; without any frivolous additions; intentionally plain and without character

Her AUSTERE style kept her from being effective in such a relaxed group.

authoritarian *(uh-THAW-rih-tayr-ree-uhn), adjective*
In favor of complete obedience; demanding of obedience to the exclusion of individuality

The greatest threat to an AUTHORITARIAN government is an independent, thinking populace.

autocrat *(AW-tuh-krat), noun*
A leader with complete and unlimited power

Throughout history, every AUTOCRAT has eventually become power-hungry and corrupt.

autodidact *(AW-toe-dih-dakt), noun*
A self-educated person.

In the twentieth century, the library was the university of the AUTODIDACT; in the twenty-first century, it is the Internet.

autonomous *(aw-TAWN-uh-mus), adjective*
Having the ability to work and exist independently

He quickly discovered his assistant was not AUTONOMOUS but instead needed daily direction.

autonomy *(aw-THAN-ah-mee), noun*
Maintaining independent thought and action; free; self-governing; without dependence on, or under control of, a higher authority.

Herb claims he wants AUTONOMY, but he goes absolutely nuts whenever his boss gives him unstructured assignments.

auxiliary *(awg-ZIL-ah-ree), adjective*
Helpful, giving assistance; held in reserve in case extra assistance is required

The AUXILIARY troops stationed in Germany hoped they would not be needed in the war.

avant-garde *(ah-vahnt GARD), adjective*
Artistically innovative, experimental, or unconventional. Used to describe members of the intelligentsia (such as writers, artists, musicians, or film makers).

It was hard for the untrained eye to determine if the art in the new museum was AVANT-GARDE, or just bad.

avarice *(A-vuh-riss), noun*
Unreasonably strong desire for money and riches. Extreme greed.

Some believe that AVARICE drove the recent corporate wrongdoings, which resulted in several CEOs being tried and convicted of crimes.

aver *(uh-VER), verb*
To declare as fact; to swear as true

Witnesses are asked to AVER that they will tell the truth in court or face charges of perjury.

aversion *(uh-VER-shun), noun*
A strong dislike or feeling of disgust; repulsion

While she was no longer afraid of spiders, she still had an AVERSION to them and knew she always would.

Know This Quote

"'Has she no faults, then (Envy says), sir?' / Yes, she has one, I must AVER: / When all the world conspires to praise her, / The woman's deaf, and does not hear."
—Alexander Pope, British poet

Which Word?

The parts of speech can be changed for many words by simply adding a different suffix. It seems obvious that kind and kindness are related words. Unfortunately, it is not always that simple. Be aware that although aver and aversion appear to be different forms of the same word, they really are not. To aver (uh-VER) means to swear something is true. Aversion (uh-VER-shun) means a strong dislike. Be careful not to get the two confused.

avert *(ah-VERT), verb*
To change or prevent; to turn away

The young woman used the scary part of the movie as an excuse to AVERT her eyes and cling to her date.

aviary *(AY-vee-ayr-ree), noun*
A large structure for housing birds

The zoo AVIARY was closed for repairs after the storm ripped through the netting.

avow *(ah-VOW), verb*
To state openly and without shame

He was brave enough to AVOW he was a Republican in a city where most people were Democrats.

avuncular *(A-VUN-cue-lar), adjective*
Kind, genial, benevolent, like an uncle.

Myron's AVUNCULAR personality makes women think of him as a friend, not as a lover.

axiom *(AHK-see-um), noun*
A statement that is considered to be true or a given without needing further proof

It is an AXIOM that people want jobs that pay well and make them happy.

"A straight line is the shortest distance between two points" is an AXIOM for both mathematicians and travelers.

B

baccalaureate *(BA-kuh-LOR-ee-it), noun*
The degree bestowed upon completion of a course of undergraduate college study (bachelor's degree). Also a farewell address to a graduating class.

I received my BACCALAUREATE in 1975 from the University of Pennsylvania, but my education truly began at commencement.

bacchanal *(bah-kan-AL), noun*
A wild celebration; a party at which the partygoers are loud and out of control, often fueled by excess alcohol consumption.

The initiation ceremony at the fraternity turned into a full-blown BACCHANAL requiring the intervention of the campus police to restore order.

badinage *(BAH-dih-nadge), noun*
Light, good-natured, even playful banter.

You could tell the young couple was in love just by listening to their BADINAGE.

Know This Quote

"If you don't care for me, you can move out now. I'm frankly not up to BADINAGE." —Harlan Ellison, American author

bailiwick *(BALE-ee-wick), noun*
A person's specific area of expertise, experience, skill, knowledge, education, or authority.

Foreign language is not my BAILIWICK, I soon realized after failing out of Hebrew School.

balderdash *(BALL-der-dash), noun*
Senseless or nonsense talking or writing; a ridiculous, senseless, or worthless idea or suggestion.

It must have been embarrassing for you when your favorite English teacher called your essay BALDERDASH!

baleful *(BAYL-ful), adjective*
Threatening; intending to intimidate or cause harm

The BALEFUL look she gave her little brother only confirmed for her parents that he was telling the truth about her sneaking in after curfew.

balm *(BAHLM), noun*
An ointment used for soothing or healing; anything that causes a pain or hurt to be eased; something that gives comfort

After the breakup, listening to classical music was a BALM for his broken heart.

banal *(BAY-nul), adjective*
Ordinary to the point of boring; dull and uninteresting

Although parents still hire them, most children find clowns BANAL and childish.

bandy *(BAN-dee), verb*
To exchange, trade, or pass words or blows. To exchange witticisms or insults.
The two brothers were known to BANDY both words and loving punches, but they never came to serious blows.

baneful *(BAYN-ful), adjective*
Ruinous or destructive; capable of spoiling or causing utter destruction. Deadly and likely to cause ruin.
The BANEFUL influence of gangs on their young members is without question.

basilisk *(BAH-sill-isk), noun*
A mythical reptile with a lethal stare or breath.
With poisonous saliva that can kill a man with one bite, the Komodo Dragon is truly a modern-day BASILISK.

bask *(BAASK), verb*
To relax and enjoy warmth, either literally or figuratively
After the long, cold winter, all they wanted to do was BASK in the Caribbean sun.

bastion *(BAS-tee-uhn), noun*
An institution, individual, or something else protecting or preserving a particular way of life, society, set of beliefs, or moral code.
Cliff, a Yale BASTION, continuously quibbles with Irene, who graduated summa cum laude from Harvard.

bathos *(BAY-thoss), noun*
A sudden change in mood from the solemn and serious to a more light-hearted, relaxed, and humorous outlook.
When the clock ticked at midnight on December 31, 1999, and we moved into the new century without the computers shutting down, the grim look and worried faces disappeared, and the IT department was suddenly enveloped in a feeling of BATHOS.

beatify *(BE-ah-taf-fy), verb*
To idolize above all; to make someone blissfully happy
Her friends wouldn't let her BEATIFY her ex but kept reminding her how annoying he could be.

beatitude *(Bee-AT-it-tood), noun*
Being in the highest possible state of happiness, good humor, and contentment.
Laura felt a deep sense of BEATITUDE when she learned her offer on the house had been accepted.

Know This Quote

"Kindness is a virtue neither modern nor urban. One almost unlearns it in a city. Towns have their own BEATITUDE; they are not unfriendly; they offer a vast and solacing anonymity or an equally vast and solacing gregariousness." —Phyllis McGinley, American author and poet

bedaub *(beh-DAHB), verb*
To smear, usually with something sticky

The groom's attendants decided to BEDAUB the steering wheel of the getaway car with honey as part of the joke.

bedraggled *(bih-DRA-guld), adjective*
Wet, dirty, unkempt, or in a general condition of disarray. She was so bedraggled she looked like she'd been dragged from bed just seconds before.

When the campers returned from three days in the woods, they were BEDRAGGLED and tired, but happy.

befuddle *(bih-FUH-dil), verb*
To confuse or perplex, mystify, or confuse. To make someone inebriated and/or unable to think clearly.

The absent-minded professor's lectures so BEFUDDLED his students that they were quickly as confused as he was.

beget *(bih-GET), verb*
To father, as in a child; to cause or inspire the existence of something.

Despite the term's biblical overtones, it is correct to say that the first edition of my book BEGAT the second edition.

beguile *(bee-GYL), verb*
To charm, often by being deceptive

The young woman didn't have to BEGUILE men because she was naturally friendly and outgoing.

belated *(bih-LAY-ted), adjective*
Late or tardy; delayed after the specified time. Past due, often too late to be effective.

BELATED gifts and good wishes should be graciously received and appreciated, though this is hard for some to do.

beleaguer *(bih-LEE-ger), verb*
To harass someone and make them feel embattled and under pressure. To constantly confront with obstacles. To besiege (surround with an army).

With the crowd becoming more and more unruly, the BELEAGUERED umpires finally called the game.

belie *(bee-LYE), verb*
To be false or misrepresent; to be intentionally inaccurate

The condition of the house BELIED her claim that no one had come over while her parents were out.

belles lettres *(BELL LET-truh), noun*
Novels, short stories, poems, and other writings read for their grace and literary style and not necessarily their content.

Many of the BELLES LETTRES published in the literary journal were not understood by those looking for strong character development and plot lines.

Know This Quote

"Learning has been as great a Loser by being . . . secluded from the World and good Company. By that Means, every Thing of what we call BELLES LETTRES became totally barbarous, being cultivated by Men without any Taste of Life or Manners." —David Hume, Scottish philosopher

bellicose *(BEH-lih-koce), adjective*
Ready or inclined to quarrel, fight, or go to war. Warlike or hostile in manner or temperament.

It is ominous when leaders engage their nations in BELLICOSE behavior, for little good can come of such actions.

belligerent *(beh-LIH-je-rent), adjective*
Ready to start a war or fight; hostile, aggressive, or pugnacious. Describes participants in a war or fight.

Football players, especially those who play on defense, often psych themselves into a BELLIGERENT state prior to each game.

bellwether *(BELL-weather), noun*
A leading indicator or important factor in determining a course of action or outcome.

The fact that Robert got thrown out of Groton and Exeter was a BELLWETHER for his lackadaisical years at Dartmouth.

bemused *(bih-MYOOZD), adjective*
Confused, puzzled, preoccupied, and unable to think clearly; bewildered, perplexed, or lost in reflection. You can be amused and bemused if confused.

College students often appear BEMUSED right before an exam, for they are focusing intently on their studies.

benediction *(beh-nih-DIK-shun), noun*
A formal blessing or expression of good wishes. A prayer at the end of a service that asks for God's blessing.

After the BENEDICTION, the congregation would meet for lunch and then work on community service projects.

benefactor *(BEHN-uh-fahk-tor), noun*
Someone who gives money to help a person or cause

Without a generous BENEFACTOR, the small art gallery would have gone out of business years ago.

beneficent *(be-NE-fih-sent), adjective*
Kindly in action, purpose, or speech.

In a BENEFICENT gesture, the neighborhood raised $10,000 to help pay for the young boy's leukemia treatments.

benevolent *(beh-NEHV-oh-lent), adjective*
Concerned with performing good or charitable acts; being kind and helpful

The teen's BENEVOLENT acts throughout the year inspired the whole community to help the less fortunate during the holidays.

benighted *(bee-NYE-ted), adjective*
To be lost, ignorant, or unenlightened.

The Medieval period was a BENIGHTED era of superstition.

benign *(beh-NIYN), adjective*
Harmless; gentle; without cruel intent or ability

The owners assured people the dog's nature was completely BENIGN but it was hard to believe considering how mean it sounded when it barked.

bequeath *(bih-QUEETH), verb*
To leave personal property to someone after death by means of a will. To hand down something from one generation to another. Bea bequeathed her teeth after she died.

Steve had always hoped that his grandfather would BEQUEATH him his classic 1965 Mustang convertible.

berate *(bur-AYT), verb*
To scold harshly; to yell, usually implies an extended scolding

His father BERATED him not just for cheating on his English test but because the young man was smart enough to not need to cheat.

bereaved *(beh-REEVD), adjective*
To be in a state of grief as the result of the death of someone you love or care deeply about.

Lucy was deeply BEREAVED over the death of her beloved pet parakeet.

Know This Quote

"Laughter would be BEREAVED if snobbery died." —Peter Ustinov, British writer and dramatist

beseech *(bih-SEECH), verb*
To beg or ask earnestly. To entreat, implore, or request forcefully.
The students BESEECHED the teacher to delay the quiz until the next day, as most were not prepared.

besotted *(bih-SOTT-ed), adjective*
Made foolish, stupid, or dull due to an infatuation with love, money, the pursuit of power, etc.
Aline thinks Jake is BESOTTED with her, but he's really BESOTTED with her father's stock portfolio.

bespoke *(bih-SPOHK), adjective*
Clothes, shoes, and other goods custom-made for a particular client.
Taylor's big secret is that though he wears BESPOKE clothing, he's only leasing his new Lexus.

bête noire *(Bett NWAR), noun*
A thing for which one has an intense dislike or great fear; a dreaded enemy or foe.
Sunlight was Dracula's greatest BÊTE NOIRE.

betoken *(bee-TOE-ken), verb*
To serve as a warning.
For Mary and Paul, the breakdown of their new Porsche while they were still two hours away from their summer home BETOKENED a disastrous vacation.

bewilder *(bee-WIL-der), verb*
To confuse; to puzzle a person
By the end of the drive, the poor directions and the winding roads had BEWILDERED us.

bibelot *(BIB-low), noun*
A small object of beauty or rarity.
The Rossington's collection of BIBELOTS contains numerous Fabergé eggs.

bibliomania *(bib-lee-oh-MAY-nee-uh), noun*
A preoccupation with the acquisition and ownership of books.
Lauren's BIBLIOMANIA extends only to her stockpile of catalogues for exclusive shops.

bibulous *(BIB-yuh-luss), adjective*
Related to drinking or to drunkenness.
Arthur thinks he's "fine," but his BIBULOUS activities are causing the club to consider permanent expulsion.

bicameral *(by-KAM-er-el), adjective*
A government or parliament with two chambers or houses.

With a Senate and a House of Representatives, the United States has a BICAMERAL legislature.

bifurcate *(BYE-fur-kate), verb*
To divide something into two branches or forks.

The college was BIFURCATED. Half the students attended the School of Arts and Sciences, the rest attended the School of Business.

Know This Quote

"François Truffaut defined a great movie as a perfect blend of truth and spectacle. Now it's become BIFURCATED. Studio films are all spectacle and no truth, and independent films are all truth and no spectacle."
—Howard Franklin, American screenwriter and director

bilateral *(By-LAT-ur-ul), adjective*
Touching, existing on, or having or being agreed to by two sides.

The President signed a BILATERAL disarmament agreement with the nation bordering to the north.

bildungsroman *(BILL-dungs-roh-man), noun*
A coming-of-age novel, such as *The Catcher in the Rye* or *A Portrait of the Artist as a Young Man*.

Alex has started writing a BILDUNGSROMAN about his experiences in prep school.

bilious *(BILL-yuss), adjective*
Having a nasty temperament or disagreeable disposition; to be "full of bile" and hated.

The polo team's BILIOUS captain made his team miserable as he proceeded to criticize their every move.

billet *(BILL-uht), noun*
A job, position, or appointment.

With his wealthy father's influence, Miles was able to secure a lucrative BILLET in a major brokerage house.

bilk *(BILK), verb*
To swindle or cheat. To defraud a person or institution of funds or goods. To escape from someone or manage to lose a pursuer.

The swindler denied that he had ever BILKED any person of money or property.

binary *(BYE-neh-ree), adjective*
Composed of two parts and elements; of or pertaining to two. Describes a number system that only uses the two digits zero and one.

It is truly amazing to think that all computer software programming has evolved from a BINARY number system, giving zero and one the power to change the world.

blandishment *(BLAN-dish-ment), noun*
Gentle flattery used to get someone to behave in a certain way

She knew better than to try BLANDISHMENT on her father just to get the car keys because he would just laugh and hand her bus fare.

blasé (*blah-ZAY), adjective*
Not worried about something, often because of previous experience. Unimpressed; bored.

Much to the surprise of her classmates, Cindy was BLASÉ about being named to be the commencement speaker.

blatant *(BLAY-tent), adjective*
Open and in-your-face to the point of being offensive

The teacher was shocked by the BLATANT cheating going on during the test.

blather *(BLA-ther), verb*
To talk nonsense in an inane manner and at great length. To gabble or talk ridiculously. People who blabber until they lather are said to blather.

While there are no warning labels on bottles of beer, people should be warned that overindulging in alcohol can cause one to BLATHER, leading to embarrassment and the need for many apologies.

blazon *(BLAY-zuhn), noun or verb*
A coat of arms; or, to proclaim something widely.

You'll find the Rutherford's family BLAZON on every one of Prescott's ties.

bleak *(BLEEK), adjective*
Cold, miserable, barren; without hope

Unless she started taking her classes seriously and raised her GPA, her outlook for graduating on time was BLEAK.

blighted *(BLY-ted), adjective*
Diseased; given over to hopelessness and despair; sickly; run down

For years after the factory closed, the small town looked BLIGHTED with the boarded up windows and empty storefronts.

blithe *(BLIYTH), adjective*
Lightheartedness to the point of indifference or uncaring; happily unconcerned and oblivious

There is something uplifting about watching the BLITHE play of young children.

bloviate *(BLOH-vee-ayt), verb*
To speak pompously and at length

Maxwell BLOVIATES about his "excellent" golf game, but everyone knows he inflates his handicap exponentially.

bludgeon *(BLUH-jun), verb*
To beat repeatedly with a heavy object. To bully or coerce someone into doing something against their will.

Forensic experts determined that the victim was BLUDGEONED with a baseball bat by someone over six feet tall and weighing about 200 pounds.

bluster *(BLUS-ter), verb*
To speak loudly, arrogantly, and boisterously. To behave in a bullying way. To blow in loud gusts, as in the wind.

Senators filibuster while bullies BLUSTER, and both verbal strategies yield little action.

bohemian *(bo-HEE-mee-un), noun*
Someone, often an artist or writer, who does not live according to conventions of society. Denotes a lifestyle free of mainstream concerns.

According to Jim, he was a BOHEMIAN; according to his parents, he was just lazy, unkempt, and lacking in ambition.

Where'd That Word Come From?

Bohemian—This word was first used during the Middle Ages to mean a gypsy or vagabond. At that time, many mistakenly believed gypsy tribes came from the ancient kingdom of Bohemia (now the Czech Republic). *Bohemian* came to be synonymous with a poor writer or artist thanks to French novelist Henri Murger's stories in *Scènes de la vie de bohème* (1848), the book that inspired Puccini's opera *La Bohème.*

boisterous *(BOY-stuhr-us), adjective*
Cheerfully loud and out of control

The party grew BOISTEROUS as more people arrived to help celebrate.

bolster *(BOL-ster), verb*
To shore up; to build up; to increase support

The candidate needed to BOLSTER his support in the Midwest if he was going to win the election.

bombast *(BOM-bast), noun*
Speech or writing full of long and pretentious words, usually meant to impress others. Haughty, overblown, or pompous language. A verbal bomb blast of long words is a *bombast.*

The senatorial candidate did not instill confidence in voters, for his announcement speech seemed little more than BOMBAST.

Where'd That Word Come From?
Bombast—Originally, this word referred to a cotton used as a padding or stuffing for clothes, derived from the word *bombyx*, for "silkworm" or "silk," which was used for cotton as well. Just as stuffing or padding in clothing was called bombast so, eventually, was padded, stuffed, inflated, grandiose speech.

bona fide *(BOE-nuh fyde), adjective*
Authentic, actual, or genuine. Not deceptive; indisputably legitimate.

Mr. and Mrs. Stevens bought a painting at a garage sale for $50, and they later found it to be a BONA FIDE masterpiece worth $50,000.

bonhomie *(bon-uh-MEE), noun*
A good-natured, genial manner.

Even though he has no family pedigree, Walker is accepted into our group because of his contagious BONHOMIE.

boorish *(BUHR-ish), adjective*
Crass, insensitive, ill-mannered, and offensive. Lacking in social graces. Boars are pigs, as are boors.

Fraternity boys are notorious for BOORISH behavior.

bourgeois *(boor-ZHWAH), adjective*
Pertaining or relating to the middle class, as opposed to the upper class or royalty on one end and the peasants or common laborers on the other.

The majority of American families are considered BOURGEOIS.

Know This Quote
"The representation of the garrison thus turned out to be incomparably more moderate and BOURGEOIS than the soldier masses." —Leon Trotsky, Bolshevik revolutionary and Marxist theorist

bovine *(BO-vyne), adjective*
Anything related to or reminiscent of cows or other dull, docile, slow-moving, grazing mammals.

Susan took so long to finish her part of the race that her teammates called her a BOVINE at the next track meet.

bowdlerize *(BOWD-luhr-EYZE), verb*
To remove parts of a work of literature considered objectionable, indecent, or offensive. Coined after Thomas Bowdler, who published an expurgated edition of Shakespeare in 1818.

> *The editor BOWDLERIZED the author's first draft to make the book marketable to a broader audience.*

braggadocio *(bra-guh-DOA-see-oo), noun*
Someone who makes overexaggerated claims or empty boasts. Also, empty boasts and swaggering self-aggrandizement. Braggarts, dolts all, are acting with braggadocio.

> *Fighters who can back up their boasts are not simply full of BRAGGADOCIO, but they are still often controversial.*

Where'd That Word Come From?

Braggadocio—In his epic poem *The Faerie Queene,* Edmund Spenser (1552–1599) gave the name Braggadochio to a loud-mouthed braggart who was revealed as a coward. The word came to refer to any braggart and finally also to mean empty or loud boasting.

braggart *(BRAG-ert), noun*
One who boasts or brags unnecessarily; one who builds himself up in order to appear impressive

> *He had a reputation as a BRAGGART, which people found so annoying it kept them from admiring his skills as much.*

brandish *(BRAN-dish), verb*
To wave something, especially a weapon, in a threatening or menacing way. To wave something in defiance, as a warning of potential future harm, or out of pride, as a sign of status.

> *The hockey player suddenly, without warning, BRANDISHED his stick and skated toward the frightened crowd.*

bravado *(bruh-VAH-do), noun*
Real or pretended display of courage. An open display of boldness. Brave Otto proved ultimately to be most courageous, with strong bravado.

> *The mayor's swaggering attitude of BRAVADO was of little help when the town was finally attacked.*

breach *(BREECH), verb*
To break through; to violate

Anyone who has seen water BREACH a levee will never forget the sight of the flooding or the damage it caused.

breviary *(BREE-vee-air-ee), noun*
A brief summary or abridgement.

She called it a BREVIARY, but Lana's recounting of her family's month on the Riviera was anything but short.

brevity *(BREHV-ih-tee), noun*
Shortness and clarity in written or spoken word

She aimed for BREVITY in her speeches so she wouldn't bore her audience since she herself hated to listen to speakers drone on and on.

BREVITY, combined with the use of the very best words, is the mark of a quality essay.

brittle *(BRIT-tuhl), adjective*
Hard but fragile and easily broken or damaged

The older a woman gets, the more BRITTLE her bones will become unless she exercises and gets enough calcium in her diet.

broach *(BROHTCH), verb*
To bring up, as a suggestion or topic of conversation; to approach a topic

He finally got up his nerve enough to BROACH the possibility of a date with her while they were instant messaging.

Brobdingnagian *(brahb-ding-NAG-ian), adjective*
Describes a thing or person of enormous size; huge.

Andre the Giant was a man of BROBDINGNAGIAN proportions, standing seven-foot-five-inches and weighing over five hundred pounds.

brouhaha *(BREW-ha-ha), noun*
A confusing, exciting, and turmoil-rife event.

Madeline caused a BROUHAHA when she told her parents she was eschewing Harvard for a state school in order to be closer to her boyfriend.

bromide *(BRO-mide), noun*
A cliché or tired saying used to express an idea without any thought or originality.

Helen's Harvard education does not stop her from peppering her speech with insipid BROMIDES.

brummagem *(BRUHM-uh-juhm), noun or adjective*
Describes something that looks great but performs poorly.

The new car Marcus bought turned out to be a bit of a BRUMMAGEM. It looked great parked in his driveway, but wouldn't go above fifty miles per hour on the highway.

Know This Quote
"Our press is certainly bankrupt in . . . reverence for nickel plate and BRUMMAGEM." —Mark Twain

brusque *(BRUSK), adjective*
Abrupt, blunt, short, or curt in manner or speech. Impatient (and showing it).

Her BRUSQUE actions appeared unfriendly at first, but later they were perceived as honest and sincere.

bucolic *(BYOO-kawl-ik), adjective*
Idealized characteristics of the country and country life; rustic and pastoral

The BUCOLIC paintings of the farm had made her want to move there but the reality made her miss the city.

bugaboo *(BU-guh-boo), noun*
Something that causes fear, annoyance, trouble, worry, or dismay. An imagined threat or problem. To those with arachnophobia, a bug causes fear, and the word "boo" causes worry, so both are bugaboos.

Not swimming for an hour after eating seemed a BUGABOO to him, rather than good advice.

bulwark *(bull-WARK), noun*
A defensive, protective barrier, wall, or force.

The two young boys built a snowfort to act as a BULWARK for their snowman.

Know This Quote
"Since he aims at great souls, he cannot miss. But if someone should slander me in this way, no one would believe him. For envy goes against the powerful. Yet slight men, apart from the great, are but a weak BULWARK." —Sophocles, Greek tragedian

bumptious *(BUMP-shus), adjective*
Loud and self-serving to the point of being obnoxious

Instead of charming and witty, the candidate just came off as BUMPTIOUS whenever he was working without a script.

buoyant *(BOY-ant), adjective*
Lighthearted and happy; or able to float

Her BUOYANT personality brought much needed cheer to the residents of the home.

The BUOYANT rubber duck was enough of a temptation that the child was finally willing to get in the bath in order to "swim with the duckie."

bureaucracy *(byoo-RAH-kruh-see), noun*
An administrative system, especially in government, that organizes work into categories and departments. The people hired to work within such a system. An organization operated by a hierarchy of officials, often characterized by adherence to routine and lack of innovation.

The student government turned into an inefficient BUREAUCRACY, not a group representing the interests of its constituents.

burgeon *(BUR-jun), verb*
To increase rapidly; to flourish and grow

The artists were surprised at the BURGEONING popularity of their cartoon on the Internet.

burnish *(BUHR-nish), verb*
To make something smooth and shiny by rubbing or polishing it

Every Sunday, her grandmother BURNISHED the silver before setting the table.

buttress *(BUH-tress), verb*
To support or reinforce a building, thought, idea, or argument

He had plenty of documentation to BUTTRESS his claims in the debate but his opponent's style won over more of the audience.

byzantine *(biz-ann-TEEN), adjective*
A convoluted plan; a scheme that is overly complicated; a puzzle or task that's difficult to figure out because of its complexity.

We found it impossible to follow the BYZANTINE plot of how Eileen made Mariah a laughingstock by replacing her Prada shoes with nearly identical knockoffs.

C

cabal *(kuh-BAHL), noun*
A secret group of plotters or conspirators

The Founding Fathers were actually just an articulate CABAL with good connections.

cabotage *(KAB-uh-tij), noun*
The right of a country to control all air traffic flying in its skies.

After 9/11, CABOTAGE became a major concern of New York City and its mayor.

cache *(KASH), noun*
Something hidden or stored.

Everyone was jealous when they learned of Moira's CACHE of acceptances to the finest schools.

cacophony *(kah-KOFF-ah-nee), noun*
A harsh, jarring, disconnected group of sounds; discordant noise

The CACOPHONY of the horns and sirens during rush hour traffic is enough to give anyone a headache.

cadacous *(kuh-DOO-kuss), adjective*
Transitory; short-lived; perishable.

Meredith's excitement over her trip was CADACOUS when she found out she wouldn't be able to take her mother's credit card with her.

Know This Quote

"Some thing, which I fancied was a part of me, falls off from me and leaves no scar. It was CADACOUS." —Ralph Waldo Emerson, American poet, essayist, and transcendentalist

cajole *(kah-JOL), verb*
To persuade someone to do something through persistent flattery, teasing, and/or repeated requests

She hoped to CAJOLE her parents into letting her go to the party after the game, even though it was past her normal curfew.

calculated *(KAL-kyoo-lay-ted), adjective*
Done with a full understanding of the consequences; carefully examined and planned

He took a CALCULATED risk when he mortgaged the house to pay for her education but it paid off when she graduated top of her class.

callow *(KAL-oh), adjective*
Inexperienced, immature, naïve; emotionally young

Teenagers from small towns tend to be far more CALLOW than teens from inner cities.

calumny *(KAL-um-nee), noun*
Slander; a false statement made intentionally to damage another's reputation

The CALUMNY and insults spouted during the debate just made both candidates look bad.

Know This Quote

"CALUMNY will sear virtue itself." –William Shakespeare

camaraderie *(kahm-ah-RAH-duh-ree), noun*

Friendly, powerful emotional bonding between people; group trust

The CAMARADERIE formed among sorority sisters is more valuable than the status gained by pledging.

canard *(kuh-NARD), noun*

A deliberately false report, rumor, or fabrication intended as a joke. Also, a small projection like a wing near the nose of an airplane. It's only a silly rumor that April 1 will be named Canard Day.

Wally's story about how the dog ate his paper was clearly a CANARD, but the teacher took pity and accepted the excuse.

Where'd That Word Come From?

Canard—In French, *canard* means "duck." Its meaning of "a ridiculously false story" comes from the French expression *vendre un canard à moitié*, literally, "to sell half a duck." The expression means to make a fool out of a buyer, or anyone else, with a false story.

candid *(KAN-did), adjective*

Completely truthful; not posed; with nothing held back

The teacher waited until she knew none of her students could hear her before she gave a CANDID opinion of her colleague.

candor *(KAN-dohr), noun*

Sincere and honest expression of thought or opinion

Although some people were put off by her CANDOR, most people appreciated knowing she would be honest with them.

Politicians who speak with CANDOR are an endangered species, one that is nearly extinct.

cannonade *(CAN-non-ayd), noun*

A continuous, relentless bombardment or effort.

A CANNONADE of questioning greeted Eva's statement that she was quitting the club's tennis team.

canon (*KAN-non), noun*

The general principals, standards, or rules by which something is judged

Societal CANON requires a certain code of conduct in public, regardless of what is acceptable in private.

capacious *(kuh-PAY-shus), adjective*
Roomy; spacious; large

Although her CAPACIOUS purse looked somewhat silly, it could carry everything she needed for the baby and herself.

capitulate *(kah-PITCH-yoo-layt), verb*
To surrender or give up; to give in

The babysitter found it easier to CAPITULATE to the child's demands than listen to him cry while his parents were out.

Finally, after long hours of discussion, the parents' committee did CAPITULATE and allow the Junior Prom to take place—though under very specific guidelines.

capricious *(kuh-PRIH-shuss), adjective*
Unpredictable, impulsive; prone to making sudden unplanned changes. That fool, who thinks he's cool, may be capricious if without thinking he jumps in the pool.

Given his CAPRICIOUS approach to life, it is not surprising that Andrew never settled into one field of employment.

Know This Quote
"I do not understand the CAPRICIOUS lewdness of the sleeping mind." —John Cheever, American novelist

captious *(KAP-shus), adjective*
Tending to nitpick or find fault; overly critical of small mistakes

The students knew their papers had to be perfect because the professor was a CAPTIOUS grader.

The stereotypical, nagging mother-in-law is CAPTIOUS to an extreme, and teens tend to think that their parents are as well.

cardiologist *(kar-dee-AHL-oh-jist), noun*
A doctor who specializes in the heart

After her grandfather's heart attack, she made a point of meeting the CARDIOLOGIST who would be handling the follow-up.

caricature *(KAR-ih-kuh-chuhr), noun*
A drawing, description, or other depiction that exaggerates someone's characteristics. An inappropriate and ridiculous version of an attempt to do something. It takes a character to draw a *caricature*, but these words are not the same.

Political cartoons always show a candidate's CARICATURE, magnifying a nose, ears, smile, or particular body or head shape.

carouse *(kuh-ROWZ), verb*
To engage in boisterous social activity.

We CAROUSED until dawn at the annual New Year's Eve party that the Weathertons hold on their yacht.

carping *(KAR-ping), verb*
Complaining or nagging in a fault-finding way; unfairly and vocally dissatisfied

Throughout the trip, their teenagers kept CARPING about how bored they were in spite of their parents' attempts to cater to teenage interests.

carte blanche *(kart BLONSH), noun*
Permission given to someone to do entirely as they wish. French for "blank document," signifies the freedom to write one's own ticket without restrictions. Carte Blanche was the name of an old credit card, and if someone gave you *carte blanche* to use it, the bill would likely be huge.

The homeowners gave CARTE BLANCHE to the talented interior decorator, knowing their new room would be beautiful as well as expensive.

cartel *(kar-TELL), noun*
A group of companies or individuals formed to control production, competition, and prices of a certain product or good. A political alliance among parties or groups with common goals. You would care if there were a car *cartel*, for it would control the automobile industry.

The oil CARTEL has for many years controlled the world's energy prices and sought to influence political developments as well.

caste *(KAST), noun*
A social class whose boundaries are defined by strong hereditary and cultural ties. In some cultures, notably in India, applies to a system that divides people into classes according to the family into which they are born.

While people in some Hindu countries are born into a certain CASTE, some believe that financial CASTES exist in all societies.

castigate *(KAS-tuh-gate), verb*
To scold or criticize harshly, with the objective of assigning blame and motivating the other person to correct their error.

The bartender was CASTIGATED by his boss for serving alcohol to two teenage girls without checking their ID first.

castigation *(KAS-tih-gay-shun), noun*
A harsh scolding or verbal punishment

She avoided her father because she knew she deserved the CASTIGATION she would get for drinking and driving.

catalyst *(KAT-ah-list), noun*
Something that causes an event or change without participating in the change or changing itself

A free press has often been the CATALYST needed for people to overthrow an ineffectual or dictatorial government.

cataract *(KAT-uh-ract), noun*
A great, rushing waterfall

Although it was a beautiful place for a picnic, the roar of the CATARACT made conversation impossible.

Which Word?

Sometimes you think you know a word and its definition—and you probably do know one of its definitions. Cataract (KAT-uh-ract) is probably one of those words. You may have heard the word cataract used in relation to an eye or vision problem. That is its most common definition. However, if you double-check the listing in the book, you'll discover it is also a raging waterfall.

catch-22 *(KATCH twen-tee-TOO), noun*
A problem whose only solution is eliminated by some characteristic of the problem itself. A situation that is illogical and self-contradictory and, often, that presents a hidden trap.

The absent-minded professor created a CATCH-22 for the teaching assistant by requiring him to be certified before taking on any students while also refusing to grant the certification until he had experience teaching students.

Where'd That Word Come From?

Catch-22—The phrase comes from Joseph Heller's 1961 novel of the same name. In this story of American pilots in Italy during World War II, the catch was this. If you were crazy, you could get out of flying any more dangerous combat missions just by asking. However, asking not to fly any more dangerous missions showed that you were clearly sane, which meant you had to fly them.

catharsis *(kuh-THAR-siss), noun*

An experience or feeling of spiritual or emotional release arising from an intense experience. A release of repressed emotions that identifies and relieves related feelings and confusions. A cleansing of the mind or soul preceded by amazing insight. A fancy way to say *emotional release.*

Characters in many novels undergo a CATHARSIS after dramatic or traumatic experiences, thereby revealing much to readers.

caustic *(KAW-stik), adjective*

Sarcastically nasty; biting; mean

The coach was fired in large part because of the CAUSTIC comments he made to his team about its abilities.

Jane's CAUSTIC speech caused all the members to reexamine their support of her candidacy.

cavalier *(KA-vuh-LEER), adjective*

Arrogant, with disregard or lack of respect for someone or something. Unconcerned about things considered important; nonchalant, especially in regard to serious matters. As a noun, interestingly enough, this word defines a gallant or chivalrous gentleman, especially one who is escorting a lady, although the adjective describes almost the opposite.

The lacrosse player's CAVALIER attitude toward school may someday interfere with his dream of playing the sport in college.

caveat *(KAV-ee-ott), noun*

A precaution or warning.

Before Arthur applied to college, his sister offered him a CAVEAT: "Many of us do not consider Columbia to be a true Ivy League school."

cavil *(KA-vuhl), verb*

To raise objections based on small and unimportant points; to find fault on trivial matters or raise petty objections. Hey, to no avail, parents who *cavil* will find fault, no matter how small.

Laura CAVILED about the length of her altered skirt, but she later realized that the extra quarter-inch made no difference.

censorious *(SEN-sor-us), adjective*

Quick to cast blame; highly critical and judgmental of others

The girl would have been more popular if she hadn't been so CENSORIOUS and had accepted others as they were.

censure *(SEN-shur), noun or verb*
A strong, official reprimand (noun) or to reprimand formally (verb)
The legislature issued a CENSURE to the senator for lying under oath during the hearings.
The school CENSURED the speaker because his presentation had been racist.

Which Word?
Many words can be used as either a noun or a verb. Censure (SEN-shur) is one of them. The verb to censure means to hand down an official reprimand or scolding. The noun censure is the official reprimand or scolding. So, one could say that Congress may censure a representative by issuing a censure. Be careful not to confuse them.

centurion *(SEN-tyur-ee-ahn), noun*
An ancient Roman commander, traditionally in charge of 100 troops
For Halloween, he dressed as a CENTURION and carried action figures to represent his 100 soldiers.

certitude *(SUR-tih-tood), noun*
The absolute certainty that something is true; complete confidence in the truth of a matter
The four-year-old knew with CERTITUDE that Santa Claus had been on the roof that Christmas Eve.

cessation *(seh-SAY-shun), noun*
A stop, pause, interruption, or permanent discontinuation. An end to something; the reaching of a point of conclusion.
The substitute teacher prayed for a CESSATION of the rude behavior in his classroom.

chagrin *(shuh-GRIN), noun*
A feeling of humiliation due to disappointment. Humiliation, embarrassment, or disappointment; anxiety about oneself. *Chagrin* does not mean that "she grin"; more appropriate would be a grimace or frown.
Much to the CHAGRIN of his family and friends, Suzanne rejected Bill's proposal.

charismatic *(kare-ihz-MA-tik), adjective*
Possessing great charm or influence, with a special quality of leadership, authority, confidence, and overall appeal. Also used to describe Christian sects whose practices include healing, prophecy, and speaking in tongues.
The CHARISMATIC entertainer was more than a singer, actress, and model; many felt she had the potential to be an elected official.

charlatan *(SHAR-luh-tun), noun*
A con artist or fraud; someone who claims to have a special skill that he or she does not have

In the old days, CHARLATANS traveled from town to town to find their next victim, but now they just use the Internet.

Ultimately, the healer was proven to be a CHARLATAN, but not before several people had suffered and died.

chary *(CHAR-ee), adjective*
Wary; cautious; on guard

Since she was CHARY about walking home by herself after dark, she never took the shortcut through the parking lot.

chicanery *(shi-KAN-er-ree), noun*
Deception or trickery, especially that achieved by clever argument or manipulation of facts or language. What most teens try when they get caught doing something wrong, though few succeed.

The actions and oratory of Professor Harold Hill, that famous character in the musical The Music Man, *are often held up as perfect illustrations of CHICANERY.*

Where'd That Word Come From?

Chicanery—This word for trickery, especially legal dodges and quibbles, came into English through a French word with the same meaning. It seems to be derived from the Persian *chaugan,* for the crooked stick used in polo. The stick's name somehow came to mean a dispute in polo and other games, then took on the meaning of a crooked practice in those games and in general.

chivalrous *(SHI-vuhl-russ), adjective*
Honorable and courteous, as in a code of behavior followed by medieval knights. Considerate, especially toward women, the poor, or the defeated.

Placing one's coat over a puddle for a lady was once thought CHIVALROUS, but it's now more likely to be thought crazy.

chivalry *(SHIV-ul-ree), noun*
Brave, kind, courteous, or gentlemanly behavior.

After Brett held the door for her at the restaurant, Maureen knew that CHIVARLY was not dead.

Know This Quote

"We hear much of CHIVALRY of men towards women; but . . . it vanishes like dew before the summer sun when one of us comes into competition with the manly sex." —Martha Coston, American author

cholers *(KOH-lers), noun*
The mood of anger, irritability, grumpiness, or being short-tempered and impatient.

When Franklin is in the grip of CHOLERS, even his closest friends avoid his table at the club.

churlish *(CHUHR-lish), adjective*
Ill-bred, surly, sullen, or miserly. Unmannered; boorish and vulgar. Boy, don't we all know someone who deserves to be called this dramatic word?

CHURLISH behavior is never acceptable, no matter the person or the circumstances, but it is very hard to stop.

circumspect *(SIR-kum-spekt), adjective*
Prudent, cautious, and well considered.

After months of meetings, her business plan was CIRCUMSPECT.

Know This Quote
"I smiled, / I waited, / I was CIRCUMSPECT; / O never, never, never write that I / missed life or loving." —Hilda Doolittle, American poet and memoirist

circuitous *(sur-KYOO-uh-tus), adjective*
Roundabout or indirect; winding

Although the walk through the park was CIRCUITOUS, it was prettier than going directly home so the young couple often took the path when they weren't in a hurry.

circumlocution *(sir-kum-low-KYOO-shun), noun*
Evasiveness in speech or writing. The use of excess language to avoid saying something directly or truthfully. Overblown and tedious writing or speech. Don't try to get around good elocution with circumlocution; speak and write directly and well.

The use of CIRCUMLOCUTION can lengthen term papers and help students meet a predetermined word count or page requirement, but it can also often lead to lower grades.

circumvent *(sir-kum-VENT), verb*
To avoid rules or laws without actually breaking them. To evade by means of a gray area or loophole. To maneuver around authority.

To CIRCUMVENT the no-short-skirt rule, many of the girls took to wearing Daisy Duke shorts.

clairvoyant *(klayr-VOY-ant), adjective or noun*
Having the ability to see or know something that cannot be seen or known with the five senses (adjective) or a person who claims to have the ability to see or know something that cannot be seen or known with the five senses (noun)

The old woman who claimed to be CLAIRVOYANT did seem to know things no one else did.

Clare's claims of seeing into the future, and her amazing talent for predicting outcomes, still didn't prove her CLAIRVOYANCE.

The CLAIRVOYANT was the amusement park's biggest moneymaker after dark.

clandestine *(klan-DESS-tin), adjective*

Hidden, secret; concealed from general view or, if illegal, from authorities.

The CLANDESTINE activities of spies may seem glamorous in books and movies, but to those who really work in intelligence gathering, life can be dull as well as dangerous.

Know This Quote

"CLANDESTINE steps upon imagined stairs / Climb through the night, because his cuckoos call." —Wallace Stevens, American poet

clarion *(KLAR-ee-uhn), adjective*

Clear and shrill, like sound.

On the day classes began at his prep school, Paul groaned at the CLARION call of his morning alarm.

clarity *(KLAYR-rih-tee), noun*

Clearness in speech, appearance, or thought

The lecturer explained her ideas with such CLARITY that the audience was able to understand the very difficult concept.

clemency *(KLEH-muhn-see), noun*

A show of mercy or leniency toward a wrongdoer or opponent, under appropriate circumstances.

Jack's parents showed CLEMENCY and allowed him to keep his car even after his speeding conviction, inspiring him to drive more carefully.

cliché *(KLIH-shay), adjective*

Trite, unoriginal, or overused

The movie plot of aliens attacking the earth and humanity fighting them off has become so CLICHÉ I'm surprised any studio still makes those films.

cloying *(KLOYE-ing), adjective*

Sickeningly sweet, sappy, or sentimental.

Mark and Tania were in love and weren't ashamed to show it, but their friends found their relationship CLOYING.

Know This Quote

"Minerva save us from the CLOYING syrup of coercive compassion!" —Camille Paglia, American author, feminist, and social critic

coalesce *(ko-ah-LESS), verb*
To bond or come together; to form a single unit

The coach loved watching a group of kids come together as strangers at training camp and COALESCE into a real team by the season opener.

coddle *(KAH-dul), verb*
To baby, pamper, or indulge; to treat more gently than necessary

Much to his annoyance, his grandmother still CODDLED him as if he was a child even though he was a teenager.

codify *(KAHD-uh-fye), verb*
To organize into a system of rules, codes, or principles; to make clear and coherent.

Fiona set out to CODIFY the rules associated with her exclusive clique.

coercion *(KOH-her-shun), noun*
The act of using violence or the threat of violence to bring about desired results

When the businessman couldn't be bought, the mafia tried COERCION to get him to sell his property.

coeval *(KOH-ee-vahl), adjective*
Being of the same time period or era; existing at the same time

It is hard to believe that a man as clean-cut as Elliot Ness was COEVAL with a man as dangerous as Al Capone.

cogent *(KOH-jent), adjective*
Clear, concise, and convincing, usually of an argument or point of view; logical and well-presented

Instead of becoming emotional, she presented a COGENT argument for getting a new car as a graduation present, and her parents agreed.

Although it took a while, he eventually convinced the rest of the student council with his COGENT arguments.

cogitate *(kah-jih-TAYT), verb*
To think over carefully; to ponder and consider; to weigh all aspects of a situation

The state representative had to COGITATE on whether he would run for national office because he refused to make a snap decision.

cognition *(kog-NIH-shun), noun*
Mental ability; the process of acquiring knowledge through reason, intuition, or perception. Can also mean knowledge. Yes, it's just a fancy way to talk about thinking, but it's definitely an impressive word.

The young parents were excited to see the process of COGNITION developing in their daughter, as she began to take tiny steps with her feet and giant leaps with her mind.

cognizant *(KAHG-nih-zant), adjective*
Aware of; having knowledge about

Youth today are far more COGNIZANT of the hardship that comes with being an adult than kids of earlier generations.

cognoscente *(kon-yuh-SHEN-tee), noun*
Person with superior knowledge or understanding of a particular field.

As a result of my many years living in the Bordeaux region of France, I am very much COGNOSCENTE of wine and winemaking.

coherent *(KOH-heer-ant), adjective*
Able to make sense, be logical; consistently logical

She chose not to drink often because she stopped being COHERENT after only one glass of wine.

cohort *(KO-hort), noun*
A supporter, accomplice, or associate of a particular leader to whom special treatment is given. A member of a united group or group sharing a common characteristic like age, income, or gender, especially in statistical surveys. Originally referred to one of ten divisions of a Roman legion, composed of soldiers with strong ties of comradeship.

Stephanie and her COHORTS on the soccer team all shared physical qualities like blonde hair, as well as mental ones, such as the drive to win.

collaborate *(koh-laa-bur-AYT), verb*
To work together or jointly, usually to create something

The writer and the artist decided to COLLABORATE on a children's book.

colloquial *(kuh-LO-kwee-uhl), adjective*
Used in ordinary speech; informal; may imply regionally used words and phrases

Many freshmen have a difficult time switching from COLLOQUIAL language to formal writing in their college research papers.

Know This Quote
"COLLOQUIAL poetry is to the real art as the barber's wax dummy is to sculpture." —Ezra Pound, American expatriate poet

colloquy (*kaw-LUH-kwee), noun*
Conversation, discussion, or conference; often formal. A literary work written in the form of dialogue. The adjective *colloquial* means breezy, informal communication. A *colloquialism* is a common phrase of a conversational nature. So from noun to adjective to noun, from colloquy to colloquial to colloquialism, the definitions become less formal and more conversational.

Our member of the House of Representatives often holds a COLLOQUY for discussing specific legislation, rather than just talking about general topics.

collusion *(kuh-LOO-zhun), noun*
Secret cooperation among a number of people, usually to accomplish something illegal or wrong. A conspiratorial or secret understanding to join a secret plot or plan. Not a collision, but sometimes a *collusion* can also yield serious results.

We suspect COLLUSION when the price of gas rises and all stations charge the same higher rates, but it may just be the power of supply and demand.

combustible *(khum-BUS-tih-bul), adjective*
Able to catch fire and/or burn easily

Smoking while filling a gas tank is not recommended because gasoline is highly COMBUSTIBLE.

Which Word?

Look out for words that look or sound similar but have very different meanings. Combustible (khum-BUS-tih-bul) and comestible (kuhm-EHS-tih-bul) can easily be confused, especially when you are reading quickly. Combustible means something that can catch fire; comestible means something that can be eaten. Read closely so you don't misread these words.

comely *(KUM-lee), adjective*
Physically good-looking, pleasing, fetching, inviting, or attractive; usually referring to women.

COMELY women hope that love is more than skin deep and that men are attracted to them for more than just their looks.

comestible *(kuhm-EHS-tih-bul), noun or adjective*
Anything that can be eaten (noun) or edible; fit for human consumption (adjective)

He really didn't impress anyone by referring to the groceries as COMESTIBLES.

Travelers to third-world countries need to make sure the food is COMESTIBLE or it can make them very sick.

commemorate *(kuh-MEM-or-rayt), verb*
To honor or mark an occasion with a celebration, ritual, or ceremony

The United States COMMEMORATES the attacks on the World Trade Center with a moment of silence every September 11.

commensurate *(kuh-MENTS-rit), adjective*
Properly or appropriately proportionate. Of the same size, with an equal measure or equivalent duration. You can say *equal,* but *commensurate* is a much more powerful word.

Stewart's grades were, unfortunately, COMMENSURATE with the small amount of time and energy he invested in his academics.

commiserate *(kuh-MIH-zeh-rate), verb*
To express sympathy or sorrow; to share in another's sorrow or disappointment.

After the game, the first thing the team did was COMMISERATE with the parents of the player who was seriously injured.

compassion *(kum-PASH-uhn), noun*
The awareness of and sympathy for other's sufferings; kindness toward others less fortunate

Even after she became successful, she never forgot the COMPASSION of the people who had supported her during the hard times.

compendious *(kuhm-PEN-dee-us), adjective*
Concise, succinct; to the point.

Sheila is unable to tell COMPENDIOUS stories about her trips to the Riviera.

compile *(kum-PYL), verb*
To gather information from several sources in order to collect in one place

He COMPILED the names of all the fraternity brothers from the last fifty years in order to invite them to the reunion.

complacency *(kum-PLAY-sen-see), noun*
The feeling of being so good one doesn't have to try any longer

After acing three tests in a row in the class, a dangerous sense of COMPLACENCY set in and she stopped studying.

complaisance *(kum-PLAY-sens), noun*
A willingness to do what others want; the willingness to go along with the crowd without complaint

Her natural COMPLAISANCE made her an easy target for manipulation.

complement *(KOM-pluh-ment), noun*
Something used to enhance or perfect another

His dry sense of humor was the perfect COMPLEMENT to her goofy personality.

Which Word?

It is easy to confuse words that sound the same, especially when their spellings are also very similar. Complement (KOM-pluh-ment) and compliment (KOM-pluh-ment) are two easily confused words. A complement is something that enhances or improves another, but a compliment is a nice thing to say about someone. Be careful not to mix up these words.

compliance *(kum-PLIY-uhns), noun*
The act of observing and following directions, requests, or advice

The doctor assured her that COMPLIANCE with the new diet and exercise regime would help her lose weight.

comport *(kum-PORT), verb*
To behave or conduct oneself in a particular manner; to act in a certain desirable way

She decided to COMPORT herself with absolute dignity in order to counter the rumors she was a party girl.

composure *(kum-POH-shur), noun*
Being calm and in control of oneself and one's emotions; a calm state of mind

Her ability to maintain her COMPOSURE during a crisis made her an excellent police officer.

comprehensive *(cahm-PREE-hen-siv), adjective*
Total; complete; all encompassing; leaving nothing out

After the fire, the insurance company wanted a COMPREHENSIVE list of belongings that had been destroyed.

compromise *(KAHM-pro-miz), noun or verb*
A settlement in which the parties all give up some of their demands (noun) or to settle a situation by having all parties give up some of their demands (verb)

The COMPROMISE they reached was that she could stay out until one in the morning but she had to call at midnight.

Since she wanted a quiet beach vacation but he wanted nightlife, they decided to COMPROMISE and take a cruise.

compunction *(kum-PUNK-shun), noun*
Feelings of guilt, shame, and regret about doing something wrong. Remorse or uncertainty about a decision or course of action. Some punks shun others, then feel guilty and express compunction.

It is extremely sad when you see friends behaving badly yet showing no COMPUNCTION.

compurgation *(kom-purr-GAY-shun), noun*
A practice by which an accused person can be found not guilty if twelve or more people take an oath testifying to the validity of his claim of innocence.

The Anglo-Saxon process of COMPURGATION is the basis of the modern American jury system.

concede *(kuhn-SEED), verb*
To reluctantly admit something is true

After seeing the movie, he had to CONCEDE that the director could indeed handle a big-budget film.

conceit *(con-SEET), noun*
Arrogance; an unreasonably high opinion of oneself

His CONCEIT in the interviews was not backed up by his performance once he got the job.

concerted *(kun-SURT-id), adjective*
Planned by two or more persons working together on an action or effort. Mutual, as in actions taken toward an established goal. Also describes music written for several soloists. Much fancier way of saying *together.*

Musicians in concert act as performers CONCERTED to achieve common creative objectives.

conciliatory *(kon-SIL-ah-toree), adjective*
Meant to appease someone or make someone feel better

Her CONCILIATORY remarks were not enough to undo the damage caused by the young man's rude behavior.

Know This Quote
"If you are not very clever, you should be CONCILIATORY." —Benjamin Disraeli, British statesmen and literary figure

concise *(kun-SIYS), adjective*
Expressing a lot of information in a few words

The assignment was to keep the essay to fewer than 200 words so the students could learn to be clear and CONCISE.

concord *(KAHN-kord), noun*
Agreement and harmony between people or groups

If the original settlers had not learned to live in CONCORD with Native Americans, the settlement would have died out within the first year.

concur *(kuhn-KUR), verb*
To agree or share an opinion

She hated to CONCUR with her little brother's opinion on anything, but this time he was indeed right about her dress being unflattering.

concupiscence *(kon-KYOO-pih-suhns), noun*
Unbridled lust in the extreme—horniness.

The CONCUPISCENCE of teenage boys is legendary.

Know This Quote
"You're talking to a young vampire, a fountain of CONCUPISCENCE." —Mario Acevedo, American fantasy author

condense *(kun-DENS), verb*
To make shorter or reduce in volume without losing the meaning of the original subject matter

He had to CONDENSE an hour-long presentation to fit the thirty-minute time slot.

condescending (*kohn-di-SEN-ding), adjective*
Having a superior and patronizing attitude

The seniors regretted being so CONDESCENDING to the juniors once they were treated the same way by the college students.

conditional *(kun-DISH-ahn-ul), adjective*
Dependent upon something else; needing other conditions to be met

Her attending the dance was CONDITIONAL on her finishing her chores and homework on time.

condone *(kun-DOHN), verb*
To overlook or even support an action without comment or complaint

Many school officials believe if condoms are available in the high schools, the students will believe the adults CONDONE premarital sex.

confabulate *(kun-FA-byoo-late), verb*
From the Latin for "to have a conversation with," to chat or discuss something informally. Can describe engaging, extravagant storytelling. Also, to invent and believe stories to fill mental gaps due to memory loss or dementia. The noun *confab* means a casual discussion or chat, or a gathering of people for a discussion. Talk about a fancy word for talking—*confabulate* takes the prize.

The two drivers stopped the flow of traffic east and west in order to CONFABULATE about who had caused the accident.

conflagration *(kon-fla-GRAY-shun), noun*
A very large, very destructive fire; uncontrollable fire

The paints and chemicals in the garage turned what could have been a small, easily contained fire into a CONFLAGRATION.

confluence *(KAHN-floo-ens), noun*
The meeting, joining, or flowing together at one point, originally used in relation to streams

The CONFLUENCE of John Adams' determination, Benjamin Franklin's vision, and Thomas Jefferson's eloquence led to the thirteen original colonies declaring themselves independent of England.

conformist *(kun-FORM-ist), noun*

A person who behaves only in ways that are socially acceptable and expected

Although he sneered when he called his sister a CONFORMIST, he was secretly jealous of her popularity.

confound *(kuhn-FOWND), verb*

To confuse or puzzle; to mix-up; to be unable to distinguish

No matter how often he drove the route, the directions continued to CONFOUND him.

congeal *(kun-JEEL), verb*

To jell or curdle; to coagulate; to form a loose solid

The dessert was supposed to have CONGEALED around the fruit but it stayed liquid and runny because he used more water than called for in the recipe.

congenital *(kun-JEN-ih-tul), adjective*

Relating to a condition or characteristic had since birth, usually referring to a disease or deformity

She was still very young when she learned to take care of her CONGENITAL diabetes on her own.

congregation *(kahn-grih-GAY-shun), noun*

A large gathering, often but not always of people for the purpose of worship

The senator's inauguration party brought in the largest CONGREGATION of politicians the town had ever seen.

The church's CONGREGATION was small but determined to keep the church open in spite of the current financial difficulties.

conjoin *(kon-JOYN), verb*

Attach, come together, join

The little boy was thrilled when he was able to CONJOIN two of the puzzle pieces.

conjure *(KON-jur), verb*

To perform illusions and magic using agile hand movements. To summon or call upon, as if by supernatural means.

On the anniversary of Houdini's death, many try to CONJURE up the image of this famous magician who spent his life exploring the potential to communicate with the dead.

connoisseur *(kahn-uh-SOOER), noun*

A person with great knowledge and training in matters of taste

The butler was, by necessity, a CONNOISSEUR of wine and cuisine.

connotation *(KAH-noh-TAY-shun), noun*
The implied, figurative, or suggested additional meaning of a word or phrase, apart from the literal dictionary meaning. In contrast, the word *denotation* means the literal definition or meaning.

As society changes, the CONNOTATIONS of particular words also change, and what was once an appropriate word sometimes becomes politically incorrect.

consecrate *(KON-seh-KRAYT), verb*
To declare something sacred, true, sacrosanct, or involuble.

The couple CONSECRATED their love at their wedding.

consensus *(kun-SENS-us), noun*
General agreement; the opinion of the majority of the group

The student government had come to a CONSENSUS that they would approach the principal about opening the parking lot to students.

console *(kun-SOL), verb*
To lessen sorrow or grief; to ease emotional pain

Her friends were unable to CONSOLE her when she was rejected by her first choice of schools.

consortium *(kun-SOR-shee-um), noun*
A group set up for a common purpose that would be beyond the capabilities of a single member. A union, partnership, or alliance. Also a legal term for the rights of married persons.

The Career and Internship Connection is a CONSORTIUM of about a dozen schools that participate in four off-campus recruiting events.

conspicuous *(kun-SPIK-yoo-us), adjective*
Obvious; standing out; unhidden

He left his report card in a CONSPICUOUS place so his mother would find it and see his improved grades.

consternation *(KOHN-ster-nay-shun), noun*
Extreme dismay or anxiety, usually caused by something unexpected occurring

The principal's CONSTERNATION at the break-in was eased somewhat when she learned none of her students had committed the crime.

constraint *(kon-STRAYNT), noun*
Physical, emotional, or logistical restraint; a binding, literally or figuratively

A feeling of CONSTRAINT filled the room as people tried not to react too harshly after the speaker made an inappropriate comment.

constrict *(kun-STRIKT), verb*
To tighten or make narrower; to close in

Jitters caused his throat to CONSTRICT before every performance but he always relaxed once he started singing.

construe *(kon-STROO), verb*
To interpret or understand meaning of a word, gesture, or action in a particular way. To translate or analyze the grammar of a piece of text. To construe is to reach a conclusion based on review.

It is often an attorney's job to CONSTRUE the meaning of a contract, then share that interpretation with a client and, if needed, with a judge or jury.

consummate *(KON-suh-mate), verb*
To bring something such as a business deal to a conclusion or desired end; to achieve, fulfill, complete, or finalize. Also, for a couple to make a marriage legally valid by having sexual relations.

By CONSUMMATING an agreement, and then signing the letter of intent, the high school All-American football player committed to attending Notre Dame.

Know This Quote
"[John F. Kennedy is] a new star with a tremendous national appeal, the skill of a CONSUMMATE showman." —Russell Baker, American author

contemptuous *(kun-TEMPT-choo-us), adjective*
Showing or having the feeling that someone or something is inferior or worthless

Although he tried not to be CONTEMPTUOUS of homeless people, he didn't always succeed.

contend *(kun-TEND), verb*
To claim or assert; to struggle against

The prosecutor expected the defense to CONTEND the evidence was irrelevant.

contentious *(kun-TEN-shus), adjective*
Argumentative or likely to cause an argument

Her CONTENTIOUS attitude made it more difficult for the group to come to an agreement.

context *(kon-TEKST), noun*
The words, phrases, or passages before and after a particular word or passage that help to explain its complete meaning. The circumstances or events related to an incident or action.

The CONTEXT of Martin Luther King, Jr.'s, famous "I Have a Dream" speech is important for understanding the full impact this oration had on its audience.

contiguous *(kun-TIG-yoo-us), adjective*
Touching, connected, or sharing a border; uninterrupted; continuous

Often, stores will ship to the CONTIGUOUS United States but not Alaska or Hawaii.

contract *(kun-TRAKT), verb*
To shrink or make smaller

The doctor knew the boy's head wound wasn't too bad when his pupils CONTRACTED in the light.

contravene *(kon-truh-VEEN), verb*
To disagree with or oppose a decision or statement; go against or deny. To oppose something by action or argument. To break a rule or law. To be mean, you would *contravene* (or deny), often making others cry.

The decisions of coaches are rarely CONTRAVENED by players.

contretemps *(KON-truh-tahn) noun*
An inopportune occurrence with embarrassing results.

Dropping the roast for the dinner party on the floor right before she was supposed to serve it was an unfortunate CONTRETEMPS.

Know This Quote

"Pan had been amongst them . . . the little god Pan, who presides over social CONTRETEMPS and unsuccessful picnics." —E. M. Forster, English novelist

contrite *(kohn-TRYT), adjective*
Feeling sorry or apologetic

He couldn't stay angry at his sister when she was so CONTRITE for spilling her drink on his homework.

contrivance *(kun-TRY-vunce), noun*
A cleverly made, unusual device or machine. A clever way to acquire something; a plot or scheme. A plan intended to deceive.

The CONTRIVANCES of alchemists were machines that attempted—and failed—to turn base metals into gold.

contumacious *(kun-tuh-MAY-shus), adjective*
Willfully and intentionally rude and disobedient

Although she had been CONTUMACIOUS in front of her friends, she dropped the brave front when she was at the police station by herself.

conundrum *(kuh-NUN-drum), noun*
A difficult problem or situation that is not easily resolved.

Knowing whether to attend MIT, Yale, or Harvard was quite a CONUNDRUM: MIT had the courses he wanted, but Harvard and Yale offered him full sports scholarships.

convalescence *(kon-vuh-LEH-sunce), noun*
Time spent resting, recovering, and regaining one's health after an illness or medical treatment. From the Latin for "to grow stronger."

Those people who believe CONVALESCENCE is done better at home don't have two-year-old twins.

convention *(kun-VEN-shun), noun*
Social norms; usual and expected behavior; that which is approved of and accepted by society at large

Female suffragettes defied CONVENTION by marching and protesting for the right to vote.

Know This Quote
"CONVALESCENCE is the part that makes the illness worthwhile." —George Bernard Shaw, Irish playwright

convergence *(kun-VER-jens), noun*
The act or process of coming together or meeting at one point or place

America's independence from England was largely a result of the CONVERGENCE of great minds and brave hearts.

conviction *(kun-VIK-shun), noun*
A strong, firmly held belief

His moral CONVICTIONS about the importance of all human life caused him to oppose the war.

convivial *(kun-VIV-yul), adjective*
Enjoyable because of friendliness and amicability; festive and sociable. Given to eating, drinking, and socializing.

It was very surprising that the prom was so CONVIVIAL, given that adolescents can often be competitive and taunting.

Know This Quote
"One does not leave a CONVIVIAL party before closing time." —Winston Churchill, British statesman and orator

convoluted *(kon-vuh-LOO-tid), adjective*
Too complex or intricate to understand easily. Complicated, with many twists or folds. Literally, folded into a coil or spiral. Most often used to express an extreme state of complication, intricacy, or interdependency.

Relationships can be CONVOLUTED and difficult, but they are ultimately worth the effort.

copious *(KO-pee-us), adjective*
Produced in large quantities; abundant.

COPIOUS notes can be a student's best study tools.

coquette *(ko-KET), noun*
A woman who dresses promiscuously or flirts excessively to make men think she is sexually available when in fact she has no intention of sleeping with them.

Marla doesn't intend to play the COQUETTE at society balls, but her alluring looks attract other debutantes' dates constantly.

cordial *(KOR-jul), adjective*
Warm and friendly; welcoming; nice

Her mother-in-law was so CORDIAL, the new bride felt comfortable immediately when she arrived at her husband's childhood home.

cornucopia *(kor-neh-KOH-pee-yah), noun*
A symbol, literally or figuratively, of abundance, wealth, and plenty; when literal, usually in the form of a horn overflowing with fruits and vegetables

The dean of the law school was a CORNUCOPIA of legal information and knowledge.

corporeal *(koh-POR-ee-uhl), adjective*
Of the body; regarding the body

A good doctor understands the connection between mental health and CORPOREAL health.

correlate *(KOR-uh-layt), verb*
To show or prove connection, relationship, or similarity

Sociologists claim it is easy to CORRELATE high school dropout rates to the rise in crime committed by teenagers.

corroborate *(kuh-RAW-buh-rate), verb*
To give evidence of the truth; confirm or increase in certainty. To provide testimony that supports previous theories or opinions.

Jim said his bother would CORROBORATE his story, proving he was nowhere near the scene of the crime.

corrode *(kor-ROHD), verb*
To rust or be eaten away by chemical reaction; to destroy slowly and systematically

It was painful for the couple's friends to watch the trust between them CORRODE as they moved toward divorce.

corrugated *(kor-uh-GAY-ted), adjective*
Shaped into ridges and grooves

The boys discovered CORRUGATED steel was good for making the walls of their fort.

countenance *(KOUN-tn-unts), noun*
A facial expression, either deliberate or unconscious, conveying the person's mood, thoughts, or emotions.

Although she did not intent to show her annoyance at the man's rudeness, her COUNTENANCE betrayed her.

Know This Quote
"We romped until the pans / Slid from the kitchen shelf; / My mother's COUNTENANCE / Could not unfrown itself." —Theodore Roethke, American poet

counterfeit *(KOUN-ter-fit), adjective, noun, or verb*
Fake; imitation; made to look like the original (adjective) or a fake; a copy of something valuable, usually made to defraud or fool (noun) or to make a copy of something valuable with the intent to defraud (verb)

She wore COUNTERFEIT jewels so people wouldn't know she had been forced to sell the real ones.

Upon closer examination, the Monet painting supposedly discovered in the family's attic was actually a COUNTERFEIT.

Printers had become so advanced that it was relatively easy for criminals to COUNTERFEIT money, so the government changed the design on the bills.

countervail *(kown-tehr-VAYL), verb*
To offset the effect of something with an equal but opposing force; to counter

The moral of many stories is that good must COUNTERVAIL evil in order for humanity to live in peace and harmony.

coup *(koo), noun*
When a person already in a position of power forcibly seizes control.

Sophia took control of her father's company while he was in the hospital, an act the investors considered a bit of a COUP.

couture *(kuh-TOUR), noun*
Clothing in the latest and most popular styles created by in-vogue fashion designers.

If Alyssia does not have the latest COUTURE prior to its debut on Paris runways, she will not deign to consider wearing it.

covenant *(KUHV-nent), noun*
A binding agreement or contract between two or more parties. In biblical terms, the promise binding the ancient Israelites to God.

Some teenagers believe promises made by parents, particularly regarding cars and curfews, should be thought of as COVENANTS.

covert *(KOH-vert), adjective*
Secret or covered over. Concealed or surreptitious. Not intended to be known or seen.

Many COVERT operations contributed to the success of D-day, but it took decades for anyone involved in them to be honored.

covet *(KUV-it), verb*
To want or desire something that belongs to another person

The young woman had always COVETED her grandmother's pearls so was delighted to receive them as her birthday present.

cower *(KOW-er), verb*
To shrink or cringe in fear

The puppy COWERED away from new people at first but adjusted within a few weeks.

cram *(KRAM), verb*
To study a subject intensively for an imminent exam. To eat food hastily and with greed. To force persons or objects into a space or container too small to comfortably fit them all.

CRAMMING for exams is an attempt to quickly force large quantities of facts into your memory, which, ideally, can retain all the pertinent information.

crass *(KRASS), adjective*
Crude and unrefined, usually used to describe a person or attitude

Women found his attitudes about gender roles CRASS and outdated.

credence *(KREE-dence), noun*
A belief in something as factual, based on the degree that something is plausible. Faith in a thing's legitimacy.

The defendant's claims of innocence lost CREDENCE as more evidence was uncovered and made public.

credulity *(kreh-DYOO-lih-tee), noun*
A tendency to be gullible; ready to believe anything

The professor's CREDULITY made it easy for students to get extensions on assignments so long as their excuses weren't too outrageous.

criterion *(kryi-TEER-ee-uhn), noun*
A standard or test by which something else is judged or compared

The judges made the CRITERION for the contest available for all the contestants so everyone would know what was expected.

Which Word?

Everyone is familiar with adding s or es to the end of a word to make a singular into a plural. However, it's not that easy with some words. Criterion (kryi-TEER-ee-uhn) means one rule or guideline. But when there are two or more rules or guidelines, they are criteria (kryi-TEER-ee-uh). Although many people say "criteria" for both the singular and the plural, it is incorrect to do so. Always read the sentence carefully since "the criterion" and "the criteria" are both correct. The first means there is only one, while the second indicates more than one.

cryptic *(KRIHP-tihk), adjective*

Vague; coded; having a mysterious meaning

> *Since she didn't know who might hear the message, she made it CRYPTIC enough that only her boyfriend would understand what she meant.*

culinary *(KYOO-luh-ner-ee), adjective*

Related to food or cooking. Commonly used to describe the type of school where chefs are trained. If you want to follow the recipe for good usage, use "culinary" rather than "cooking."

> *The sale of CULINARY books and related items increased dramatically as the popularity of television cooking shows rose.*

cull *(KULL), verb*

To gather, amass, or collect.

> *Consumer behavior data was CULLED from online surveys and focus groups.*

culminate *(KUL-min-ayt), verb*

To come to the end or completion; to reach the climax of an event or happening

> *Everyone knew the graduation ceremony would CULMINATE with tears of joy as well as the traditional tossing of the mortar boards.*

culpable *(KUL-puh-bull), adjective*

Deserving blame or punishment for something wrong; accountable for errors or misdeeds.

> *Mr. Hartland was CULPABLE for the errors he made while grading the English exams, so he gave the students an extra ten points on each essay.*

cultural literacy *(KUHLCH-rul LIH-tuh-reh-see), phrase*

As conceived and defined by Professor E.D. Hirsch, Jr., "the background knowledge necessary for functional literacy and effective national communication"; from the subtitle of his book, *What Every American Needs to Know.* The information authors assume readers have at certain stages of education; the educational background necessary for effective communication of ideas.

> *The debate regarding CULTURAL LITERACY and its part in our elementary and secondary school curricula continues to this day.*

cumbersome *(KUM-ber-sum), adjective*
Awkward to carry or handle; hard to manage because of bulk, weight, size, or shape. Difficult to deal with because of length or complexity. Not a *cummerbund*—that's a pleated, often colored sash worn by men as part of formal attire.

While desktop computers have become smaller and lighter, they are still CUMBERSOME when compared to laptop models.

cupidity *(kyoo-PIH-duh-tee), noun*
Greed; extreme desire for money and possessions. Cupid is a symbol of love, and cupidity is the love of money and things.

Unrealistic CUPIDITY of youth, often expressed by spoiled children, should with time be replaced by the work ethic of an adult.

curative *(KYOOR-uh-tive), adjective*
Able to restore health; curing; serving to provide a remedy.

The CURATIVE regimen of the spa involved diet and hot baths, as well as exercise.

cursory *(KUR-sur-ree), adjective*
Brief; without attention to detail; not thorough

In spite of her mother's request, the young woman only gave her room a CURSORY cleaning before heading out to the mall.

curtail *(kur-TAYL), verb*
To cut short; to reduce the time or quantity

The concert tour had to be CURTAILED when the lead singer lost his voice and was given doctor's orders not to sing for six weeks.

cyberspace *(SY-ber-spase), noun*
The theoretical realm where electronic information exists or is shared. The imaginary world of virtual reality.

It's fun to think of e-mails as floating in CYBERSPACE, but they are actually a series of impulses sent and received over a variety of fiber-optic or traditional telephone lines.

cynicism *(SIN-ih-si-zim), noun*
A negative and suspicious attitude; the expectation of the worst

As she got older, it became harder and harder not to let her natural trust of people to turn into CYNICISM.

cynosure *(SIN-uh-shoor), noun*
An object or person that has all the attention; the focal point

The new baby was the CYNOSURE of the entire party.

Know This Quote

"This lighthouse was the CYNOSURE of all eyes." —Henry David Thoreau, American author and transcendentalist

D

doctrinaire abstemious levity hubris panacea veracity cerebellum labyrinth criterion nonagenarian meticulous

quondam colloquial palpable incipient salutary redact fervent beleaguered yawnful elixir beneficent

dalliance *(DA-lee-unce), noun*
A lighthearted undertaking; carefree, frivolous, inconsequential, or idle wasting of time. An amorous flirtation, distraction, or affair.

Stephanie could not forgive her husband's DALLIANCE, so she asked for a divorce.

dank *(DANK), adjective*
Damp and chilly; unpleasantly cold and moist. Dank is damp, but not necessarily dark.

The Williams' basement was DANK even before the rainy winter season.

dauntless *(DAWNT-liss), adjective*
Fearless, intrepid, and bold.

When it came to bungee jumping, Carlos was DAUNTLESS.

Know This Quote
"For Thought has a pair of DAUNTLESS wings." —Robert Frost, American poet

de facto *(dee FAK-toe), adjective*
Existing in fact.

Although we eschew titles, Sasha clearly is the DE FACTO head of our arts-patronage club.

de rigueur *(duh rih-GUR), adjective*
Conforming to current standards of behavior, fashion, style, and etiquette.

A two-carat diamond engagement ring that cost a young man a year's salary was DE RIGUEUR for proposing to a girl in the 1950s.

dearth *(DERTH), noun*
A lack or shortage; not having enough of something

Her sons were pleased that after her trip to the grocery store, there was no longer a DEARTH of snack food in the house.

debacle *(dee-BAH-kuhl), noun*
Something that becomes a disaster, defeat, or failure. Utter collapse or rout; complete, often humiliating failure.

Wars often seem justified at first, but they tend to become DEBACLES if an exit strategy is not devised and implemented.

debauchery *(deh-BOW-chair-ee), noun*
Frequent indulgence in sensual pleasures.

The group of college kids engaged in DEBAUCHERY at the beach house.

Know This Quote
"The geniuses, the mad dreamers, those who speak of DEBAUCHERY in the spirit, they are the condemned of our times." —Harlan Ellison, American author

debilitate *(dih-BIH-lih-tate), verb*

To weaken or sap strength from someone or something.

ALS, also known as Lou Gehrig's disease, DEBILITATES those who suffer from it, and it is ultimately fatal.

debunk *(DEE-bunk), verb*

To prove false; to disprove exaggerated claims

Medical advances and personal experiences have managed to DEBUNK the earliest claims that cigarette smoking was actually good for you.

deciduous *(dih-SIH-juh-wus), adjective*

Shedding or losing foliage at the end of the growing season. Falling off or shedding at a particular time, season, or stage of growth. Not lasting; ephemeral.

Some Native American tribes marked the change of seasons by the DECIDUOUS clues around them, including deer shedding antlers, leaves falling from certain trees, and feathers molting from specific birds.

decimate *(DEHS-ih-mayt), verb*

To utterly destroy or ruin; to inflict great damage

The coach taught her team it was better to show good sportsmanship and win with grace rather than try to DECIMATE the other team.

Know This Quote

"Every doctor will allow a colleague to DECIMATE a whole countryside sooner than violate the bond of professional etiquette by giving him away."
—George Bernard Shaw, Irish playwright

déclassé *(day-klass-AY), adjective*

Of a fallen social position or inferior status.

Jean thought her imitation designer bag looked exactly like the real thing, but the other girls in her exclusive private school quickly ridiculed Jean—and her bag—for being DÉCLASSÉ.

decorous *(DEH-kore-us), adjective*

Behaving in a manner acceptable to polite society; having good taste and good manners.

"Another week with these DECOROUS drones and I'll jump out the window," the young girl complained to her mother of her fellow debutantes.

decorum *(deh-KOR-um), noun*

Appropriate and proper behavior

In spite of his long hair and tattoos, he could act with DECORUM and dignity when the situation called for it.

decrepit *(dih-KREH-pit), adjective*
In very poor condition; old, overused, or not working efficiently. Lessened in strength or ability, as in old age. Used to describe a person, object, or idea that is weak and past its prime. Please don't call someone *decrepit* if they are just old; use this word appropriately.

Most of the buildings in the so-called poor part of town were indeed DECREPIT and dangerous to live in.

deduce *(di-DOOCE), verb*
To reach a logical conclusion by using what is known, without all necessary information. To infer or derive from evidence or assumption. To deduce is not to take your best guess; it means a logical leap.

It is the job of detectives to DEDUCE the circumstances of crimes, for they rarely have all the facts.

defamation *(de-fuh-MAY-shun), noun*
False, baseless attack on a person's or group's reputation, name, or character. The act of defaming or bringing disgrace.

DEFAMATION seems to be the purpose of many newspapers that focus on sensational stories about stars and celebrities.

defer *(DEH-fur), verb*
To put off or postpone; to reschedule for a later time

She decided to DEFER college for a year in order to travel through Europe with her friends.

deference *(DEH-fuh-rence), noun*
Polite respect or submission to the judgment, opinion, or wishes of another. The act of yielding to another higher, senior, or more authoritative person.

In DEFERENCE to the memory of his brother, Ken did not speak about the details of his accident with anyone.

deflation *(dee-FLAY-shun), noun*
A weakened economy in which prices fall because of a decline in consumer spending.

We were pleased to learn that DEFLATION has not harmed sales at Wempe's on Fifth Avenue, our favorite purveyor of watches.

defunct *(dih-FUNKT), adjective*
An institution, object, etc., that has ceased to exist.

Many once-bustling companies are now DEFUNCT due to a poor economic climate.

Know This Quote

"Practical men, who believe themselves to be quite exempt from any intellectual influence, are usually the slaves of some DEFUNCT economist."
—John Maynard Keynes, British economist

degradation *(deh-grih-DAY-shun), noun*
The process of insulting or putting someone down; the state of being put down, insulted, or humiliated

She couldn't bring herself to rush a sorority because she didn't believe in the DEGRADATION the pledges went through.

dehydrate *(dee-HIY-drayt), verb*
To cause something to dry out and lose water

Before hiking or camping, they would DEHYDRATE fruit to carry with them to have as easy snacks.

deification *(DEE-if-ih-kay-shin), noun*
The process of making someone or something into—and worshipping them as—a god.

Many Christians feel the DEIFICATION of a statue or other object is wrong.

Know This Quote
"Poetry is the DEIFICATION of reality." —Edith Sitwell, British poet

deign *(DAYN), verb*
To do something that is believed to be below one's station or dignity

Some of the more stuck-up seniors wouldn't DEIGN to speak to freshmen in spite of being only a few years older.

delectable *(dih-LEK-tuh-bull), adjective*
Delicious; absolutely delightful, pleasing, or attractive. From the Latin for "delightful."

Italian and Jewish grandmas are famous for their DELECTABLE dishes, served with a bit of guilt on the side.

deleterious *(duh-lee-TREE-us), adjective*
Harmful or damaging

He studied for every test because he realized that one bad grade would be DELETERIOUS to his GPA and lower his chances of getting into an Ivy League college.

delineate *(dih-LI-nee-ate), verb*
To describe or explain something in detail. To outline, sketch, graph, chart, or draw something. To describe the principal points of something.

The proctor clearly DELINEATED the instructions for the essay exam, in writing and out loud.

deluge *(DAY-looj), noun*
A great flood or fall of water; anything that overwhelms like a great flood

When the paper leaked that the movie star was in town, the hotel received a DELUGE of phone calls from people hoping to talk to him.

demagogue *(DEHM-ah-gog), noun*
A leader who uses the emotions, fears, and prejudices of a populace, rather than logic, intellect, or facts to gain support

Eva Peron, or Evita as she is better known, was one of the most successful DEMAGOGUES of modern history.

Know This Quote

"A DEMAGOGUE is a person with whom we disagree as to which gang should mismanage the country." —Don Marquis, American journalist and humorist

demiurge *(DEM-ee-urj), noun*
A powerful creative force or a creative personality.

After trying a few different professions, Jackson realized that his ability with artifice, combined with his family connections, would make him a marketing DEMIURGE.

demotic *(dih-MAH-tik), adjective*
Language used by ordinary people.

Eileen always avoids the DEMOTIC because she does not want to be mistaken for someone from the middle class.

demure *(dih-MYOOR), adjective*
Modest, reserved, or shy in appearance. Used to describe sober, retiring, or sedate behavior.

DEMURE actions and attitudes are much more proper than oppositional and defiant behavior.

Know This Quote

"Assent, and you are sane; / DEMUR,—you're straightway dangerous, / And handled with a chain." —Emily Dickinson, American poet

denigrate *(DEN-ih-grayt), adjective*
Insulting; put down; demean; belittle.

Lucy became upset when the boys at the mall DENIGRATED her best friend for her curly hair.

denizen *(DEN-ih-zen), noun*
A native or one who is in a particular place often enough to practically be a resident.

The DENIZENS of the Bronx have a culture separate from the rest of New York.

denote *(dih-NOTE), verb*
To designate or refer to somebody or something in particular. To define something literally, as in a dictionary definition. To announce or make known. The opposite of *connote,* which means to imply or suggest something in addition to its literal meaning.

Before the camping trip, each student received specific instructions regarding what would DENOTE a rules infraction that would be punished by being sent home.

dénouement *(DAY-noo-mah) or (DAY-nyoo-mah), noun*
The final part of a story or movie in which all the loose ends are tied up and all the questions answered

The DÉNOUEMENT of most mysteries occurs when the detective reveals which character is the murderer.

dénouement *(day-new-MAH), noun*
The conclusion of a complex series of events.

Marjorie was disappointed with the opera because she felt its DÉNOUEMENT left too many loose ends

denounce *(dee-NOWNS), verb*
To declare publicly that something is wrong, evil, or incorrect

After much soul-searching, the senator DENOUNCED her own party's stance on immigration.

deplete *(deh-PLEET), verb*
To use up or greatly diminish in quantity

There is some concern that we will DEPLETE the earth's resources if the population of the planet continues to grow at its current rate.

deplore *(dih-PLOHR), verb*
To feel strong disapproval; to condemn; to be strongly against

While most people DEPLORE poverty and injustice, few people are willing to sacrifice anything in order to help reduce it in society.

depose *(deh-POZ), verb*
To remove from office; to remove from power; to dethrone

The President sent troops into the impoverished country to DEPOSE the tyrannical dictator.

deposition *(dep-uh-ZISH-uhn), noun*
A statement or testimony under oath

He didn't have to appear in court because the attorneys were satisfied with his DEPOSITION given earlier in the investigation.

deprave *(dih-PRAYV), verb*
To make wicked; to morally corrupt

She kept a close eye on her teenage son to ensure the influences of growing up in the inner city wouldn't DEPRAVE him.

deprecate *(DEH-prih-kate), verb*
To belittle or express disapproval of someone or something. To cut down verbally. Teens can *deprecate* those they hate, or, in humor, those they date. Most high school humor is *deprecating* in nature. Get it, geek?

Verbal bullies DEPRECATE others rather than using their fists, but the words hurt just the same.

Know This Quote

"Those who profess to favor freedom and yet DEPRECATE agitation, are men who want crops without plowing up the ground."
—Frederick Douglass, American abolitionist and orator

dereliction *(dare-uh-LIK-shun), noun*
deserting a building.

DERELICTION of duty is a serious charge for those in the military.

deride *(deh-RYID), verb*
To ridicule; to speak or treat with contempt; to tease cruelly; to scorn

Under school policy, no student was allowed to DERIDE another for any reason.

derision *(duh-RIZSH-un), noun*
Mockery, contempt, ridicule

Although many people treated him with DERISION because of his disability, he had learned to ignore them.

derivative *(duh-RHIV-ih-tiv), adjective*
Originating from another source; copied or adapted from something else

A paragraph in her essay was so obviously DERIVATIVE that the teacher feared plagiarism.

descant *(des-KANT), verb*
To talk freely and without inhibition.

Eloise is always more than willing to DESCANT concerning her past liaisons.

descry *(duh-SKRY), verb*
To finally see; to catch sight of; to figure out through detection

After she turned him down for the third time, he finally was able to DESCRY that she just wasn't interested in a date.

desiccated *(DES-ih-kayt-ed), adjective*
Dried; dehydrated; having all water removed from

The explorers were not surprised to discover the ancient mummies were DESICCATED after centuries within the tombs.

desideratum *(deh-sih-deh-RAH-tum), noun*
Something that one covets or desires.

Ever since she was an adolescent, Evangeline's DESIDERATUM has been a first edition of Virginia Woolf's first novel, The Voyage Out.

despondent *(dih-SPON-dunt), adjective*
Extremely unhappy, depressed, dejected, or discouraged. Despairing, with the feeling that all hope is in vain.

Divorce respondents are often DESPONDENT, if depressed about the breakup, or, most likely, the attorney fees.

despotism *(DESS-puh-tih-zum), noun*
Authoritarian rule by a tyrant, dictator, or despot. Rule by one dominant person who exercises complete power. High school students sometimes describe principals, parents, or coaches as despots, and occasionally they are right.

The rise of DESPOTISM is often linked to poverty, when the poor hope a powerful leader can bring positive change.

desuetude *(DEH-sweh-tood), noun*
Disuse; inactivity

Rules of etiquette have fallen into DESUETUDE as society has become more relaxed about gender and class roles.

desultory *(DES-uhl-tor-ee), adjective*
Disconnected; half-hearted; seemingly random

Her presentation was so DESULTORY even her professor realized she hadn't spent enough time preparing it.

Know This Quote
"Find time still to be learning somewhat good, and give up being DESULTORY." —Marcus Aurelius, Roman Emperor

detached *(dee-TATCHED), adjective*
Disconnected either emotionally or physically; separate and apart

Doctors and other health-care professionals need to remain DETACHED from their patients or else they become too emotionally involved.

deterrent *(duh-TER-ahnt), noun*
Something that discourages or dissuades

For most students, the threat of expulsion is an effective DETERRENT against cheating on exams.

detrimental *(det-treh-MEN-tul), adjective*
Harmful; damaging; negative in some way

At this point, everyone knows that smoking is DETRIMENTAL to a person's health but some people still smoke anyway.

deus ex machina *(DAY-oos eks ma-KEEN-uh), noun*
An unexpected and fortunate event solving a problem or saving someone from disaster; a stroke of good luck.

The author used a DEUS EX MACHINA to work his way out of the mess he got the characters in toward the end of the novel.

devious *(DEE-vee-us), adjective*
Sneaky; underhanded

Her little brother could be DEVIOUS when it came to getting her in trouble and making himself look like an angel.

devise *(de-VIYZ), verb*
To plan, create, or design, usually referring to the mental process of creation

The city government DEVISED a plan to expand the pedestrian mall in order to bring in more shoppers.

dexterity *(dek-STAYR-ih-tee), noun*
Skill, ability, or grace, especially physical or mental

Most visitors to the zoo are amazed by the DEXTERITY of the animals in the primate house.

diaphanous *(diy-AHF-un-us), adjective*
Delicate and filmy to the point of being nearly transparent; gauzy

She had always dreamed her wedding dress would have a cathedral length train and a DIAPHANOUS veil.

Know This Quote

"To behold the day-break! / The little light fades the immense and DIAPHANOUS shadows, / The air tastes good to my palate."
—Walt Whitman, American poet and humanist

diatribe *(DIE-uh-tribe), noun*
A bitter verbal or written attack; a denunciation. Also, a pointed and abusive critique.

Angry at being caught cheating, the student launched a profanity-laced DIATRIBE on the test proctor.

dichotomy *(die-KAH-tuh-mee), noun*
Two parts, ideas, or concepts that differ from, contradict, or perfectly complement each other. Contrasting halves, pairs, or sets. A division of mutually exclusive ideas or groups.

The DICHOTOMY of good and evil is a theme in almost all classic novels read in high school.

didactic *(die-DAK-tik), adjective*
Focused on communicating a moral, political, or educational message. Presenting a clear vision of right and wrong; projecting morality. Not to be confused with *eclectic,* which means composed of elements from varied sources, or *dialectic,* which is the tension between conflicting elements, forces, or ideas.

> **Know This Quote**
> "The essential function of art is moral . . . . But a passionate, implicit morality, not DIDACTIC."
> —D. H. Lawrence, British author

Some authors and lecturers are subtly DIDACTIC, while others are more obvious and preachy.

diffident *(DIH-fuh-dent), adjective*
Lacking self-confidence. Shy, unassertive, or with a low sense of self-worth. Reserved or restrained in the way one behaves. Don't confuse with *defendant,* which is a person answering criminal charges, or *dissident,* a person who disagrees with an established political or religious authority.

DIFFIDENT individuals don't belong in sales positions, which require assertiveness and risk-taking.

diffuse *(dih-FYOOZ), adjective or verb*
Spread without specific direction; not concentrated (adjective)
To scatter or spread out; to cause to spread; to thin out (verb)

The DIFFUSE light cast a lovely glow over the evening making the dinner that much more romantic.

The mediator knew he had to DIFFUSE the anger between the couple if he was going to help them come to a mutually satisfying settlement.

digression *(di-GRESH-un), noun*
A turning away or diversion from the main topic

The students discovered it was easy to distract their teacher with an interesting DIGRESSION into current events.

dilate *(DI-layt), verb*
To expand; to make wider or larger

In the dark, our pupils DILATE to let in what light is available.

dilatory *(DIHL-uh-tor-ee), adjective*
Meant to cause delay or postpone; used for the purpose of putting off an event

The young man used a DILATORY question to postpone her leaving until he had gained the courage to ask her out.

dilettante *(DIL-eh-tahnt), noun*
An amateur or uneducated follower of a field of interest, usually the arts; someone who has an interest in but no real knowledge about a field of interest

His artwork was mediocre at best and would only appeal to the DILETTANTES at the showing.

diligence *(DIL-ih-jens), noun*
Persistent and attentive work or effort; determination about one's goals

Her academic DILIGENCE paid off when she graduated at the top of her class.

diminutive *(dih-MIH-nyoo-tiv), adjective*
Very small, or smaller than usual. This idea is often communicated by attaching a suffix to the noun being described, as in *kitchenette* (suffix "-ette") or *booklet* (suffix "let").

The DIMINUTIVE yet amazing basketball player proved the axiom "Good things do come in small packages."

disabuse *(dis-uh-BYOOZ), verb*
To convince or persuade someone an idea, thought, or belief is false

She hated to DISABUSE him of his fantasy but she knew his screenplay would never be optioned.

disallow *(dis-uh-LOUH), verb*
To state something is false; to refute

The police decided to DISALLOW that alcohol had been involved in the accident in order to silence the rumors that the woman had been drinking.

discern *(dis-URN), verb*
To be able to recognize and understand differences, either visually or mentally

Very young children cannot DISCERN the difference between fact and fiction, so what first appears as lying may actually be the misunderstanding that an event didn't really happen.

disclose *(dis-KLOWZ), verb*
To share a secret; to make a secret known

It wasn't until the reunion that she was able to DISCLOSE she had had a crush on the quarterback when they were in school.

discombobulate *(DISS-kum-BAH-byoo-late), verb*
To throw someone into a state of confusion; to utterly take aback. A great word to use, but don't confuse, or you will discombobulate or give someone the blues.

The attempt to see everything at Disneyland in one day can DISCOMBOBULATE even the calmest parents.

discomfit *(dis-KUM-fit), verb*
To embarrass or make uncomfortable; to defeat soundly

The couple was so aggressive in their kissing while on the train that many people were DISCOMFITED by it.

The football team's goal was to DISCOMFIT their last opponent and move on to the state finals.

disconcerting *(diss-kon-SER-ting), adjective*
Causing unease, confusion, or dismay. Upsetting harmony or balance.

Many actions that are typical of teens are DISCONCERTING to their parents and teachers.

disconsolate *(dis-KON-so-luht), adjective*
Deeply sad to the point of being unable to find or accept comfort

She was DISCONSOLATE for over a year after her father died.

discordant *(dis-KORD-uhnt), adjective*
Disagreeing; in conflict; unpleasant or harsh, especially in describing sound

He composed the music to be especially DISCORDANT in order to highlight the strife in the scene.

discount *(dis-KOUNT), verb*
To disregard, see as exaggerated, or dismiss

She was afraid he would DISCOUNT how important his help had been with her writing the book.

discountenance *(dis-KOUN-te-nans), noun*
Disapproval

Her expression showed her DISCOUNTENANCE even though her words were favorable.

discourse *(dis-KORS), noun*
A written or spoken communication; a verbal exchange

As the debate team president, he was a master of DISCOURSE and could talk rings around most other students and even some professors.

discredit *(dis-CRED-it), verb*
To damage a reputation; to cause disbelief; to cause another to appear untrustworthy

The candidate hoped to DISCREDIT his opponent's positive stance on the environment by proving the other candidate supported deforestation.

discreet *(dis-KREET), adjective*
Careful; subtle; showing self-restraint

The teachers were DISCREET about their personal relationship so the students never even knew they were dating.

discrepancy *(dis-CREP-uhn-see), noun*
A difference between what is stated and what is fact; a difference between facts

The accountant was concerned about the DISCREPANCY between the figures in the books and the amount in the bank account.

discretion *(dis-KREH-shun), noun*
The ability to act or think responsibly; the ability to act or behave prudently

After his secrets were told all over school, he used greater DISCRETION when deciding who he would confide in.

discriminating *(dis-CRIM-uh-nay-ting), adjective*
Able to show judgment and distinction; capable of making wise decisions

The socialite was known and respected for her impeccable style and DISCRIMINATING tastes.

discursive *(dis-KER-siv), adjective*
A manner or style of lecturing in which the speaker jumps back and forth between many topics.

Paul's DISCURSIVE lectures on American history jumped from century to century, yet it all came together in an understandable and fresh fashion.

disdain *(dis-DAYN), noun*
Held in contempt; looked down on

The proper, older woman looked with DISDAIN on the fashions of teenagers.

disenfranchise *(dis-en-FRAN-chyz), verb*
To deny someone a right or privilege; to make someone feel rejected and apart.

The lack of decent health care made those with lower incomes feel DISENFRANCHISED.

Know This Quote
"Some states specify felonies that condemn the citizen to DISENFRANCHISEMENT for life."
—Andrew Hacker, American political scientist

dishabille *(dis-uh-BEE-uhl), noun*
Casual dress, or a casual manner.

Jensen is such a stickler for proper attire he feels he is in a state of DISHABILLE if he leaves the house without an ascot.

disheveled *(dih-SHEHV-uhld), adjective*
Messy or untidy, usually used in describing physical appearance

We all knew he had pulled an all-nighter when he showed up to class DISHEVELED and bleary-eyed.

disinclination *(dis-in-klih-NAY-shun), noun*
Reluctance or unwillingness to do something

Her DISINCLINATION to babysit on a Friday night was overridden by her need to make some extra money.

disingenuous *(dih-sen-JEN-yoo-wus), adjective*
Less than honest, scheming, insincere, crafty, or sly. Withholding known information; intending to deceive. If dis or dat is less than genuine and honest, it is disingenuous.

Mary did not look Jim in the eye when she explained why she missed their date, so he suspected she was being DISINGENUOUS.

disinterested *(dis-IN-truh-sted), adjective*
Lack of interest or curiosity; being emotionally removed from something

Although he tried to appear enthusiastic, he simply could not hide how DISINTERESTED he was in her shopping spree.

dismiss *(dis-MISS), verb*
To demand or allow someone to leave; or to write off; to consider unimportant or unworthy of attention

The king DISMISSED the courtiers for the afternoon because he was tired of being surrounded by people.

It is best to simply DISMISS e-mail offers as spam rather than be taken in by outrageous claims.

disparate *(dis-PAYR-uht), adjective*
Essentially different or dissimilar; not easy or even impossible to compare

The two girls' personalities were so DISPARATE, it was hard to believe they were sisters.

Know This Quote

"As if, as if, as if the DISPARATE halves / Of things were waiting in a betrothal known / To none."
—Wallace Stevens, American modernist poet

disport *(dih-SPORT), verb*
To show off, draw attention to oneself, or behave in a playful way. If dis sport is a diversion, you're said to disport at a sporting event.

Those two teens are acting like little kids as they DISPORT at Disneyland.

disputation *(dis-PYOO-tay-shun), noun*
Formal debate or argument, often on an academic level

The professor encouraged her students to enter into worthy DISPUTATIONS with her during class but was not interested in wasting time with simple concepts.

disquiet *(dis-KWIY-eht), noun*
A feeling of anxiety, worry, or unrest

At lights out, a sense of DISQUIET spread throughout the camp because of the ghost stories that had been told around the campfire.

dissemble *(dis-EM-bul), verb*
To create or hide behind a fake appearance, attitude, or personality

It is sad that some young women still feel the need to DISSEMBLE instead of being honest about their intelligence and strength.

disseminate *(dih-SEH-muh-nate), verb*
To distribute or spread information or something else; to spread far and wide.

Once information about colleges was received, the counselor had to decide how to DISSEMINATE the brochures and flyers.

dissent *(dih-SENT), verb*
To disagree, usually with a formal or official statement

It takes courage for a congressman to openly DISSENT against the party's platform.

dissolution *(dis-uh-LOO-shun), noun*
The ending of an official organization or body; the breaking up of an established group

The DISSOLUTION of the band was caused by budget cuts in the school's music department.

dissonance *(DIH-suh-nunce), noun*
Incompatibility among ideas, actions, or beliefs; disharmony between several sounds. The antonym of *consonance,* which means agreement, harmony, close similarity, or pleasing and simultaneous sounds. *Dissonance* is truly an annoyance, for it is disharmonious.

Adolescence is often described as a period of DISSONANCE, when young men and women face challenges, confusion, and conflict as they forge new beliefs that are often incompatible with past behaviors.

dissuade *(dih-SWADE), verb*
To persuade someone against a course of action; to convince an audience not to think, feel, or believe a certain thing. To convince another to take alternate action.

Tim's classmates DISSUADED him from cutting class and risking a detention.

distend *(dis-TEND), verb*
To cause swelling or expansion from the inside

Severe malnutrition causes the stomach to DISTEND in addition to causing other major physical conditions.

distraught *(dis-TROHT), adjective*
Deeply agitated; emotionally upset

The girl was DISTRAUGHT until the animal shelter called with the news they had found her lost puppy.

diurnal *(die-URN-al), adjective*
Taking place or being active during daylight hours.

The house staff knows not even to approach Nora's bedroom door before twilight because she totally rejects a DIURNAL lifestyle.

divergent *(diy-VER-gent), adjective*
Dividing off from a common point; moving in different directions from a single starting point

Although the brothers had similar interests growing up, they took DIVERGENT paths once they graduated.

divest *(diy-VEST), verb*
To deprive, usually the power or rights of another person

The black majority was DIVESTED of their basic human rights in South Africa during apartheid.

divulge *(diy-VULJ), verb*
To share or make known a secret or something else private

She waited to DIVULGE the fact that she was pregnant until she had told her family first.

DNA *(dee enn AY), noun*
The acronym for "deoxyribonucleic acid," the molecule that carries genetic information in all life forms. The workings of *DNA* are central concerns of biology and genetics.

DNA is commonly referred to as the "blueprint for life," for it carries the genetic codes associated with the post-fertilization development of an organism.

docile *(DAW-sul), adjective*
Quiet, easy to control or teach; unlikely to cause trouble. A crocodile is rarely docile.

It is unusual to find a truly DOCILE wolf, for these animals are wild by nature.

doctrine *(DOK-trihn), noun*
The beliefs or principles held and taught by some governing body, usually political or religious

Most people agree with parts of a political party's DOCTRINE but not necessarily every aspect of it.

document *(dok-YOO-ment), verb*
To supply written proof; to keep a paper trail

The employees had to DOCUMENT their gas mileage to be reimbursed for it.

dogmatic *(dog-MA-tik), adjective*
Strong expression or adherence to beliefs or opinions. Related to or expressing religious, political, philosophical, or moral dogma.

Students believe some teachers are DOGMATIC, not willing to change their views or consider ideas counter to their own.

domicile *(DAH-muh-cile), noun*
An occupied house, apartment, or residence; a legal, permanent home. Don't confuse it with docile, for a home is not easy to teach or control.

Homeless individuals, by definition, have no DOMICILE, so it is difficult if not impossible for them to get certain financial benefits.

dormant *(DOR-ment), adjective*
Having physical vital signs slowed dramatically; waiting to be roused

Many plants become DORMANT in winter, blooming again in spring.

dossier *(DOSS-yay), noun*
A collection of documents related to a particular person or topic.

The personnel office keeps a DOSSIER on all employees.

douceur *(doo-SIR), noun*
A bribe or a conciliatory gift.

After Francine's father refused to buy her another polo pony, he offered her the DOUCEUR of a weekend at an exclusive spa.

doyen/doyenne *(doy-EN), noun*
A man or woman who is the senior member of a group, based on rank, age, experience, etc.

Though she is the youngest member of our group, Brittany is our DOYENNE, based on her extensive family connections.

Draconian *(drah-KONE-ee-an), adjective*
Strict; mean-spirited; excessively harsh; cruel; punishment or restriction meant to cause misery to those receiving it.

Ophelia was distraught over the DRACONIAN way that her father forced her to stay with her chaperone throughout their vacation on the Greek Isles.

droll *(DROLE), adjective*
Amusing in a wry, odd, or funny way. Trolls might be droll, if they are funny and amusing.

Norma's peers considered her DROLL, for she was always able to make them laugh with her offbeat comments.

dubious *(DOO-bee-us), adjective*
Uncertain; causing doubt; questionable

Her excuses were always DUBIOUS but her teachers never caught her in an outright lie.

duffer *(DUFF-uhr), noun*
An incompetent or ineffectual person.

Maxwell can't help being a DUFFER. After all, his family has only been wealthy for two generations.

dupe *(DOOP), verb or noun*
To deceive or trick someone (verb) or a person who has been deceived or tricked; someone easily fooled (noun)

The class decided to DUPE the substitute teacher by pretending one of the students was deaf.

Her trustworthy nature made her an easy DUPE for con artists.

duplicity *(doo-PLIS-ih-tee), noun*
A state of being two-faced or deliberately deceptive

She couldn't stand the DUPLICITY required to juggle more than one boyfriend at a time.

dyslexia *(dis-LEK-see-uh), noun*
A learning disorder marked by difficulty in spelling or reading.

Her learning disabilities, including DYSLEXIA, frequently caused her to transpose letters in words.

dyslogistic *(diz-luh-JISS-tick), adjective*
Showing disapproval or censure.

We gave Elizabeth DYSLOGISTIC glances when she told us she had decided to stop shopping at Cartier.

E

earmark *(EER-mark), verb*
To set aside money to be used for a specific purpose.
Milly's earnings from her job were EARMARKED for her son's college tuition.

earthenware *(UR-then-wayr), noun*
Pottery made from a specific, porous clay
The EARTHENWARE plates combined with the heavy pewter flatware gave the table a rustic, welcoming look.

ebullient *(eh-BOOL-yunt), adjective*
Full of cheer, enthusiasm, or optimism, as expressed in speech, writing, or behavior.
EBULLIENT game-show hosts are talented in very special ways.

eccentric *(ek-SEN-trik), adjective*
Following a different, unusual path; straying from the norm or that which is expected
The opera singer was as famous for her ECCENTRIC style as she was for her singing abilities.

eccentricity *(ek-sen-TRIH-suh-tee), noun*
Unconventional, unpredictable, or erratic behavior or quality. The behavior of a person who is prone to odd behavior. A very fancy way of saying *strange,* and a word that often describes characters in novels. Remember Jay Gatsby?
William was thought to be odd in general, but one of his ECCENTRICITIES, his making of unusual noises, could have been a symptom of Tourette's syndrome.

echelon *(ESH-uh-lonn), noun*
A level of command or authority.
Family connections helped Michael ascend quickly to the upper ECHELON of his brokerage firm.

éclat *(ay-KLAH), noun*
Great public acclaim; or, great public notoriety.
Although they are the height of Paris fashion, Martina's five-inch heels earned her much ÉCLAT in the society pages.

eclectic *(ih-KLEK-tik), adjective*
Drawing from or combining elements from many places or situations; multifaceted
Many people were surprised at how ECLECTIC his musical tastes were as they encompassed classical and house and everything in between.

edacious *(eh-DAY-shus), adjective*
Voracious; greedy for; devouring

After months in isolation, the prisoners were EDACIOUS for news from the outside world as well as nutritious food.

edible *(EHD-ih-bul), adjective*
Able to be eaten; fit for consumption

Although the hungry hikers ate it willingly, the rest of us found the burned stew barely EDIBLE.

edification *(eh-dih-fuh-KAY-shun), noun*
Instruction or enlightenment, often involving moral or spiritual teachings. Not a word to be confused with *edifice,* an impressive building or large complex structure, but similar to its soundalike, *education.*

The evangelical preacher's EDIFICATION of church members and others in the community was known to all.

educe *(eh-DOOS), verb*
To bring out or draw out; to coax

Her goal as a dance instructor was not just to teach ballet but to EDUCE a sense of self-confidence in all her students.

efface *(eh-FAYS), verb*
To erase or rub out

The years had not managed to EFFACE the memories of the fabulous summer she had spent in Europe with her friends.

effervesce *(ehf-fer-VES), verb*
To bubble up; emit small bubbles

The little girl was fascinated by the way the seltzer would EFFERVESCE as her grandfather poured it into their glasses.

Know This Quote

"It is also true that one can write nothing readable unless one constantly struggles to EFFACE one's own personality. Good prose is like a windowpane." —George Orwell, British author

effervescent (*ef-ur-VES-ent), adjective.*
Bubbly; upbeat; cheerful; possessing a positive attitude and joyful personality.

After getting the acceptance letter from Cornell, Sabrina was positively EFFERVESCENT and celebrated with a trip to Neiman Marcus.

effete *(eh-FEET), adjective*
Worn out; out of date; lacking effectiveness; or overly refined, pretentious; characterized by affectation

The teaching style of rote memorization was proven to be EFFETE and so was replaced.

efficacious *(eff-ih-KAY-shuss), adjective*
Capable of having a desired effect.

The candlelit room was EFFICACIOUS.

efficacy *(eff-ih-KASEE), noun*
Effectiveness; the ability to create the desired effect

The EFFICACY of the drug was called into question when only half of the test patients responded well to treatment.

efflorescent *(ef-luh-RES-uhnt), adjective.*
Describes something that has reached the final stage of its development or is at the peak of perfection.

Thomas is convinced that the Bugati Veyron Fbg represents the EFFLORESCENT automobile.

Know This Quote
"Example is always more EFFICACIOUS than precept." —Samuel Johnson, British moralist and poet

effrontery *(ih-FRON-tuh-ree), noun*
An attitude or action notable for being bold, impudent, shameless, or arrogant. Effrontery in front of others is insulting.

Sean had the EFFRONTERY to ask his parents for a new car immediately after he had an accident that was a result of drinking and driving.

effulgence *(ef-FOOL-jens), adjective*
Bright and radiant; glowing

The EFFULGENCE of her personality lit up every room she entered.

effusive *(eh-FEW-siv), adjective*
Profuse and overflowing, without reservation.

In an effort to butter up the senator, the lobbyist was transparently EFFUSIVE in his praise of the new bill.

egalitarian *(ih-ga-luh-TARE-ee-un), adjective*
Related to or arising from a belief that all people are equal and should enjoy equal rights. Fair toward all parties. Not related to eagles, unless you believe that metaphorically all persons should be as free as these amazing birds.

It is unusual to see EGALITARIAN behavior among high school students, who often act as if rights are related to grade, age, and how cool someone seems.

Know This Quote
"Chinks in America's EGALITARIAN armor are not hard to find. Democracy is the fig leaf of elitism." —Florence King, American author

egocentric *(EE-go-SEN-trik), adjective*
Selfish; interested only in oneself, and not in the needs or feelings of others. Narrow-mindedly focused on self rather than other people. Sounds like *eccentric,* and while egocentrics can be odd or unusual, the two words are not synonyms—you shouldn't confuse them.

Not surprisingly, the EGOCENTRIC author's greatest achievement was an autobiography.

egotism *(EE-gah-tizm), noun*
An inflated sense of self-worth; a tendency to only speak or care about oneself

The artist's EGOTISM eventually gained her a reputation for being difficult to work with and lost her several job opportunities.

egregious *(ih-GREE-juss), adjective*
Incorrect to an extraordinary level. Bad in a flagrant, blatant, or ridiculous way.

An EGREGIOUS error is one so obvious it should not have been made, nor should it be easily forgiven.

egress *(EE-gres), noun*
The exit; the path out

During the evacuation, all the roads were open for EGRESS so there were no roads leading into the city.

eidetic *(aye-DETT-ick), adjective*
Of visual imagery that is nearly photographic in detail.

We were displeased with the Howlands' recent art purchase because the so-called artist harkens back to the tired old school of EIDETIC representation.

eidolon *(eye-DOH-luhn), noun*
A phantom or apparition; or, the image of an ideal

Maggie was upset after she watched an EIDOLON pass through her bedroom wall.

Know This Quote

"By a route obscure and lonely, / Haunted by ill angels only, / Where an EIDOLON, named Night, / On a black throne reigns upright." —Edgar Allan Poe, American author and poet

élan, *(ey-LAN), noun*
Enthusiasm, energy, flair, zest.

Bryanna reacted with ÉLAN when she was tapped to be part of a feature for Elite Travel Magazine.

elated *(ee-LAY-ted), adjective or verb*
Joyous; extremely happy (adjective) or to make joyous or extremely happy (verb)

Everyone in the family was ELATED when she received her acceptance to the college of her choice.

Being nominated for the award ELATED the scientist because it meant his work was finally being recognized.

elegy *(EL-eh-gee), noun*

A poem or song written in honor of someone who has died

It was common for bards and poets to compose ELEGIES at the death of a monarch.

Which Word?

Many words have definitions that seem identical, but they cannot always be used interchangeably. This is the case for elegy (EL-eh-gee) and eulogy (yoo-LEH-gee). An elegy is a song or poem written in honor of a person who has died. This song may be written by anyone, at any time after the person's death. A eulogy, however, is a statement or speech made about a person who has died. Traditionally, the eulogy is given by someone who knew the deceased at the time of his or her death.

elicit *(ih-lih-SIHT), verb*

To draw out, usually a response from a person

The verdict of guilty ELICITED both cheers and cries of outrage from the large crowd that had gathered outside the courthouse.

The calling of each graduate's name ELICITED cheers and applause from family and friends.

elide *(ee-LIDE), verb*

To leave out a sound or syllable when speaking; to eliminate the distinctive barrier separating levels.

When Catherine ELIDES the "g's" at the end of certain words, she betrays her Southern origins.

elocution *(eh-luh-KYOO-shun), noun*

A manner or style of speaking, especially public speaking; the art of speaking well in public. *Elocution* refers to the way language is spoken; *eloquence* refers to the way ideas are expressed.

The candidate's ELOCUTION was so poor that it diminished her ability to convey a coherent message.

eloquence *(EH-luh-kwents), noun*

The ability to speak forcefully, expressively, and persuasively. Convincing and pleasant language.

The professor's ELOQUENCE made her very popular among students and, ultimately, led to her being granted tenure.

elucidate *(ih-LOO-si-date), verb*
To explain, clarify, or provide key information. To throw light on and clarify a subject. Related to the adjective *lucid,* meaning emitting light, rational, or clear and easily understood. Ed would elucidate his feelings, transforming Stephanie into a lucid date.

Only Jordan could ELUCIDATE upon his motivations and why he behaved in certain ways.

Know This Quote
"It [was] the mission of the twentieth century to ELUCIDATE the irrational." —Maurice Merleau-Ponty, French philosopher

elucubrate *(ih-LOO-kyoo-brait), verb*
To produce a written work through lengthy, intensive effort.

Thanks to a few hundred bucks passed along to a classmate, Miles did not have to ELUCUBRATE his term paper and could, instead, attend parties with us.

elusive *(eh-LOO-siv), adjective*
Difficult to find, discover, or capture; just out of reach; unable to be grasped

To this day, some people believe the Loch Ness Monster to be a hoax while others believe it to simply be an ELUSIVE and crafty being.

emaciate *(ih-MAY-see-ayt), verb*
Make abnormally thin, usually due to starvation or illness

The need to be accepted and beautiful causes many young women to EMACIATE themselves in order to look like the models in magazines.

emanate *(EH-muh-nate), verb*
To come from or come out of someone, something, or somewhere. To flow from a specific source.

The glow and heat that EMANATED from the fireplace made everyone feel warm and safe.

emancipate *(ih-MAN-si-pate), verb*
To free or liberate from slavery, restraint, oppression, or bondage.

Many young people feel that an eighteenth birthday has the power to EMANCIPATE them from their parents' rules.

embellish *(em-BEL-ish), verb*
To decorate with ornamentation; to add to; to make more colorful or decorative

The urge to EMBELLISH a story to make it even more interesting is one every author must fight, especially when speaking with friends.

embezzle *(em-BEZ-uhl), verb*
To take or steal, usually money, that has been entrusted to one's care

No one knew exactly when the president of the company had decided to EMBEZZLE the payroll funds but they quickly realized it had been going on for years.

emblazon *(em-BLAY-zen), verb*
To display obviously; to put something somewhere it cannot be missed

The student body decided to EMBLAZON the front doors with a welcome sign for the visiting dignitaries.

emend *(ih-MEND), verb*
To alter or edit with the intent to improve

The teacher asked for rough drafts so she could EMEND any glaring mistakes that might count against the students' final papers.

emollient *(ih-MOL-yent), noun*
Any substance that softens or soothes the skin

Lotion with aloe is an excellent EMOLLIENT, especially during the dry months of winter.

empathize *(EM-puh-thize), verb*
To identify with and understand another's feelings, emotions, and challenges. Not to be confused or misused with *emphasize*, which means to stress or give importance to something.

The counselor tried to EMPATHIZE with students in order to earn their trust.

empathy *(EM-puth-ee), noun*
The ability to identify, understand, and share the feelings of another

A therapist who can balance EMPATHY with objectivity is usually more effective than one who is strictly clinical.

empirical *(em-PEER-uh-cul), adjective*
Based on verifiable facts rather than theory; fact based

The students had to complete an EMPIRICAL study on sunscreens with varying levels of protection for an easy summer assignment.

empressement *(ahn-press-MAH), noun*
A display of effusive cordiality.

Those at the party who belonged to the nouveau riche set were easy to recognize, due to their constant and distasteful EMPRESSEMENT.

empyreal *(em-PEER-ee-uhl), adjective*
Elevated and sublime; or, of the sky

The beautiful three-carat sapphire her fiancé gave her shone with an EMPYREAL, almost celestial, light.

emulate *(EM-yoo-layt), verb*
To imitate or copy in a flattering way; to strive to be like

Her goal was to EMULATE Angelina Jolie in fashion, personality, and beauty.

en masse *(on MASS), adverb*
As a body or group; together. A French term that translates loosely as "in the form of a crowd." Definitely try this one in your next conversation or paper, and then see the reactions. They will be positive *en masse.*

Teenage girls seem to move EN MASSE, almost always in a group.

encipher *(en-SY-fur), verb*
To scramble or convert data into a secret code, prior to transmission, thereby making it impossible for unauthorized users to understand or decipher.

Mathematicians were employed by the Army to crack ENCIPHERED messages during the war.

encomium *(en-KOH-mee-um), noun*
A formal speech or statement in praise of someone

The dean fought back tears while reading the ENCOMIUM at the professor's retirement celebration.

encumbrance *(ehn-KUM-bruhns), noun*
A burden; something that makes another thing more difficult

At first she thought watching her little sister three days a week would be an ENCUMBRANCE but she quickly came to enjoy the time they shared.

endemic *(en-DEH-mik), adjective*
Indigenous to a certain place, region, or group, as in characteristics, species, or disease. Something that describes and is confined to a particular area. In contrast, *pandemic* means existing in a wide area, such as in many countries.

Pines of that type were ENDEMIC to only a specific region, one that was clearly identifiable by what was called the treeline.

endorse *(en-DORS), verb*
To give or declare public approval; to give backing to; to support

The candidate hoped her stance on fair employment practices would convince the trade unions to ENDORSE her.

enervate *(EH-nur-vate), verb*
To weaken someone's physical, mental, or moral vitality. To deprive or diminish vitality, strength, or endurance. The antonym of *energize,* it is still sometimes misused to mean pepping somebody up when in fact it means bringing that person down.

Activity-packed family vacations that are intended to provide rest and recuperation often ENERVATE all involved.

engender *(ehn-JEN-dehr), verb*
To cause, usually a feeling; to bring into existence

Watching his wife and new baby ENGENDERED such love for his family that it sometimes took his breath away.

engrave *(en-GRAYV), verb*
To etch or mark permanently; to carve into something hard

The award was ENGRAVED with his name and the date he won the competition.

enjoin *(ehn-JOYN), verb*
To direct or order someone to do something.

After purchasing one too many Bentleys, Alex's father ENJOINED him to be more frugal.

enhance *(en-HANS), verb*
To intensify or increase the value, beauty, or look of something

The sunlight shining on her hair only served to ENHANCE her natural beauty.

enigma *(eh-NIG-mah), noun*
A puzzle or mystery, usually a person; someone that is difficult to understand

It is a sad fact that women are ENIGMAS to most men and vice versa.

The Mona Lisa's smile is probably the most popular ENIGMA in the world of art.

enigmatic *(en-ig-MATT-ik), adjective*
Mysterious, puzzling, and difficult to figure out.

She found the recipes in the new cookbook curiously ENIGMATIC.

Know This Quote

"The interest in life does not lie in what people do, nor even in their relations to each other, but largely in the power to communicate with a third party, antagonistic, ENIGMATIC, yet perhaps persuadable, which one may call life in general." —Virginia Woolf, British essayist and novelist

enmesh *(en-MESH), verb*
To involve, entangle, or implicate someone in a way that makes it hard for them to extricate themselves. Literally, it means to catch with a mesh net. Enmeshed in mesh nets, it was hard for fish to get loose.

When Julie got home, she was immediately ENMESHED in the raging argument between her brother and sister.

enmity *(EN-mi-tee), noun*
Extreme ill will, hatred, and mutual antagonism between enemies. Not to be confused with *enigma,* which means a mystery, puzzle, or confusing person or thing. Sadly, it is a powerful and applicable word, today and every day.

The ENMITY between terrorists and those they consider enemies grows day by day.

ennui *(OHN-wee) or (ohn-WEE), noun*
Boredom; lack of interest, usually caused by having nothing to occupy one's time or thoughts

Although the students had looked forward to summer vacation, relaxation quickly turned into ENNUI as the allure of having nothing to do dwindled.

Know This Quote

"And he spoke of ENNUI, of jaded appetites, of nights and days aboard a moonstone vessel as large as a city." —Harlan Ellison, American author

ensconce *(en-SKONTS), verb*
To settle oneself warmly or snugly; or, to hide something in a secure place

Julia ENSCONSED herself in a leather chair in the family's library and perused recent catalogues.

enshrine *(en-SHRlNE), verb*
To protect and preserve from change; to cherish as though sacred.

The most significant honor an athlete can receive is to be ENSHRINED in a sport's hall of fame.

entangle *(en-TANG-gul), verb*
To tangle or twist together; to become a tangled mess

She didn't know how she had become ENTANGLED in the politics of the sorority but she knew she didn't care for it.

enthralling *(ihn-THRALL-ing), adjective*
Delightful, fascinating, or engaging someone's attention; beautiful, captivating, mesmerizing, or spellbinding.

For most teenage boys, the beauty of swimsuit models is ENTHRALLING, to say the least.

entreat *(en-TREET), verb*
To ask earnestly; to request wholeheartedly; to plead

The police ENTREATED anyone who had any information about the crime to come forward.

entropy *(EN-troh-pee), noun*
The tendency of any system to run down and revert to total chaos.

Each winter her garden leaned toward ENTROPY.

enunciate *(ee-NUN-see-ate), verb*
To pronounce distinctly; articulate. To give a speech that explains something clearly and lucidly. When you enunciate, you also elucidate and educate, so don't wait.

The speech therapist worked with Sam on his inability to properly ENUNCIATE words that began with the letter T.

envisage *(en-VIZ-ij), verb*
To envision, imagine, or create a mental picture.

Karen ENVISAGED a perfect future for her and Dave, but her friends thought she was mistaken.

ephemeral *(ef-FEM-er-al), adjective*
Short-lived or temporary; passing quickly

Although he knew it was EPHEMERAL, he enjoyed the quiet between the time his son left for work and his daughter got home from band rehearsals.

Know This Quote
"There remain some truths too EPHEMERAL to be captured in the cold pages of a court transcript."
—Irving Kaufman, Chief Judge, United States Court of Appeals

epicure *(EH-pih-kyoor), noun*
Someone with a refined taste for food and drink; a connoisseur. An epicure often needs an epic cure for heartburn and hangovers, even after eating good food and drinking fine wines.

To an EPICURE, a fast-food restaurant is an affront and not worthy of discussion.

Where'd That Word Come From?
Epicure—The ancient Greek philosopher Epicurus argued that true pleasure means peace of mind and freedom from want and pain, to be achieved through noble thoughts, self-control, and moderation. Students distorted his teachings completely, using them as an excuse for selfish indulgence, so that an *epicure* became one devoted to gluttony and debauchery. Centuries later, the word took on its current meaning of gourmet or connoisseur, one with refined tastes and knowledge of food and drink.

epicurean *(eh-pih-CURE-ee-an), noun*
Devoted to the enjoyment of good food and comfort.

Mother's Thanksgiving meal at the Cape Cod compound was an annual EPICUREAN delight.

epiphany *(ih-PIH-fuh-nee), noun*
A sudden intuitive leap of understanding, often with credit given to divine inspiration. A sudden manifestation of the essence or meaning of something; a revelation. When capitalized, refers to the Christian festival celebrating the manifestation of Christ to the Gentiles.

Seemingly miraculous circumstances, such as an unexplained recuperation from serious illness, often lead a person to an EPIPHANY regarding the blessings of life.

epistolary *(eh-PISS-toe-lar-ee), adjective*
Having to do with the writing or letters or other literary works.

Madeline continues the EPISTOLARY tradition by eschewing e-mail, opting for fine parchment and her great-grandfather's diamond-encrusted quill pen for her correspondence.

epithet *(EP-ih-thet), noun*
Phrase used to describe a person, often a nickname picked up by the general population

The late President Ronald Reagan carried the EPITHET "the Great Communicator" due to his skill at debate and diplomacy.

epitome *(ih-PIT-oh-mee), noun*
A person or thing that is the ideal all others are compared to

Even so long after his death, many people still consider James Dean the EPITOME of cool.

eponymous *(eh-PON-eh-muss), adjective*
To be named after something, such as a child being named after his grandfather or the mythical Romulus giving his name to Rome.

Josephine spends as much time as possible sailing in her EPONYMOUS yacht.

equable *(EHK-kwah-bul), adjective*
Not easily disturbed or agitated; free from extreme emotional highs and lows

His EQUABLE nature made him an excellent camp counselor because not even the teenagers could frazzle him.

Know This Quote

"He spake of love, such love as spirits feel / In worlds whose course is EQUABLE and pure."
—William Wordsworth, British Romantic poet

equanimity *(ee-kwa-NIH-muh-tee), noun*
Even temper and calm, usually displayed under stress; composure in a difficult situation. Not to be confused with *equality,* to value all in a group equally, or *anonymity,* the state of being unknown or not identifiable.

EQUANIMITY is a quality to be revered and one that can be taught, practiced, and perfected.

equilibrium *(ee-kwi-LIB-bree-um), noun*
A state of emotional, mental, or physical balance

The easiest way to keep EQUILIBRIUM in the house was to ensure the twins received the exact same amount of everything.

equine *(EE-kwiyn), adjective*
Having to do with horses; relating to horses

His EQUINE laugh was distinctive enough to be identified from anywhere in the room.

equinox *(EE-kwih-noks), noun*
Either of the two days in a year when the sun crosses the celestial equator and day and night are approximately equal.

The vernal EQUINOX occurs in the spring, and the autumnal EQUINOX occurs in the fall.

equitable *(EK-kwit-uh-bul), adjective*
Even, equal, or fair

The mediator's job was to ensure the divorce settlement was EQUITABLE and both sides came away satisfied.

equivocal *(ih-KWIV-ih-cul), adjective*
Uncertain; having more than one interpretation, often intentionally in order to mislead

Teenagers will often give EQUIVOCAL answers when asked about their sex, drinking, and drug habits.

equivocate *(ih-KWIV-oh-kayt), verb*
To intentionally use language that may deceive or be open to more than one interpretation

She knew she could no longer trust him when he began to EQUIVOCATE instead of giving her straight answers.

eradicate *(ih-RAD-ih-kayt), verb*
To destroy, often at the very core of something; to eliminate completely

The president swore to ERADICATE illiteracy but his programs and ideas were unrealistic.

errant *(AYR-unt), adjective*
Moving away or straying from what is expected or considered the norm

Her ERRANT behavior might have made her popular with other students but it got her in trouble with her teachers and the principal.

erratic *(ih-RA-tik), adjective*
Uneven; having no set or fixed course, either in direction or behavior

The man's ERRATIC driving caused the police to pull him over because they suspected he was driving under the influence.

erroneous *(ir-ROHN-ee-us), adjective*
Incorrect or mistaken; full of errors

The results of the test were ERRONEOUS because the sample was tainted.

ersatz *(EHR-sats), adjective*
Being an imitation or substitute for something of better quality. Characteristic of an unconvincing substitute that is not the real deal. If you err and sit on the *ersatz* chair, you might fall and hurt your derriere.

Margarine is really just ERSATZ butter, so it doesn't taste as good.

erudite *(AYR-oo-dyt), adjective*
Having great knowledge and intelligence; well spoken and knowledgeable

The university prided itself on having well-rounded, ERUDITE graduates.

eschew *(es-CHOO), verb*
To deliberately avoid using; to reject the use of

After the war, the veteran spoke on the importance of ESCHEWING violence.

esoteric *(eh-suh-TARE-ik), adjective*
Intended to be understood by a select and initiated few. Secret or highly confidential; accessible to insiders only. Using the word *esoteric* is quite *esoteric*. Get it? If so, you're among the select few who do!

ESOTERIC historians are not overly popular among college freshmen, but senior history majors tend to like them.

Know This Quote

"My ESOTERIC doctrine, is that if you entertain any doubt, it is safest to take the unpopular side in the first instance." —William Lamb Melbourne, British prime minister

espouse *(ihs-POWZ), verb*
To adopt, support, or advocate a particular belief or cause. Also, to take in marriage.

Presidential candidates tend to ESPOUSE centrist causes as the election draws nearer.

espy *(ih-SPY), verb*
To notice; catch sight of; most commonly used in poetry

Romeo waited after the ball, hoping to ESPY Juliet in her window.

estrange *(iss-TRANGE), verb*
To cause someone to stop feeling friendly, affectionate, or sympathetic; to alienate or remove from a relationship.

Today it is not unusual for family members to be ESTRANGED, either not living with or not caring about each other.

ethereal *(eh-THEER-ee-uhl), adjective*
Light and airy; possessing a heavenly or celestial quality.

Katie's wedding dress was designed to give her an ETHEREAL look as she walked down the aisle.

ethos *(EE-thos), noun*
The core principles or beliefs of a religion, culture, or community.

Even the eating of cheese violates the ETHOS of the vegan culture.

etiolate *(EE-tee-uh-late), verb*
To cause to become weak and appear sickly.

Over time, Brad's excesses increasingly ETIOLATED his once-handsome appearance.

etymology *(eh-tih-MAH-luh-gee), noun*
The study of word origins and how words have evolved into their current forms or meanings. The lineage of a word; description of origin and how the word came into its current use.

Those who have studied Greek or Latin can make educated and often correct guesses regarding a word's ETYMOLOGY.

eulogy *(yoo-LEH-gee), noun*
A speech praising another person, traditionally one who has just died

The EULOGY given at my father's funeral by his favorite student made us laugh and cry at the same time.

euphemism *(YOO-fem-iz-um), noun*
A mild, inoffensive term for something that might be considered rude, inappropriate, or vulgar

Many people prefer to use the EUPHEMISM "the little girls' room" instead of asking for the restroom or bathroom.

euphonious *(YOO-fon-ee-us), adjective*
Pleasing to the ear; nice to listen to

The sound of birds singing was particularly EUPHONIOUS after the long, cold winter.

euphuism *(YOU-few-iz-im), noun*
A phrase, sentence, or thought expressed in an ornate, flowery, overly elaborate style of writing, often making the exact meaning difficult to discern.

Felicia's words are full of EUPHUISM, particularly when describing the architecture of her family's various houses.

euphony *(YOU-fone-ee), noun*
The habit of changing the pronunciation of words or the wording of phrases so they are pleasing to the ear and roll off the tongue with greater ease.

In finishing school, Alsace learned the art of EUPHONY, and she has parlayed that into a hobby of earning roles in television commercials.

eustasy *(YEW-stah-see), noun*
A change in sea level caused by melting of ice, movement of ocean floors, or major deposits of sediment.

Global warming is already triggering EUSTASY with the melting of the polar ice caps.

evanescent *(EH-vuh-NEH-sent), adjective*
Disappearing after only a short time; likely to vanish, like vapor. The name of a popular musical group, this word also describes the fate of most such groups.

Some stellar phenomena appear to astronomers, even those using the most sophisticated equipment, as EVANESCENT events, visible for only fractions of seconds.

Know This Quote

"Nobody thinks it's silly to invest two hours' work in two minutes' enjoyment; but if cooking is EVANESCENT, well, so is the ballet."
—Julia Child, American cook, author, and television personality

evince *(ih-VINS), verb*
To show clearly; to reveal; to put out in the open

Often, a society's mercy or lack thereof is EVINCED in the condition of its prisoners and how it treats its convicts.

evoke *(EE-vohk), verb*
To call or bring forth; to bring to mind or remind

The young politician's energy and demeanor EVOKED memories of John F. Kennedy and his campaign.

For college freshmen, first visits back to high school EVOKE many positive memories and sentimental feelings.

exacerbate *(ig-ZA-sur-bate), verb*
To worsen or aggravate an already bad situation. To make something even more unpleasant or severe.

Lying almost always EXACERBATES a bad situation; that's one reason that honesty is the best policy.

exalt *(ig-ZAHLT), verb*
To praise someone or something; to hold someone or something in high regard

Americans tend to EXALT sports players and disregard teachers, nurses, and those in other important professions.

exasperation *(ig-zas-pur-RAY-shun), noun*
Intense annoyance or irritation

His mother's EXASPERATION was only intensified when he admitted not only was his homework not done, but he hadn't started on a major report that was due the next day.

excerpt *(EK-surpt), noun*
A short section taken from a larger piece of work, such as a movie, book, or other written work

The EXCERPT she read in the magazine was so engaging that she rushed out to buy the book.

excoriate *(eggs-KORE-ee-ate), verb*
To criticize; to attempt to censure or punish.

We EXCORIATED Melanie for inviting people with no family connections to her birthday party.

exculpate *(ECK-skul-pate), verb*
To free from blame or accusation of guilt. To clear one's name.

DNA evidence has been used to EXCULPATE those accused and convicted of many serious crimes.

execrate *(EGGS-eh-krayt), verb*
To loathe; to subject to scorn and derision.

We EXECRATED William for weeks due to his casual rejection of an invitation to join Yale's Skull and Bones.

execute *(EKS-ih-kyoot), verb*
To carry out or perform an action or deed

The gymnast was confident she could EXECUTE the routine flawlessly even under the pressure of competition.

exemplary *(ek-ZEM-pla-ree), adjective*
Close enough to ideal to serve as a model for others

At school, her behavior and attendance were EXEMPLARY, so no one suspected she was a wild child on the weekends.

exemplify *(ek-ZEM-pleh-fiy), verb*
To be or serve as an example

The application required three writing samples that EXEMPLIFIED the student's writing styles.

exhaustive *(eks-ZOH-stiv), adjective*
Practically complete; including nearly all elements or aspects; thorough

The editor's EXHAUSTIVE research unearthed several little-known facts about the late senator.

exhilarating *(ek-ZIL-er-ay-ting), adjective*
Invigorating; happy, rejuvenating, and energetic

The fast roller coaster was even more EXHILARATING than the riders had expected.

exhort *(ig-ZORT), verb*
To urge someone strongly and earnestly to follow a course of action. To give urgent or earnest advice.

Some believe it is an axiom that a crowd of cheering fans can EXHORT players to achieve their maximum capability.

exigency *(eck-ZIH-jen-see), noun*
An urgent situation requiring immediate action or attention. An unexpected development that puts pressure on those involved. An exigency sounds like its near synonym, *emergency*. Don't confuse with the meaning of the adjective *exiguous,* which means scanty or meager.

When the woman on the plane complained of labor pains, the flight attendant fully understood the EXIGENCY of the situation.

Know This Quote

"We should never despair, our Situation before has been unpromising and has changed for the better, so I trust, it will again. If new difficulties arise, we must only put forth New Exertions and proportion our Efforts to the EXIGENCY of the times."
—George Washington, American president

exigent *(EG-sih-jent), adjective*
Demanding immediate attention, usually referring to an emergency or dangerous situation

Knowing basic first aid is essential in order to be helpful during an EXIGENT situation.

exonerate *(ig-ZAH-nuh-rate), verb*
Officially declare someone not guilty of a crime or blameless for an act. To relieve someone from obligation or responsibility. Similar to *exculpate,* but used in an official context.

The jury EXONERATED him of any guilt in the case, but many people believed he was still somehow responsible.

exorbitant *(eg-ZOR-bih-tant), adjective*
Unreasonably high, generally refers to prices or financial cost

During the gas shortage, the government froze prices so that no one could charge EXORBITANT prices for gasoline.

expatiate *(eks-PAY-shee-ayt), verb*
To be long-winded; to speak or write at length on a topic

The old man tended to EXPATIATE in answer to very simple questions.

expedient *(ek-SPEE-dee-yent), adjective*
Practical as a way to meet one's own needs; serving one's own self-interest

It was EXPEDIENT for her to do her chores without complaint since she wanted her mother's permission to go to the party that night.

expedite *(egs-PEH-diyt), verb*
To make something happen faster than usual; to rush or hurry

In order to get the package across the country in time for Christmas, the store had to EXPEDITE the shipment.

expeditious *(eck-spuh-DIH-shuss), adjective*
Speedy, prompt, and efficient.

My EXPEDITIOUS completion of my homework meant I could leave the house immediately after dinner.

expiate *(EK-spee-ayt), verb*
To right a wrong; to make up for an intentional error; to cancel out

She volunteered at the store hoping it would EXPIATE her guilt at having shoplifted there.

expletive *(EK-splih-tive), noun*
An exclamation, interjection, or profanity. In grammar, the part of speech that conveys or expresses emotion without having a strict literal meaning, as in *Oh!* or *Ah ha!*

One of the editor's jobs was to expurgate EXPLETIVES from the manuscript in order to make the final copy acceptable to all readers.

explicate *(EKS-plih-kayt), verb*
To analyze an idea or written work in order to understand it clearly

The assignment was to present and then EXPLICATE one of Shakespeare's sonnets so the class could understand the strange-sounding language more easily.

explicit *(ek-SPLIH-siht), adjective*
Clearly and with no room for interpretation; obvious; with nothing hidden

Even with EXPLICIT directions to the airport, he still got lost on the way.

exploit *(eks-PLOYT), verb or (EKS-ployt), noun*
To use, often unethically or immorally, toward one's own ends (verb) or a brave, adventurous deed (noun)

Child labor laws were enacted to prevent businesses from being able to EXPLOIT young children.

Regardless of if they are fact or fiction, Robin Hood's EXPLOITS have entertained people for generations.

expostulate *(eks-POS-choo-layt), verb*
To express strong disagreement with the goal of changing another person's mind or attitude

Most activists prefer to EXPOSTULATE with the other side rather than resort to violence.

expropriate *(eks-PRO-pree-ayt), verb*
To take away from the rightful owner, usually an action performed by a government

Generally speaking, it is illegal for the government to simply EXPROPRIATE property without offering its owners a fair market value.

expunge *(eks-PUNJ), verb*
To rid oneself of an annoyance; to cast out; to get rid of; to forcibly eject.

Clifford tried to EXPUNGE himself of his old car, but couldn't get a decent trade-in amount for it.

expurgate *(ECK-spur-GATE), verb*
To cleanse something, like a book or music lyrics, of material that is vulgar, obscene, or otherwise objectionable. A very fancy way to say *censor.*

The Federal Communications Commission motivates broadcasters to EXPURGATE offensive material by levying fines on stations that receive complaints from listeners.

Know This Quote

"There is no man, however wise, who has not at some period of his youth said things, or lived in a way the consciousness of which is so unpleasant to him in later life that he would gladly, if he could, EXPUNGE it from his memory." —Marcel Proust, French novelist, essayist, and critic

extant *(EKS-tent) or (eks-TENT), adjective*
Still in existence; not lost or destroyed, usually refers to a document

EXTANT historical documents are important because they offer a glimpse into a former way of life.

extemporaneous *(ek-stemp-ohr-RAY-nee-uhs), adjective*
Performed or spoken with little or no preparation; done without notes

The motivational speaker was so good at her job that most people didn't realize her speeches were EXTEMPORANEOUS.

extenuate *(ick-STEN-yoo-ate), verb*
To make a mistake, fault, or error seem less serious by providing mitigating excuses.

Dylan managed to EXTENUATE his tardiness and avoid a week's detention.

extenuating *(ek-STEN-yoo-ay-ting), adjective*
Something that lessens the seriousness or guilt of something else

Although she was late to her daughter's graduation, everyone understood there were EXTENUATING circumstances once she explained the overflowing toilet.

extinct *(ek-STINKT), adjective*
No longer living or active

Geologists thought the volcano was EXTINCT until it erupted, surprising everyone.

extinguish *(ek-STING-gwish), verb*
To put out; to put an end to

When the runner fell during the trials, his hopes for a gold medal were EXTINGUISHED before he ever made it to the Olympics.

extirpate *(EK-stuhr-payt), verb*
To destroy at the core; to tear out from the roots

After the attacks on the World Trade Center, the United States stated it would EXTIRPATE terrorists and terrorism wherever they were hiding.

extol *(ek-STOHL), verb*
To praise greatly

The realtor EXTOLLED the benefits of living in the neighborhood to the point it sounded like heaven on earth.

extort *(ek-STORT), verb*
To obtain by threat or intimidation

The gang used the threat of violence to EXTORT a "protection fee" from the local businesses.

extraneous *(ek-STRAY-nee-us), adjective*
Extra; not essential; not pertaining to the central topic

He knew the paragraph describing the farm itself was EXTRANEOUS to his report on George Washington but he needed to make the report longer.

extrapolate *(ick-STRA-puh-late), verb*
To use known facts as a starting point, and then draw conclusions about something unknown. To estimate by examining unknown values that fall outside a range of known variables.

Crime scene investigators are known for their abilities to EXTRAPOLATE information about a victim's last hours, based upon forensic evidence.

extricate *(ek-STRIH-kayt), verb*
To free from an entanglement or difficulty, may be physical or theoretical

She knew she had to EXTRICATE herself from the in-fighting at the office but she didn't know how to do so without risking her job.

exuberance *(eg-ZOO-buhr-ans), noun*
Joyous, unbridled enthusiasm

Seeing the children's EXUBERANCE when they finally arrived at the amusement park made the planning and expense worthwhile.

F

facet *(FA-sit), noun*
A component, dimension, or aspect; one of several parts. One face of a cut stone or smooth, polished surface.

In order to do well on the history exam, Jay had to study all FACETS of the Civil War and the antebellum period.

facetious *(fuh-SEE-shus), adjective*
Treating serious issues in a humorous manner; lighthearted in a way that is not always appropriate

The employees of the funeral home made FACETIOUS jokes when they were alone in order to stay detached from their work.

Know This Quote

"Boarding school manners and attitudes—stoic denial, FACETIOUS irony—are still deeply entrenched in the character of the country." —Jonathan Raban, British travel writer and novelist

facile *(FA-sihl), adjective*
Easy to accomplish, often superficial and disregarding of the full issue

The FACILE solution presented by the school board disregarded the complex issues the principal dealt with on a day-to-day basis.

facilitate *(fuh-SIL-ih-tayt), verb*
To bring about; to make something easier to happen

The union's acceptance of the contract FACILITATED a quick resolution to the negotiations.

faction *(FAK-shin), noun*
A small dissenting group within a larger one.

Within the office, there was a small FACTION that disapproved of their colleagues eating lunch at their desks.

Know This Quote

"I will keep where there is wit stirring, and leave the FACTION of fools." —William Shakespeare

factious *(FAK-shus), adjective*
Produced by dissatisfaction within a larger group; internal strife or dissatisfaction

The complaints of the three members created a FACTIOUS feeling among the entire board.

factitious *(fack-TISH-uss), adjective*
Contrived; fabricated.

At first, we thought the rumor FACTITIOUS, but then we learned that couture-producer Hermes does, in fact, plan to design and market a helicopter.

fait accompli *(FATE uh-com-PLEE), noun*
Something done, decided, already concluded, or seemingly unalterable. From the French for "accomplished fact," an act or event presented as beyond change or dispute. While *done deal* is nice, *fait accompli* will suffice if you wish to impress teachers and others.

Applying to some colleges for early decision means that if admitted, it is a FAIT ACCOMPLI that you will attend.

fallacious *(fuhl-AY-shus), adjective*
Based on something misunderstood or incorrect

She held the FALLACIOUS belief that Texas was the largest state in the country.

fallacy *(FAHL-uh-see), noun*
Something that is untrue, usually believed due to false logic or bad information

It is a FALLACY that most states make it financially appealing to be on welfare, although it is a commonly held opinion.

fallible *(FAL-ih-bull), adjective*
Capable of screwing up, making errors, or being wrong.

At a fairly young age children realize their parents are eminently FALLIBLE.

fallow *(FAHL-oo), adjective*
Prepared for planting but left unsown in order to give the earth time to rejuvenate; inactive

The farmer left his southern fields FALLOW hoping to get a healthier crop in the freshened soil next season.

falter *(FAHL-ter), verb*
To hesitate or be unsteady, usually from fear; to lose courage and be unable to act

She felt her courage FALTER as they passed her the microphone but managed to give her opinion to the crowd anyway.

fanaticism *(fa-NAT-ih-sizm), noun*
Extreme, often irrational belief in something, characterized by criticism of differing viewpoints

Religious FANATICISM exists in every country and religion in the world.

farcical *(FAR-sih-kuhl), adjective*
Ludicrous, absurd, or laughably inept.

The performance of her assistant was so FARCICAL that her friends were surprised she hadn't fired him yet.

Know This Quote

"To conjure up such ridiculous questions, the answers to which we all know or should know are in the negative, is to build up a whimsical and FARCICAL straw man which is not only grim but Grimm." —Tom C. Clark, Supreme Court Justice

farouche *(fah-ROSH), adjective*
To become sullen, shy, or withdrawn in the presence of company.

His FAROUCHE demeanor gave people the impression that he didn't like them, when in fact, he was merely an introvert.

fastidious *(fa-STIH-dee-uss), adjective*
Concerned over the perfection of even the smallest detail. Meticulous and exacting; compulsive in terms of cleanliness.

Robbie's mom is known as a FASTIDIOUS housekeeper, so we all took our shoes off at the door.

fathom *(FA-thum), verb*
To understand on a deep level; to truly comprehend

By his early twenties, the man finally realized he would never truly FATHOM the way women thought.

fatuous *(FA-choo-uss), adjective*
Revealing a lack of intelligence, as well as a lack of awareness. Stupid, foolish, or idiotic; without personal responsibility. Many teens are *fatuous* when expressing what they think is humor.

Comedians that are FATUOUS, rather than thoughtfully sarcastic or clever, are not funny or worthy of their audience's approval.

Faustian *(FOW-stee-in), adjective*
Evil; malicious; dark and brooding with malevolent intent; demonic; satanic; having sold one's soul to the devil—metaphorically or literally—in exchange for wealth and power.

In the movie The End of Days *a group of police officers make a FAUSTIAN bargain with Satan himself.*

faux *(FOH), adjective*
Fake; phony; artificial.

She wore a cheap second-hand dress and a FAUX pearl necklace made out of white beads.

faux pas *(foh PAW), noun*
An embarrassing social blunder; a behavioral error. French for "false step."

Stepping on kitty's four paws is clearly a FAUX PAS.

To avoid committing a FAUX PAS, Wendi read several etiquette books before embarking on her trip to Europe.

fawn *(FAWN), verb*
To flatter in a subservient manner in order to gain favor; may include putting oneself down in order to build the other person up

When he first won the award he enjoyed having everyone FAWN over him but it rapidly became annoying and he longed for his old, down-to-earth friends.

Which Word?

Sometimes a word you know may be used in an unfamiliar way. You may be unaware of its other definitions. Fawn (FAWN) is probably one of those words. You know that a fawn is a baby deer. That is its most common definition. However, it is also a verb meaning to suck up to someone. Remember, even if you think you know the word, check the definition as well—just in case.

feasible *(FEE-zih-bul), adjective*
Possible to do or accomplish; easy to bring about

If she saved her babysitting money, spending a week on the beach was a FEASIBLE vacation.

fealty *(FEE-ul-tea), noun*
A sense of obligation or loyalty, usually existing because one person feels beholden to another.

The only reason that Bryson pledged FEALTY to David is because David's social connections helped Bryson get a job on Wall Street.

feckless *(FEK-less), adjective*
Unable or unwilling to do anything useful. Lacking the thought or organization necessary to succeed. Ineffective or feeble. Without initiative or ability in a specific field.

It is frustrating when the most vocal person in a group of volunteers also proves to be the most FECKLESS.

fecundity *(Fe-KUN-di-tee), noun*
A person, organization, resource, or activity that is exceptionally productive, creative, fertile, or fruitful.

The FECUNDITY of her vegetable garden surprised even the most avid of her horticulturally inclined friends.

Know This Quote

"Blistering heat suddenly took the place of Carboniferous moisture and FECUNDITY." —Simon Winchester, British author and journalist

feint *(FAYNT), noun or verb*
A false, misleading move intended to draw attention away from the real action or activity, usually used in sporting events (noun); to make a misleading move with the intention of drawing away from the real action (verb)

The goalie had expected a FEINT on the penalty kick so was able to block the ball when it indeed came to her weak side instead.

The boxer had studied his opponent so he was ready when the other man tried to FEINT with his left and attack with his right.

felicity *(fih-LIH-suh-tee), noun*
Happiness, contentment, and bliss. Something that inspires sublime contentment. An appropriate or pleasing manner. Use this word in lieu of *happiness,* and those around you will be felicitous.

The baby's after-meal FELICITY was a relief to his tired mother.

Know This Quote

"Never lose sight of the fact that all human FELICITY lies in man's imagination, and that he cannot think to attain it unless he heeds all his caprices." - Marquis de Sade, French aristocrat and revolutionary

fell *(FEHL), verb*
To cut or knock down; to topple

The hurricane FELLED trees and ripped roofs from houses but no lives were lost.

felon *(FEHL-un), noun*
A person who has committed a serious crime

The residents of the town locked their doors and windows until the escaped FELON had been recaptured.

feral *(FEER-uhl), adjective*
Having the qualities of a wild beast; undomesticated. Feral ferrets are fearsome, so watch out.

Legends of FERAL children, those reared by wolves or apes, are common in folklore and literature.

ferocity *(fur-AH-sih-tee), noun*
The state of being fierce or violent

The lion's FEROCITY was more intimidating in the wild than it had been at the zoo.

fervent *(FUHR-vent), adjective*
Having great emotion or passion; caring a great deal

The mother's FERVENT pleas for an organ donor moved everyone who heard them.

Which Word?

Two words with similar definitions may seem identical, but they are not used in exactly the same way. Fervent (FUHR-vent) and fervid (FUR-vid) are two of these words. The word fervent can be used to encompass a wide range of emotions. A person can be fervent in her anger, her joy, her grief, or her support—any number of strong emotions. Fervid, however, implies feeling a positive emotion. Fervid means enthusiastic, overjoyed, or another extreme sense of happiness.

fervid *(FUR-vid), adjective*

Intensely enthusiastic; wildly supportive or excited

The FERVID crowd broke through the fence and stormed the field when the team won in the last seconds of the game.

fervor *(FUR-vuhr), noun*

Intense and passionate emotion

The FERVOR in Boston when the Red Sox finally won the World Series cannot be understood if you weren't there to experience it.

Overcome by the FERVOR of the game, not the heat, the players on the winning team took off their jerseys and threw them to the crowd.

fiasco *(fee-ASS-koe), noun*

A total, humiliating, or ludicrous failure.

It was harsh, but accurate, to call their first date a FIASCO, for both Barbara and Charles agreed to never speak to each other again.

Where'd That Word Come From?

Fiasco—This word, meaning "a total, foolish failure," derives from the Italian word *fiasco,* for "bottle," but no one seems to know why. Used in England as a theatrical term in the late nineteenth century, the word may have something to do with a bottle breaking—either accidentally or as part of the plot—in some forgotten yet very bad play. It might also be that a brand of wine in some bottles was flat or sour—a complete failure or fiasco—or that imperfect bottles made by glassblowers were called *fiascos.*

fiat *(FEE-aht), noun*

An authoritative decree or order.

Everyone interested in receiving a sizeable portion of his inheritance simply allows grandfather to rule the household by FIAT.

fidelity *(fih-DEL-ih-tee), noun*
Faithfulness and loyalty, expressed by continued support

She showed her FIDELITY to her alma mater with a generous check every year.

filibuster *(FIL-eh-buhs-ter), noun*
Delaying tactics, usually the making of long speeches, used in the legislature to postpone or prevent action being taken

The senator was three hours into the FILIBUSTER and showed no signs of yielding the floor to let the vote take place.

finesse *(fin-ESS), noun*
Refinement and delicacy; grace and skill

It took all the FINESSE the building manager had to juggle the needs and egos of all the artists performing at the benefit concert.

fitful *(FIT-ful), adjective*
Irregular; broken up; not steady

Her sleep was always FITFUL during exams because she was so stressed about the tests.

flagitious *(fluh-JISH-uss), adjective*
Shamefully wicked or particularly heinous.

Now that that the paparazzi hangs on her every move, Natasha goes out of her way to engage in FLAGITIOUS behavior.

flagrant *(FLAY-grehnt), adjective*
Obviously bad or wrong; conspicuously offensive

Some people consider the verdict in the O.J. Simpson trial a FLAGRANT miscarriage of justice while others consider it proof the criminal justice system works.

flamboyant *(flam-BOI-ant), adjective*
Elaborate; highly energetic; tending to draw attention

His eccentric aunt's house was as FLAMBOYANT as she was.

flaunt *(FLONT), verb*
To display in an ostentatious way; to lack shame, modesty, or humility. To show off a characteristic or possession in an outrageous way. Not to be confused, as often happens, with *flout* (defined on the next page).

Rappers FLAUNT their income with what they call "bling," and what others call ostentatious jewelry.

fledgling *(FLEJ-ling), noun*
A young bird whose flight feathers have just grown in. A young or inexperienced person. The fledging of the fledgling's feathers forecast flight for that night.

The FLEDGLING golfer became frustrated after most shots but quite excited when a ball landed close to the hole.

flippant *(FLIP-uhnt), adjective*
Disrespectful but often humorous; not showing seriousness

The young woman's FLIPPANT remark in response to his offer hurt him deeply but he refused to show it.

florid *(FLOH-rid), adjective*
Flushed with color, usually reddish; ruddy

His FLORID complexion made his mother realize he hadn't just been studying with his tutor.

flout *(FLOWT), verb*
To openly disregard or show contempt for

She dyed her hair purple as a safe way to FLOUT the school's dress code.

fluidly *(FLOO-id-lee), adverb*
In a graceful, flowing way

The large cat moved FLUIDLY through the grass as it stalked its prey.

foible *(FOI-bull), noun*
An idiosyncrasy, small weakness, failing, fault, or character flaw that is comparatively insignificant.

A common FOIBLE is to surround yourself with those who flatter, rather than those who will be honest.

foist *(FOYST), verb*
To unload something undesirable, false, or inferior on the pretence that it is genuine, valuable, or desirable; to pawn off something undesirable.

This project was FOISTED off on us because everyone believed it was impossible and because we were considered the worst department in the organization.

foment *(foh-MENT), verb*
To incite or instigate; to stir up, usually to action

The speakers FOMENTED the crowd, turning a peaceful gathering into a violent riot.

Know This Quote

"If perticuliar care and attention is not paid to the Laidies we are determined to FOMENT a Rebelion, and will not hold ourselves bound by any Laws in which we have no voice, or Representation." —Abigail Adams, second First Lady of the United States

foolhardy *(fool-HARD-ee), adjective*
Rash; uncaring of the consequences; daring in an irresponsible way

His leap from the balcony into the pool was easily the most FOOLHARDY thing any of the students did while on spring break.

foppish *(FOHP-ish), adjective*
Overly concerned with looks, style, and mannerism

Underneath the Scarlet Pimpernel's FOPPISH exterior was a brave and daring man.

foray *(FORE-ay), noun*
An initial attempt at a new activity or occupation. A short trip or visit to a place; a particular purpose. A sudden military attack or raid.

Elizabeth's FORAY into the world of publishing was not without some disheartening moments.

forbear *(for-BEAR), verb*
To not do something; to do without.

The landlord decided to FORBEAR raising the rent until the repairs to the building had been completed.

forbearance *(for-BAYR-ens), noun*
Patience and self-control, especially when faced with an annoyance

I was grateful to my tutor for treating me with such FORBEARANCE while I struggled to understand calculus.

forestall *(for-STAWL), verb*
To thwart an action in advance; or, to buy up goods in order to increase their resale price.

Arthur's family thrives during financially insecure times because it always seems to FORESTALL exactly the right commodities.

forfeit *(FOR-fit), verb or noun*
To surrender or give up (verb) or something that is surrendered or given up, usually in payment (noun)

When the opposing team had to FORFEIT, our school felt cheated out of a good game.

The courts ruled that the FORFEIT of the farmer's land would be due the first day of the next month.

forgery *(FOR-juh-ree), noun*
Something that is a fake, made with the intention of presenting it as authentic

The Picasso FORGERY was so well made that even experts couldn't recognize it as fake just by looking at it.

forswear *(for-SWAYR), verb*
To deny, renounce, or agree to give up, usually in a formal setting such as under oath or before God

In order to save her life, Katherine Parr had to FORSWEAR that she was not Protestant but had only studied the teachings in order to better debate King Henry VIII.

fortuitous *(for-TYOO-ih-tus), adjective*
Occurring by lucky chance or happening; unexpected and unplanned but good

It was FORTUITOUS that they were both walking in the park at the same time or they might never have met in a city the size of Houston.

Know This Quote

"The most FORTUITOUS event of my entire life was meeting my wife Eleanor." —Franklin Delano Roosevelt

founder *(FOUN-der), verb*
To fail utterly or to become a complete wreck.

William had always wanted to open his own business, but his first attempt FOUNDERED hopelessly.

fractious *(FRAK-shuss), adjective*
Irritable and quarrelsome. Likely to misbehave or complain; unruly. Likely to cause disturbance or trouble. Not related in meaning to *fraction,* a number that is not a whole number or a small portion of an entire thing.

For some strange reason, the saying "Boys will be boys" is often used to describe FRACTIOUS male teens who act out in public.

fragile *(FRAH-jul), adjective*
Easily broken or destroyed; flimsy

She didn't allow the children to carry the china because it was FRAGILE and they were clumsy.

frangible *(FRAN-juh-bull), adjective*
Easily breakable.

The Worthingtons' staff knows to be excessively careful around the family's collection of FRANGIBLE Ming vases.

frantic *(FRAN-tik), adjective*
Overcome with fear, anxiety, or another negative emotion

The young woman became FRANTIC when her computer crashed with the only copy of her thesis on it.

frenetic *(fruh-NET-ick), adjective*
Frantic and frenzied.

As Ruth's deadline approached, her work became even more FRENETIC.

frippery *(FRIHP-uh-ree), noun*
Ostentatious or affected elegance.

The FRIPPERY of Lara's couture belied her nouveau riche origins.

frisson *(FREE-son), noun*
A sudden strong feeling of excitement, conflict, or danger.

As Paul approached the abandoned house, he felt a overwhelming sense of FRISSON.

Know This Quote

"Pregnant women! They had that weird FRISSON, an aura of magic that combined awkwardly with an earthy sense of duty." —Ruth Morgan, American novelist

frivolous *(FRIV-uh-lus), adjective*
Carefree; having no serious purpose

The ceramic purple and blue giraffe might have been a FRIVOLOUS purchase but it made her very happy, so it was worth the money.

frugality *(FROO-gal-ih-tee), noun*
The ability to spend very little money; the ability to save without wasting much

He decided it was better to learn FRUGALITY than have to ask his parents for money again.

fruition *(froo-IH-shun), noun*
The point at which something comes to maturity or reaches a desired outcome. The achievement of something desired or labored. Literally and figuratively, "to reap the fruit of one's labors."

All those years of studying reached FRUITION when Ted was accepted to the college he had dreamed of.

fugacious *(fyoo-GAY-shus), adjective*
Passing away quickly; fleeting; short lived

Between the heat in September and the snow in early November, autumn seemed even more FUGACIOUS than usual this year.

fulminate *(fool-mih-NAYT), verb*
To express violent disapproval; to protest vehemently

The murder of the little girl caused the mayor to FULMINATE against street crime at every opportunity.

fulsome *(FOOL-sum), adjective*
Excessive and insincere, used to define flattery or praise

His obviously FULSOME praise of his boss backfired when he didn't get the promotion because he was such a brownnoser.

funereal *(fyoo-NIR-ee-uhl), adjective*
Reminiscent of, related to, or suitable for a funeral. Solemn, mournful, dark, brooding, and dismal. Clearly a very dramatic adjective—just be careful to spell it correctly, or you may be mournful.

After they lost the state championship, the football team's locker room could be accurately described as FUNEREAL.

fungible *(FUHN-jih-bull), adjective*
Freely exchangeable for another of like nature; interchangeable.

Stella was incensed to find that not all Cartier watches are FUNGIBLE.

furtive *(FUR-tiv), adjective*
Hidden due to guilt or the belief that being seen or known would cause trouble

Although happily married himself, he couldn't help but steal FURTIVE glances at his friend's beautiful wife.

Know This Quote

"For a while the two stared at each other—Denison embarrassed, Selene almost FURTIVE."
—Isaac Asimov, Russian-born American author and biochemist

fussbudget *(FUSS-buh-jet), noun*
Someone who typically worries about trivial things. A word most famously applied to Charlie Brown's friend Lucy.

Most FUSSBUDGETS seem to have an unlimited supply of fuss and bother because they never run out of either.

fuzzy-headed *(FUH-zee HED-ehd), adjective*
Not thinking clearly, or not expressing ideas or thoughts clearly; inarticulate.

A FUZZY-HEADED morning often follows a fun night.

G

gable *(GAY-bull), noun*
The triangular upper part of a wall at the end of a rigid roof.
The Sandersons could not resist purchasing a second Cape Cod home because they fell in love with the home's colorful GABLES.

gainsay *(GAYN-say), verb*
To deny, contradict, or state something is false
She wanted to GAINSAY the accusations against her friend but couldn't because she knew they were true.

galivant *(GAL-ih-vant), verb*
To wander widely; to constantly travel to many different places, without an itinerary or plan; to freely go wherever and whenever the mood strikes you, and doing so frequently.
Some accuse us of GALIVANTING around the world, but cultural knowledge is de rigueur for cocktail conversation.

gallantry *(GAL-luhn-tree), noun*
Courtesy, thoughtfulness, and bravery; nobility or chivalry, especially in actions toward women. Grand, majestic, or showy dress, style, or action.
Some say that chivalry and GALLANTRY are dead, but if you look hard you can see that they are still alive and well in many modern attitudes and actions.

galleon *(GAL-ee-un), noun*
A Mediterranean sailing vessel used by explorers for ocean voyages.
The GALLEONS of the Spanish fleet sailed annually from Seville to Panama and Cartagena.

galumph *(ga-LUMF), verb*
To walk or run in a clumsy and boisterous way. To move heavily, with thudding steps.
Today's athletes GALUMPH in triumph after a touchdown, basket, or goal; they have no concern for the sportsmanship of the past.

galvanize *(GAL-vuh-nize), verb*
To stimulate someone or something into action, especially muscle fibers, by means of electric current. In a technical sense, to coat a metal with zinc to prevent corrosion.
The hardships of winter GALVANIZE the isolated residents of Maine to help one another whenever needed.

gambit *(GAM-bit), noun*
A remark used to redirect a conversation; or, a maneuver used to seek advantage.

When it seemed as though Margie was about to tell Richard's secret, he used a GAMBIT and turned the conversation to sports instead.

gambol *(GAM-bowl), verb*
To run, skip, or jump about in a playful or joyous fashion.

When Sarah and William found out they were going to be parents, they were so excited that they GAMBOLLED in their living room.

Know This Quote
"We all have these places where shy humiliations GAMBOL on sunny afternoons." —W. H. Auden, Anglo-American poet

gamesmanship *(GAYMZ-muhn-ship), noun*
Strategies used to gain an advantage in sports, life, business, or politics. Unconventional but not strictly illegal tactics employed to gain an advantage.

Pre-game chatter with opposing team members is a sure sign of GAMESMANSHIP, and it can backfire at times.

gamesome *(GAYM-suhm), adjective*
Playful and frolicsome.

Paula's new puppy was especially GAMESOME.

gamine *(gah-MEEN), noun*
A girl with a boyish demeanor and mischievous nature who is somehow still appealing.

Her GAMINE behavior and looks only made her that much more attractive to teenage boys her age.

gamut *(GA-mut), noun*
The full range or extent. A critic once famously slammed an early performance of Katharine Hepburn's as running the "gamut of emotions from A to B." In music, refers to the entire series of standard musical notes.

His house featured an entertainment center whose components ran the GAMUT of state-of-the-art equipment.

garner *(GAHR-ner), verb*
To earn, acquire, collect, amass, gather, or accumulate something by effort. To gather something into storage.

Jamie, always a good student, GARNERED many honors at commencement, including that of valedictorian.

garnish *(GAHR-nish), verb*
To add something to food or drink to enhance flavor or appearance; to decorate something, usually food, with an ornament.

Tony would GARNISH his wedding cakes with rose blossoms, enhancing their appearance as well as fragrance.

garrulity *(gah-ROO-lih-tee), noun*
The habit of talking way too much.

Wanda was often annoyed by Carl's GARRULITY and frequently asked him to stop interrupting her.

garrulous *(GAR-uh-lus), adjective*
Excessively talkative; using many, many, many, too many words.

Drunks are often described as GARRULOUS.

Know This Quote

"The interview is an intimate conversation between journalist and politician wherein the journalist seeks to take advantage of the GARRULITY of the politician and the politician of the credulity of the journalist" —Emory Klein, American journalist

gastronomy *(gas-TRAH-nah-mee), noun*
The art or appreciation of preparing and eating good food. Those who practice *gastronomy* don't necessarily have gas, but their efforts do focus on things "gastro," relating to the stomach or belly.

Those knowledgeable in GASTRONOMY don't consider hot dogs bought and eaten at a sporting event to be epicurean delights, but true fans do.

gauche *(GOASH), adjective*
Lacking grace or tact in a social situation. Describes a socially inappropriate remark or action.

Justin's constant belching at the table was clearly GAUCHE, but he believed such behavior was normal for a teenager.

gaudy *(GAHW-dee), adjective*
Brightly colored, showy; decorated in a tasteless or vulgar way. Tacky or excessively ornamental.

Those who win the lottery or acquire other unexpected riches often quickly adorn themselves with GAUDY jewelry.

gazetteer*(gaz-ih-TEERr), noun*
A geographical index or dictionary of places organized by name.

The Rothschilds prefer their pilot simply head for the sun, rather than consult a GAZETTEER prior to short flights.

gelid *(JELL-uhd), adjective*
Extremely cold; icy.

The Vangelders' yacht sluiced easily through the GELID waters of the Cape.

genome *(GEE-nome), noun*
The collection of chromosomes that makes an individual organism unique from all others except its clone or identical twin.

Blake has become convinced that the GENOMES of those among his most important social contacts have more commonalities than differences.

genteel *(jen-TEEL), adjective*
Refined, good-mannered; typical of high social standing. Overdoing the refined behavior considered typical of the upper class. At the risk of provoking giggles, *please* do not confuse this well-mannered word with *genital,* which refers to external sexual organs.

Cynthia took care to make sure she ate properly and conversed politely at her first experience with her GENTEEL future in-laws.

Know This Quote

"[I am] a journalist in the field of etiquette. I try to find out what the most GENTEEL people regularly do, what traditions they have discarded, what compromises they have made." —Amy Vanderbilt, American etiquette expert

geopolitical *(gee-oh-poh-LIH-tih-kull), adjective*
Anything having to do with the politics affecting the relationships of two or more countries, especially when influenced by geographical factors.

GEOPOLITICAL instability in the Middle East is fueling rising crude oil prices.

geostationary *(GEE-oh-STAY-shin-air-ee), adjective*
A satellite in orbit 22,300 miles above the Earth's surface so that the satellite is always directly over the same spot of ground.

Arthur C. Clarke was the first to propose that three GEOSTATIONARY satellites orbiting Earth could provide a global communications network effectively covering every location on the planet.

germane *(jer-MAYN), adjective*
Relevant to the topic at hand; pertinent to what is being discussed

Students' participation in class is GERMANE when considering their grades.

Let's see what Bill has to say, as his contributions are always GERMANE.

germinal *(JUHRM-nuhl), adjective*
Related to the earliest stage of development

Roland's foray into art-buying is in its GERMINAL phase.

gerrymander *(JAIR-ee-MAN-der), verb*
To divide an electoral district so as to give a political advantage to a particular party. To divide a geographic area into voting districts so as to give advantage to one party in elections.

The state legislature's attempt to GERRYMANDER was deemed illegal and voided by the state supreme court.

gestalt *(geh-STALT), noun*
A unified whole.

"If we don't show a GESTALT, how are they ever going to take us seriously!" Beth exclaimed as the workers wavered in their support of the strike.

Know This Quote

"Feminism is an entire world view or GESTALT, not just a laundry list of women's issues."
—Charlotte Bunch, American feminist

gestation *(jes-TAY-shun), noun*
The carrying of offspring in the womb. The necessary period of time for the development of a fetus during pregnancy. Also, the development of a concept, idea, or plan. Not a "gas station," where you purchase gas.

The GESTATION of one's candidacy for President begins well before and goes well beyond the primary elections.

gesticulate *(jes-TIK-yoo-layt), verb*
To use gestures while speaking, especially for emphasis

The more passionate she was about a topic, the more she GESTICULATED when discussing it.

gesticulation *(jes-TICK-yoo-lay-shun), noun*
A movement of hands or arms that accompanies speech, usually for emphasis. An expression made with hands and arms, and not a vulgar one-finger gesture.

Great orators are versed in GESTICULATION as well as verbal eloquence.

gimcrack *(JIHM-krack), noun*
A showy object of little or no value.

Susan bought the old vase thinking it would be worth a great deal of money. Imagine how disappointed she was when she found out it was only a GIMCRACK.

gizmo *(GIZZ-moe), noun*
An overly complicated device, usually mechanical. A gadget is a *gizmo*, and a *gizmo* is a gadget. Yes, they are synonyms.

Justin's father is always designing and building GIZMOS that cost more than things he could just get from the store.

glacial *(GLAY-shul), adjective*
Extremely cold, either in demeanor, manner, or temperature

The GLACIAL stare she sent him when he walked in the room made it clear to the rest of us their relationship had ended badly.

glasnost *(GLAZ-noast), noun*
A Soviet policy permitting greater openness, discussion, and disclosure of ideas and information. Used by Mikhail Gorbachev, former Soviet premier, to describe the less repressive policies of the Soviet Union in the 1980s.

A period of GLASNOST preceded the downfall of the Soviet Union and foretold of an independent and democratic Russia.

glean *(GLEEN), verb*
To discover or learn slowly and deliberately.

Bentley GLEANED from the drop in Ferrari sales that a looming recession even had some of his social contacts feeling nervous.

glib *(GLIHB), adjective*
Natural to the point of being off-handed; without much depth, shallow

The girl's GLIB response when questioned about her homework concerned her father because he knew she hadn't started on the report.

glimmer *(GLIHM-ehr), noun*
An intermittent flicker of light; or a faint glimpse

The GLIMMER of the Christmas tree lights and the glow of the fire made the room cozy and romantic.

The young man had a GLIMMER of hope that she might be interested in him when she gave him her phone number.

gloaming *(GLOW-ming), noun*
The time of fading light after sunset, just before dark.

The GLOAMING is sometimes gloomy, but often serene.

globalization *(glow-bull-ih-ZAY-shin), noun*
The movement toward a true world economy with open and free trading across national borders.

The company longed for GLOBALIZATION as they were currently unable to ship their goods to certain countries.

globule *(GLAHB-yewl), noun*
A small globe or ball

Hillary's favorite possession was a small GLOBULE with a snowman inside.

glossary *(GLAU-suh-ree), noun*
An alphabetical collection of specialist terms and meanings, often an appendix to a book—or, in the case of this publication, an entire book.

A GLOSSARY is a special list for specialists, containing words and definitions.

Know This Quote

"In yourself is the law of all nature, and you know not yet how a GLOBULE of sap ascends."
—Ralph Waldo Emerson, American poet, essayist, and transcendentalist

glutton *(GLUT-un), noun*
A person who eats an enormous amount; or a person who can withstand or even longs for a large amount of something

All-you-can-eat buffets tend to be heaven for GLUTTONS.

When he started dating yet another self-centered woman, his friends started wondering if he was a GLUTTON for punishment.

Gnosticism *(NAH-stih-sih-zim), noun*
The religious belief that salvation is attained through secret knowledge rather than through prayer, ritual, faith, divine grace, or good works.

Many of the key principles of Christianity were formed as a direct response to GNOSTICISM.

goad *(GODE), verb*
To provoke, invite, stimulate, urge, or prod, especially toward a specific action. Originally, the word meant a pointed stick used to prod animals.

As a form of initiation, or hazing, members of the football team would GOAD freshmen into running naked across the field.

goliath *(guh-LIE-uth), noun*
Something or someone large in size and stature; giant. When capitalized, refers to the biblical giant who was slain by David with a sling and stone.

The GOLIATH sundae, made with four flavors of ice cream and five toppings, was too large for one person to finish.

gorgonize *(GORE-guh-nize), verb*
To paralyze or mesmerize with one's looks or personality.

Even without her family's wealth and connections, Marla would likely GORGONIZE all the men who enter her orbit.

gormandize *(GORE-mun-dize), verb*
To eat like a glutton, as if one was starving.

We find GORMANDIZING on even the finest French cuisine to be quite tasteless and, therefore, to be avoided.

gossamer *(GOS-ih-mer), noun*
Something light, flimsy, and delicate, often referring to very delicate material

At the sight of the flowers on her desk, her bad mood dissolved like GOSSAMER.

gossipmonger *(GOHS-sip-MOHN-guhr), noun*
Someone who conducts a conversation about personal or intimate rumors or facts, especially those that are malicious to and about others.

Stacie was a notorious GOSSIPMONGER, yet she still had the ears of many in the twelfth grade.

gourmand *(gor-MAND), noun*
A person who loves good food

The newspaper's food critic was well-suited to the job because she was such a GOURMAND.

gradation *(gray-DAY-shun), noun*
A series of gradual and progressive degrees, steps, or stages. A move that is made in measured, distinct stages. *Gradation* is gradual progress, and not to be confused with *graduation*, which is often the result of a four-year process.

The GRADATION of colors in the sunset covered the whole range of the spectrum.

graft *(GRAFT), noun*
The use of dishonest or illegal means to gain money or property, often by someone in a position of power or elected office. Personal profit made in an illicit way because of official standing.

The game had been sold out for months, and the mayor's easy acquisition of choice tickets led to whisperings of GRAFT in the administration.

grandeur *(GRAN-jur), noun*
The quality of being great, grand, or very impressive; extravagance in scale or appearance.

The GRANDEUR of Buckingham Palace impresses all who have the honor to visit.

grandiloquence *(grand-EHL-ih-kwens), noun*
A pompous and pretentious way of speaking; a manner of talking that suggests the speaker is trying too hard to impress

The speaker's GRANDILOQUENCE impressed some but merely put off others.

grandiose *(GRAN-dee-OCE), adjective*
Pretentious, pompous, and imposing. Can be used to describe pretensions or ambitions that go beyond abilities or means.

It is surprising when GRANDIOSE schemes become realities, but that is why so many reach for the stars.

granular *(GRAN-you-ler), adjective*
The ability to divide, organize, and search through something at a fine level of detail.

Julian's GRANULAR abilities allow him to extract the absolute best from among even the largest pile of uncut diamonds.

gratify *(GRA-tih-fiy), verb*
To please or satisfy

The teacher was always GRATIFIED when her students were accepted into college.

gratuitous *(grah-TOO-ih-tus), adjective*
Unnecessary and uncalled for; unwanted; extra or unneeded

Sadly, movie makers have learned that GRATUITOUS sex and violence sells tickets.

gravitas *(GRAH-vih-tahs), noun*
A serious and solemn attitude or way of behaving.

A funeral is an appropriate place for GRAVITAS.

gravity *(gra-VUH-tee), noun*
Seriousness, great importance

The drunken teens' parents called the police in order to help reinforce the GRAVITY of the situation.

Know This Quote

"Being accused of making money by selling sex in Hollywood, home of the casting couch and the GRATUITOUS nude scene, is so rich with irony that it's a better subject for a comic novel than a column." —Anna Quindlen, American author and opinion columnist

Which Word?

Words often have a second (or third) meaning that is less common than its best-known definition. Gravity (gra-VUH-tee) is one of those words. You know that gravity is the force that keeps everything on the planet from floating off the earth. However, it also means seriousness or importance.

gregarious *(gri-GARE-ee-uss), adjective*
Very friendly, sociable, outgoing, or cordial; happy in the company of others.

GREGARIOUS individuals are often suspected of having hidden agendas when they are really just being friendly.

grievous *(GREE-vus), adjective*
Devastating; causing severe pain, either emotional or physical

Only time will tell if the city will ever recover from the GRIEVOUS loss caused by the hurricane that struck this year.

grisly *(GRIHS-lee), adjective*
Gruesomely unpleasant or creating a sense of horror. Not to be confused with *grizzly*, which is a type of bear.

Seeing grizzlies eating the carcasses of their prey is a GRISLY sight.

grouse *(GRAUSS), verb*
To complain or grumble about one's situation.

We decided not to return to the restaurant after the maître d' continuously GROUSED about the slovenliness of his wait staff.

grovel *(GRAH-vul), verb*
To act in a servile way. To show exaggerated and false respect, intending to please or out of fear. To crawl or lie face down in humility or fear.

Prisoners were forced to GROVEL before their guards, fearing torture and abuse if they did not.

guerilla *(guh-RILL-uh), noun*
One who engages in warfare through small acts of harassment and sabotage.

With her keen eye for detail and authenticity, Lorissa has begun to wage a GUERILLA war against stores that proffer knockoffs as legitimate couture.

guffaw *(guh-FAWE), noun*
A loud and raucous laugh.

Robert's GUFFAW was embarrassing to his wife, so she grimaced whenever they went to a humorous play.

guile *(GILE), noun*
Cunning, deceitful, and treacherous quality or type of behavior. Skill and cleverness used to trick, deceive, or mislead people.

No matter how smart you think you are, you are no match for the GUILE of an experienced street con seeking to separate you from your money.

Know This Quote

"Gaze no more in the bitter glass / The demons, with their subtle GUILE, / Lift up before us when they pass, / Or only gaze a little while." —William Butler Yeats, Irish poet and dramatist

gullible *(GUL-uh-bul), adjective*
Easily made to believe something false; easy to fool

Con artists count on people being GULLIBLE enough to believe their scams.

gustatory *(GUSS-tuh-tore-ee), adjective*
Of the sense of taste.

Mark found the blueberry pie to be a GUSTATORY delight.

gyrating *(jye-RAY-shun), adjective*
Of a circular or spiral pattern.

When he first appeared on the Ed Sullivan show, Elvis Presley's GYRATING hips during his act caused quite a stir.

H

habeas corpus *(HAY-bee-us CORE-puss), noun*
A written order requiring a prisoner or person under arrest or confinement to be brought before a judge to assess whether the restraint of said person is lawful and proper.

Following the nightclub brawl, Chad and Wendell managed to receive a writ of HABEAS CORPUS only after their father called the authorities and reminded them of his social contacts.

habile *(HAB-ill), adjective*
Skillful and able; handy.

Our HABILE gardener has helped render our topiary into the shapes of dollar and pound signs.

habitude *(HAB-uh-tyood), noun*
Customary behavior or customary procedure.

Alistair's HABITUDE is for the servants to awake him just prior to noon.

hackneyed *(HAK-need), adjective*
Made commonplace, less significant, and stale by overuse or common use. Strictly, refers either to a carriage for hire or to a horse suited only for routine riding or driving.

Soap operas are now HACKNEYED caricatures of dramas appearing on television daily.

haggard *(HA-gurd), adjective*
Showing signs of tiredness, anxiety, or hunger. Wild and unruly in appearance.

After a twelve-hour shift at the hospital, anyone would look HAGGARD.

Where'd That Word Come From?

Haggard—This words originates with the 3,000-year-old sport of falconry. A haggard bird is one trapped as an adult and very difficult to train, unlike a bird captured as a nestling. The word came to mean a wild, intractable person, and it later took on the meaning of a terrified, anxious, or exhausted expression on a human face. This finally evolved to mean gaunt, drawn, wasted, or exhausted.

hagiography *(hag-ee-OG-ruh-fee), noun*
A biography that idealizes its subject.

The Van Gelders were disappointed with the volume written about their illustrious descendants because the book fell far short of being a HAGIOGRAPHY.

halation *(hal-AYE-shun), noun*
A blurred image or ring of light caused by the reflection or dispersal of light.

The mysterious white ring he claims is a ghost is merely HALATION caused by the photographer's lighting.

halcyon *(HAL-see-yon), adjective*
Idyllic; peaceful and calm; often used when describing a particular time from the past

Many people look back on the summers of their childhoods and consider them HALCYON days, forgetting that those same days were often boring at the time.

Know This Quote

"It was the most HALCYON summer I ever spent." —Rick Bass, American author and environmental activist

hale *(HAYL), adjective*
In robust good health. Used most often in the phrase "*hale* and hardy." A robust word to use in writing or speech.

After recovering from a bout of flu, Mitch was finally feeling HALE again.

halitosis *(HA-lih-toe-sis), noun*
A formal and fancy way of referring to very bad breath. If you use this word about your friend it might not embarrass him as much; on the other hand, if he had used a mint, you wouldn't have to use this word at all.

Knowing about Skip's HALITOSIS, I decided to wait for the next elevator after I saw him get on one.

hallmark *(HAWL-mahrk), noun*
A mark showing something is of high quality, or one identifying purity of certain metals or the maker of specific crafted items. A feature of something that distinguishes it from similar items. No, it's not just a type of greeting card. The *hallmark* of Mark's hall was an amazing mural.

Each college has a building that serves as a HALLMARK of that institution.

Where'd That Word Come From?

Hallmark—These "marks of excellence on products," originated as the official stamp of the Goldsmiths' Company of London. In 1300, Edward I ordered that all gold and silver be struck with such a mark to indicate its purity. They were called *hallmarks* because the stamping was done at Goldsmiths' Hall in London.

hallow *(HA-low), verb*

To make someone or something holy. To have great respect or reverence, the highest possible honor for a person or thing.

Many football fans HALLOW the frozen tundra of Lambeau Field where the Green Bay Packers play.

halo effect *(HAY-low ih-FEKT), noun*

The tendency to judge someone as being totally good because one particular aspect of his or her character is good, or because those around him or her are also good.

The HALO EFFECT helps us assume that young men and women who sing in church choirs and participate in church youth groups are free of behavioral problems, but it's not always true.

hamlet *(HAM-luht), noun*

A small village or group of houses, homesteads, or households. Not just the name of Shakespeare's melancholy Dane. If you describe certain residences as a *hamlet*, it will be quite quaint and impress your readers or listeners.

During their summer trip to North Carolina, the Harrisons visited many HAMLETS and stayed at some phenomenal bed-and-breakfast inns.

hamper *(HAM-per), verb*

To hinder or prevent free movement; to hold back, literally or figuratively

Her friends told her that the umbrella would only HAMPER her on the hike but she insisted on taking it anyway.

Which Word?

Even if you think you know a word, you may find it used in an unfamiliar context. Check the definition—it may have a second meaning you were unaware of. Hamper (HAM-per) may be one of those words. You know that a hamper is a container, usually where you throw your dirty laundry. That is its most common definition. But it is also a verb that means to hold back or make difficult.

haphazard *(hap-HA-zurd), adjective*

Happening or done in a way not planned; irregular; governed by chance. Something not guided by a regular or predetermined method. *Haphazard* golfers often happen to be in a hazard.

After several rounds using a HAPHAZARD approach to the game, Mark decided that golf lessons were definitely in order.

hapless *(HA-pluss), adjective*
Unlucky, unfortunate, or inauspicious. Haphazard hunters may appear *hapless*, but a little planning may give them better luck.

High school freshmen seem so HAPLESS during the first few weeks of school, but they later appear more confident.

Know This Quote

"Exile is the noble and dignified term, while a refugee is more HAPLESS." —Mary McCarthy, American author

harangue *(hu-RANG), noun*
A long, critical speech or lecture

The young man refused to return his sister's phone call because he knew it would just be another hour-long HARANGUE about what a bad brother he was.

Peter's parents would regularly HARANGUE him regarding inappropriate dress and behavior, but it never seemed to help.

harbinger *(HAR-bin-jur), noun*
Someone or something that brings about a major change. One that foreshadows or anticipates something still to come.

Employment figures are accepted as HARBINGERS of economic trends and, during election years, of political success or failure.

hardy *(HAR-dee), adjective*
Capable of living in just about any condition

Aloe plants are HARDY, which makes them ideal for city apartments that don't get much light or fresh air.

harpy *(HAR-pee), noun*
A greedy and predatory person; or, a scolding and shrewish woman.

"That HARPY Charlotte can't wait to get her claws into Bruce," Nancy observed.

harry *(HAR-ee), verb*
To torment with constant attacks.

Sara was HARRIED by worry about her test.

Know This Quote

"At middle night great cats with silver claws, / Bodies of shadow and blind eyes like pearls, / Came up out of the hole, and red-eared hounds / With long white bodies came out of the air / Suddenly, and ran at them and HARRIED them." —William Butler Yeats, Irish poet and dramatist

haughtiness *(HAW-tee-ness), noun*
Arrogance; superiority; condescending pride

The HAUGHTINESS of the contestant lost her points in the personality category.

haughty *(HAW-tee), adjective*
Superior, condescending, or arrogant. Rather than using the "B" word, it's more polite to describe someone as haughty.

The HAUGHTY behavior of those who were members of the country club was not appreciated by their friends.

haute couture *(OAT koo-TOOR), noun*
Highly fashionable clothing on the cutting edge of the latest design fads and trends.

Sophia love the HAUTE COUTURE she was wearing when she went out on the town.

Know This Quote

"HAUTE COUTURE should be fun, foolish, and almost unwearable." —Christian Lacroix, French fashion designer

haute cuisine *(OAT kwi-ZEEN), noun*
Traditional, classic, high-quality French cooking or general gourmet preparation of food. Can refer to the preparation of meals like artwork.

Gourmets, though not necessarily gourmands, prefer HAUTE CUISINE, because they believe more in quality rather than quantity.

HAZMAT *(HAZ-maht), abbreviation*
Stands for "hazardous material." The label given a team of professionals who deal with hazardous material.

More than ever, HAZMAT training and team members are critical.

headlong *(HED-long), adjective*
Rashly and without much thought; or headfirst

The young couple rushed HEADLONG into marriage without considering that they were making a lifetime commitment at only eighteen years old.

She fell HEADLONG down the stairs but only received a few bruises.

hearsay *(HEER-say), adjective*
Describing information that is heard from other people, and not from the person or persons who made the original statement. Information gained from another party, not as a result of observing the original action.

HEARSAY evidence is not admissible in a court of law.

hedonist *(HEED-on-ist), noun*
A person who believes only in the pursuit of pleasure

The socialite had a reputation as a HEDONIST only because she kept her numerous charitable activities private.

Know This Quote

"[Bad] taste supervenes upon good taste as a daring and witty HEDONISM. It makes the man of good taste cheerful, where before he ran the risk of being chronically frustrated." —Susan Sontag, American literary theorist, philosopher, and political activist

hegemony *(heh-JOHM-eh-nee), noun*
Leadership or dominance, usually in regards to government or the relationship between nations

When a nation is very wealthy and powerful, it is important that it not abuse its state of HEGEMONY on the global stage.

England has throughout history been accused of trying to achieve HEGEMONY, particularly with regard to past members of the British Empire.

heinous *(HAY-nus), adjective*
Particularly vicious or offensive on a societal level, not just a personal one

The police released few details to the public due to the HEINOUS nature of the crime.

heirloom *(ARE-lume), noun*
Something valuable handed down from one generation to the next. An item that is a part of an estate, with a legal heir to inherit it. An ancient hair loom, used to make hair rugs, could be a valued *heirloom.*

The cameo brooch that Mrs. Powell wore was an HEIRLOOM passed on by her grandmother to her mother and from her mother to her.

hellacious *(hel-AYE-shus), adjective*
Extremely brutal, violent, and severe.

Madison's foray into the corporate world was so HELLACIOUS that she quickly went back to being supported solely by her trust fund.

heraldry *(HEHR-uhl-dree), noun*
The practice of creating coats of arms and determining those who are entitled to bear them. Coats of arms and symbols associated with specific birth rights. Pomp and ceremony.

The study of medieval HERALDRY can be fascinating.

herbivorous *(EHR-bihv-rus), adjective*
Eating only grass and plants, not meat. An antonym of *carnivorous.*

Even HERBIVOROUS dinosaurs would have been intimidating by virtue of their size, though not necessarily their eating habits.

herculean *(hur-kyuh-LEE-un), adjective*
Strong and powerful; relating to or resembling Hercules. Daunting, formidable, extremely difficult, requiring a great deal of strength, stamina, effort, or resources.

The HERCULEAN efforts of the 1969 Mets to win the World Series will go down in baseball history.

heresy *(HAYR-ih-see), noun*
A belief or statement that goes against religious doctrine

In ancient times, HERESY was a crime punished by torture and execution.

heretic *(HER-eh-tik), noun*
A person who boldly, loudly, and publicly defies the conventions of a religion, society, culture, or set of beliefs.

People who stand on the street exclaiming that the world is ending are often considered HERETICS.

heretical *(huh-RHET-ih-cul), adjective*
Characterized by beliefs that differ from accepted religious beliefs, generally holds a negative connotation

Strict followers of a religion tend to find other faiths HERETICAL and in need of saving and redemption.

hermetic *(her-MET-ick), adjective*
Isolated, or unaffected by outside influences.

The new writer's first novel was lauded for its HERMETIC writing.

Know This Quote

"Reality, whether approached imaginatively or empirically, remains a surface, HERMETIC." —Samuel Beckett, Irish writer, dramatist, and poet

herstory *(HER-steh-ree), noun*
History presented from a feminist perspective or with an emphasis on the point of view of women. The study or recording of life experiences, achievements, or ambitions of a particular woman or group of women. A new word that originated in the feminist lexicon, yet is now commonly used.

The HERSTORY of the women's suffrage movement is in many ways the story of Susan B. Anthony's life.

heterogeneous *(het-tuh-ROH-jee-nus), adjective*
Diverse; consisting of many, dissimilar parts

She loved living in the city partly because of its HETEROGENEOUS population and diverse neighborhoods.

heyday *(HAY-day), noun*
The time of someone's or something's greatest popularity, success, or power.

While it was thought that the 1960s were the HEYDAY of the bell-bottom, this fashion trend seems to be making a revival today.

hiatus *(hie-AY-tuss), noun*
A break in something where there should be continuity; an interruption or gap.
After his refusal to submit to the draft and his long HIATUS from boxing, Muhammad Ali returned to the ring and won back the heavyweight title.

hidebound *(HIDE-bound), adjective*
Inflexible and holding narrow opinions.
Wallace can be rather HIDEBOUND when pontificating on the virtues of classic Mercedes-Benz models versus the condition of the automobile company at present.

hierarchy *(HIE-eh-rahr-kee), noun*
An organization or group with members arranged by ranks, in order of seniority or power. Categorization by order of importance or status. A normal chain of command. Originally referred to the division of angels into ranks.
The military HIERARCHY is clear and obvious by title and uniform.

hindsight *(HYND-syte), noun*
The realization or analysis of an event after it has happened. Perception of the past, in retrospect.
HINDSIGHT is twenty-twenty, and lessons learned by analyzing history should prove valuable when planning for the future.

hirsute *(hur-SOOT), adjective*
Hairy, covered in hair
HIRSUTE caterpillars didn't bother him but bare, slimy worms made him cringe.

histrionic *(hiss-tree-ON-ick), noun*
Overdramatic in reaction or behavior; theatrical. Related to acting or actors.
The HISTRIONICS associated with two adolescents breaking up is hard for adults to deal with.

homogeneous *(HO-mah-jee-nus), adjective*
Similar; consisting of many, similar parts
With the Internet, chat rooms, and easier international communication, few people have a HOMOGENEOUS social circle any longer.

HIV *(AYCH eye vee), acronym*
Acronym for "human immunodeficiency virus." Refers to a retrovirus that destroys the immune system and causes AIDS (acquired immune deficiency syndrome).
Although we are working hard to discover a cure for HIV, we must continue to be careful about sexually transmitted diseases.

hoax *(HOACKS), verb*
To trick someone into believing something is real when it is not.
They HOAXED us by burying false fossils in the old excavation site.

hoi polloi *(HOY puh-LOY), noun*
A pejorative term used to describe the masses or the common people.
"My practice is to ignore the pathetic wishes and desires of the HOI POLLOI," the governor said haughtily.

holarctic *(hole-ARK-tik), adjective*
Anything relating to the geographical distribution of animals in the Arctic region.
Our so-called Arctic safari was a bust. No one told us that, due to HOLARCTIC conditions, we would find no polar bears near our encampment.

holistic *(ho-LISS-tik), adjective*
Involving all of something; specifically, all of someone's physical, mental, and social conditions, not just the physical when treating an illness.
HOLISTIC medicine, addressing all contributing factors of illness, is increasingly popular.

homage *(AH-mij), noun*
Show of reverence, honor, and respect; a formal public acknowledgment, reverence, allegiance, or honor.
By visiting the lacrosse hall of fame, the team paid HOMAGE to the sport they played.

homeopathy *(HOME-ee-oh-path-ee), noun*
The medical practice of giving patients minerals, metals, herbs, and other bioactive compounds in extremely diluted form.
Most modern scientists believe the effectiveness of HOMEOPATHY in some cases is due mainly to the placebo effect.

homeostatis *(ho-me-oh-STAY-sis), noun*
A dynamic system in which balance between input and output has been achieved, so no net changes take place.
When HOMEOSTATIS is achieved in a sealed biosphere, the animals and plants can live without outside air, food, or water.

hominid *(HAH-muh-nid), noun*
A primate belonging to a particular biological family, all extinct except for modern human beings. Humans and their ancestors.
The more archeologists and anthropologists study, the more they agree that Africa was the birthplace of HOMINIDS.

homonym *(HAH-muh-nim), noun*
A word that sounds and is spelled the same as another word but with a different meaning.

"Tee fore too" and "tea for two" are phrases full of HOMONYMS.

honorific *(on-err-IF-ik), adjective*
A tribute or reward given in an effort to honor someone as a sign of deep respect.

Lifetime achievement awards aren't for any single work, but an HONORIFIC for long service and a track record of excellence.

hoodwink *(HUHD-wink), verb*
To trick or deceive; to fool; to put one over on

Her attempts to HOODWINK her parents failed when they discovered she had sneaked out after midnight.

hospitable *(hahs-PIT-a-bul), adjective*
Friendly and welcoming; or having an open mind; being willing to hear new ideas

The innkeepers had to be HOSPITABLE, even when they were having bad days themselves.

The principal was HOSPITABLE to suggestions from the seniors regarding a new venue for the prom.

hubris *(HYOO-bris), noun*
Arrogant or overwhelming pride

In many Greek myths, the HUBRIS of mortals causes them to think they can successfully challenge the gods, but they always lose in the end.

humanism *(HEW-man-iz-um), noun*
The philosophy or belief that the highest ideals of human existence can be fulfilled without regard to religion or supernatural intervention.

Harold was an atheist, but he liked to think of himself as a HUMANIST instead.

Know This Quote

"The four characteristics of HUMANISM are curiosity, a free mind, belief in good taste, and belief in the human race."
—E. M. Forster, English novelist

humectant *(hue-MEK-tant), noun*
A substance that absorbs moisture or retains water.

Sorbitol, a HUMECTANT, is used in the processing of dried fruit.

hygroscopic *(high-grow-SKOP-ick), adjective*
Capable of absorbing moisture from the air.

Prescription pills are often packed with a container of HYGROSCOPIC material to keep the drugs dry.

hyperbaric *(hi-per-BARE-ik), adjective*
Related to artificially high atmospheric pressure, used to treat certain diseases.

Divers who ascend to the surface too rapidly may be placed in a HYPERBARIC chamber to prevent the bends.

hyperbole *(hie-PUR-buh-lee), noun*
Deliberate and obvious exaggeration used for effect; an extravagant overstatement.

The HYPERBOLE associated with being worth one's weight in gold is one that some would like to test in reality.

Hyperborean *(high-per-BORE-ee-an), noun*
A person or animal who lives at or near the North Pole.

The polar bear, one of the great HYPERBOREANS, is in danger of extinction as the melting of the polar cap makes the ice floes on which they live disappear.

hypercritical *(high-purr-KRIT-ih-kuhl), adjective*
Excessively or meticulously critical.

When painting, David was HYPERCRITICAL to the point where others barely dared compliment him.

Know This Quote

"Good writers have two things in common: they would rather be understood than admired, and they do not write for hairsplitting and HYPERCRITICAL readers."
—Friedrich Nietzche, German philosopher

hypnopompic *(hip-nuh-PAHM-pick), adjective*
Having to do with the semiconscious state that precedes wakefulness.

With all of her partying at exclusive clubs, Madison spends most of her life in a HYPNOPOMPIC state.

hypocrisy *(hih-POK-ruh-see), noun*
The act of saying one thing and doing another; the practice of stating a certain belief and then acting differently from that belief

When a smoker discourages someone from lighting up, it is not HYPOCRISY but an earnest desire to prevent someone from making the same mistake the smoker made.

hypocritical *(hip-ih-KRIT-ih-kul), adjective*
To express feelings one doesn't really have or feel; to behave in a way one has criticized

The young woman's friends ignored her HYPOCRITICAL comments about flirting because they knew she behaved the same way when they weren't around.

Which Word?

Don't get tripped up by words that look or sound almost identical! Hypocritical (hip-ih-KRIT-ih-kul) and hypothetical (hiy-po-THET-ih-kul) can easily be confused, especially when you are reading quickly. To be hypocritical is to be two-faced and behave in ways that you have condemned. If something is hypothetical, it is based on an assumption or theory.

hypothecation *(hi-POTH-ih-KAY-shun), noun*
The practice of using property or other assets as the collateral for a loan.

Buying stock on margin is a useful form of HYPOTHECATION that encourages unsophisticated individual investors to buy more stock than they can afford.

hypothermia *(hie-po-THER-mee-uh), noun*
Dangerously low body temperature caused by prolonged exposure to cold; extreme loss of body heat. From the Greek for "below heat."

Most of the fatalities associated with the sinking of the Titanic were as a result of HYPOTHERMIA.

hypothesis *(high-POTH-uh-sis), noun*
A principle derived from limited evidence, seen as sensible based on an analysis of available data, but not proven to the point where it is an accepted theory, rule, or law.

He wasn't sure his HYPOTHESIS would prove true, but he was going to test it anyway.

hypothetical *(hiy-po-THET-ih-kul), adjective*
Based on a supposition; not real

It is easier to make difficult decisions in HYPOTHETICAL situations because there are no real consequences.

I

Iberian *(EYE-beer-ee-uhn) noun*
Someone who lives or was born or raised in Spain or Portugal, or one who lived on the Iberian Peninsula.

While IBERIANS share a common geography, those from Spain and Portugal want to be perceived as a unique people.

ichthus *(ICK-thaas), noun*
A simple symbol of Christianity that resembles a fish, consisting of two curves that bisect each other.

People sometimes put ICHTHUS bumper stickers on their cars, often to let others know they are born-again Christians.

iconoclast *(eye-kah-nuh-KLAST), noun*
Someone who challenges or overturns traditional customs, beliefs, and values.

ICONOCLASTS are always controversial, and often they are perceived as dangerous.

Where'd That Word Come From?

Iconoclast—This word for a debunker, one who attacks cherished beliefs, dates from the time of Byzantine emperor Leo III, who in 726 began a program of destroying icons, or images, in churches because he believed his people actually worshipped the icons, not the religious figures they represented. The monks fanatically opposed Leo and called him, among other things, an *iconoclast*, "image breaker."

ideology *(EYE-dee-ah-luh-gee), noun*
A closely organized system of beliefs, values, and ideas, especially one that forms the basis of a social, economic, or political philosophy. A system of thought that shapes the way an individual group thinks, acts, and views the world. Not to be confused with *idolatry,* the worship of idols or false gods, or the extreme admiration or fanatical devotion to someone or something.

For some extreme fans, Star Trek is the foundation of an IDEOLOGY and not just a science fiction television show.

idiom *(IH-dee-uhm), noun*
A phrase whose usage is peculiar to a particular language, in terms of grammar or in meaning. An expression whose meaning cannot be figured out from the grammatical combination of individual words, such as "He puts me in stitches." The way of using a language that comes naturally to native speakers and involves knowledge of grammar and usage.

For the recent immigrant from Brazil, IDIOMS such as "beating a dead horse" were quite difficult to understand and sometimes rather disturbing.

idiosyncrasy *(id-dee-oh-SINK-ra-see), noun*
A characteristic specific to a certain person; a quirk

One of her IDIOSYNCRASIES was that she liked to burn candles while she worked at her desk.

idolatrous *(iy-DAHL-eh-trus), adjective*
Adoring a person or thing to the level of worship

Tabloid magazines helped create the IDOLATROUS feelings society tends to have toward movie and television stars.

idyllic *(EYE-dih-lick), adjective*
Serenely beautiful, untroubled, and happy. Like an idyll, which is a scene, event, or experience characterized by tranquility and simple beauty.

As they arrived at the bed and breakfast at sunset, it seemed an IDYLLIC place to stay for their honeymoon.

ignoble *(ig-NOH-bul), adjective*
Common, ordinary, or plain; not overly honorable or impressive

People were shocked to see the candidate doing something as IGNOBLE as shopping at the mall.

ignominious *(ig-nuh-MIH-nee-uss), adjective*
Characterized by a total loss of dignity and pride; shamefully weak, ineffective, or disgraceful. Used to describe public humiliation or failure.

Richard Nixon's IGNOMINIOUS resignation of the presidency will forever remind those in high office to be honest and not cover up errors in judgment.

ignoramus *(ig-nuh-RAY-muss), noun*
An idiot, dolt, or someone who is ignorant.

Someone who ignores his studying may not be smart, but he should not be called an IGNORAMUS.

illicit *(ih-LIS-it), adjective*
Forbidden or illegal; prohibited; immoral or improper

The teacher knew the paper had been obtained through ILLICIT means because the same one had been turned in the previous year by another student.

illusory *(ih-LOO-suh-ree), adjective*
Not real; based on an illusion or wish; based in fantasy rather than fact

The safety the women had felt on campus was proven to be ILLUSORY when a young woman was attacked.

imbibe *(im-BIBE), verb*
To drink something, especially alcohol or alcoholic beverages. To take in or absorb something into the mind, like an idea. It's hard to thrive when you regularly imbibe.

Although it sounds better to say "IMBIBE" and "inebriated," you might just as well say "booze it up" and "drunk."

imbroglio *(im-BROHL-yoh), noun*
A complicated, entangled, confusing, and often embarrassing situation

The Iran-Contra IMBROGLIO will always be important in the study of the politics of the late 1980s.

imbue *(im-BYOO), verb*
Influence deeply, pervade; inspired by; often used with "with" or "by"

Her discussions were IMBUED with ideas first taught by the great philosophers.

immaculate *(ih-MAH-kyoo-leht), adjective*
Perfectly clean, spotless; free from stain or marking

While he hadn't expected his son's dorm room to be IMMACULATE, he was still shocked at how messy it was.

immigrant *(ih-MIH-grunt), noun*
Someone who comes to a country to settle there. Sounds like its antonym, *emigrant,* which is someone who leaves a place, especially his or her native land, to live in another country.

Almost every American IMMIGRANT dreams of success, wealth, and happiness.

imminent *(ih-MIH-nent), adjective*
About to happen; immediate; due to occur at any moment

The crowd knew the President's arrival was IMMINENT when the Secret Service started clearing everyone from the path.

immure *(ih-MYOOR), verb*
To confine, imprison, or enclose behind walls.

Whitney remained IMMURED in her room as she pondered the itinerary for her luxury vacation to Italy.

immutable *(ih-MYOO-tah-bul), adjective*
Set and stable; not subject to change

It is an IMMUTABLE fact that teenagers will find some way to rebel against their parents and societal expectations.

impair *(im-PAYR), verb*
To weaken or diminish; to make less effective
Her cold medication left her groggy and IMPAIRED her ability to drive to the doctor's office, so her friend drove her instead.

impalpable *(im-PAL-puh-bull), adjective*
Not capable of being perceived with the sense of touch, or not capable of being perceived by the senses. Difficult to understand or grasp; difficult to perceive or interpret.
The IMPALPABLE dark left him with only the vague impression that someone else had just left the room.

Know This Quote
"The soul is so IMPALPABLE, so often useless, and sometimes such a nuisance, that I felt no more emotion on losing it than if, on a stroll, I had mislaid my visiting card." —Charles Baudelaire, French poet, critic, and translator

imparity *(ihm-PAR-ih-tee), noun*
Inequality or disparity.
There is little, if any, IMPARITY between the chateaubriand offered at the two bistros.

impart *(im-PART), verb*
To give or bestow a particular quality upon something. To communicate information or knowledge.
Professor Green daily sought to IMPART wisdom to his students.

impasse *(IM-pass), noun*
A point or situation with no solution, or when no further progress can be made or agreement reached. A situation that seems to offer no solution or escape. A road or passage that has no way out: literally, a dead-end street or passage.
The research team's efforts had come to an IMPASSE, so they brought in new members to inspire innovative approaches.

impassive *(im-PAS-iv), adjective*
Showing no emotion; having no particular expression
The principal stayed IMPASSIVE even though he wanted to laugh during the young man's outlandish explanation.

impeach *(im-PEACH), verb*
To charge a government official with serious misconduct while in office. To remove an official, including a president, from public office for having committed high crimes and misdemeanors. To make an accusation against, challenge the validity of, or discredit someone or some document.
It is the responsibility of a good attorney to IMPEACH the credibility of witnesses, although it often appears to be an aggressive and mean-spirited strategy.

impeccable *(im-PEK-uh-bul), adjective*
Meeting the highest standards; perfect

Her outfits were always so IMPECCABLE that she looked like she could have stepped out of a fashion magazine.

impecunious *(im-peh-KYOO-nee-us), adjective*
Having little money; poor

Although his family was in an IMPECUNIOUS situation after the layoffs, he still managed to get birthday presents for his children.

impede *(im-PEED), noun*
To delay or prevent something from continuing

The United Nations refused to let the threat of violence IMPEDE the elections in the small country.

imperative *(im-PAYR-ih-tiv), adjective*
Absolutely necessary; required; urgent

She wore a medical alert bracelet because it was IMPERATIVE that doctors know she was allergic to penicillin in the case of a medical emergency.

impertinence *(im-PURR-tih-nent), noun*
Boldness or rudeness; brash behavior showing a shocking lack of respect for a superior. Disrespectful action or comment. Inappropriate to a particular matter or issue.

Too often confused with courage, IMPERTINENCE is unacceptable in most circumstances.

imperturbable *(im-per-TUR-bih-bul), adjective*
Calm and collected at all times; unable to be shocked or disturbed

Part of what made him an effective teacher was his ability to make his students believe he was truly IMPERTURBABLE, regardless of what stunts they pulled.

impervious *(im-PER-vee-us), adjective*
Impossible to affect; immune to reaction

Having grown up in New England, she was IMPERVIOUS to southern winters.

Everyone knows Superman was IMPERVIOUS to pain, except that caused by Kryptonite.

impetuous *(im-PEH-choo-wus), adjective*
Tending to act on the spur of the moment, without consideration of consequences. Impulsive; passionate. Characterized by great force and energy.

Some believe the phrase "IMPETUOUS youth" is redundant, for acting without thinking is one way to define adolescence.

impetus *(IHM-puh-tus), noun*
The motivation or stimulus behind movement or change

The sleeveless bridesmaid's dress was the IMPETUS she needed to lose the twenty pounds that had been plaguing her.

impiety *(ihm-PIY-ih-tee), noun*
Lack of reverence or respect, especially toward God

Although teenagers often speak with IMPIETY, studies show that their faith is strong and religion is important to many of them.

impinge *(im-PINJ), verb*
To strike or run into something, with force. To have an effect on something. Also, to encroach upon the limits of something, especially a right or law; to cause some kind of restriction.

Censorship most definitely IMPINGES on the right of free speech, which is why we hold the first amendment sacred.

implacable *(ihm-PLAHK-ih-bul), adjective*
Impossible or unable to appease; or relentless and unstoppable

The professor had a reputation for being IMPLACABLE because of her high and uncompromising standards.

Once the dam was breeched, the river was IMPLACABLE on its path toward the town.

implausible *(ihm-PLOH-zih-bul), adjective*
Unbelievable; not seeming reasonable or true

As the school year went on, her excuses for not doing her work became more and more IMPLAUSIBLE.

Know This Quote
"At first glance, most famous fairy tales seem so IMPLAUSIBLE and irrelevant to contemporary life that their survival is hard to understand." —Alison Lurie, American novelist and academic

implement *(IHM-pleh-ment), noun or verb*
A tool used for work; a way to achieve a goal (noun) or to put into practice or action, generally plans or ideas (verb)

A prepared worker always has the right IMPLEMENT for each job.

The boss of the organization decided to IMPLEMENT new ideas in order to keep the company state of the art.

implicate *(IHM-plih-kayt), verb*
To show a close connection between two things, usually in an incriminating, criminal, or negative way

She took the proof of illegal hazing to the school dean even though she knew doing so would IMPLICATE her own sorority.

implicit *(im-PLIH-sit), adjective*
Implied though not stated directly; or inherent; essentially part of something even if not obvious; or without doubt; having no questions or reservations

The threat IMPLICIT in dealing with Al Capone was one every person in Chicago understood during Prohibition.

When someone joins the military just to pay for college, he needs to understand the IMPLICIT risk of being sent to war instead.

Children's IMPLICIT faith in Santa Claus is heartwarming and helps remind adults of simpler times.

implore *(im-PLORE), verb*
To beg or pray for something fervently. To plead urgently.

No matter how Bob IMPLORED her, the teacher would not allow him to make up the exam.

importunate *(ihm-POR-cheh-nant), adjective*
Persistent to the point of being annoying

His niece was IMPORTUNATE in her requests for specific and elaborate birthday presents.

importune *(ihm-por-TOON), verb*
To frequently and repeatedly ask, urge, or request something of another person, usually implies being annoying

She considered repeating her request for a raise but didn't want to IMPORTUNE her boss with the issue.

imprecation *(IM-pre-kay-shun), noun*
A curse spoken aloud.

Thomas muttered IMPRECATIONS as he circled the airfield, waiting for clearance to land his Airbus 380.

Know This Quote

"Sisters are always drying their hair. / Locked into rooms, alone, / They pose at the mirror, shoulders bare, / Trying this way and that their hair, / Or fly IMPORTUNATE down the stair / To answer the telephone." —Phyllis McGinley, American poet

impregnable *(im-PREG-nuh-bul), adjective*
Impossible to be attacked or brought down, referring to a structure, idea, or argument

Although she made her case badly, the core facts were truly IMPREGNABLE so she won the debate in spite of her poor performance.

impromptu *(ihm-promp-TOO), adjective*
Spur of the moment; happening without a plan, purpose, or rehearsal

The IMPROMPTU party that developed on his floor canceled out the plans for studying he had made earlier in the week.

improvident *(ihm-PRAHV-ih-dent), adjective*
Showing little or no forethought or planning; not thinking of the future

Her shopping spree was IMPROVIDENT in light of her tuition bill being due at the end of the month.

imprudent *(im-PROO-dent), adjective*
Showing no care, forethought, or judgment. Lacking discretion. As a teenager, even dear Prudence was imprudent, always acting without thinking. (Not to be confused with *impudent*. See below.)

Buying cigarettes and alcohol for her teenage friends was certainly IMPRUDENT, as well as illegal and improper.

impudence *(IM-pyeh-dens), noun*
Uncaringly disrespectful; offensively bold or forthright

The young man's IMPUDENCE was an indication that his mother had lost control over his behavior.

impugn *(im-PYOON), verb*
To suggest that someone or something cannot be trusted. To challenge someone's honesty or motives. Not to be confused with the next entry, *impunity*, which sounds alike but basically means "unable to be impugned."

The defense attorney sought to IMPUGN the prosecutor's witness.

Know This Quote
"I do not IMPUGN the motives of any one opposed to me. It is no pleasure to me to triumph over any one." –Abraham Lincoln

impunity *(im-PYOO-nih-tee), noun*
Exempt from punishment; free from consequence

She had always acted with IMPUNITY because of her father's standing in the community, so getting into trouble at college was a rude awakening for her.

impute *(ihm-PYOOT), verb*
To assign or attribute, usually fault, blame, or responsibility, to another

Children often try to IMPUTE bad behaviors to imaginary friends.

in vitro *(inn VEE-troe), adjective*
An artificial environment, such as a test tube, rather than inside a living organism. Describes an egg that is fertilized outside of the mother and then implanted in the womb.

IN VITRO fertilization is a miraculous procedure for those who thought they would never be able to conceive a child.

inadvertently *(IN-ad-ver-tant-lee), adverb*
Accidentally; unintentionally; caused by being unintentionally negligent

He immediately regretted the offhanded comment that had INADVERTENTLY caused his friend so much pain.

inane *(in-NAYN), adjective*
Without substance; silly; pointless

The sitcom's INANE humor and shallow characters appealed to some people but not enough to keep it on the air.

inarguable *(in-ARG-yoo-uh-bull), adjective*
Impossible to deny or take an opposing view from. The position of most parents, when a teenager comes home hours after curfew.

Alex's assertions regarding who manufactured a particular car model were INARGUABLE.

inauspicious *(ih-nah-SPIH-shuss), adjective*
Suggesting that the future is not very promising or that success is unlikely. Marked by a sign of some kind that things might not work out as well as planned.

The INAUSPICIOUS beginning of their trip was marked by a speeding ticket and a flat tire, making them fear what would next go wrong.

Where'd That Word Come From?

Inauspicious—Like many words used today, this word, meaning "unlikely to lead to success," made its debut in the works of Shakespeare. In *Romeo and Juliet*, Romeo cries: "Here, here, will I remain. And shake the yoke of inauspicious stars. From this world-wearied flesh." Shakespeare probably invented *inauspicious*, as he did *auspicious* (in *The Tempest*), meaning favorable, marked by lucky signs or good omens, conducive to success. Its roots are in the Latin *auspex*, a corruption of *avispex*, for the Roman birdwatcher who deduced omens from the flight of birds.

incendiary *(in-SEN-dee-air-ee), adjective*
Describes the deliberate burning of property. Designed to excite or inflame, as in causing civil unrest. Able to catch fire spontaneously or easily.

His INCENDIARY remarks were certainly not necessary, as the crowd was already emotionally charged.

incessant *(in-SEH-sunt), adjective*
Continuing unstopped for a long time. From the Latin roots for "without end."

The children's INCESSANT singing on the bus gave the teacher and chaperone headaches.

inchoate *(in-KOH-ayt), adjective*
New enough to not be fully formed or established; at an early stage

It is unfair to judge an INCHOATE democracy by the same standards the United States can manage with ease.

incidental *(IN-sih-dent-uhl), adjective*
Happening along with but secondary to the major event; minor and less significant

The movie being filmed on site became INCIDENTAL to the team winning the World Series.

incipient *(in-SEH-pee-unt), adjective*
Beginning to appear or develop; at an early stage. Sounds like and shares a root with *inception,* the beginning of something.

INCIPIENT bad behavior of puppies must be addressed quickly, as it quickly becomes difficult to change their habits.

incisive *(in-SIY-sihv), adjective*
Accurate, sharp, and penetrating, in regards to a mind, concept, or theory

The professor really looked forward to his senior classes because of his students' INCISIVE, thought-provoking comments on world politics.

incite *(in-SIYT), verb*
To stir up or provoke; to encourage or urge on, usually violent behavior or dissension

Tensions were so high during the trial that the police presence actually INCITED the crowds to violence rather than keeping the peace.

Which Word?

It's often possible to change the parts of speech of a word simply by adding a suffix. But similar looking words are not always related. Although incisive and incite appear to be different forms of the same word, they really are not. Incisive (in-SIY-sihv) means penetrating. To incite (in-SIYT) means to stir up or provoke. Be careful not to confuse the two.

inclusive *(in-KLOO-sihv), adjective*
Including all aspects; comprehensive; including the limits at the extremes

Some sociologists believe that unless the two major political parties find a way to be more INCLUSIVE, it is just a matter of time before a third-party candidate wins a major election.

The assignment was to work problems one through twenty-five, INCLUSIVE, but many students stopped at number twenty-four.

incognito *(in-cog-NEE-to), adjective*
With one's identity disguised or hidden, as when using a false name. Describes the action of taking an assumed name or intentionally changing appearance and hiding from public recognition by making one's real identity unknown.

Rock stars, actors, and other famous people wear sunglasses and hats, seeking to be INCOGNITO at restaurants; these disguises rarely work, though, and they are often recognized.

incommensurable *(in-co-MEN-ser-uh-bull), adjective*
Two things that cannot be measured or judged by the same standards.

There are some who think that homemade apple pie and store bought apple pie are INCOMMENSURABLE.

Know This Quote
"Two men who perceive the same situation differently but employ the same vocabulary in its discussion speak from INCOMMENSURABLE viewpoints." —Thomas Kuhn, American philosopher

incompatible *(in-kohm-PAT-ih-bul), adjective*
Unable to exist at the same time; incapable of living or associating in harmony

Living in Dallas, Texas, tends to be INCOMPATIBLE with being a Washington Redskins fan.

incongruous *(in-KOHN-groo-uhs), adjective*
Out of place or inappropriate; deeply unexpected; not in line with what is expected or appropriate

The fast-food restaurant was INCONGRUOUS with the quaint surroundings of the New England village.

inconsequential *(in-KOHN-sih-kwen-shul), adjective*
Unimportant; trivial

In light of her overall GPA, the one B+ was INCONSEQUENTIAL to the universities that were courting her.

incontrovertible *(in-KAHN-truh-VER-tuh-bull), adjective*
Certain, undeniable, and not open to question or controversy. Impossible to dispute; unquestionable.

The district attorney attempted to present INCONTROVERTIBLE proof of the defendant's guilt.

Know This Quote
"Some minds are as little logical or argumentative as nature; they can offer no reason or 'guess,' but they exhibit the solemn and INCONTROVERTIBLE fact." —Henry David Thoreau, American author and transcendentalist

incorrigible *(in-KOHR-ih-jeh-bul), adjective*
Incapable of being reformed, corrected, or improved; used when describing a person or behavior

When the public school deemed the young woman INCORRIGIBLE, her parents chose to send her to private school rather than risk her getting involved with gang activity during her suspension.

incredulity *(in-kreh-DYOO-lih-tee), noun*
The state of disbelief, doubt regarding truth; the state of being unwilling or unable to believe

He didn't blame anyone for having a sense of INCREDULITY when he passed science since he had struggled with the subject all year.

incredulous *(in-KRE-joo-lus), adjective*
Unable or unwilling to believe something. Unconvinced, or demonstrating disbelief. This is a look you've seen often on your parents' faces; now you know what to call it.

The teenager was INCREDULOUS when accused of cheating, for he was a good student.

inculcate *(IN-kul-kate), verb*
To fix something firmly in someone's mind using frequent and forceful repetition. To teach by means of repetition or instruction. To impress an idea upon someone with urging or earnest example.

Police use "scared straight" strategies with at-risk youth, INCULCATING them with lessons related to the negative consequences of their actions, and instilling the fear of incarceration.

inculpate *(in-KUL-pate), verb*
To incriminate someone or put the blame for something on someone. Blame for a wrongdoing.

Motive and opportunity are two of the critical factors determined to INCULPATE suspects for murder.

indefatigable *(in-dih-FA-tih-guh-bul), adjective*
Never showing signs of getting tired, or of relaxing an effort; unyielding stamina.
Michael Jordan seemed INDEFATIGABLE, playing as hard in the fourth quarter as he did in the first.

indelible *(in-DEHL-ih-bul), adjective*
Impossible to erase, mark out, remove, or forget
The girl's first meeting of Mickey Mouse was an INDELIBLE memory she secretly carried with her throughout her life.

indict *(in-DIYT), verb*
To charge or accuse of wrongdoing, often a crime but not necessarily
Instead of just presenting the award as planned, the actor took a moment at the podium to INDICT the government for its handling of the war.

indifferent *(in-DIHF-her-ehnt), adjective*
Having no feelings one way or another; uncaring or unconcerned
She realized she was truly over her ex-boyfriend when she learned he was dating someone else and she was actually INDIFFERENT to the fact.

indigenous *(in-DIJ-ih-nus), adjective*
Naturally occurring in a specific place; native
Many plants INDIGENOUS to the rain forests cannot be found anywhere else on the planet.

indigent *(IN-deh-jent), adjective*
Impoverished; in need or wanting; poor
Many people find great satisfaction in helping INDIGENT families during the holidays.

indiscriminate *(in-dis-KRIM-ih-nat), adjective*
Happening randomly, without plan or logic; seemingly confused or without a specific pattern
Her INDISCRIMINATE taste in music made it difficult to know if she would like a particular band or not.

indistinct *(in-dih-STINKT), adjective*
Unclear, foggy, or hazy; not well defined, referring to a thought, concept, or physical entity
The directions were vague, leaving them only the most INDISTINCT idea of how to get to the party.

indite *(in-DITE), verb*
To write or compose a literary work.

It was with high hopes and and not much talent that he began to INDITE.

Know This Quote

"But if, both for your love and skill, your name / You seek to nurse at fullest breasts of Fame, / Stella behold, and then begin to INDITE." —Sir Philip Sidney, English courtier, soldier, and poet

indolence *(IN-dul-ens), noun*
Laziness; the state of avoiding work or exertion

He stopped working out because of a muscle injury, but sheer INDOLENCE kept him from returning to it once he was healed.

indolent *(IN-duh-lent), adjective*
Lazy, lethargic, not showing interest in making an effort, as a way of life. Inactive and unlikely to exert oneself. Also used to describe a disease or condition that is slow to develop or heal, yet causes no pain. "*Indolent* adolescent" seems a little redundant.

INDOLENT youths don't participate in athletics or in anything else.

indomitable *(in-DOM-ih-tuh-bul), adjective*
Impossible to beat, conquer, or break down; unable to be subdued

Most cancer survivors possessed an INDOMITABLE will to live during their treatment in spite of their diagnosis or prognosis.

induce *(in-DOOS), verb*
To cause or bring about; to convince or persuade someone to take an action

He helped her with her homework secretly hoping to INDUCE her to break up with her boyfriend.

indulgent *(in-DUL-jent), adjective*
Being overly lenient; not being able to say no to someone's wishes or wants

People disagree about how INDULGENT parents can be with their children before the children become spoiled.

inebriate *(ih-NEE-bree-ate), verb*
To cause someone to become drunk or intoxicated; to make excited or exhilarated.

Prior to the state championship game, the anticipation and excitement INEBRIATED all of the players.

ineffable *(in-EHF-ah-bul), adjective*
Unable to be described in words, usually because something is so great, glorious, or overwhelming

Tourists are often made speechless by the INEFFABLE beauty of the Grand Canyon at first sight.

ineluctable *(in-uh-LUK-tuh-bul), adjective*
Unavoidable and inescapable; unable to turn back or stop

Romeo and Juliet's fate and INELUCTABLE heartbreak were sealed from the moment they fell in love.

inept *(in-EPT), adjective*
Having little or no skill, sense, or judgment; incompetent

Superman hid his abilities behind the INEPT persona of Clark Kent.

inert *(in-ERT), adjective*
Without the ability or desire to move; still and lethargic; showing or having no reaction

After finals week, the students sat INERT in front of the television for the whole day.

inevitable *(in-EHV-ih-tah-bul), adjective*
Unable to be stopped, unavoidable; certain to occur

The new father knew it was INEVITABLE that his baby girl would grow up so he enjoyed every moment of her childhood.

inexorable *(ih-NEKS-or-ruh-bul), adjective*
Unyielding. Something that is stubborn or unwavering is *inexorable*. This is a good word to describe the power of a chocolate chip cookie over the average chocoholic.

"The INEXORABLE advance of our troops," the Union general said happily, "will complicate things for Mr. Davis."

inexplicable *(ih-nik-SPLIH-kuh-bul), adjective*
Incapable of being explained, justified, or interpreted. For someone who is not a chocoholic, the power of chocolate is *inexplicable*.

Peter's failure to show up for his final exam was INEXPLICABLE.

inextricably *(in-eks-TRIK-uh-blee), adverb*
Something that is strongly linked to something else, with the bond between quite difficult to break.

Some say the bond that the twin sisters had was INEXTRICABLY strong.

Know This Quote

"At its best, [Japanese cooking] is INEXTRICABLY meshed with aesthetics, with religion, with tradition and history." —M. F. K. Fisher, American author

infallible *(in-FA-luh-bul), adjective*
Incapable of making a mistake. Certain not to fail. Beyond error in religious matters of doctrine or dogma.

Those who believe computers are INFALLIBLE have never had a software virus.

infelicitous *(in-feh-LIS-ih-tuhs), adjective*
Inappropriate, not thought out, or poorly chosen

They realized just how INFELICITOUS it had been to toilet paper the principal's yard when she drove up and caught them in the act.

infer *(in-FUR), verb*
To conclude something on the basis of evidence or reasoning. To suggest or lead to a conclusion. Too often confused with *imply,* which means to make something understood without expressing it directly.

You can INFER from her absence that she does not support the actions of her neighbors to remove the old oak trees.

inference *(IN-fer-ence), noun*
The process of reaching a logical conclusion by examining and analyzing the evidence.

Watson solved cases through INFERENCE, while Sherlock Holmes was seemingly gifted with flashes of brilliant insight.

infrastructure *(IN-fruh-struk-chur), noun*
The foundation or structure of a system or organization. The large-scale public systems, services, and facilities of a country or region necessary for economic activity. The essential primary components of a system, organization, or structure.

A city's INFRASTRUCTURE influences its potential for future growth and greatness, or decline and failure.

infuse *(in-FYOOZ), verb*
To fill up or permeate; to spread throughout

As more decorations went up, the room became INFUSED with the lights, colors, and sounds of the holidays.

ingénue *(AHN-jzeh-nyoo), noun*
An innocent young woman; often the role or character of an innocent young woman in a play

The actress knew with her voluptuous figure and throaty laugh she was more suited to playing the sidekick than the INGÉNUE.

ingenuous *(in-JEN-yoo-uhs), adjective*
Innocent, unworldly, and trusting; open to the point of being gullible; usually has a positive connotation rather than a negative one

It was endearing to see how truly INGENUOUS the teenagers were the first time they saw New York City.

ingratiate *(in-GRAY-she-ate), verb*

To try to gain someone's favor, especially in order to gain an advantage. Sounds like but not the same as *ingrate,* a person who does not show or express gratitude.

When he first met his fiancée's parents, Chuck tried to INGRATIATE himself with his future father-in-law.

inherent *(in-HEYR-ent), adjective*

A natural and vital part of something else; an essential part of a larger whole that cannot be removed

The INHERENT risk in extreme sports is part of their allure for many participants.

Dwayne's INHERENT reluctance to entrust newcomers with tasks of any significance was a major problem for the company.

Which Word?

Many words are virtually synonymous—but this doesn't mean they are interchangeable. This is the case for inherent (in-HEYR-ent) and innate (ih-NAYT). Use the word inherent when you are describing an aspect of a thing, an activity, or an idea. An inherent aspect is one that cannot be completely removed from this thing, activity, or idea. Generally speaking, however, innate describes an aspect or a part of a person or other living creature. An innate aspect is one that is not learned but is with a person from birth, and therefore cannot be completely removed from that person.

inimical *(ih-NIHM-ih-cul), adjective*

Counterproductive; causing harm or the opposite of the desired effect

His girlfriend's urgings that he attend the party were INIMICAL to his studying for the test he had the next day.

innate *(ih-NAYT), adjective*

Existing from birth; natural and inborn; essentially a part of something; coming naturally, not learned

His parents discovered he had an INNATE ear for music when he sat down at a piano and began to play when he was only five.

innocuous *(ih-NAWK-yoo-uhs), adjective*

Completely harmless to the point of being disregarded; tame; not offensive

It took several bad relationships before she finally saw nice guys as being more than totally INNOCUOUS.

innovation *(in-oh-VAY-shun), noun*
A new creation, usually that moves a field forward in some way
Scientists expect medical INNOVATIONS to increase human life expectancies by many years.

inscrutable *(in-SKROOT-uh-bul), adjective*
Difficult or impossible to understand or know; incomprehensible; hard to get a handle on, as in a person, attitude, or concept
The contestants tried to read the judges in order to guess the result, but their faces were INSCRUTABLE throughout the competition.

Know This Quote
"I suppose I now have the reputation of being an INSCRUTABLE dipsomaniac. One woman here originated the rumour that I am extremely lazy and will never do or finish anything." —James Joyce, Irish author and playwright

insensible *(in-SENS-uh-bul), adjective*
Too small to be noticed or to register; imperceptible; or temporarily unconscious or without feeling, usually due to external factors such as alcohol, violence, or extreme temperature; or unaware, insensitive to or indifferent; uncaring; unfeeling emotionally
None of them noticed the INSENSIBLE change in the light as the sun set until they realized they were sitting in the dark and had to turn on a light.
The blow to the head knocked the boxer INSENSIBLE for several minutes.
She wasn't INSENSIBLE toward her students' complaints but knew they needed the extra work if they were going to pass the test.

insinuate *(in-SIN-yoo-ayt), verb*
To hint, suggest, or subtly make known, generally regarding something negative; or to introduce oneself into a setting through crafty and somewhat unwelcome or negative means
Although his words seemed innocent enough, everyone knew he was trying to INSINUATE that the director was doing a poor job.
She was able to INSINUATE herself into the queen's inner circle through subtle bribery and indirect threats.

insipid *(in-SIP-id), adjective*
Unexciting; lacking in flavor, life, or vigor; boring and dull
After living in the city, she found life in a small town INSIPID and unbearable.

insolent *(IN-suh-lent), adjective*
Showing aggressive lack of respect; rude and arrogant in speech or behavior or disrespectful.

Many adolescent boys appear INSOLENT, when some are just naturally challenging authority.

insolvent *(in-SOL-vent), adjective*
Unable to pay debts or what is owed; without money or assets

The president of the small company knew if they did not win a contract soon, the company would become INSOLVENT and would have to close.

insouciant *(in-SOO-see-aynt), adjective*
Casual indifference or unconcerned; nonchalant

Although he tried to be INSOUCIANT about his acceptance to an Ivy League college, his friends knew he was very excited about it.

inspiration *(in-spuh-RAY-shun), noun*
Something that stimulates creative thoughts and actions, or the making of a work of art. A sudden brilliant idea. Someone or something that inspires somebody. Divine guidance and influence.

Some idiosyncratic artists think procrastination precedes INSPIRATION.

instigate *(in-STIH-gayt), verb*
To stir up or urge; to start, begin, or initiate

Even after years of marriage, they couldn't agree on which one of them INSTIGATED their first kiss.

insular *(INN-suh-ler), adjective*
Self-contained and therefore isolated from the world and unaffected by outside influences, usually to one's detriment.

The Pricewaters moved from the family's traditional enclave to a more INSULAR compound further up the coast.

insularity *(IN-sul-ayr-ih-tee) or (INS-yoo-layr-ih-tee), noun*
The state of being detached, either physically or emotionally; characterized by having little or no contact with others

In a world as intertwined as earth, no government can afford an attitude of complete INSULARITY and expect its nation to thrive.

insuperable *(in-SOO-per-ah-bul), adjective*
Impossible to beat, overcome, or rise above, such as a challenge or obstacle

Stories of heroes facing INSUPERABLE odds and still succeeding have long been used to motivate individuals to achieve great things.

insurgent *(in-SUR-junt), noun*
Someone who rebels against authority or leadership. Refers especially to those involved in an uprising against a government. Member of a political party who rebels against party leaders or policies.

> *The government admitted that some parts of the country were under the control of INSURGENTS.*

insurrection *(in-suhr-REK-shun), noun*
A violent uprising or revolt against a government or group in power

> *Many INSURRECTIONS in East Germany were put down before the Berlin Wall finally fell in the latter part of the twentieth century.*

integrity *(in-TEG-rih-tee), noun*
The state of having and living by a strong sense of morals and values; walking the walk as well as talking the talk; or the state of being complete and strong, without noticeable weaknesses or flaws, generally refers to a structure or concept

> *He enjoyed doing business with people who had a sense of INTEGRITY that was as strong as his own.*
>
> *After the earthquake, the INTEGRITY of the bridge was called into question, so it was closed until tests could be performed and analyzed.*

intelligentsia *(in-tell-ih-GENT-see-uh), noun*
The class of people who are cultured, educated, intellectual, and interested in art and literature.

> *Paul, who had only earned his GED, often felt uncomfortable around the INTELLIGENTSIA.*

Know This Quote

"You see these gray hairs? Well, making whoopee with the INTELLIGENTSIA was the way I earned them." —Dorothy Parker, American author and poet

intercession *(IN-ter-SEH-shun), noun*
The act of pleading on someone's behalf. The attempt to settle a dispute; mediation of a conflict by acting or speaking in someone's behalf.

> *The coach's quick INTERCESSION stopped the fight before anyone from either team was ejected.*

interim *(IN-ter-ihm), noun or adjective*
The time between the end of one event or period and the beginning of another (noun) or temporary, occurring between the end of one event and the beginning of another (adjective)

> *He knew he would be working very hard up until the end of the semester and would start working hard again once his job started in September, so he decided to relax during the INTERIM.*
>
> *The United Nations set up an INTERIM government at the end of the hostilities until the country could hold its own elections.*

interpolate *(in-TER-puh-layt), verb*
To insert something, often unnecessary, between two elements. To add comments or extra words to a written text or conversation, altering or falsifying its meaning. To estimate the value of a mathematical function that lies between known values, usually done by projecting graph points.

Actuaries use statistics to INTERPOLATE customers' potential life expectancy, and that's how they figure out how much to charge for an insurance policy.

intervene *(in-tehr-VEEN), verb*
To come between two things, often to prevent something from occurring

The camp counselor waited to INTERVENE in the argument to see if the two boys could work it out between them.

intimidate *(in-TIHM-ih-dayt), verb*
To frighten or make nervous; to make someone afraid by using threats

Although she wasn't easily INTIMIDATED, the thought of meeting the president made her more than a little nervous.

intractable *(in-TRAKT-ah-bul), adjective*
Hard to manage, control, or handle; stubborn; resistant

The mother was INTRACTABLE when it came to making compromises about her children's health and well-being.

intransigent *(in-TRAN-zih-jent), adjective*
Unwilling to change or alter; uncompromising; stubbornly refusing to be persuaded or changed

Once he had made up his mind, he was INTRANSIGENT regardless of what new information might be presented to him.

intrepid *(in-TREH-pid), adjective*
Unusually courageous or bold; fearless; not able to be intimidated or frightened, may be used humorously or tongue in cheek

His INTREPID approach to women had gained him a reputation as a lady's man.

intrinsic *(in-TRIN-zik), adjective*
Belonging to something as a basic and essential element. By itself, rather than because of an association or consequences. Essential in nature; fundamental in character.

The INTRINSIC conflict between good and evil is a constant theme in literature.

Know This Quote

"We are the men of INTRINSIC value, who can strike our fortunes out of ourselves, whose worth is independent of accidents in life, or revolutions in government: we have heads to get money, and hearts to spend it." —George Farquhar, Irish dramatist

introspection *(in-troh-SPEK-shun), noun*
The honest examination of one's own thoughts, feelings, motivations, and beliefs

It was only after much INTROSPECTION that she could admit she wanted to be a doctor, not a teacher, as everyone had always expected.

intuition *(in-TOO-wih-shun), noun*
State of being aware of or knowing something through direct insight without any reasoning. Something believed or known instinctively without tangible evidence. Immediate knowledge of something.

Martin's INTUITION inspired him to buy an initial public offering of a stock that quickly rose greatly in value.

intuitive *(in-TOO-ih-tiv), adjective*
Based on gut feeling, instinct, or emotion rather than fact and specific information; or easily understood; user friendly

Successful police officers often work with their INTUITIVE feelings as well as the facts presented to them in order to solve a case.

The website was INTUITIVE and therefore easy for users to navigate.

inundate *(IN-un-dayt), verb*
To overwhelm or flood; can be literal or figurative

Every year, colleges and universities are INUNDATED with requests for information and applications.

inundation *(in-nun-DAY-shun), noun*
A flood. Also, an overwhelming amount of things to deal with.

The newlyweds returned home to an INUNDATION of family and friends who wanted to see them, but they wanted some time alone.

inure *(in-YOOR), verb*
To become used to or accustomed to something, usually something very unpleasant, through repetition or constant exposure

Although visitors to the ranch noticed the smell, she had become INURED to it after several weeks of working there.

inurement *(inn-UR-meant), noun*
Acceptance without resistance or fighting back of punishment, poor treatment, or unpleasant circumstances or conditions.

"Perhaps others might respond to this treatment with INUREMENT," Eloise hissed, "but I will buy my diamonds at another boutique from this point forward."

invalid *(IN-vuh-lihd), noun or (in-VAL-id), adjective*
Someone who is disabled by sickness or injury, often used to describe a weak person who needs caretaking (noun) or not legitimate legally or factually; untrue; based on faulty logic or reasoning (adjective)

She refused to be called an INVALID just because she was in a wheelchair after the accident.

Debates with him were often frustrating because he was unable to see that his arguments were generally INVALID in light of the facts.

invective *(in-VEK-tiv), noun*
Abusive expression, or language used to denounce, attack, or blame someone. Extremely harsh speech or writing.

Angry over being charged with a foul, the basketball team's best player shouted INVECTIVES at the referee, and he was immediately ejected from the game.

Know This Quote
"The art of INVECTIVE resembles the art of boxing. Very few fights are won with the straight left. It is too obvious, and it can be too easily countered." —Gilbert Highet, Scottish-born, American biographer and essayist

inveigh *(in-VAY), verb*
To write or speak out against something with great anger and passion; to be against an attitude, belief, or behavior in the strongest possible way; to condemn

South Africa was liberated from apartheid because brave men and women were willing to INVEIGH against the injustice inherent in the system.

inveigle *(in-VAY-gul), verb*
To gain or obtain something through flattery; to win over with sweet talk, often false or put on for the occasion

His friends were always amazed at how he was able to INVEIGLE so many phone numbers from different women in one night.

invert *(in-VERT), verb*
To swap or reverse the order; or to turn inside out; or to turn upside down; or to turn inward

The young woman decided to INVERT two of the digits in her phone number to make sure he couldn't reach her later.

Everyone in the dorm pretended not to notice that her blouse was INVERTED when she came home from her date.

The young man INVERTED a cross that he wore around his neck because he knew it drove his parents crazy.

The clerk's foot was INVERTED, giving him a slightly pigeon-toed look.

inveterate *(in-VEH-ter-uht), adjective*
Long-standing, deep-rooted, and unlikely to change

Even though she was over eighty years old, she was still an INVETERATE flirt.

invidious *(in-VIH-dee-us), adjective*
Likely to make others angry, jealous, or envious; creating hostility among others; or containing or hinting at discrimination

He was so well liked that his election wasn't INVIDIOUS, even to the people who were running against him.

Her comments about her lesbian roommate seemed innocent enough but were actually subtly INVIDIOUS.

invincible *(in-VIN-sih-bul), adjective*
Incapable of being beaten, subdued, or overcome

The baseball team's INVINCIBLE spirit took them into the playoffs when other, more skilled teams failed to get there.

invious *(IN-vee-uhs), adjective*
Unwalked, and thus, pristine.

The Wallenstones' new compound contains many INVIOUS tracts perfect for hiking or fox hunting.

iota *(IY-oh-dah), noun*
An insignificant amount; so small as to be imperceptible. Also the ninth letter of the Greek alphabet.

Her arguments for a later curfew didn't change her parents' opinion even an IOTA.

irascible *(ih-RAS-ih-bul), adjective*
Angry and mean; easily made upset or angry

The young children in the neighborhood avoided going near the IRASCIBLE old man's house, but the older kids considered it a great challenge.

Which Word?

Their definitions may seem identical, but that doesn't mean two words can be used exactly the same way. Irascible (ih-RAS-ih-bul) and irate (iy-RAYT) are two of these words. The word irascible describes someone's overall personality. Irate, however, just means a person is very angry at the moment about something specific. Be aware of the subtle differences between words that seem the same.

irate *(iy-RAYT), adjective*
Enraged; extremely angry; furious

The judge became IRATE at the continued outbursts in her courtroom.

ire *(IYR), noun*
Fury; anger; wrath

By the time they were seniors, every student had learned not to bring on the IRE of the principal.

irksome *(URK-sum), adjective*
Annoying, irritating, and bothersome; tedious and boring to the point of annoyance

Although she loved teaching, she found grading papers IRKSOME and monotonous.

ironic *(iy-RON-ik), adjective*
The opposite of what is expected, in an emotionally moving, poignant way

He had been so outspoken against the war that it was IRONIC when he discovered joining the military was the only way he could pay for college.

irony *(eye-roh-nee), noun*
The use of words to suggest the opposite of their literal meaning, often used in humor. Something that happens that is not what might be expected, especially when it seems absurd, laughable, or coincidental. That you can't iron iron could be called an *irony*.

The IRONY was that even as leaders of the former Soviet Union protested American capitalism, Levi jeans were the hottest and most expensive items on Moscow's black market.

irremediable *(ihr-ree-MEE-dee-uh-bull), adjective*
Impossible to cure or remedy.

Sylvia's outdated concept of couture is completely IRREMEDIABLE.

irreproachable *(eer-ree-PROH-chah-bul), adjective*
Beyond fault or criticism; perfect and without blemish

The press quickly learned the candidate's personal life was IRREPROACHABLE so had to look for scandal elsewhere.

irreverent *(ih-REV-runt), adjective*
Lacking in respect. Displaying behavior that is disrespectful. A reverend is rarely irreverent.

IRREVERENT comedians often use words that are considered expletives.

isochronous *(EYE-so-krone-us), adjective*
Occurring consistently at regular intervals.

The ticking of a clock is ISOCHRONOUS, but the arrival of the elevator at different floors is not.

isolationism *(eye-so-LAY-shin-iz-um), noun*
A foreign policy in which a country deliberately keeps its relationships and interactions with other nations to a bare minimum, effectively isolating itself from world affairs.

In the early twentieth century, American ISOLATIONISM stopped the U.S. from joining the League of Nations.

iteration *(ih-tuh-RAY-shun), noun*
An instance or the act of repeating something. A series of steps that is repeated to get closer to a desired outcome. A different version of something, as in a newer version of a video game.

After several ITERATIONS, the chefs found the best recipe for chocolate cheesecake.

Know This Quote

"Thou hast damnable ITERATION, and art indeed able to corrupt a saint." —William Shakespeare

itinerant *(iy-TIN-er-ehnt), adjective*
Characterized by moving from place to place, usually in order to perform one's job

Actors who join touring companies must accept and enjoy an ITINERANT way of life or else they quickly change professions.

itinerate *(iy-TIN-er-ayt), verb*
To move from one place to another, one town to another, usually to perform one's job

The salesman had to ITINERATE seven out of every eight weeks in order to meet his quota.

J / K

jactitation *(jak-ti-TAY-shun), noun*
A false boast, especially one that is harmful to others.

Beatrice tried impress her classmates by telling them her last name was Kennedy. However, her JACTITATION was discovered and her peers returned to ignoring her.

jaundiced *(JAWN-dist), adjective*
Demonstrating prejudice, due to envy or resentment.

The Blythingtons' view of our dinner parties is JAUNDICED by the fact that our personal chef is superior to theirs.

jaunt *(JAWNT), noun*
A short journey taken for pleasure.

Nicole plans to take a JAUNT across the southern tip of Africa next year.

jawbone *(JAW-bon), verb*
To attempt to get someone to do something through persuasion rather than by force.

No matter how much he JAWBONED, Karl could not get Alison to sell her stock prior to the unveiling of the company's disastrous new line of parvenu fashion.

jejune *(jih-JOON), adjective*
Uninteresting and intellectually undemanding. Dull or lackluster. Can also mean lacking in sophistication or insight. Lacking proper nourishment. Not very fertile.

Many of those taking their first music lessons have JEJUNE dreams of fame, fortune, and standing room only gigs.

jeremiad *(jer-uh-MY-uhd), noun*
A document or speech in which the author bitterly rails against the injustices of society or warns of impending death, destruction, or doom.

The Unabomber's Manifesto was an intelligently written JEREMIAD.

jingoism *(JIN-go-ih-zuhm), noun*
Zealous patriotism, especially in hostility toward other countries. Aggressive and overbearing patriotism; blindly nationalistic.

JINGOISM usually manifests at times of war or just prior to war.

Where'd That Word Come From?

Jingoism—A refrain from a British music hall song that urged Great Britain to fight the Russians and prevent them from taking Constantinople goes: "We don't want to fight, yet by Jingo, if we do, we've got the ships, we've got the men, and the money, too." This is the origin of this expression for "chauvinism or excessive patriotism." *Jingo* is a euphemism for "by Jesus" that dates back to the late seventeenth century.

jinn *(JIN), noun*
A mythical creature created from fire long before man inhabited the Earth.

Failing in their rebellion against God, the JINN were banished to the deserts.

jobbery *(JAH-buh-ree), noun*
The corrupt practice of making private gains from public office. This one's easy to remember: *Jobbery* is robbery by a politician.

The senator was accused of JOBBERY by his opponent, yet he was never charged formally.

jocose *(joe-KOSS), adjective*
Humorous, playful, and characterized by good humor.

The pony's JOCOSE antics marked it for a career in polo, rather than on the racetrack.

jocular *(JAHK-yoo-lur), adjective*
Good-natured, humorous; given to jokes; generally happy; funny and playful

The old man's JOCULAR nature made him a favorite with all the children of the neighborhood, not just his own grandchildren.

Stan's always JOCULAR behavior and attitude was out of place during serious times.

jocund *(JOE-kund), adjective*
Having a lust for life; possessing a positive attitude and desire to enjoy life to the fullest.

Ron's JOCUND façade shattered when he found himself the victim of identity theft.

joie de vivre *(ZSHWA duh VEEV), noun*
Energy and love of life. Originally a French phrase, but now commonly used in English.

The JOIE DE VIVRE she demonstrated in the most difficult circumstances was an inspiration to everyone around her.

jovial *(JOH-vee-ahl), adjective*
Joyful, happy, full of good cheer; friendly; sincerely warm emotionally

The party's success was based largely on the JOVIAL hostess, who made everyone feel so welcome in her home.

Which Word?

Don't confuse words that have similar meanings. Jocular (JAHK-yoo-lur) and jovial (JOH-vee-ahl) are two of these words. The word jocular tends to describe someone who will actually make jokes or make people laugh as well as just be a happy, warm person. Jovial, however, does not carry the implication of jokes or humor.

jubilation *(joo-bih-LAY-shun), noun*
Extreme joy and happiness; nearly overwhelming elation; rejoicing

As reserved as the man usually was, he couldn't hide his JUBILATION at the news he was going to be a father.

judicious *(JOO-di-shus), adjective*
Showing wisdom, good sense, or discretion, often with the intention of avoiding trouble or waste.

Since his earlier troubles, Jonah was very JUDICIOUS whenever he partied with friends.

judiciously *(joo-DISH-us-lee), adverb*
Marked by good sense; having sound judgment; using reason and logic to come to or behave in an appropriate way

The company hired her full-time after they saw her handle the crisis JUDICIOUSLY and calmly.

juggernaut *(JUH-guhr-not), noun*
A force that is relentlessly destructive and that crushes all obstacles in its way.

The Green Bay Packers of the early 1960s were considered a professional football JUGGERNAUT.

junta *(JUN-tuh) or (HUN-tuh), noun*
A group, usually military, that takes control of the government by force in order to rule the country

The weak government of the small island was easy prey for the general and his JUNTA.

jurisdiction *(joor-iss-DICK-shun), noun*
The authority to enforce laws or pronounce legal judgments; power or authority generally.

Judge Judy's JURISDICTION seemed to reach far beyond specific geographic boundaries.

jurisprudence *(joor-iss-PROO-dense), noun*
The philosophy and methodology behind the practice of law.

The study of JURISPRUDENCE was interminably dull to John; he longed to work with real clients and real court cases.

jurist *(JOOR-ust), noun*
An expert in the science or philosophy of law, especially a judge or legal scholar. Not to be confused with *juror,* who is someone sworn to an oath to serve on a jury.

All Supreme Court justices are JURISTS and legal scholars beyond question.

jury-rig *(JOOR-ee rihg), verb*
To build something in a makeshift way, or fit something with makeshift equipment. Despite including the word *jury,* the term has nothing to do with law.

Stranded in the desert, the team had to JURY-RIG tools and parts to repair the truck when it broke down.

juvenilia *(joo-vuh-NILL-yuh), noun*
Early work by a creative artist, typically produced when the artist or writer was young.

Lorna turned toward the stock market and away from poetry after we read her JUVENILIA and laughed uproariously.

juxtapose *(JUK-stuh-pose), verb*
To place (or pose) two or more things together, side by side for comparison and contrast, or to suggest a link between them.

JUXTAPOSED, the pictures of Jay and his son showed an amazing family resemblance.

Know This Quote
"A manic JUXTAPOSITION turned Hill House into a place of despair." —Shirley Jackson, American author

kabbalism *(KAH-bah-liz-um), noun*
A Jewish mystical tradition, based on revelation instead of reason, in which mystical feats can be performed by manipulating the letters of the Hebrew alphabet.

Through meditation, KABBALISM enables practitioners to become one with God.

kaffeeklatsch *(CAW-fee-klatch), noun*
An informal social gathering, typically including coffee and gossip.

Jeanette is not welcome at our KAFFEEKLATSCH because she refuses to gossip about her social contacts.

Kafkaesque *(kahf-KAH-esk), adjective*
Related to, typical of, or similar to the work of Franz Kafka, a writer whose novels and plays were quite complicated and often disturbing. Overly complex, seemingly pointless, and impersonal. If you use this word, you'll sound smart, especially if you know who Kafka is and if you've read one of his works. How about *The Metamorphosis*?

Her short story had a very KAFKAESQUE atmosphere, but it still wasn't very good.

kangaroo court *(kan-guh-ROO CORT), noun*
An unofficial court that is set up on the spot to deliver a judgment that had already been decided in advance. A situation when someone is prejudged and unable to receive a fair hearing or trial. From history, when those convicted of crimes were sent from Britain to Australia, where this large leaping animal is indigenous.

Recently, a defense attorney was placed in jail for referring to the proceedings as a KANGAROO COURT.

kapellmeister *(kuh-PELL-my-ster), noun*
The director of a choir or orchestra.

Ever since the Prithingtons hired a personal KAPELLMEISTER for their Christmas parties, everyone else has had to follow suit.

keepsake *(KEEP-sake), noun*
A small item or gift kept to evoke memories of something, an event, or someone.

Before she left for college, Samantha gave her mom the tassel from her high school graduation cap as a KEEPSAKE.

kelvin *(KEL-vin), noun*
A temperature scale in which absolute zero is zero degrees, and there are no negative values.

When we questioned Rachel about her purse, suggesting that it is a knockoff, she gave us a stare cold enough to measure on the KELVIN scale.

kenning *(KEN-ing), noun*
A metaphorical compound word or phrase, used often in epic poetry.

Cliff's letter to Natasha included such KENNINGS as "pearl-eyed dove" and "crinkly gowned angel." It's no wonder she broke up with him soon after.

kerning *(KER-ning), noun*
In typography, the amount of spacing between letters in a word or line of type.

If the KERNING is too large or too small, words are difficult to read.

kibosh *(kih-BOSH), noun*
Something that serves to stop something else.

Father put the KIBOSH on my plans to extend my summer trip to Europe by another three months.

kickback *(KIHK-bahk), noun*
A reaction that is quick and violent, as when a chainsaw bites into metal. Also money received illegally in return for a secret agreement (also usually illegal).

The contractor was accused of taking KICKBACKS from suppliers who charged excessive prices.

kinesiology *(kih-nee-see-OL-uh-jee), noun*
The science of muscles and their function, physical movement, and muscular development.

As a body builder, he studied both nutrition and KINESIOLOGY.

kinetic *(kih-NEH-tik), adjective*
Relating to or characterized by motion

The toddler's KINETIC activities quickly tired his babysitter but hardly seemed to slow him down at all.

kismet *(KIHZ-met), noun*
Fate or destiny.

Elaine's parvenu background hardly seemed destined to make her part of our group, but KISMET has made her an important social contact.

kith *(KIHTH), noun*
Friends and close acquaintances; almost always used in the phrase kith and kin, meaning friends and family

The young woman's KITH and kin gathered from all over the country to see her receive the award from the President.

kitsch *(KIHCH), noun*
Art, artifacts, or other objects of a cheap or junky nature produced by the popular culture.

His room was filled with KITSCH: lava lamps, Farrah Fawcett and Cheryl Tiegs posters, and plastic models of Frankenstein and Dracula.

knavish *(NAY-vish), adjective*
Untrustworthy, dishonest, and mischievous.

Despite, or perhaps because of, his KNAVISH behavior, Jonathan is always a success at our society balls.

knell *(NELL), noun*
The sound of a bell, especially when rung solemnly at a funeral.

She knew as she stood there, listening to the bell's KNELL at her father's funeral, that she would forever associate August with passings.

Know This Quote

"They are of sick and diseased imaginations who would toll the world's KNELL so soon." —Henry David Thoreau, American author and transcendentalist

knobbly *(NOB-blee), adjective*
Having lumps or bumps that resemble knobs

The fruit from the island was KNOBBLY enough that some of the tourists couldn't figure out how to eat it until their guide showed them how to peel the rind by pulling one of the bumps.

kohl *(KOL), noun*
A black powder, used especially in Egypt and the Middle East, to darken and outline the eyes

In ancient Egypt, both the male and female members of a royal family would use KOHL around their eyes in order to enhance their looks.

kowtow *(KOW-tow), verb*
To act in a particularly subservient manner in hopes of gaining favor; to brownnose

The entire department was embarrassed watching the director KOWTOW to the CEO when she made her yearly visit of all the programs.

Where'd That Word Come From?

Kowtow—The Chinese *k'-o-t'ou*, spelled in English as *kowtow*, means "know your head"—that is, to kneel and bow before a superior by touching the floor with your forehead. Mandarins required the *k'-o-t'ou* of their "inferiors." Explorers visiting China at the end of the nineteenth century brought back the word. To *kowtow* to someone has come to mean to act in an obsequious and groveling way—that is, doing pretty much everything short of touching your head on the floor.

kraken *(KRAH-ken), noun*
A gigantic creature, somewhat like the Loch Ness Monster, reputedly sighted off the coast of Norway.

Most of the KRAKEN reported as washed up on beaches were probably giant squid.

kudos *(KOO-dos), noun*
Praise, credit, glory, honor, or accolades for an achievement. A black belt in judo earns tons of *kudos*.

KUDOS were offered to all graduates at the commencement ceremony and during the receptions that followed it.

Kwanzaa *(KWAN-zah), noun*
An African holiday observed by many African-Americans from December 26 to January 1.

We feel we are doing our part to foster multiculturalism by allowing the stray KWANZAA decoration at our Christmas parties.

kyphosis *(ki-FOE-sis), noun*
Excessive curvature of the spine suffered by hunchbacks.

After William's father forced him to help out the family gardener, William complained for weeks afterward that the outdoor work gave him KYPHOSIS.

L

labanotation *(la-bah-no-TAY-shun), noun*
A nomenclature used to choreograph ballets, modern dance, and other performances so the dancers can follow the steps.

Even with the best-available LABANOTATION, Walker was unable to adequately perform a Viennese waltz at Natasha's coming-out party.

laborious *(lah-BORE-ee-us), adjective*
Requiring a great deal of effort. Showing signs of effort or difficulty, rather than easy, naturalness, or fluency.

Most high school boys find any work, no matter how hard or long it is, to be LABORIOUS.

labyrinth *(LAB-ih-rinth), noun*
A complicated and difficult path that is very hard to find the way through; a maze; or anything that is overly complex, difficult to navigate

One of the most popular destinations for teenagers during Halloween was the haunted LABYRINTH the town set up each year.

When dealing with bureaucracies, finding one's way through the LABYRINTH of red tape can be a frustrating and time-consuming event.

lachrymose *(LAK-ree-mohs), adjective*
Crying, weeping, in tears; or sorrowful; prone to cause tears or crying

The news of the latest terrorist attack had most of the nation LACHRYMOSE.

Hoping to counter the LACHRYMOSE air, he told humorous stories about his friend at the funeral.

lackadaisical *(lak-uh-DAY-zihk-uhl), adjective*
Lacking care or energy; carelessly lazy; unconcernedly indifferent

Her parents were concerned that her LACKADAISICAL approach to her schoolwork would prevent her from being accepted to the college of her choice.

laconic *(luh-KON-ik), adjective*
Using very few words; concise or terse writing or speech.

A LACONIC politician is hard to find, so if you can identify a candidate who is concise and honest, vote for him or her.

lactation *(lak-TAY-shun), noun*
The production of milk from the breasts of a mother mammal so her young can feed by sucking on the nipple.

When mother took us to visit the farm on one part of our property, she shielded our young eyes from the LACTATION of the various animals.

laggard *(LAG-urd), noun*
Someone who or something that falls behind and does not keep up with others. One who lags behind or loiters. Most often used as a negative description.

It was insensitive and unprofessional of the teacher to refer to those who were falling behind in the difficult mathematics class as LAGGARDS.

Know This Quote
"Reviewers . . . must normally function as huff-and-puff artists blowing LAGGARD theatergoers stageward." —Walter Kerr, American theater critic

lagniappe *(lan-YAP), noun*
An unexpected bonus gift or extra benefit; the icing on the cake.

Frederick would have bought the Porsche Panamera, even without the LAGNIAPPE of a free voice-activated navigation system.

laissez-faire *(leh-zay FARE), noun*
The principle that the best economy is one that does not regulate private industry and leaves markets free. Noninterference in the affairs of others; letting others do as they wish.

Ironically, many who believe in economical LAISSEZ-FAIRE often support governmental interference in the affairs of other nations.

laity *(LAY-uh-tee), noun*
Followers of a religion who are not clergy; lay persons. All who are not members of a specific profession.

The LAITY of the Catholic Church is growing more and more independent and less likely to follow the dictates of the Pope.

lambaste *(LAM-baste), verb*
To criticize someone or something severely; to reprimand sharply or attack verbally. To beat or whip someone. Originally meant "to beat harshly."

Teenagers are LAMBASTED for staying out past curfew so commonly that it might be called a rite of passage.

lament *(luh-MENT), verb or noun*
To grieve or mourn, openly and often loudly; or to deeply regret; to feel great remorse (verb) or the feeling or expression of deep, heart-wrenching grief; or a work, such as a song or poem, expressing deep sadness, grief (noun)

Flowers and notes were left at the memorial by numerous fans LAMENTING the singer for years after his murder.

The LAMENT that spread through the town the first few days after the hurricane was soon replaced by a desire to rebuild and move on with life.

The composer was known for his LAMENTS, so few people knew he could also write cheerful airs and waltzes.

lammergeyer *(LAM-er-GEE-er), noun*
A large black bird of the vulture family.

He saw the LAMMERGEYER and felt a chill run up his spine.

Know This Quote

"The world is just that LAMMER-GEYER, or bearded vulture, in the sky." —Pico Iyer, British-born essayist of Indian descent

lampoon *(lahm-POON), noun or verb*
A work that makes fun of a person, event, or situation in a joking, satirical manner (noun) or to tease or make fun of something; to satirize or mock jokingly (verb)

The sketch performed at orientation was a LAMPOON of college life, written to calm the freshmen's nerves about starting school.

He knew he was in trouble when the teacher he was LAMPOONING caught him in the act.

Which Word?

Many words can be used as either a noun or a verb. Lampoon (lahm-POON) is one of them. The verb to lampoon means to make fun of something. The noun lampoon is the skit, joke, cartoon—or anything else—that is being used to make fun. In other words, the comedian can lampoon the politician in a lampoon.

languid *(LANG-gwid), adjective*
Lacking vigor and energy. Listless, indifferent, sluggish, or slow.

Those who are frequently LANGUID may be suffering from some malady or disability.

languish *(LANG-gwish), verb*
To undergo hardship as a result of being deprived of something, typically independence, attention, or freedom. To decline steadily, becoming less vital, strong, or successful. To long for something being denied.

Famous musicians often LANGUISHED for years in obscurity before being discovered and catapulted overnight to stardom.

lapping *(LAH-ping), noun*
The practice of falsifying accounting records to conceal a shortage caused by theft or loss, usually by posting a financial transaction to an accounting period other than the one during which it actually took place.

Even after Skyler was indicted, he could not accept that LAPPING was an objectionable practice.

largess *(lar-ZHESS), noun*
Generous gifts, often in the form of money or favors. The gifts given as a result of someone's generosity. Generosity in spirit or attitude; a generous nature. Largish gifts reveal largess of givers.

The LARGESS of wealthy individuals is often surprising, for some believe them to be less than generous.

lascivious *(luh-SIHV-ee-us), adjective*
Feeling or showing overt, inappropriate, and usually offensive lust or sexual desire

The LASCIVIOUS looks she received at the bar made the group decide to get their drinks elsewhere.

lassitude *(LAS-ih-tood), noun*
The state of being overly tired, drained, or lacking energy; physically or mentally tired and worn out

A feeling of LASSITUDE filled the locker room after the team's heartbreaking loss in overtime.

Know This Quote
"We know what boredom is: it is a dull / Impatience or a fierce velleity, / A champing wish, stalled by our LASSITUDE, / To make or do." —Richard Wilbur, American poet

latent *(LAY-tent), adjective*
In existence but hidden or unknown; potential; undiscovered or undeveloped

It only took a few classes for her to realize she had a LATENT talent for interior decorating and design.

latency *(LAY-ten-see), noun*
A period of dormancy that precedes a period of great growth or action.

We knew that Abigail's focus on extremely liberal causes was merely a LATENCY that would end with her focus solely on charitable giving to the proper charities.

latifundia *(lah-ti-FUN-dee-uh), noun*
A large estate, plantation, or farm run by wealthy owners and staffed with underpaid or semi-servile workers.

Billings argued that his family's sugar cane plantation in Caribbean is not a LATIFUNDIA because the factory pays its workers what is considered a living wage for the country.

laudable *(LAW-dih-bul), adjective*
Deserving of praise; commendable; noteworthy

Although the quarterback's performance was LAUDABLE, it couldn't make up for the defense's poor showing.

laudatory *(LAW-dih-toh-ree), adjective*

Giving or expressing praise or compliments; complimentary

The actor's apartment was filled with LAUDATORY reviews he had clipped from various newspapers over the years.

lavish *(LA-vish), adjective or verb*

Abundant and overflowing; extravagant; excessively lush (adjective) or to shower with abundance; to give without reserve (verb)

The gardens at Versailles in France are known throughout the world as being some of the most LAVISH and beautiful ever grown.

As an aunt, the woman considered it her responsibility to LAVISH her nephews with not only love but adventure as well.

lax *(LAKS), adjective*

Not strict, tight, or tense; not easily controlled. Lacking attention to detail.

After the investigation it was concluded that Bob had been LAX when inspecting the bridge for structural faults.

learned *(LUR-nid), adjective*

Well-educated and very knowledgeable. Describes behavior or knowledge that is acquired through training.

The LEARNED scholar was greatly respected among those who studied anthropology.

lector *(LEK-tohr), noun*

A university lecturer or one who reads passages from the Bible to a congregation at a service, or during a meal.

The LECTOR stood very formally, in academic regalia, ready to deliver the annual lecture on abstinence and temperance.

LED *(EL-ee-dee), noun*

Acronym for "light-emitting diode." A semiconductor that emits light when a current passes through it. Used as indicators on electronic devices.

Once a novelty, LED displays in automobiles are now standard equipment.

left-brain *(LEFT-brayn), adjective*

Relating to or involving skills or knowledge that is analytical or linguistic, believed associated with the left half of the cerebrum.

LEFT-BRAIN thought was required for mathematics exams, while right-brain effort was required for the music appreciation tests.

leftism *(LEF-tih-zum), noun*
The principles of the Left; liberal, socialist, or communist political and social movements or reform.

It seems that conservatives are always accusing those who disagree with them of LEFTISM.

legacy *(LEG-ah-see), noun*
Anything, material or otherwise, handed down from one generation to the next

The United States has a long LEGACY of protecting the rights and freedoms of individuals.

legerdemain *(le-juhr-duh-MAYN) noun*
Magic tricks; or, generally speaking, trickery and deception.

The Wilkinsons are one of the few of our families whose initial wealth did not come as a result of financial LEGERDEMAIN.

leniency *(LEE-nee-uhnt-see), noun*
Punishment, judgment, or action that is not too severe. Personal quality of being lenient and forgiving; mercy.

The suspect admitted his guilt, hoping that it would lead to LENIENCY at sentencing.

lenient *(LEE-nee-uhnt) or (LEEN-yunht), adjective*
Permissive and indulgent; inclined not to be harsh or strict

While some children need structure and strict discipline, others thrive under more LENIENT situations where they can make their own decisions.

lethargic *(leh-THAR-jik), adjective*
Lacking in energy; tired; slow and sluggish

She knew her son was sick when he was achy and LETHARGIC and didn't mind staying in bed on a Saturday.

After many long hours of work, Pat and Corey were LETHARGIC but still unable to accept the necessity of calling it a night.

Know This Quote
"Great talents, by the rust of long disuse, / Grow LETHARGIC and shrink from what they were."
—Ovid, Roman poet

levant *(leh-VANT), noun*
The countries on the eastern coast of the Mediterranean Sea.

Ties between Western Europe and the LEVANT were first established during the Crusades.

levee *(LEH-vee), noun*
A structure built to hold back a body of water; a dike; a barrier created to prevent an area from being flooded by a river or sea

When the LEVEES collapsed in 2005, the city of New Orleans was devastated by the rising sea waters.

leviathan (*lih-VIE-uh-thun), noun*
Large beast or sea monster, originally from the Bible. Something extremely large and powerful in comparison to others of its kind. A whale or other large sea animal.

Cruise ships are getting bigger and bigger, appearing as LEVIATHANS as they move across the ocean's horizon.

levity *(LEHV-ih-tee), noun*
Humor or a joking manner, often in an inappropriate place or time; amusement; foolishness

His attempt to inject some LEVITY into the emergency meeting was met with disapproval and a concern that he wasn't taking the matter seriously.

lexicon *(LEKS-ih-kon), noun*
The vocabulary or words used by a specific group or within a specific field

One of the many difficulties faced by adults is keeping up with the current and ever-changing LEXICON of teenagers.

The LEXICON of rap music seems a different language to many parents, but it is an adaptation of street English.

liaison *(LEE-uh-ZON), noun*
An exchange of information among separate groups or individuals. A person responsible for maintaining communication between one group and another. An intimate, romantic relationship between unmarried people.

Nurse Sheffield was appointed to be the pediatric department's LIAISON with the transplant unit.

libation *(lie-BAY-shun), noun*
An alcoholic beverage offered or accepted in celebration. Originally, pouring out of liquid such as wine or oil as a sacrifice to a god or in honor of the dead in a religious ceremony.

Some think it is adult to consume a LIBATION every evening, and others think it quite immature.

libel *(LIY-buhl), noun or verb*
Any publication, be it written word or picture, that is false and damaging to a person's reputation or well-being (noun) or to write or publish lies or other false information about a person (verb)

Tabloid magazines must be careful when printing rumors because they can be sued for LIBEL if the information is not true.

The bloggers didn't care if they were LIBELING the candidate or not so long as what they wrote contributed to her losing the election.

liberalism *(LIH-buh-rah-LIH-zum), noun*
A theory found in both economics and in politics. In economics, it emphasizes the freedom of the individual consumer and of the market. In politics, it is founded on the protection of civil liberties and on a belief in progress toward a better society.

Economic and social LIBERALISM are not at all the same things.

libertine *(LIB-er-teen), noun, adjective*
Licentious and free of moral restraint; or, a person so characterized.

Lisa's grandmother thought Lisa was a LIBERTINE because she enjoyed a glass of wine when she got home from work.

Know This Quote
"It is easier to make a saint out of a LIBERTINE than out of a prig." —George Santayana, author and philosopher

libido *(lih-BEE-doh), noun*
Sexual drive. The psychic and emotional energy associated with basic human instincts, including the sex drive.

The LIBIDO of adolescents is sometimes difficult to understand and to control.

libration *(ly-BRAY-shun), noun*
The oscillation of Earth's moon around its axis.

LIBRATIONS are caused by changes in the intensity of Earth's gravitational pull on the moon.

licentious *(LIY-sen-shus), adjective*
Having little or no care for rules and morals when it comes to sexual behaviors

In this day and age of AIDS and other STDs, LICENTIOUS behavior can result in more than just a bad reputation.

Wealth and power are not acceptable excuses for LICENTIOUS behavior.

lien *(LEEN), noun*
The legal right to hold a person's property until a debt is paid

The bank had a LIEN on the couple's house in case they could not pay back the loan.

Lilliputian *(lil-ee-PEW-shun), adjective*
Small in stature; tiny in comparison to one's peers.
Jules Verne's LILLIPUTIAN appearance made people treat him like a child.

limpid *(LIM-pid), adjective*
Clear and transparent; free from obscurity.
The Motsingers are fond of saying that they are capable of eschewing all of the most LIMPID tax dodges.

lineage *(LIN-ee-ij), noun*
Ancestry; your family tree.
We still consider Rachel nouveau riche because her family can only trace its American LINEAGE to the mid-eighteenth century.

linger *(LIHN-ger), verb*
To stay in a place longer than necessary, usually because of a reluctance to leave; to take one's time; or to hang around; to persist
He LINGERED outside his classroom hoping to catch a glimpse of the teacher he had a crush on.

liquidity *(lih-KWI-dih-tee), noun*
The relative ease with which a person can sell an asset.
Despite a firm belief in wealth LIQUIDITY, Dotson continues to buy such depreciable items as yachts and Porsches.

lissome *(LISS-um), adjective*
Lithe; supple; flexible.
Moira acquired her LISSOME frame from years of swimming in her family's Olympic-sized pool.

listless *(LIST-luhs), adjective*
Having no energy or enthusiasm; uncaring and disinterested; having low spirits
She was LISTLESS for weeks after the breakup until her friends finally took her out for a night on the town so she could enjoy life again.

litany *(LIH-tuh-nee), noun*
A responsive prayer marked by much repetition. A long and repetitious list of things such as complaints or problems.
Whenever his father got angry, Brad had to listen to the entire LITANY of his faults.

Know This Quote

"With the supermarket as our temple and the singing commercial as our LITANY, are we likely to fire the world with an irresistible vision of America's exalted purpose and inspiring way of life?" —Adlai Stevenson, American politician

literate *(LIH-tuh-rut), adjective*
Having the ability to read and write. Well educated; skilled and cultured, particularly in regard to literature and writing. A good understanding of a particular subject.

LITERATE students are a teacher's delight.

literati *(lih-ter-AH-tee), noun*
The segment of society comprised of learned or literary men and women.

We attract the LITERATI because of our constantly carefree and exciting exploits.

lithe *(LIYTH), adjective*
Graceful, moving with ease; flexible; limber; willowy

Her LITHE movements and constant poise marked her as a dancer even when she was offstage.

litigious *(lih-TIH-jus), adjective*
Overly inclined to quarrel and argue. Tending to engage in lawsuits. Related to litigation.

It's difficult to say how much attorneys have promoted the LITIGIOUS trends apparent today, or whether they are the responsibility of society in general.

liturgy *(LIH-tur-jee), noun*
The performance of a Christian religious service in a church.

During the LITURGY, the singing of the Christmas hymns filled the church with the sound of joy.

livid *(LIH-vid), adjective*
Discolored, as in a bruise. Also a change from normal coloring, whether from a lack of it or an excess. Very angry.

Justin's father was LIVID when he found out his son was buying alcohol with a counterfeit driver's license.

lobby *(LAH-bee) verb*
To attempt to persuade a political representative or influential person to support a fight, particular cause, or specific vote. Guess how this activity got its name? From where it usually happened—in the lobby prior to a vote.

The firearms LOBBY in the United States is so strong that it has always managed to defeat most gun control legislation.

lobbyist *(LAH-bee-ist), noun*
A professional hired by a group to persuade politicians to pass laws and regulations the group favors

His concern for the environment, along with his ability to be persuasive, made him an excellent LOBBYIST for conservation groups.

locution *(loe-KYOO-shun), noun*
A phrase or expression typically used by a group of people. The way someone or some groups speak; style of speaking. Also a particular word, expression, or phrase.

Because Jacqueline was unfamiliar with this group's particular LOCUTIONS, much of what they said was odd to her.

lofty *(LAWF-tee), adjective*
Very tall or very high; imposing; or noble; of high character; impressive and respectable; or self-important; arrogant; pompous

The LOFTY buildings towered over the small church in the center of the square.

His LOFTY ideas could never have been realized without his partner's common sense and business skills.

In fairy tales, evil stepmothers often treat the heroine with LOFTY distain.

longevity *(lon-JEHV-ih-tee), noun*
Long life; duration, usually of life; or an overly long period of time within a position or situation

Doctors are striving not just to achieve LONGEVITY but also a good quality of life for their patients.

Her LONGEVITY with the company was rewarded with a huge retirement party and a substantial pension.

loquacious *(loh-KWAY-shus), adjective*
Talkative; excessively wordy; prone to going on and on

The professor was so LOQUACIOUS it was difficult for students to separate the important facts from fluff.

lucid *(LOO-sid), adjective*
Clear and easy to understand; well explained or thought out; or sane and mentally stable, used to describe moments between bouts of delusion or unconsciousness; aware of one's surroundings and situation

The defendant's explanation of his alibi was LUCID but strangely emotionless and dry considering what was at stake.

Even though she was perfectly LUCID, the EMTs took her to the hospital for observation after she hit her head.

lucre *(LOO-ker), noun*
Monetary reward or gain.

Sam never intended to be a bounty hunter, but was driven by LUCRE.

Luddite *(LUHD-eyt), noun*
A person who refuses to use or embrace modern technology.

We would not stop calling Annabel a LUDDITE until she finally got herself a Vertu cell phone like the rest of us.

Know This Quote

"I fear the popular notion of success stands in direct opposition in all points to the real and wholesome success. One adores public opinion, the other, private opinion; one, fame, the other, desert; one, feats, the other, humility; one, LUCRE, the other, love." —Ralph Waldo Emerson, American poet, essayist, and transcendentalist

ludicrous *(LOO-dih-kruss), adjective*
Utterly ridiculous, absurd, incongruous, implausible, impractical, or unsuitable.

It's LUDICROUS to expect that teenagers will behave all of the time, in all circumstances.

lugubrious *(loo-GOO-bree-us), adjective*
Extremely sad or gloomy. Lugubrious describes someone who is mournful to an inappropriate degree. Realizing that you're ludicrous may make you lugubrious.

It was too bad that the football team lost in the season finale, but it doesn't really justify going around with a LUGUBRIOUS expression for weeks afterward.

luminary *(LOO-mih-nayr-ee), noun*
A person who inspires or influences others, often but not necessarily in a specific group; or a celestial object that gives off natural light

Many political leaders from the twentieth century will be LUMINARIES to the leaders of future generations.

The earth's sun is the most well-known and recognizable LUMINARY in the galaxy.

luminescent *(LOOM-in-ess-sent), adjective*
Emitting light produced by means other than heat.

LUMINESCENT paint that glows under special lights was popular in the 1960s.

lumerpa *(loo-MER-pa), noun*
A mythological radiant bird from Asia that shines so brightly that it absorbs its own shadow.

The presence of numerous Waterford crystal chandeliers made the ballroom shine like a LUMERPA.

luminary *(LOO-muh-nair-ee), noun*
A person recognized as an inspirational leader in his or her field.

Frederick's father is a LUMINARY in the field of circumventing most income tax.

lumpenproletariat *(LUM-pen-pro-lih-tear-ee-ut), noun*
Term used by Karl Marx to describe uneducated common people.

It's difficult to pretend to be a member of the LUMPENPROLETARIAT when your car costs more than your next-door neighbor's house.

lurid *(LYOO-rid), adjective*
Shocking, explicit, or gruesome; graphic beyond necessity; or glaringly ornate; overdone with color, usually creating an unnatural, often unpleasant effect

Although the mainstream media showed tact in reporting the crime, the tabloids published all the LURID details.

The colors chosen for the playground turned out to be LURID and slightly eerie instead of bright and happy as intended.

lustration *(luh-STRAY-shun), noun*
Purification through symbolic or ceremonial means or remembrances.

After Melanie spent six months working with charities in third-world countries, we put her through LUSTRATION by reintroducing her to our favorite luxury boutiques.

lustrous *(LUHS-trus), adjective*
Glowing, as from an inner light; shining and bright; having a soft light

The snow and the full moon gave the gardens a LUSTROUS, romantic look that made them perfect for the couple's date, in spite of the cold.

luxuriant *(lug-ZHOOR-ee-ant), adjective*
Thick and healthy growth; lush; or characterized by luxury; decadent and delightful

The young man's thick, LUXURIANT hair made him the envy of most women who knew him.

The woman couldn't believe she actually owned something as LUXURIANT as her new cashmere robe.

lyceum *(LIE-see-um), noun*
A school or other place of learning.

She was shocked to learn that her son considered the back of the bus to be his main LYCEUM.

Know This Quote

"[Television] should be our LYCEUM, our Chautauqua, our Minsky's, and our Camelot."
—E. B. White, American author

M

macabre *(muh-KAHB), adjective*
Using death as subject, as in movies, books, or conversation; focused on the morbid and grisly. Horrifying.

MACABRE movies are very popular with almost all teen viewers, male and female.

Machiavellian *(mack-ee-uh-VEL-ee-uhn), adjective*
A somewhat unscrupulous and self-centered individual who is always looking out for his or her own good.

We can hardly be called MACHIAVELLIAN simply because we do what we need to do to hold on to the luxurious lifestyle which we have become accustomed.

machismo *(mah-CHEEZ-mow), noun*
Exaggerated sense or display of masculinity. An emphasis on qualities typically considered male, such as strength, courage, aggressiveness, and lack of emotion.

Driving a motorcycle is, for some, a demonstration of MACHISMO.

macroeconomics *(MA-kroe-eh-kuh-NAH-micks), noun*
The study of economics that focuses on the big picture, especially the systems that make up a national or international economy. Also, a study of the ways different parts of the overall system are connected.

Those studying MACROECONOMICS learn about supply and demand and other factors that impact the nation's economy.

maelstrom *(MAIL-struhm), noun*
A situation marked by violence, turbulence, and uncertainty.

Many families who lost their fortunes during the MAELSTROM of the 1929 stock market crash are still trying to regain their social status today.

maestro *(MYS-troe), noun*
An expert in an art, especially music; a conductor, composer, or music teacher of high regard.

The violin students eagerly awaited the MAESTRO, who was teaching them a complex arrangement that he would then conduct at their spring performance.

Magna Carta *(MAG-nah KAR-tah), noun*
Any constitution that guarantees rights and liberties.

The club's charter is a MAGNA CARTA that will ensure we are able to keep our tennis courts and swimming pools open only to our most significant social contacts.

magnanimous *(mag-NAH-nuh-mus), adjective*
Very generous, kind, or forgiving. Has nothing to do with volcanoes or magma.

In a MAGNANIMOUS gesture, the wealthy alumnus, who had once been suspended for bad grades, donated $10,000,000 to his alma mater.

Know This Quote
"In a serious struggle there is no worse cruelty than to be MAGNANIMOUS at an inopportune time." —Leon Trotsky, Bolshevik revolutionary and Marxist theorist

magnate *(MAG-nayt), noun*
A wealthy and prosperous business leader; a tycoon.

Oil MAGNATE T. Boone Pickens is now investing in wind power.

magniloquent *(mag-NILL-uh-kwuhnt), adjective*
Pompous, bombastic, and boastful.

The nouveau riche try to atone for their lack of polish with MAGNILOQUENT speech, but the result is ludicrous.

magnum *(MAG-num), noun*
An extra-large wine bottle twice the size of a regular wine bottle; a powerful handgun firing large bullets.

We doubted the taste of the event planner when we saw that the tables were filled with distasteful MAGNUMS of wines of questionable vintage.

mainframe *(MANE-FRAYM), noun*
Fast powerful computer with a large storage capacity that has a number of terminals for individual users connected to it.

As personal computers became faster and cheaper, the university had less need (and less room) for its MAINFRAMES.

malady *(MA-luh-dee), noun*
A disease or illness of the body or the mind. An unhealthy, problematic condition that causes discomfort and requires a remedy.

New doctors sometimes fear that an undiagnosed MALADY will cause a patient's death.

malaise *(MUH-layze), noun*
General feeling of illness or sickness. Vague sense of worry, discontent, or dissatisfaction and the bad feelings that come with it. Not to be confused with Malaysian, a person from Malaysia.

Doctors could not diagnose any particular disorder, yet Page still suffered from a MALAISE she could not overcome.

malapropism *(MA-la-prah-pi-zuhm), noun*
Misuse of a word through confusion with another word that sounds similar, especially with a humorous or ridiculous effect. "The physical year ends in June" is a malapropism for "The fiscal year ends in June."

Those who confuse and misuse words make many a MALAPROPISM.

malcontent *(MAL-kon-tent), noun or adjective*
A person who is discontented or unhappy, generally with the government and the status quo and makes those views known thorough words and actions; a rebel (noun) or dissatisfied and disgusted, especially with authority or the government; discontented (adjective)

The protestors spoke calmly and rationally in order to be taken seriously and to avoid being seen as a group of MALCONTENTS.

Many analysts predicted MALCONTENT Democrats would vote for a third-party candidate in order to make a statement about the new party platform.

maleficence *(muh-LEF-ih-sense), noun*
To act in a way that deliberately causes harm; behavior driven by evil intentions.

Our upstairs maid's various acts of MALEFICENCE finally caused her to be released from our family's employment.

malevolent *(muh-LEHV-oh-lent), adjective*
Characterized by having, showing, or carrying ill-will and a desire to do harm to others; evil; wishing others harm

All of the great villains in fiction have a MALEVOLENT streak in them that becomes focused most strongly on the hero.

Which Word?

Two words with similar meanings are not always interchangeable. This is the case for malevolent (muh-LEHV-oh-lent) and malicious (muh-LISH-us). The word malevolent describes someone who is generally cruel or nasty. A malevolent person doesn't care or hold a grudge against any particular person. On the other hand, malicious describes someone who is mean or hurtful to a specific person or about a specific thing.

malfeasance *(mal-FEE-zinss), noun*
Misbehavior; wrongdoing; illegal, unethical, or immoral conduct.

Gavin insists that insider trading is not MALFEASANCE; it's merely making good use of all available information.

malicious *(muh-LISH-us), adjective*
Deliberately and intentionally harmful; knowingly hurtful and damaging

Although she claimed her statements had not been MALICIOUS, but simply misunderstood, no one who knew her true feelings believed her.

malign *(MUH-liyn), verb or adjective*
To make intentionally harmful, cruel, and often untrue statements about a person; to criticize in an intentionally harsh or hurtful way (verb) or influential in an evil way; characterized by having evil nature or intent (adjective)

The star was grateful for her friends who stood by her when the press MALIGNED her for unpopular statements she had allegedly made in college.

The witches in the play Macbeth *are considered to have a MALIGN influence over the lead characters.*

malleable *(MAH-lee-ah-bul), adjective*
Able to shape and form without breaking, referring to a substance; or unformed; impressionable; easily swayed or taught; able to be manipulated

Even the hardest steel becomes MALLEABLE when heated above a certain temperature.

The professor enjoyed teaching philosophy to freshmen because their ideas were fresh and their minds still MALLEABLE.

Know This Quote
"I did not know that mankind was suffering for want of gold. I have seen a little of it. I know that it is very MALLEABLE, but not so MALLEABLE as wit." —Henry David Thoreau, American author and transcendentalist

manic *(MA-nik), adjective*
Relating to or affective by mania; extremely or excessively happy, busy, active, agitated, of high excitement or nervous energy.

Chaperones are suspicious of MANIC behavior in teens at dances, for sometimes it means they have been drinking.

manifest *(MAN-ih-fehst), adjective, verb, or noun*
Plainly and clearly obvious; easily seen or understood (adjective) or to express, show, or reveal; to personify by one's actions; to demonstrate (verb) or the list of cargo and/or passengers on a ship or plane (noun)

The glaring error in the headline was so MANIFEST to everyone, the editor knew someone would be fired for missing it before the paper went to print.

Although emotions may MANIFEST differently in different people, even the most subdued or private person has feelings.

The captain checked off the MANIFEST several times to ensure everything was on board before sailing on the long ocean voyage.

manifesto *(ma-nuh-FES-toh), noun*
A public, written declaration of principles, policies, and objectives. Often issued by a political movement, candidate, or leader.

The Communist *MANIFESTO, by Karl Marx and Friedrich Engels, inspired a political and economic movement that lasted decades yet ultimately proved finite.*

manumit *(man-yoo-MIHT), verb*
To set free, as from slavery, bondage, or servitude

Most human rights watch groups believe that no human is truly free until all slaves are MANUMIT and free to live as human beings and not property.

mar *(MAHR), verb or noun*
To damage or disfigure; to spoil or cause harm to something (verb) or a mark or spot that spoils the overall look, situation, or experience (noun)

The bride refused to let a few clouds and light sprinkles MAR the overall beauty of her wedding day.

Due to a MAR on the back of the cabinet, she was able to buy it at well under normal retail price.

marginal *(MARJ-nul), adjective*
Very small in scale or importance, as written in a margin. Not of central importance or relevance. Close to the lowest acceptable value or limit. In business terms, barely able to cover the costs of production when sold or when producing goods for sale; not truly profitable.

Trudy studied harder, but there was only MARGINAL improvement in her grades, so she agreed to get a tutor.

marginalize *(MAR-jin-ul-eyes), verb*
To dismiss something as less important than it actually is.

Francine has too many connections for us to snub her completely, but we have done our best to MARGINALIZE her influence.

marshal *(MAR-shul), verb*
To gather all the resources at one's disposal to achieve a goal.

Patricia MARSHALED all of her social contacts to try to get a front-row ticket for fashion week.

marsupial *(mar-SOUP-ee-uhl), noun*
A mammal who carries its young with her after its birth in a pouch on the outside of her body, where the baby continues to develop.

The kangaroo is the best-known MARSUPIAL, but wombats also carry their babies in a pouch.

martial *(MAR-shul), adjective*
Having to do with or regarding war or soldiering; suggestive of war and/or being a soldier; warlike; soldier-like

The search and rescue team showed MARTIAL courage, risking their own lives to save people trapped by the storm.

martyr *(MAR-tuhr), noun*
Someone who chooses to die rather than deny religious, political, or other strong beliefs. Someone who suffers or sacrifices to advance a cause or principle. Someone who experiences great and constant pain. Someone who complains a great deal to solicit sympathy.

Seeking to become MARTYRS, kamikaze pilots of World War II flew their explosive-laden planes into enemy targets.

Where'd That Word Come From?

Martyr—Derived from the Greek word for "witness," early Christians used this word to honor those who preferred to accept the penalty of death rather than renounce their faith.

masticate *(MASS-tuh-kate), verb*
To grind, pulverize, or chew using the teeth and jaws. To grind or crush something until it turns to pulp.

Grandpa, always an extravagant speaker, referred to his dentures as his "MASTICATING companions."

matriculate *(muh-TRIH-kyoo-late), verb*
To enroll as a member of a specific group or body, especially a college or university. Don't confuse with *masticate*, which means to chew.

After all of the admissions challenges and decisions, it was a relief for Kim to finally MATRICULATE to the University of Rochester.

matrix *(MAY-ricks), noun*
A situation, circumstance, or substance that allows for origin, development, or growth of something. A substance within which something is embedded or enclosed. It's more than just a movie title!

Necessity often seems to be the MATRIX of innovative thinking.

maudlin *(MAWD-lin), adjective*
Excessively sentimental, usually to the point of tears, often involving an element of self-pity; weepy for sad, sentimental, and perhaps self-absorbed reasons; often associated with drunkenness

No one enjoyed her company after her third drink because she became MAUDLIN talking about her years as a young dancer and what could have been.

Know This Quote
"It is a MAUDLIN and indecent verity that comes out through the strength of wine." —Joseph Conrad, Polish-born English novelist

maunder *(MAWN-dehr), verb*
To move, speak, or act in a random, meaningless manner.

Ricardo's speech MAUNDERS so much that you'd never know he was heir to one of Central America's largest fortunes.

maverick *(MA-ver-ik), noun or adjective*
A freethinking, slightly rebellious person; a person who refuses to conform to a particular idea or standard; or a calf or other livestock that has yet to be branded, traditionally considered the property of whoever first brands it if it roams free (noun) or independent and freethinking; slightly radical or rebellious (adjective)

People who truly want to make their mark on the world and society cannot be afraid to be labeled MAVERICKS by those who are happy with the way things have always been.

The rancher always kept a close eye on his MAVERICKS so no other rancher could brand them and claim them.

His MAVERICK attitude toward the criminal justice system made him a popular, if unpredictable, judge.

mawkish *(MAW-kish), adjective*
Sentimental in a sappy, even offensive way; sickly sweet emotion

It was difficult to buy his grandmother a Mother's Day card because most of them were so MAWKISH that they didn't fit her straightforward personality.

mea culpa *(MAY-ah CUL-pah), noun*
An admission of one's own guilt. Formal apology or acknowledgement of responsibility. Latin for "on my head."

Bradley offered a MEA CULPA after he lost the tickets to the concert.

mean *(MEEN), noun*
In arithmetic, the average value of a series of numbers, determined by taking the sum of a series and dividing by the number of items in the series.

The MEAN of the Bakersfields' fortune is nowhere near that of ours, but we tolerate the family anyway because several members are excellent golfers.

meander *(mee-AN-dehr), verb*
To move or flow in a random path; to wander aimlessly without a set direction

The young couple chose to MEANDER through the gardens, holding hands and enjoying each other's company, rather than head straight back to the dorms.

median *(MEE-dee-en), noun*
In arithmetic, the middle number in a series of numbers arranged in order from smallest to largest.

When philanthropists Brock, Cliff, and Edward were honored at a luncheon, Cliff was called upon to speak second as his donation was the MEDIAN of the three.

melanin *(MEL-uh-nin), noun*
The pigment that determines the color of one's hair, eyes, and skin.

Tamara is unwilling to accept that, no matter how much time she spends on the sunny beaches of the Mediterranean, she will not achieve her desired tan due to her lack of MELANIN.

melee *(MAY-lay), noun*
A confused struggle involving many people.

When Ester heard about the MELEE at the club where her son worked, she was afraid he had been hurt and called the hospital.

Know This Quote
"The man who is in the MELEE knows what blows are being struck and what blood is being drawn." —Woodrow Wilson

meliorism *(mel-ee-OR-iz-um), noun*
A philosophy of optimism that says the world is gradually improving through divine intervention or human effort—or both.

Thomas Hardy's philosophy was distinctly MELIORIST because he believed ultimately in the goodness of humankind.

mellifluous *(muh-LIF-loo-uhs), adjective*
Pleasant sounding; flowing and musical sounding; flowing sweetly, smoothly

The overnight DJ's MELLIFLUOUS voice helped soothe many people who were restless and could not sleep during the long, dark nights.

The voices of passionate preachers are MELLIFLUOUS, making the congregation feel as if they were singing their sermons.

mendacity *(men-DAS-ih-tee), noun*
Lies; untruthfulness; dishonesty

She was often amazed at the MENDACITY that would come from her brother's mouth and more so that her parents would believe him.

mendicant *(MEN-dih-kuhnt), adjective or noun*
Dependent upon alms or charity for a living (adjective) or one who asks for alms or charity, usually a man from a religious group, in order to live (noun)

In the Middle Ages, the MENDICANT religious orders could face hard, poor winters if people had not shown them charity during the previous seasons.

The MENDICANT traveled from town to town, stopping to preach wherever he would be given some food and a little money.

mentat *(MEN-tat), noun*
A human being capable of performing mental tasks with the accuracy and speed of a computer.

Our accountant is a veritable MENTAT! Did you see how fast he determined all of our charitable deductions?

mentor *(MEN-tor), noun*
Someone, often older or more experienced, who is trusted to advise, counsel, and teach another person who is younger or less experienced.

Each freshman was assigned a MENTOR from the senior class who was meant to provide help in adjusting to campus life more quickly and easily.

Where'd That Word Come From?

Mentor—Mentor, in Greek mythology, was the friend of Odysseus who took charge of his household when the hero of Homer's *Odyssey* went off to war. When problems arose, Pallas Athena descended from heaven to inhabit Mentor's body and, through him, to give good advice to Odysseus's son Telemachus. Mentor has since meant an adviser, teacher, or coach.

mercenary *(MUR-seh-nar-ee), adjective or noun*
Solely interested in monetary gain, even at the expense of morals and ethics (adjective) or a soldier hired by another country who is interested only in the money offered, not the politics or ideals involved (noun)

He bought and sold companies with a MERCENARY indifference to the employees or their families.

Generally speaking, MERCENARIES do not fight with the same heart as the soldiers who are fighting for their homes and their country.

mercurial *(mer-KYOOR-ee-uhl), adjective*
Lively, witty, fast-talking, hard to catch, and likely to do the unexpected. Caused by or containing mercury. Originally, relating to the god Mercury or born under that planet.

His MERCURIAL ways made Matthew hard to understand and even harder to get to know.

meretricious *(mayr-eh-TRISH-us), adjective*
Attractive on the surface but having no real value; attracting attention in a gaudy and flashy way; or reasonable to believe yet insincere and fake; phony, referring to an argument

Every summer, the beaches are filled with stalls selling MERETRICIOUS souvenirs to the tourists.

She never quite believed his MERETRICIOUS statements of friendship even though others called her cynical.

meridian *(mer-ID-ee-en), noun*
Any line that runs from north to south on a map or globe.

He sailed his yacht straight along a MERIDIAN to the Arctic Circle.

meritocracy *(mer-ih-TOK-ruh-see), noun*
Government or leadership by people have great merit, rather than by people with great wealth.

Corporate leadership in a family-owned business is determined by nepotism, not MERITOCRACY.

meritorious *(mair-uh-TORE-ee-uhss), adjective*
Worthy of praise or reward.

The work she did on her thesis was MERITORIOUS.

Know This Quote

"Arrogance on the part of the MERITORIOUS is even more offensive to us than the arrogance of those without merit: for merit itself is offensive." —Friedrich Nietzsche, nineteenth-century German philosopher

mesmerize *(MEZ-mer-iyz), adjective*
To entrance or enthrall; to hypnotize; to strongly attract

The young girls were MESMERIZED by the colors, lights, and sounds of their first performance of the ballet.

metachromasis *(meh-tah-CROWM-ah-sis), noun*
The phenomenon of different substances becoming different colors and shades when stained by the same dye.

An identical cotton blend was used in the entire lot of shirts to avoid METACHROMASIS ruining the color.

metallism *(MEH-tah-liz-um), noun*
The belief that money must either be made of precious metal or backed by precious metal held in reserve—usually gold or silver.

Richard Nixon abolished the gold standard for U.S. currency, and METALLISM declined as a result.

metamorphosis *(meh-tuh-MORE-fuh-sus), noun*
A complete or significant change of the body, appearance, character, or condition. A transformation caused by supposed magic or supernatural powers. Franz Kafka's famous story, *The Metamorphosis,* describes a man who changes into a cockroach.

The caterpillar's METAMORPHOSIS into a butterfly is one of nature's most amazing transformations.

metaphysics *(Met-a-FIZ-iks), noun*
The study of arguments, thoughts, and principles based primarily on thinking and abstract reasoning rather than hard facts that can be demonstrated through physical evidence.

Tom, a biology major, often feuded with his girlfriend, who studied METAPHYSICS about the basis of scientific facts.

Know This Quote
"During my METAPHYSICS final, I cheated by looking into the soul of the person sitting next to me."
—Woody Allen, American film director, writer, and comedian

metastasize *(meh-TA-sti-size), verb*
The tendency of cancer cells to spread from a tumor throughout the body.

Byron's ugly nature quickly METASTASIZED in our group, as he spread lies and gossip among more and more of our social contacts.

mete *(MEET), verb*
To distribute or allot.

After Elyssia ran up several of her father's platinum cards, he METED out substantial punishment for her by not allowing her to shop at exclusive boutiques for an entire week.

meticulous *(meh-TIK-yoo-lus), adjective*
Having or showing great concern for details; taking great care; being precise

The young woman's METICULOUS nature was evident by how clean her room and desk were even in the middle of finals.

métier *(MAY-tee-yay), noun*
One's occupation, profession, field of work, etc.

Since her family started one of Wall Street's most profitable houses, it's only natural that Ellen's MÉTIER would be finance.

mettle *(MEH-tul), noun*
The ability to cope well with adversity or challenges; courage; spirit and heart; the ability to rise to an occasion

The runner showed his true METTLE when he managed to qualify for the competition even though he tripped during trials.

mettlesome *(MEH-tul-som), adjective*
Having an unbroken spirit; characterized by courage and heart

The METTLESOME soccer team managed to play their way into the finals in spite of injuries and other setbacks.

miasma *(my-AZ-mah), noun*
An unhealthy atmosphere or environment; an unpleasant feeling pervading the air.

A MIASMA of distrust pervaded the room after the theft had taken place.

microcosm *(MIYK-roh-kah-zim), noun*
A situation, community, or system that represents a larger whole; a smaller, representative sample

College campuses, with their diverse populations, politics, and hierarchies, are MICROCOSMS of society at large.

Know This Quote

"These appearances, which bewilder you, are merely electrical phenomena not uncommon—or it may be there they have their ghastly origin in the rank MIASMA of the tarn"
—Edgar Allan Poe, American author and poet

micromanage *(MY-crow-ma-nij), verb*
To manage a business or organization by paying extreme (and usually excessive) attention to small details. To retain personal responsibility for overseeing all details of an organization or project.

Some who MICROMANAGE contribute a great deal, yet others do more harm than good.

mien *(MEEN), adjective*
Bearing or conduct; look or appearance, especially as it relates to personality or character

The dean's austere MIEN caused most students to avoid dealing with him directly.

migratory *(MY-gruh-toar-ee), adjective*
Moving as part of a bird, fish, or animal population from one region to another every year. Relating to movement of people or animals from one place to another. Tending to wander from one region to another without settling down for any length of time.

MIGRATORY birds are good indicators of seasonal changes.

milestone *(MYEL-stone), noun*
A stone or other marker on a road that indicates the number of miles to a given place. A significant or important event in someone's life or in the history of a country, a family, or an organization.

The bar mitzvah celebrated by Jewish young men when they are thirteen is a MILESTONE for the entire family.

milieu *(meel-YUH), noun*
The surroundings or environment that someone lives in and is influenced by. Describing the circumstances or environment around a person or thing. A fancy way of saying "what's around you."

The principal thought a positive and friendly MILIEU would benefit the new students, so she approved some renovations to the cafeteria.

millenarianism *(mil-uh-NAIR-ee-uhn-ism), noun*
Any apocalyptic religious, philosophical, or social movement that predicts radical disaster, particularly at the end of the current millennium or the beginning of the new one.

As they worried about the impact of computer errors on the family fortune during the change from 1999 to 2000, the Cadburys briefly believed in MILLENARIANISM.

millenium *(mil-EN-ee-um), noun*
A period of a thousand years.

Millicent takes a MILLENIUM to get ready for society balls, but the results, typically, are worth the wait.

mimic *(MIH-mik), verb*
To imitate someone; to copy someone's voice, gestures, or appearance. To resemble someone or something to be a deliberate copy.

Many popular comedians tell stories of how they used to MIMIC teachers, friends, and family when they were young.

minimalism *(MIN-ih-mull-iz-um), noun*
A school of art in which "less is more"—clean and uncluttered paintings; sculpture with simple lines; fiction written in a lean and spare style; and music with uncomplicated scores and minimal instruments.

John Cage's MINIMALIST composition 4'33" consists of four and a half minutes of silence.

minutiae *(mih-NOO-shuh), noun*
Small, trifling matters that one encounters on an average day.

The MINUTIAE of golf, tennis, and spa treatments at the club can become utterly tiresome.

mire *(MYRE), verb*
To get stuck in mud, either yourself or something else. To make something muddy or dirty. To involve or entangle someone or something in difficulty. Often a part of the phrase "muck and *mire*."

Many college students become MIRED in credit card debt soon after commencement.

mirth *(MERTH), noun*
Great joy, happiness, and cheer, especially expressed through laughter
For many people, the Christmas holidays are a time of MIRTH, friendship, and giving thanks for one another.

misanthrope *(MIS-ahn-throhp), noun*
Someone who dislikes humanity and people in general

She claimed to be a MISANTHROPE but her friends knew she had just been hurt badly by an old boyfriend.

mischievous *(MIS-chihv-us), adjective*
Playful in a naughty manner; having a fondness for causing trouble in a cheerful and prankish way

His MISCHIEVOUS sense of humor and the twinkle in his eye got him into—and out of—trouble as a teenager.

misconstrue *(miss-kun-STROO), verb*
To understand or interpret incorrectly; misinterpret. To make an error of analysis.

Many of the candidate's statements were MISCONSTRUED, and she lost the election by a landslide.

miscreant *(MIS-kree-ant), noun*
Someone who behaves badly; a person who breaks the law or behaves in other socially unacceptable ways

Although he was trying to be tough and cool, he only succeeded in getting himself a reputation as a MISCREANT.

miser *(MIY-zur), noun*
A person, usually wealthy, who saves money to an extreme degree; someone who spends as little money as possible for the purpose of keeping the wealth

Ebenezer Scrooge was well-known as a MISER until the ghosts taught him there was more to life than money.

miserly *(MIY-zur-lee), adjective*
Characterized by greediness, lack of generosity, or penny-pinching

The MISERLY old landlady kept them all cold in the winter because she didn't want to pay a high heating bill.

mishmash *(MISH-mash), noun*
A disorderly collection or confused mixture of things; a jumble. Not to be confused with *mismatch,* which means a pairing or combination of people or things that are incompatible or ill-suited.

When young children dress themselves, parents are not surprised to find they choose a MISHMASH of colors and styles.

misnomer *(mis-NOH-mer), noun*
An unsuitable and incorrect or misleading name for any given object

Considering the length of the wait at many drive-thrus, "fast food" is quickly becoming a MISNOMER.

misogyny *(muh-SAH-juh-nee), noun*
Hatred of women. A bitter contempt for all women.

Trying to drown his sorrows after breaking up with his girlfriend, Jim's inebriated ranting sounded much like MISOGYNY.

missive *(MISS-iv), noun*
An official or formal letter.

He sent out a MISSIVE informing all employees that, henceforth, there would be no smoking in their quarters—but he forgot to remove the ashtrays.

mitigate *(MIT-ih-gayt), verb*
To make easier; to soothe; to alleviate; to lessen a burden

The pain of losing first place was MITIGATED when she overheard her father praising her performance anyway.

mitosis *(my-TOH-sus), noun*
The process by which a cell divides into two cells, with each having the same number of chromosomes as the original cell.

MITOSIS is fundamental to the subject of biology, and students must understand it if they plan to learn about genetics.

mnemonic *(nih-MAH-nik), noun*
Any device, like a rhyme or phrase, meant to make memorizing easier. It could be as simple as tying a string on one's finger, or using an acronym, anagram, or sentence.

ROY G. BIV is a MNEMONIC used to remember all of the colors in the rainbow: red, orange, yellow, green, blue, indigo, and violet.

moderation *(mod-eh-RAY-shun), noun*

Characterized by not being at either extreme; an avoidance of excess

It was difficult for her to eat ice cream in MODERATION, especially in the summer with a shop open on almost every corner.

modicum *(MOH-dih-kum), noun*

A small amount, often used when describing something valuable or desired; a token or trivial amount

As sad as her stories sometimes were, there was always at least a MODICUM of humor in each that could make people smile.

The police had hoped to hear at least a MODICUM of truth as they questioned the suspects about the robbery.

Know This Quote

"To be human is to have one's little MODICUM of romance secreted away in one's composition." —Mark Twain

moiety *(MOY-ih-tee) noun*

Either of the two parts, not necessarily equal, into which something is divided. A part, portion, or share. Either of two kinship groups divided by and defined by descent, that together make up a tribe or society.

The hungry fishermen divided their small catch, and each ate his MOIETY with great appreciation.

mollify *(MAWL-ih-fiy), noun*

To soften temper or anger; to soothe anxiety; to relieve tension in a situation

Whenever the clerks needed to MOLLIFY a customer, they always called on Tom because he was the most diplomatic of all of the employees.

molt *(MOHLT), verb*

To shed skin, fur, feathers, or other outer covering in order to allow new growth

The Saint Bernard shed often, but in the spring when it was time for him to MOLT, the house was positively covered in fur.

monastic *(moh-NAS-tik), adjective*

Relating to the practice of withdrawing from society to live a quiet, contemplative life, often dedicated to religious faith.

Saint Pachomius founded the first organized Christian MONASTIC community.

monistic *(moh-NIS-tik), noun*

The idea that everything—including philosophy, religion, and mysticism—can be reduced to a single substance or explained by a single principle.

Of course we believe the world is MONISTIC. Wealth is the source of everything in the universe.

monograph *(MAH-nuh-graff), noun*
A scholarly academic-focused article, paper, or essay on a single topic. It is easy to imagine most monographs being read in a monotone.

Professor Smith's MONOGRAPH on religious philosophy was his first serious academic publication since his doctoral thesis.

monolithic *(mon-oh-LITH-ik), adjective*
Massive and imposing in size, either literal or figurative, when literal, often formed from a single piece of stone or other material; large, solid, and imposing

The MONOLITHIC doors leading into the capitol building left many visitors stunned and in awe.

monomania *(mon-uh-MAY-nee-ya), noun*
An obsession or intense preoccupation with a single subject matter

Her parents were concerned that her interest in religion was beginning to shift into MONOMANIA.

monotheism *(MOH-no-THEE-iz-um), noun*
A belief in one omnipotent, omniscient God who is actively involved in the workings of both the physical universe that He created and the society of men who dwell in it.

Christians, Jews, and Muslims all believe in MONOTHEISM.

moot *(MOOT), adjective*
A fact or point that is uncertain or no longer relevant.

Whether to continue injecting growth hormones became a MOOT point as Alex grew from five feet to five-nine in eighteen months.

mordant *(MOHR-dnt), adjective*
Sharp, sarcastic, and piercing, used when describing wit or humor

The comedian's MORDANT observations made people recognize the truth in his statements even as they made people laugh.

Know This Quote

"The ocean looked dead too, dead gray waves hissing MORDANTLY along the beach." —John Fowles, British novelist and essayist

mores *(MORE-ayz), noun*
The accepted norms of social behavior for the time and society in which you live.

Grant learned the hard way that MORES vary from country to country when he made the faux pas of trying to shake the hand of the Thai businessman.

moribund *(MORE-uh-bund), adjective*
Nearly dead. Having lost all sense of purpose or vitality. Becoming obsolete or about to die. Literally, "bound toward death."

It was sad to visit Grandpa after his stroke, for this once energetic man lay MORIBUND in bed, hardly speaking or moving.

morose *(muh-ROHS), adjective*
Dejected or downhearted in a sullen, moody way; moody and depressed; brooding

He became so MOROSE when he wasn't accepted to his first choice of college that no one wanted to approach him for weeks.

mortal *(MORE-tuhl), adjective*
Certain to die eventually. Being the cause of death, as in a mortal wound or injury. Extreme, as in a mortal enemy, or intensely felt, as in mortal terror.

Teenagers who often cross the street without looking seem unaware that they are MORTAL.

mortgage *(MOR-gaj), noun*
Agreement that lets someone borrow money against a valuable piece of property, such as a house, giving the lender the right to seize the property if the loan is not paid. A written contract between borrower and lender, or the total amount of money lent. Also the amount paid by the borrower, usually every month, until the sum is repaid.

If they could get a MORTGAGE, the newlyweds would be able to buy their dream house.

mortification *(MORE-tuh-fuh-KAY-shun), noun*
To control or put an end to bodily desires by means of abstinence from pleasure and self-inflicted pain. Deep shame and humiliation caused by a blow to one's pride.

A deep sense of MORTIFICATION overcame the congregation when they learned how little had been pledged for the new rectory.

mosaic *(moh-ZAY-ik), noun*
A piece of artwork created by attaching pieces of glass, tile, stone, or other substance on a surface in a pattern or design

The MOSAIC that hung over her bed was made from sea glass she had collected while vacationing in the Caribbean.

mot juste *(MOW zshoost), noun*
The perfect word or phrase to communicate precisely what you mean to say.

Years of elocution lessons have left Paulina capable of leavening every occasion with a suitable MOT JUSTE.

motif *(mow-TEEF), noun*
A dominant or frequently repeated theme, design, image, or idea.

The Whittingtons' china has a diamond-shaped MOTIF that is a testament to how the family made its fortune.

motley *(MOT-lee), adjective*
Composed of people or things that are very different and don't seem to belong together. Made of different colors.

As a caring Little League coach, Paul was highly motivated to turn his MOTLEY group of kids into a confident team.

multifaceted *(mul-tee-FA-sih-tid), adjective*
With many different talents, qualities, or features; possessing many facets, dimensions, or cut surfaces.

Spencer Tracy was a MULTIFACETED actor, equally proficient at drama or comedy.

multifarious *(muhl-tuh-FAYR-ree-uhs), adjective*
Extremely diverse; having many aspects to its nature; created from differing parts

Immigrants to the United States are, to this day, often drawn to New York City because of its MULTIFARIOUS and multicultural nature.

multilateral *(mull-tea-LAH-terr-ul), adjective*
An agreement or accord requiring two nations or states to take the same position or action on an issue or problem.

A pacifist, he frequently spoke out for MULTILATERAL nuclear disarmament.

mundane *(mun-DANE), adjective*
Commonplace, boring; ordinary or everyday. Relating to or pertaining to concerns of the workaday world.

After visiting Stephanie at college, her parents were surprised at how MUNDANE the life of this high school partier had become.

munificent *(myoo-NIHF-ih-sint), adjective*
Showing great and overwhelming generosity; giving liberally

The critics were MUNIFICENT in their praise for the child actor who had taken on such a challenging role.

mutable *(MYOO-tuh-bull), adjective*
Subject to change at a moment's notice.

Kara and Lis couldn't tell Ashley what they were doing that night; their plans were MUTABLE.

myopia *(mye-OH-pee-uh), noun*
A common condition that causes an inability to see things clearly from far away; nearsightedness. To lack foresight or long-term planning.

After the strategic planning meeting, it became evident that the sales team suffered from MYOPIA and could not see their manager's vision for success.

Know This Quote

"For is the same! For, be it joy or sorrow, / The path of its departure still is free: / Man's yesterday may ne'er be like his morrow; / Nought may endure but MUTABILITY." —Percy Bysshe Shelley, English Romantic poet

myriad *(meer-REE-ad), adjective*
An enormous amount; an incalculable amount; an indefinite number

The stores at the mall had MYRIAD choices for the young women shopping for prom dresses.

Where'd That Word Come From?

Myriad—Before the idea of a million was introduced in about the twelfth century, the largest number word was *myriad,* which derives from a Greek word meaning countless, infinite, and was also the Greek word for 10,000. Today, *myriad* is used chiefly to mean countless or innumerable.

N

nacelle *(NAY-sell), noun*
The pod-shaped outer hull of an airplane engine.

Bentley always has his family crest imprinted on the NACELLE of each of his private planes.

nadir *(NAY-der), noun*
In astronomy, the point directly underneath the observer on the sphere; or the lowest point possible; extreme adversity; the rock bottom

From the North Pole, the South Pole is the NADIR of planet earth.

Running out of gas and having to walk three miles in her dress shoes had to be the NADIR of a very bad night.

nanosecond *(NA-noh-seh-kund), noun*
One billionth of a second. Informally, the shortest conceivable period of time. Nay, no second is shorter than a nanosecond.

It just takes a NANOSECOND for a car accident to happen, so please be focused and careful.

nanotechnology *(NA-noh-tek-NAH-nuh-jee), noun*
The ability to manipulate materials on a very small scale, with the goal of building microscopic objects such as machinery. The science of building devices, such as electronic circuits, from individual atoms and molecules.

It is believed that someday NANOTECHNOLOGY will make organ transplantation unnecessary.

narcissism *(NAHR-suh-SIH-zum), noun*
Excessive self-admiration and self-centeredness; being possessed by self-love. In medicine, a personality disorder characterized by an overestimation of one's appearance and abilities, and an excessive need for admiration.

NARCISSISM goes well beyond confidence and positive thought; it's quite obvious and disturbing.

narcolepsy *(NAHR-kuh-lehp-see), noun*
A disorder characterized by frequent, brief, and uncontrollable bouts of deep sleep.

While stories about people with NARCOLEPSY can be quite funny, the disorder is truly nothing to laugh at.

narrative *(NAR-uh-tiv), noun*
Story or account of a sequence of events, presented in the order in which they happened. The art of telling a story or giving a vivid account of something. The portion of a literary work concerned with telling a story.

The art of the NARRATIVE is a writing talent that must be nurtured.

nascent *(NAY-suhnt), adjective*
Just coming to be; newly but not yet fully developed; beginning to grow and show signs of potential; generally used when describing a process or organization

Many common items people take for granted today, such as the computer and cell phones, were only NASCENT technologies as recently as the 1980s.

NASDAQ *(NAA-zdack), acronym*
An acronym for "National Association of Securities Dealers Automated Quotation System," a collection of publicly traded stocks that includes a lot of high-tech companies. The electronic communications system that links all over-the-counter securities dealers to form a national market.

Each day economists analyze NASDAQ trading to determine the nature of the market.

nationalism *(NASH-nuh-lizum), noun*
Proud loyalty and devotion to a nation; in particular, excessive devotion to a nation and belief it is superior to all others. The desire to achieve independence, particularly by a country under foreign control.

NATIONALISM can be positive when celebrating good, but too often it is an excuse for terrorism and harm.

NATO *(NAY-toe), acronym*
An acronym for "North Atlantic Treaty Organization," an international organization established after World War II to promote mutual defense and collective security for the United States and Western Europe.

Since the fall of the Soviet Union, NATO has expanded dramatically to include nations that were once considered foes.

natter *(NAH-ter), verb*
To talk ceaselessly; babble.

The way Emily NATTERS endlessly about her family's new yacht is revolting to those of us who have owned several yachts over the years.

natty *(NA-tee), adjective*
Neat and fashionable appearance or dress. A natty dresser would never wear clothes that looked ratty.

Jayson's NATTY attire was always a welcome sight, especially in comparison to those of his friends who didn't seem to care about their appearance.

natural selection *(NA-chu-rul suh-leck-shun), noun*
A theory developed by Charles Darwin to explain the evolution of species, also known as "survival of the fittest." The organisms best suited to survive in a particular environment reproduce in greater numbers than others that are less well suited, thus creating future generations of better-adapted offspring.

> *Eventually, NATURAL SELECTION survived as the accepted theory, yet it remains controversial to those who accept creationism.*

navigable *(NA-vih-guh-bull), adjective*
Passable by ship or boat; waters deep and wide enough to allow vessels to pass. Able to be steered or controlled.

> *Prior to backing out of the crammed parking lot, Dennis first determined that it was NAVIGABLE.*

naysayer *(NAY-say-er), noun*
Someone who votes no or who speaks against something. Naysayer Jay says "No," "Never," and "Nay" every day.

> *She was always so negative that it became easy to call her a NAYSAYER.*

nebulous *(NEB-yoo-lus), adjective*
Foggy, cloudy, or hazy; unclear and undefined; blurred; indistinct; may be used literally to describe atmosphere or figuratively to describe concepts, words, or ideas

> *His brothers refused to sneak out with him because the plan for getting past their parents' bedroom was NEBULOUS at best.*

necromancy *(NEH-kruh-man-see), noun*
The practice of attempting to communicate with the spirits of the dead in order to predict or influence the future. Witchcraft or sorcery in general.

> *NECROMANCY seems impossible, yet many who want so much to communicate with dead loved ones, and who hope to foretell the future, still believe.*

Know This Quote
"The so-called science of poll-taking is not a science at all but mere NECROMANCY."
—E. B. White, American author

ne'er-do-well *(NERR-due-wel), noun*
A lazy and irresponsible person. You will do well to ne'er get called this word.

> *Lindsay's parents thought her fiancé was a NE'ER-DO-WELL, and they tried to tell her so.*

nefarious *(neh-FAYR-ree-us), adjective*
Wicked or evil; villainous; may imply infamous as well as cruel

> *The documentary focused on the NEFARIOUS crimes of serial killers in the twentieth century.*

negligent *(NEH-gluh-jent), adjective*
Habitually careless or irresponsible. Guilty of failing to provide a proper or reasonable level of care.

Investigators deemed that the nursing home staff had not been NEGLIGENT and thus was not responsible for the accident.

nemesis *(NEH-muh-sus), noun*
A bitter enemy, especially one who seems unbeatable. An opponent motivated by revenge; one who will stop at nothing to settle a score or inflict punishment.

Although he fought many other criminals, Batman's NEMESIS was truly the Joker.

Where'd That Word Come From?

Nemesis—Nemesis was the Greek goddess of justice or revenge, and her name comes from the Greek for vengeance. Thus, *nemesis* means anyone who avenges or punishes.

neoconservative *(NEE-oh-kon-SERVE-ah-tiz-um), noun*
A liberal who has become a conservative.

We've removed Bradley from our list of social contacts because he has become such a NEOCONSERVATIVE.

neologism *(nee-AWL-eh-jizm), noun*
A word or phrase that has just been created; "to coin a phrase"; a new word

The advancements, slang, and discoveries of every generation have added NEOLOGISMS that have become commonplace in the language used by ordinary people.

neonatal *(NEE-oh-NAY-tul), adjective*
Of, or relating to newborn children.

Honestly, the Atkinsons treat their grown children as though they still require NEONATAL care. No wonder they never get invited to any of our galas.

neophyte *(NEE-uh-fite), noun*
A beginner or novice at some task or endeavor. Someone who has recently converted or who has recently joined a religious order but has not yet taken vows to join an order.

A veteran boxer might be glad to fight a NEOPHYTE.

Freshmen are truly NEOPHYTES in college, but they manage to adjust and learn very quickly.

Know This Quote

"Like footmen and upstairs maids, wine stewards are portrayed as acolytes of the privileged, ever eager to intimidate the NEOPHYTE and spurn the unwary." —Frank J. Prial, former *New York Times* wine columnist

nepotism *(NEH-puh-tih-zum), noun*
Favoritism shown by someone in power to relatives and friends in professional matters, especially when appointing them to good positions.

When senior managers all share the last name of a company's founder, it's unusual if no one is accused of NEPOTISM.

netiquette *(NET-uh-kit), noun*
A set of rules for communicating properly in the electronic communication environment known as the World Wide Web, most often when using e-mail or instant message capabilities.

There should be a class in NETIQUETTE, but it would most likely be an online course.

nettle *(NET-uhl), verb*
To provoke, irritate, or annoy.

Beth was NETTLED by Rachel's behavior at the party, but didn't mention it afterward.

Know This Quote

"The comic spirit is given to us in order that we may analyze, weigh, and clarify things in us which NETTLE us, or which we are outgrowing, or trying to reshape." —Thornton Wilder, American playwright and novelist

neural *(NUR-ul) adjective*
Related to or located in a nerve or the nervous system.

When studying biology, the students were very interested in learning about NEURAL anatomy and connections.

newbie *(NUE-bee), noun*
A new user of the Internet, or someone new to any circumstance, organization, or institution.

Those planning the orientation session thought the term "NEWBIE" was appropriate, so it became the theme for the program.

nexus *(NEK-sus), noun*
A connection or link; also a group or series of connected people or things. The center or focus. If you've ever been hit in the solar plexus, you know it's the nexus of your ability to breathe.

For many, a shared love of sports is the NEXUS of their friendship and the inspiration for many conversations.

niggling *(NIG-ling), adjective*
Demanding a great deal of care, attention, or time; or, trifling and insignificant.

People just don't understand how difficult it is for us to attend to all the NIGGLING needs of our servants.

nihilism *(NIE-uh-lih-zum), noun*
The belief that life is pointless and human values worthless. A belief that there is no objective basis for truth, or a belief that all authority is corrupt and must be destroyed to build a just society. The word *annihilate* comes from the same roots, meaning "nothing."

Know This Quote
"NIHILISM is best done by professionals." —Iggy Pop, American singer and songwriter

Some believe that Henry David Thoreau, who wrote Walden, *recounting his life celebrating nature and his ability to live independent of society, was an advocate of NIHILISM.*

nimbus *(NIM-bus), noun*
A halo of light surrounding the head of a saint or other holy person.

"Sally is such a goody two-shoes, you'd think she would have a NIMBUS on top of her head," Nancy said to the girls.

nitid *(NIT-id), adjective*
Bright and lustrous.

Brock and Jenny flew through NITID moonbeams in Brock's new Gulfstream GIV personal jet.

nitty-gritty *(NIH-tee-GRIH-tee), noun*
The basic and most important details of something. The thing or approach that is most practical, direct, and down to earth.

The coach believed wins were a result of paying attention to the NITTY-GRITTY, so he always began practice with rudimentary drills.

noblesse oblige *(noh-BLESS oh-BLEEZH), noun*
The idea that people born to nobility or upper classes must behave generously toward those less privileged. From the French for "nobility obliges."

Many of the most famous foundations, named for the wealthiest families, like Carnegie and Rockefeller, were founded on the principle of NOBLESSE OBLIGE.

nocturnal *(nahk-TUR-nal), adjective*
Occurring at night, in the dark, active during the night. The antonym of *diurnal,* which describes things that happen during the day.

Once puberty kicks in, it seems that teenagers turn into members of a NOCTURNAL species.

noisome *(NOY-suhm), adjective*
Offensive and foul; harmful, possibly toxic; usually used when describing an odor, smell, or fumes

The lab was filled with a NOISOME odor for days after the student spilled the formaldehyde during an experiment.

nom de plume *(nahm duh PLOOM), noun*
Pseudonym; the name used by a writer instead of his or her real name. French for "pen name."

Authors who write romance novels often use a NOM DE PLUME, for they are a bit embarrassed to be associated with this genre.

nomad *(NOH-mad), noun*
Member of a group that moves from place to place, in search of pasture, food, or water. Someone who wanders from one place to another.

The player, who was just traded to his third team in one season, seemed like a NOMAD.

nomenclature *(NOH-mun-klay-chur), noun*
Name or designation; the act of naming. A system of names for purposes of organization. A system of names created to describe a new scientific or artistic discipline.

The NOMENCLATURE of the Internet includes terms like "pop-up," "hyperlink," and "bandwidth."

Upon entering graduate school, Mark realized that he had to learn an entire new NOMENCLATURE if he was to succeed.

nominal *(NAH-mih-nuhl), adjective*
Insignificant, trifling, or token; or existing for show but having no real depth; or lower than actual or expected value; or having to do with a specific name

The attorney charged her friend only a NOMINAL fee because she knew drawing up the will would take very little time.

His girlfriend only showed a NOMINAL interest in football so he finally stopped trying to explain the rules to her.

The service at the restaurant was so poor that the couple only left a NOMINAL tip for the server.

He would only donate to the building fund if the college promised to give the building an anonymous title rather than a NOMINAL one identifying him as the donor.

nominalism *(NAHM-ih-nl-iz-um), noun*
A philosophy that denies the existence of universal truths.

Some scientists suspect that, rather than being universal, the laws of physics may vary in different regions of the universe—a strong supporting argument for NOMINALISM.

non compos mentis *(NAHN KAHM-pohs MEN-tiss), adjective*
Crazy; insane; not in one's right mind.

When Bryce suggested he was considering the ministry, rather than joining the family bond business, we were certain he was NON COMPOS MENTIS.

non sequitur *(nahn SEH-kwit-ur), noun*
A conclusion or statement that does not seem to follow from that which preceded it.

Hilary's belief that she was now welcome in our group was, clearly, a NON SEQUITUR on her part.

nonagenarian *(none-uh-jen-AIR-ee-en), noun*
A person in his or her nineties.

When you're a NONAGENARIAN, it begins to occur to you that you could in fact live to be one hundred.

nondescript *(non-dih-SKRIPT), adjective*
Lacking distinction; ordinary.

The police had a hard time tracking down the burglar as he was quite NONDESCRIPT.

Know This Quote

"Actors ought to be larger than life. You come across quite enough ordinary, NONDESCRIPT people in daily life and I don't see why you should be subjected to them on the stage too."
—Donald Sinden, British actor

nostalgia *(NAH-stahl-juh), noun*
Mixed feeling of happiness, sadness, and longing when recalling persons, places, or events of the past. Something intended to arouse feelings associated with the past. A longing for home or family when away.

Buying and selling items that inspire NOSTALGIA has become a very lucrative business.

nostrum *(NOH-strum), noun*
Any medicine with unknown ingredients and results; usually fake medicine that promises the quick fix; medicine touted by its creator as a cure-all but with no scientific backing or proof; or a popular but unproven or ineffective solution to problems or evils

Even though the pill was a NOSTRUM, its makers guaranteed it would cause weight loss so people spent huge amounts of money on it.

Boot camps for troubled teens are a NOSTRUM for juvenile delinquency but their long-term effectiveness is still unknown.

notarize *(NOH-tuh-rize), verb*
To certify something, like a signature on a legal document, and verify to its authenticity. To certify or attest to the validity of a signature on a document as a notary public.

Paralegals who are also notaries might NOTARIZE hundreds of documents each week.

notoriety *(no-ter-RIY-ih-tee), noun*
Being known for an undesirable reason

She could have lived without the NOTORIETY that resulted from being asked to testify in front of the honor board.

nouveau riche *(NOO-voh REESH), noun*
A class of people whose extreme wealth has been recently earned, often a former member of a lower or middle class who ostentatiously displays newly acquired trappings of wealth. Also a member of this class.

Anyone who disdains the NOUVEAU RICHE must hate the way these people just keep smiling—all the way to the bank.

noxious *(NOK-shuss), adjective*
Harmful to life or health; poisonous. Likely to cause moral or spiritual harm; corrupting or debilitating influence. As a teenager, you encounter many things that smell this way. Think locker room, sweat socks, or a long-forgotten tuna sandwich.

The NOXIOUS gas was odorless and almost invisible, so it was stored very carefully.

nuance *(NOO-ahnts), noun*
A very slight difference in meaning, tone, color, or feeling. Awareness or ability to express subtle shades, meanings, and feelings, as in an artist or performer.

Jim's ability to see the NUANCES in certain photographs made him an exceptional magazine editor.

Know This Quote

"[Venice] in winter is rich with the bittersweet NUANCE and somber beauty of the once-was."
—Terry Weeks, American travel writer

nubile *(NOO-bile), adjective*
Of sexually developed and attractive youth.

We have explained time and again to Melinda that she must get a personal trainer like the rest of us to be truly NUBILE.

nugatory *(NOO-guh-tor-ee), adjective*
Insignificant; having little importance; pointless or without purpose; or ineffective or meaningless; powerless; figuratively, without teeth; worthless

The world ignored Hitler's earliest writings as NUGATORY but quickly realized this had been a mistake of enormous proportions.

Some people are beginning to wonder if the speed limit has become a NUGATORY law considering most people drive very fast on highways and interstates regardless.

null *(NUHL), adjective*
Having no legal validity; of no value or importance. Amounting to nothing in terms of context or character. At the level of zero or nothing.

The judge ruled that, in the context of this trial, all of the attorney's objections were NULL.

nullify *(NUH-luh-fie), verb*
To make something legally invalid or ineffective; to cancel something out.

Once the deadline passed, without payment being made, Jane could NULLIFY the contract with a simple phone call.

numismatist *(noo-miz-muh-tist), noun*
Someone who studies or collects coins, paper money, or medals.

I guess it takes money to become a NUMISMATIST.

nuptial *(NUP-shul), adjective*
Related to marriage or weddings.

Renting a tuxedo always seemed NUPTIAL to Stephen, even if he was just doing so for a formal dance.

nymph *(NIMF), noun*
A spirit linked to a particular place or element.

Betsy loved swimming so much that her parents considered her a water NYMPH.

Know This Quote

"Reason is a supple NYMPH, and slippery as a fish by nature."
—D. H. Lawrence, British author

O

obdurate *(AHB-dur-iht), adjective*
Stubborn and refusing to change, especially when faced with a gentler or more compassionate option

King Henry VIII was OBDURATE in his decision that his enemies be executed, refusing even to meet with them or read their letters after their imprisonment.

Know This Quote

"The fates are not quite OBDURATE; / They have a grim, sardonic way / Of granting them who supplicate / The thing they wanted yesterday." —Roselle Mercier Montgomery, American poet

obeisance *(oh-BEE-sance), noun*
Deferential respect or homage, or an act or gesture expressing the same.

Rachael practiced OBEISANCE by allowing the elderly woman to sit in her plush opera box, rather than in the mezzanine.

obesity *(oh-BEE-suh-tee), noun*
A condition of extreme excess body fat. Technically, a body weight that is 20 percent or more higher than recommended for that person's height.

OBESITY is becoming a serious issue for America's youth.

obfuscate *(AHB-fyoo-skayt), verb*
To intentionally make something unclear or confusing; to purposefully make facts or a situation difficult to understand

The principal wasn't sure if the young man was just confused about the facts or if he was trying to OBFUSCATE the story in order to protect his friends.

objet d'art *(OB-zhay dahr), noun*
An article that has artistic value. French for "object of art."

Phillip thought of his purchase at the garage sale as an OBJET D'ART, but others thought it a garish piece of junk.

oblique *(oh-BLEEK), adjective*
Not straightforward or direct; indirect and unclear. In mathematics, sloping or adjoining at an angle that is not a right angle; not perpendicular nor parallel.

Professor Blake's description of the relationship between the two novels was so OBLIQUE that few students comprehended.

oblivion *(uh-BLIH-vee-un), noun*
The state of being utterly forgotten. Complete forgetfulness; utter lack of awareness of one's surroundings.

For a time it was as if roller-skating had been relegated to OBLIVION, and then in-line skates became popular.

obsequious *(ub-SEE-kwee-uss), adjective*
Excessively eager to please or to obey all instructions. Compliant and servile to superiors, in order to curry favor.

For some, it is difficult to distinguish OBSEQUIOUS behavior from sincere and excellent customer service.

Know This Quote
"[The political mind] is a strange mixture of vanity and timidity, of an OBSEQUIOUS attitude at one time and a delusion of grandeur at another time." —Calvin Coolidge

obsolescence *(ob-suh-LESS-uhnts), noun*
The state of being no longer useful.

Roderick found, to his dismay, that some of the new Maserati models had lapsed into OBSOLESCENCE almost as soon as they hit the showroom floor.

obsolescent *(ob-suh-LESS-unt), adjective*
Having fallen into a state of disuse as a result of replacement by something new; in short, becoming obsolete. Adolescence becomes obsolescent—or should—as soon as your teen years are behind you.

Many think the piano was made OBSOLESCENT by the electronic keyboard, but not everyone agrees.

obstinate *(OB-stih-nut), adjective*
Determined not to agree with other people's wishes or accept their suspicions. Unwilling to change or give up an idea or attitude despite obstacles. Difficult to control, get rid of, solve, or cure. Not to be confused with *abstinent,* which describes restraint over desires, such as for sex or alcohol.

Arthur was OBSTINATE in his claim that he did not cheat on the exam, so he agreed to a formal review of the case.

obstreperous *(uhb-STREP-er-us), adjective*
Stubborn to the point of defiance; intentionally difficult to handle; noisy and aggressive

The teenagers were OBSTREPEROUS when they were together but once their teacher separated them, each one settled down.

obtrude *(ub-TROOD), verb*
To intrude or become noticeable in an unpleasant, unwelcome way; to force upon

The roommates' lifestyles threatened to OBTRUDE upon each other until the young women came up with an arrangement that respected everyone's rights and feelings.

obtrusive *(ob-TROO-suhv), adjective*
Tending to force one's presence or opinions on others. Highly noticeable, often with a bad or unwelcome effect.

James's Uncle Herbert was quite OBTRUSIVE, and, frankly, unwelcome at almost all family events.

obtuse *(ob-TOOS), adjective*
Slow in understanding or perceiving something; with poor powers of intellect or perceptions. In mathematics, describes an angle of greater than 90 degrees and less than 180 degrees. A word that could be used as a fancy description of a few of your friends, no doubt.

Bob was called OBTUSE for not quite understanding the basics of algebra, but many others find this form of mathematics challenging as well.

obviate *(AHB-vee-ayt), verb*
To get rid of, eliminate, or make unnecessary; to do away with a need or necessity; or to prevent from occurring; to forestall

He soon discovered working at the daycare OBVIATED his need for extra time in the gym.

Seatbelts can OBVIATE serious injury in the case of a car accident.

It was hoped that constant review of emergency procedures would OBVIATE any need for evacuation at the nuclear plant.

occlude *(uh-KLOOD), verb*
To obscure or block the path of; or to stop up, close, or make unpassable

She bought the tickets to see her favorite band even though the sight line was OCCLUDED.

Once the doctors realized the patient's arteries were OCCLUDED, a proper course of treatment could begin.

occultation *(ahk-uhl-TAY-shin), noun*
The act of hiding or blocking from view.

With disguises offering a bit of needed OCCULTATION, we were able to hit Manhattan's hot spots away from the glare of the dreaded paparazzi.

OCD *(OH-see-dee), acronym*
Acronym for "obsessive-compulsive disorder": a psychological condition characterized by uncontrolled repeated behaviors, such as hand-washing.

Her friends thought she was exhibiting the telltale signs of OCD, but Elaine just thought it appropriate to check her makeup regularly.

odal *(OH-dull), noun*
Absolute ownership of a property that is beyond dispute and can never be revoked.
Among the Norse, land allotted to a warrior at the time of conquest became ODAL after his family had held it for three generations.

odious *(OH-dee-us), adjective*
Disgusting, repellant, reprehensible; causing extreme dislike or displeasure
She was shocked that in spite of the ODIOUS way her brother treated women, he always seemed to have a girlfriend.

Know This Quote
"To depend upon a profession is a less ODIOUS form of slavery than to depend upon a father."
—Virginia Woolf, British essayist and novelist

odium *(OH-dee-yum), noun*
Contempt and disgust for a person, concept, or idea, often widespread and commonly felt
The ODIUM felt for telemarketers makes it that much more difficult for them to perform their jobs well.

odoriferous *(oh-duh-RIH-fuh-russ), adjective*
Having or diffusing a strong odor. Can also refer to actions that are immoral or offensive. Hey, it beats saying "you stink."
While few agreed on whether it was in a good or bad way, everyone thought the candle shop quite ODORIFEROUS.

odyssey *(AH-duh-see), noun*
A long journey; a series of travels, adventures, or dangerous travails. Derives from Homer's epic poem, the *Odyssey*, which describes such a grand journey undertaken by the character Odysseus.
High school for almost all students is an ODYSSEY from childhood to young adulthood, full of many unexpected challenges.

oeniphile *(EE-nuh-file), noun*
A connoisseur of wines.
Despite his relatively young age, Brad's family has brought him up to be a consummate OENIPHILE.

oeuvre *(OO-vruh), noun*
An artist's, writer's, or composer's body of work, treated as a whole.
Esmerelda is familiar with and adores all of Puccini's OEUVRE, but many find his operas overly mawkish.

officiate *(uh-FIH-shee-ate), verb*
To preside in an official capacity, especially at a particular ceremony.
It was agreed that Judge Jerome would OFFICIATE at the wedding.

officious *(oh-FISH-us), adjective*
Overly eager to offer advice or assistance, to the point of being annoying; intrusively helpful, especially regarding trivial matters
She cringed when she realized the person assigned to her department was the man everyone considered an OFFICIOUS know-it-all.

Know This Quote
"There is immunity in reading, immunity in formal society, in office routine, in the company of old friends and in the giving of OFFICIOUS help to strangers, but there is no sanctuary in one bed from the memory of another."
—Cyril Connolly, British literary critic and writer

ogle *(OH-guhl), verb*
To look at in an amorous or impertinent way.
No one would want to trade places with us if they only knew how tiresome it becomes to have the paparazzi constantly OGLING you.

old-school *(OHLD skool), adjective*
Adhering to traditional or old-fashioned values and practices. Yes, it's a movie title as well.
Stephen's parents were considered OLD-SCHOOL because they insisted on his having a midnight curfew.

olfaction *(ahl-FAK-shun), noun*
The sense of smell. The action of smelling something.
The lacrosse coaches sometimes dreamed of temporarily suspending their OLFACTION, particularly in the locker room after games.

olfactory *(ole-FAK-tore-ee), adjective*
Related to the sense of smell.
Miranda and Jonathan savored the OLFACTORY pleasures wafting from early-opening bakeries on the Upper West Side.

oligarchy *(AH-luh-gar-kee), noun*
A small group that governs a nation, or controls an organization. Government by a few, especially by a small faction of persons or families. Depending on the kind of high school you attend, the oligarchy might be composed of beautiful people, jocks, or super brains.
Historically, those who were displeased with an aristocracy have called it OLIGARCHY, and fought for democracy.

oligopoly *(oh-lih-GAH-poll-lee), noun*
Control of an industry, sector, or market by a small number of companies dominating that particular niche.

One can argue that Intel and Microsoft collectively are an OLIGOPOLY in personal computing.

Olympian *(oh-LIHM-pee-un), adjective*
Extraordinarily great or demanding, befitting an Olympic athlete. Superior or grand, above everyday events, concerns, or abilities. Related to ancient Olympia or Mount Olympus.

Many thought Betsy's getting to medical school an OLYMPIAN feat, but her friends knew she would do it easily.

ombudsman *(ohm-BUDZ-min), noun*
A person who is charged with mediating disputes between businesses and consumers, students and a university, etc.

All it took to get Brock off of academic probation at U Penn was to have his father remind the OMBUDSMAN of how much money the family had donated to the university over the years.

ominous *(AH-mih-nus), adjective*
Hinting at something evil or dangerous; presenting a feeling of foreboding; eerie

The tree-lined shortcut was perfectly safe during the day but always felt OMINOUS after dark.

omnipotent *(ahm-NIH-puh-tent), adjective*
Possessing complete, universal, unlimited power and authority. All-powerful; often used in reference to a deity.

The framers of the United States Constitution sought to avoid making any branch of government OMNIPOTENT, so they created a system of checks and balances between the executive, legislative, and judicial branches.

omniscient *(ahm-NIH-shent), adjective*
Describes someone who knows everything.

Tom thought he was OMNISCIENT, but Mary strongly disagreed.

Know This Quote

"The god of love, if omnipotent and OMNISCIENT, must be the god of cancer and epilepsy as well." —George Bernard Shaw, Irish playwright

omnivore *(AHM-nih-vore), noun*
An animal that feeds on any or many different foods, including plants and animals. Someone who has wide interests, who will read, study, absorb, or devour anything available. From the Latin for "eating everything." A related word is *voracious,* meaning desiring or consuming food in great quantities, or eager about a particular activity.

Most humans are by nature OMNIVORES, but some choose to be herbivorous vegetarians instead.

onerous *(AH-nuh-rus), adjective*
Burdensome; a lot of trouble. Describes a situation or agreement in which the cons could easily outweigh the pros. Something with heavy obligation.

Although she loved her dog, Elizabeth thought that cleaning up the back yard after him was an ONEROUS task.

online *(ohn-LYNE), adjective*
Accessible over the Internet. Can describe resources, such as bank accounts, or activities, such as participation in chat rooms or games. Attached to or available through a central computer or computer network. Used to describe an electronic device or sensor that is connected directly to something being measured.

ONLINE applications for admissions to college are becoming more prevalent than those completed on paper.

onomatopoeia *(on-uh-mot-uh-PEE-uh), noun*
The naming of a thing by creating a vocal imitation of its sound. Examples are *hiss, buzz, whack*, and *splat*. One of the most fun words to know, use, and spell. How long is the list of onomatopoeic words you know?

Comic books, which are filled with ONOMATOPOEIA, are thought to be the origin of many words of this kind.

onslaught *(ON-slot), noun*
A powerful attack that overwhelms someone or something. A large quantity of people or things that is difficult to deal with or process.

The ONSLAUGHT of online concert-ticket requests temporarily crashed the computerized ticket sale system.

onus *(OH-nus), noun*
A difficult responsibility or duty; obligation; burden of proof

The ONUS was on the teacher to prove the two students had cheated on their exams.

opaque *(oh-PAKE), adjective*
Impenetrable to light, so images cannot be seen through it. Dull and without luster. Obscure and unintelligible in meaning.

People who live in glass houses should not throw stones, and they should also dress behind OPAQUE curtains.

Know This Quote
"The bottom of being is left logically OPAQUE to us, as something which we simply come upon and find, and about which (if we wish to act) we should pause and wonder as little as possible." —William James, American psychologist and philosopher

operatic *(ah-puh-RA-tik), adjective*
Belonging or related to the opera. Overly flamboyant or extravagant in behavior or appearance. Think "diva."

Some of the students in Cathy's high school seemed rather OPERATIC to their parents and teachers, and it wasn't a school for the performing arts.

operose *(OP-uh-roass), adjective*
Hard-working and industrious.

What's the point of being OPEROSE when our social connections help us to achieve success with little effort?

opine *(oh-PYNE), verb*
To give your opinion.

The way that Charlotte OPINES about fashion, you'd think she created couture rather than just purchasing it.

opportunist *(opp-er-TOON-ist), noun*
A person who takes advantage of a situation to achieve his or her own goals, regardless of the consequences

She was accused of being an OPPORTUNIST when she applied for the position before the vacancy was even made public.

opprobrium *(uh-PROH-bree-um), noun*
Harsh and scornful criticism; extreme disapproval; or disgrace and shame created by acting in a particularly dishonorable way, usually a public disgrace

Her bigoted and close-minded statements were met with OPPROBRIUM from every organization in the school.

The scandal caused him such OPPROBRIUM that the senator chose to resign from Congress and retire from public life.

optics *(AHP-ticks), noun*
The study of light and electromagnetic reactions in the visible, infrared, and ultraviolet realms.

OPTICS has yielded inventions of common simplicity and good, like grocery store scanners, and some quite dangerous and powerful, like laser-guided missiles.

optimal *(OP-tih-mul), adjective*
Most desirable, best, favored, or best possible. While everybody likes different kinds of ice cream, most of us consider it optimal to have plenty of it in the freezer.

OPTIMAL game-time conditions would be sunny, but not hot, with little or no wind.

optimize *(AHP-tuh-mize), verb*
To make something function as effectively as possible, or to use something at its best advantage. To find the best solution to a technical problem from a number of conflicting options.

It took hours, but the mechanic eventually was able to OPTIMIZE the car's gas consumption by regulating the carburetor.

opulent *(AHP-yoo-lent), adjective*
Showing a lavish display of wealth or affluence; extravagant. Abundant in supply. Oprah is famous for her opulent gifts.

The OPULENT lifestyles of musical performers and professional athletes are revealed in many television shows.

opus *(OH-puss), noun*
A major work of music written by a composer.

The Breckinridges commissioned the composer's next OPUS, which will be debuted at the family's fall ball.

orator *(OR-ay-tor), noun*
A skilled public speaker; one who makes speeches

The candidate was an eloquent and charismatic ORATOR who could impress even his staunchest critics.

oratory *(ORE-uh-tor-ee), noun*
The art of speaking in public with style, knowledge, and grace. Eloquence in public speaking. It can also mean a pompous, boring, or inappropriately long speech.

Martin Luther King, Jr.'s ORATORY lives well into the present day.

ordinance *(OR-dih-nance), noun*
A specific law or regulation.

The lavish tree house Roger built for his kids was in clear violation of at least half a dozen local ORDINANCES.

orgiastic *(or-jee-AS-tick), adjective*
Arousing unrestrained emotional release.

William becomes loathsomely ORGIASTIC when he attends and bids at art auctions.

orientation *(OH-ree-yun-TAY-shun), noun*
Positioning of something, or the direction something is heading. Direction in which someone's interests or tendencies lie. Process of becoming accustomed to a new situation or surroundings, or a meeting to do so.

It was the goal of almost everyone to be named as an advisor at the freshmen ORIENTATION, for it was an honor and a lot of fun.

ornate *(or-NAYT), adjective*
Highly decorated; showy, flashy, and intricate; heavily ornamented; or flowery and complex, referring to writing style

The ORNATE picture frame displayed in the window looked out of place in the run-down junk shop.

Freshmen often try to impress their professors with an ORNATE writing style but the smart students learn that this usually has the opposite effect.

ornithology *(ore-nuh-THAH-luh-jee), noun*
The branch of zoology that deals with the scientific study of birds.

Few realize that Charles Darwin was well respected for his work in ORNITHOLOGY, in particular his detailed study of finches.

orotund *(OR-uh-tund), adjective*
Characterizes a voice distinguished by strength, fullness, and clearness.

In a beguilingly OROTUND voice, the conductor offered a synopsis of the evening's opera.

orthodox *(OR-thuh-docks), adjective*
Mainstream; conventional; adhering to the strictest interpretation of a law or religion.

ORTHODOX medicine has long ignored the obvious effect diet and nutrition have on health and illness.

orthography *(ore-THAH-gruh-fee), noun*
Writing according to the standard usage of a given language, using appropriate letters and symbols. The use of letters and symbols to represent the sounds of a language. The study of letters and spelling.

The ORTHOGRAPHY of Spanish includes the letters rr and ñ, which have sounds different from those common in English.

oscillate *(AHS-uh-layt), verb*
To swing steadily at an uninterrupted pace; to move back and forth at a regular speed; or to be unable to decide between two choices; to waver between separate and often opposing ideas

She bought a fan that OSCILLATED in order to cool more of the overheated room.

Politicians are known to sometimes OSCILLATE on hot-button issues, depending on the politics of the group they are addressing at the time.

Where'd That Word Come From?

Oscillate—This word for swinging back and forth derives from the custom Roman farmers had of hanging little masks representing Bacchus, the god of wine, from their vines. These little masks, called *oscilla,* would sway back and forth in the wind.

osmosis *(oss-MOE-siss), noun*
The movement of a substance through a semipermeable barrier. The gradual, often unconscious, absorption of knowledge or ideas through continual exposure rather than deliberate focused efforts.

Too many high school students think OSMOSIS an appropriate study technique; reading, writing, and rote memorization are still best.

ossify *(AWH-sih-fiy), verb*
To become set in one's ways; to become rigid and unwilling or unable to change; to become unalterable

The man's attitudes had begun to OSSIFY in his fifties so by the time he was old, he wouldn't even listen to other ideas or arguments.

ostensible *(uh-STEN-suh-bul), adjective*
Presented as being true or appearing to be true, but usually hiding a different motive or meaning.

The audience and critics thought the OSTENSIBLE purpose of the performers was to entertain, while the accountants thought it was to make money.

ostensibly *(ah-STEN-sih-blee), adverb*
Something that exists or has been done for what would seem an obvious reason.

The nouveau riche always seek to spend time with us, OSTENSIBLY to be absorbed into our world, but they will never fully be a part of our community.

ostentatious *(oss-ten-TAY-shuss), adjective*
Marked by a vulgar display of wealth, talents, possessions, or success designed to impress people; showy.

You shouldn't take the Rolls to the party; it will be seen as OSTENTATIOUS.

Know This Quote

"The man who is OSTENTATIOUS of his modesty is twin to the statue that wears a fig-leaf."
—Mark Twain

ostracism *(AWHS-trah-sih-zum), noun*
The act of banishing a person or subgroup from a larger group or community

Although she had been right to report the cheating, the OSTRACISM she faced afterward made it very difficult to believe she had acted wisely.

ostracize *(AWHS-trah-sihz), verb*
To banish or exclude, from a group, community, or society

Sadly, many countries around the world still OSTRACIZE people with physical, mental, and emotional disabilities.

Where'd That Word Come From?

Ostracize—It seems that a vote of banishment in ancient Athens had to be in writing. Because paper was scarce, the banishment ballot was written on pieces of tile called *ostrakon,* a name first applied to the shell of the oyster, which the tile resembled. It followed that the act of banishing someone from a group came to be called *ostrakismos.* Eventually, this evolved to "ostracize."

oxidation *(oks-ih-DAY-shin), noun*
A chemical reaction that increases the oxygen content of a compound or material.

When Carlton viewed the wreck of the Titanic *from the window of a submersible, he was shocked to see how OXIDATION had ravaged the ship.*

oxidize *(OKS-uh-dyz), verb*
To react or cause a chemical to react with oxygen. To combine with oxygen; make into an oxide.

When copper begins to OXIDIZE, it takes on what is called a patina, turning to a beautiful green color.

oxymoron *(ok-see-MORE-on), noun*

A phrase made by combining two words that are contradictory or incongruous.

Melissa sheepishly used the OXYMORON "accidentally on purpose" to explain to her father why her emergency credit card included a charge for $500 Manolo Blahnik heels.

ozone layer *(OH-zone LAY-er), noun*

The layer of the upper atmosphere above the earth's service where ozone collects and absorbs harmful ultraviolet radiation from the sun.

Concerns over the depletion of the OZONE LAYER grow annually, yet some still believe them to be unfounded.

P

pacifist *(PAS-ih-fist), noun*
A person who believes that war and violence cannot ever be justified under any circumstance and that all disagreements can and should be settled in a nonviolent way

As a PACIFIST, she often got into debates regarding the necessity of even having a military, let alone going to war.

paean *(PEE-uhn), noun*
A song or other expression of great joy and praise

His writings were practically a PAEAN to fatherhood and the pleasure he took in raising his children.

pagan *(PAY-gun), noun*
A follower of a religion or sect that worships multiple gods. A heathen, or one who has little to no belief in religion, choosing instead to enjoy the pleasures of the flesh.

The Crusades were fought by Christians against those they thought were PAGANS, yet today Islam is among the three major accepted religions.

pageantry *(PA-jun-tree), noun*
Highly colorful, stately, or splendid display or ceremony, often with a historical or traditional theme. Most people enjoy the pageantry of a holiday pageant.

The PAGEANTRY of graduation ceremonies is one of the reasons that they are so emotional for parents.

paginate *(PA-jih-nate), verb*
To number pages of a book or document.

Bill was amazed to see how easily the new word-processing software would automatically PAGINATE.

painstaking *(PAYN-stay-king), adjective*
Involving or showing great care and attention to detail.

The superstitious hockey player's preparation of his skates and stick before every game was PAINSTAKING.

palatable *(puh-LA-tuh-bull), adjective*
Having a good enough taste to be eaten or drunk. Acceptable to someone's sensibilities. Those with discriminating palates find only the finest food and drink palatable.

Very few of the actions of combatants in war would be considered PALATABLE in peacetime.

palate *(PAHL-eht), noun*

The roof of the mouth; or appreciation for; taste or liking

She burned her PALATE as well as her tongue gulping the hot coffee too quickly.

He developed a refined PALATE after months of eating in the finest restaurants in Paris.

Which Word?

Adding a suffix is a simple way to change the part of speech of many words. It seems obvious that pollute and pollution are related words. But it's not always that simple. Although palate and palatial appear to be different forms of the same word, they really are not. Palate (PAHL-eht) is the roof of the mouth or an appreciation for something. Palatial (puh-LAY-shul) means easily compared to a palace.

palatial *(puh-LAY-shul), adjective*

Easily compared to a palace; large and impressive

The realtor knew that the PALATIAL estate would sell quickly.

palaver *(pa-LAH-ver), noun*

A rambling, meandering stream-of-consciousness conversation spoken to prove or make a point.

Don't ask Eileen about collecting art. The result will be twenty minutes of mind-numbing PALAVER.

palimpsest *(PAL-imp-sest), noun*

A parchment manuscript on which the text is written over older, earlier text, much like an oil portrait or landscape painted over another painting.

The newest addition to the Pattersons' rare manuscript collection turned out to be a PALIMPSEST, covering a text nearly one thousand years old.

palindrome *(pal-in-DROHM), noun*

A word or sentence that reads the same forwards as backwards.

At private school, Evelyn learned about PALINDROMES, including, "Madam, I'm Adam."

palliate *(PAHL-ee-ayt), verb*

To make a crime or wrongdoing less severe, serious, or harsh; or to moderate or alleviate, generally fears, concerns, or suspicions; or to remove the symptoms of a disease or an illness without providing a cure

The attorney argued that the defendant's history of abuse and neglect should serve to PALLIATE the crime.

The babysitter tried to PALLIATE the young couple's concerns about going out without the baby for the first time.

Cold medicines effectively PALLIATE most characteristics of a cold so a person can continue to function even while sick.

palliative *(PAL-ya-tev), adjective*

Calming. Capable of soothing anxieties or other intense emotions. Alleviating pain and symptoms without eliminating the cause.

The little girl found her mother's singing of "Twinkle, Twinkle Little Star" PALLIATIVE even during the times when she was most upset.

pallid *(PAL-id), adjective*

A wan, sickly, washed-out appearance indicating illness or weakness, or lack of energy, strength, and vitality.

Many of us maintain a PALLID pallor because we want to make it clear that we do not need to go outdoors unless we so choose.

palmistry *(PAHL-muh-stree), noun*

Practice of examining the features of the palm to predict a person's destiny. At street fairs and carnivals, practitioners of palmistry are usually called fortune tellers.

While many doubt the authenticity of PALMISTRY, many others regularly visit those who practice this art.

palpable *(PAL-puh-bul), adjective*

Able to be felt, touched, or seen by humans; tangible; or so intense, it can practically be felt, touched, or seen; or obvious, plain, clearly seen

When the baby first kicked, the young parents were thrilled to have PALPABLE evidence of its health and well-being.

The love between her grandparents was PALPABLE to anyone who spent more than five minutes in their presence.

Although the scratches were PALPABLE, he couldn't get his head around the fact that someone had vandalized his brand-new car.

palpate *(PAL-pate), verb*

To examine the body with the hands and fingers, especially in a medical context. Not to be confused or misused as *palpitate,* defined next.

Medical students must learn to trust their fingers when they PALPATE patients, and not just depend on sophisticated lab tests for diagnoses.

palpitate *(PAL-puh-tate), verb*
To have the heart beat in an irregular or unusual way, because of a medical condition, exertion, fear, or anxiety.

> *Those who have been in life-and-death situations say that they heard their hearts PALPITATE and actually tasted fear.*

paltry *(PAWL-tree), adjective*
Insignificant or unimportant. Low and contemptible. Often applied to ridiculously small amounts of money or lowly people.

> *Some high school students think minimum wage is a PALTRY sum to be paid for an hour's work.*

panacea *(pan-ah-SEE-ah), noun*
A cure or remedy for every ailment or discomfort

> *In his grandmother's opinion, a strong cup of tea was the PANACEA, regardless of the problem.*

pandemic *(pan-DEM-ik), adjective*
Widespread. Something general, common, or all-encompassing, specifically an epidemic that affects people in many different regions or countries. The antonym of *endemic,* which is something occurring in a specific area or locale.

> *During times of crisis, fear is PANDEMIC and often the cause of more harm than good.*

pandemonium *(pan-duh-MOA-nee-um), noun*
Wild uproar, chaos, or tumult. A place or situation that is noisy, boisterous, and chaotic. The perfect description of almost any high school sleepover, at least those that are any fun.

> *The celebration after the Giants won the Super Bowl could only be described as PANDEMONIUM.*

Where'd That Word Come From?

Pandemonium—English poet John Milton gave us this word for wild lawlessness, tumult, or chaos when he named the capital of hell "Pandaemonium" in his epic poem, *Paradise Lost.* He coined the word from the Greek for "all demons."

pander *(PAN-der), verb*
To indulge someone's weaknesses or questionable wishes or tastes. To appeal to the worst in someone. To serve as a pimp. Even if you speak with a Boston accent, it should not be confused with *panda,* that black-and-white bear indigenous to China.

The director refused to PANDER to the wishes of some of his greedy advisors, and he left the film PG so that children could see it.

Pandora's box *(PAN-door-uhs bocks), noun*
In Greek mythology, a box that Pandora unwittingly opened that released all kinds of evil and hardship into the world. In common usage, a powerful source of potential problems.

Teens are warned that starting to use drugs is like opening PANDORA'S BOX, with consequences difficult to reverse.

panegyric *(pan-ih-JIHR-ik) or (pan-ih-JIY-rik), noun or adjective*
A formal statement of praise, usually made in the form of a public speech or a published work (noun) or praising; highly complimentary (adjective)

The actor took out a full page ad as a PANEGYRIC about how he had enjoyed working with his costar on their latest movie.

The PANEGYRIC nature of the dean's introduction of her son made the woman swell with pride and happiness.

Pangaea *(pan-GEE-uh), noun*
A single massive continent that comprised all the land on the Earth before the crust shifted and the *Pangaea* divided into many smaller continents.

The PANGAEA existed until Mesozoic times, when it divided into two separate continents.

panoply *(PAN-ah-plee), noun*
A large, sometimes complete, impressive display or collection; or complete ceremonial attire; or a protective covering

The opening ceremony of the Olympics creates the magnificent PANOPLY of colors and sounds as the nations of the world gather to celebrate and compete.

The prince rarely appeared in full PANOPLY, preferring instead to wear a plain black, pinstripe suit to most functions.

The spiky PANOPLY of a cactus makes an inconvenient source of food or water for desert animals.

panorama *(pa-noh-RAH-mah), noun*
An unobstructed view that extends in all directions. An all-encompassing survey of a particular topic, site, or issue. A wide-view photograph.

The Hendersons purchased the house on the hill because of the PANORAMA that could be seen from the glass-enclosed den.

pantheon *(PAN-thee-on), noun*
The group of all the gods of a particular religion or culture, or a group of important people in a particular field or region.

The sons of Odin, Thor and Loki, represent good and evil in the PANTHEON of the Norse gods.

papal *(PAY-pull), adjective*
Related to or pertaining to the pope or the papacy.

The PAPAL visit to New York City was a dream come true for millions of Catholics throughout the northeastern United States.

paparazzo *(pah-puh-RAHT-so), noun*
A freelance photographer who follows famous people hoping to get a newsworthy photograph, story, or something shocking or scandalous. The plural is paparazzi.

Jim's family was a bit surprised that he chose to become a PAPARAZZO, because his sister was a movie star who constantly sought to avoid photographers of this kind.

papier mâché *(PAY-purr muh-SHAY), noun*
Sheets of paper stiffened with glue or starch and molded into small objects including masks, bowls, and figures, as well as large objectives including floats.

The PAPIER MÂCHÉ piñata was filled with candy and was the hit of the birthday party.

paradigm *(PARE-uh-dime), noun*
A clear example that illustrates how something should work; an ideal instance, or a pattern worthy of study. In science, a generally accepted model of how ideas relate to one another, forming a framework with which research is conducted.

Kennedy's handling of the Cuban Missile Crisis is a PARADIGM for presidents who have to address challenges with courage, intelligence, and conviction.

paradox *(PAR-uh-doks), noun*
A statement, possibly true, that seems absurd or self-contradictory. A person or thing with contradictory qualities that are difficult to justify. Not to be confused with a "pair of ducks," unless you are the Marx Brothers.

Parents often face the PARADOX that punishment may be the kindest act of all.

paragon *(PARE-uh-gone), noun*
The very best example of something; a peerless model or pattern of perfection. Also, a perfect diamond or large pearl that is perfectly round.

Michael Jordan seemed a PARAGON among athletes, combining skill in basketball and competitive fire.

paralegal *(pair-uh-LEE-gul), noun*
Someone who assists and supports attorneys with their research and preparatory efforts. The Greek root *para-* means "beside," which means paralegals and lawyers work side by side.

The role of PARALEGAL is not given as much credit as it deserves, for attorneys are more prestigious.

parameter *(puh-RA-muh-tur), noun*
Limit or boundary. Some physical property, such as size or color, that determines a thing's behavior. Not to be confused with *perimeter,* which means a boundary enclosing an area.

In the military, there are very clear PARAMETERS for acceptable behavior and etiquette.

paranormal *(PAR-uh-NOR-mul), adjective*
Beyond the realm of things that can be explained by scientific knowledge. Having to do with the occult, magic, or supernatural.

It's hard for some to accept that PARANORMAL phenomena do exist, and that all claims of poltergeists are not fake.

parenthetical *(pair-un-THEH-tuh-cul), noun*
An explanation added to text as a commentary, usually set off by punctuation such as parentheses. A remark that departs from the sense of a passage.

Sometimes PARENTHETICAL additions to writing are significant, and others are just afterthoughts.

pariah *(puh-RIY-ah), noun*
A social outcast; one who is completely rejected from a community or a society at large

Many whistleblowers discover they have suddenly become PARIAHS in the same cities and towns where they were once well-respected members of the community.

parity *(PAH-rih-tee), noun*
The condition of everyone being more or less equal.

The firemen received a raise to help them achieve pay PARITY with the sanitation workers and police department.

parlance *(PAR-lunce), noun*
A particular style of speech or writing, especially that used by persons in a specific context or profession. A way of speech, especially daily conversations, that is familiar to speakers who share common characteristics.

The special PARLANCE of doctors is one that laypersons find difficult to understand.

parody *(PAR-oh-dee), noun*
A humorous or satirical take-off on something well known, such as a person or song. A literary or musical style or type. A poor attempt or imitation that appears ridiculous.

The Saturday Night Live PARODY of the evening news has been a very popular segment of the show since its inception.

paroxysm *(PAHR-oks-izm), noun*
A sudden and unexpected display of emotion; or an unexpected convulsion, generally related to a disease or illness

His story was so funny that his friends were all in the grip of PAROXYSMS of laughter by the end of it.

The PAROXYSM was brought on when the doctors could not lower the child's fever.

parsimonious *(par-sih-MOAN-ee-us), adjective*
To be conservative in spending and tight with a dollar; to agree to part with money or other resources only grudgingly and after much cajoling.

Esmerelda can be surprisingly PARSIMONIOUS, considering that her family's fortune is among the greatest possessed by our social contacts.

parsimony *(PAR-suh-moh-nee), noun*
Great frugality, stinginess, or unwillingness to spend money. The state of being exceptionally frugal or thrifty. *Parsimony* is the ability to keep your pennies in your pocket; never parting with or parceling money.

Mr. Bench was, to all who knew him, the personification of PARSIMONY, stingy and frugal to the extreme.

partiality *(par-shee-A-luh-tee), noun*
A liking for something or someone. An unfair preference for one person or thing over another.

High school students often accuse certain teachers of PARTIALITY, when, in truth, these educators try to be impartial.

partisan *(PAHR-tih-zen), noun or adjective*
An avid and devout follower of a group, cause, or political party (noun) or devoted to a particular cause to the point of being biased against anything else (adjective)

The PARTISANS following the general were willing to risk their lives to bring him to power.

His PARTISAN devotion to human rights and heartfelt speeches made him a leader many oppressed people could believe in and follow.

passé *(pah-SAY), adjective*
Out of date or no longer fashionable. No longer in prime condition.

It was once thought that bell-bottoms were PASSÉ, but fashion trends do return when least expected.

pastoral *(PAS-tur-ul), adjective*
Relating to rural or country living; having to do with keeping sheep or cattle. Relating to religious ministers or priests and their duties, or to the duties of a teacher. Pastoral scenes are often set in pastures.

The PASTORAL settings portrayed in the oil painting made them very popular among urban art buyers.

patent *(PA-tunt), noun*
Exclusive right to make or sell an invention. Official document setting out terms of a patent. Any official document that grants a right to someone. A government grant that gives someone title to public lands.

Some who have PATENTS are millionaires, while others are just proud that they invented something.

pathological *(pa-thuh-LAH-jih-kul), adjective*
Uncontrolled or unreasonable. Related to disease or arising from diseases. Related to pathology.

It seemed as if her lying was PATHOLOGICAL, and it was impossible for her to tell the truth.

pathos *(PAY-thohs) or (PAY-thuhs), noun*
A certain quality or experience that invokes or creates feelings of pity and sympathy, often used to describe a reaction to artwork; or the pity and sympathy created by such art

No one in the audience was immune to the PATHOS of the ballet's death scene as the beautiful swan danced her last dance and died.

His PATHOS at the sight of the painting soon turned to amusement when he discovered it hadn't been drawn by one of the masters but by a seven-year-old girl.

patrilineage *(pa-truh-LIH-nee-yuj), noun*
Descent traced through the male line. A group of people who are related to each other on the father's side of the family.

It is interesting to trace the PATRILINEAGE of one's family, seeing who was on your father's side.

patrimony *(PAT-rih-mo-nee), noun*
An inheritance from a father or male ancestor. The things that one generation inherits from its ancestors. An estate or endowment belonging to the church.

Much to the surprise of the children, who had never met their father, their PATRIMONY came to more than a million dollars.

patronage *(PA-truh-nij), noun*
The support, often financial, given by a patron, often to an artist or someone else struggling to express or invent something new. Support or kindness offered in a condescending way. The regular purchasing of goods from a business or store. Political power to grant privileges or appointments to positions.

To encourage the PATRONAGE of young shoppers, Abercrombie and Fitch was known to hire very attractive salespersons.

patronize *(PA-truh-nize), verb*
To act as someone's patron. Also, to be haughty and condescending to people perceived as less important or intelligent. To be a regular customer at a business or store.

Those who PATRONIZE others often don't have confidence in their own intellectual abilities, so they put others down.

paucity *(PAW-si-tee), noun*
An inadequacy, shortage, or lack of something. Small number of something. If you have a lot of pets in your house, you have no paucity of paws.

We were forced to head back down the mountain due to a PAUCITY of supplies.

Know This Quote
"It is very strange, and very melancholy, that the PAUCITY of human pleasures should persuade us ever to call hunting one of them." —Samuel Johnson, British moralist and poet

peccadillo *(pek-uh-DIL-oh), noun*
A small, virtually insignificant error; a petty misdeed or sin

An action that for a common man would be considered a PECCADILLO can become a scandal when performed by a world leader.

peculiarity *(pih-kyool-YAIR-uh-tee), noun*
A characteristic or trait belonging distinctively to a particular person, place, or thing. The quality of being unusual or strange.

> *George's need to whistle was thought the only PECULIARITY this well-respected man ever demonstrated.*

pecuniary *(pih-KYOO-nee-air-ee), noun*
Relating to or pertaining to money. Involving a financial penalty, such as a fine or fee. That which consists of or concerns money is pecuniary.

> *PECUNIARY matters are rarely discussed by well-mannered families in public.*

Where'd That Word Come From?

Pecuniary—*Pecu* is Latin for "cattle." Cattle were once a common means of barter, so an estate's value was measured by its number of cattle. This led to the Latin word *pecunia,* for "money or property." *Pecunia* gave birth to numerous English words, such as *pecuniary,* "relating to, involving, or pertaining to money"; *impecunious,* "without money"; *peculate,* "to embezzle"; and *peculiar,* "pertaining to that which is one's own."

pedagogy *(ped-ih-GAH-gee) or (ped-ih-GOH-gee), noun*
The method and principles of teaching, especially subjects requiring intellectual thought as opposed to straight facts or rote learning; or the teaching profession, especially at postsecondary levels

> *She grasped philosophy so quickly that her professors were shocked that these were her first experiences with philosophical PEDAGOGY.*
>
> *Although he had never expected to go into PEDAGOGY, teaching at the seminary was a logical progression in his career.*

pedantic *(ped-DAN-tik), adjective*
Characterized by a narrow, somewhat petty, attention to facts and book learning; focused only on the trivial facts of a certain topic; marked by a tiresome need to prove book smarts about a topic

> *The lecturer's PEDANTIC style bored those in the field and simply confused those who weren't in the field.*

pedantry *(PEh-dan-tree), noun*
An obsessive behavior of being proper and technically correct down to the last detail.

> *Samuel Taylor Coleridge defined PEDANTRY as "the use of words unsuitable to the time, place, and company."*

pedestrian *(puh-DES-tree-uhn), adjective*
Something ordinary, unimaginative, or uninspired. Pedestrian people are not necessarily pedestrians.

The worst comment someone can make about an author's work is that it is PEDESTRIAN.

peerless *(PEER-luss), adjective*
Incomparable, matchless, without equal; literally "without a peer."

For old-timers, Babe Ruth was the Sultan of Swat, but for younger fans Barry Bonds is PEERLESS in his ability to hit home runs.

peevish *(PEA-vish), adjective*
Bad-tempered, irritable, or tending to complain; irritated by a peeve, or annoyance.

Some parents think that all teenagers are PEEVISH before 9 A.M. on weekdays and twelve noon on weekends.

pejorative *(pih-JORE-uh-tiv), adjective*
Critical or disapproving; disparaging. A word or phrase that defames.

It is sometimes difficult to distinguish between a sarcastic and a PEJORATIVE remark, but both can hurt one's feelings.

pellucid *(peh-LOO-sid), adjective*
Clear, see-through, admitting light; able to look through; or easy to understand; clearly stated; plain and obvious

The PELLUCID waters surrounding the island revealed a host of sea life not common in lakes or rivers.

The author's PELLUCID style won her critical praise but the public found her work to be sparse and cold.

penchant *(PEN-chuhnt), noun*
A strong liking; an intense but healthy interest in a subject matter; a tendency to participate in a specific event with gusto and enjoyment

In spite of his academic, slightly nerdy appearance, he had a strong PENCHANT for sports, following his favorite teams closely every season.

penitence *(PEH-nuh-tents), noun*
Regret or sorrow for having committed sins, misdeeds, or wrongdoing.

The time he spent working with youth groups reflected his PENITENCE for the indiscretions of his youth.

penitent *(PEN-ih-tent), adjective*
Feeling sorry and regretful that you have done something wrong.

According to Ambrose Bierce's jaded view, the PENITENT are typically those undergoing or awaiting punishment.

penultimate *(pih-NUL-tuh-mut), adjective*
Second to last. Not to be confused with *ultimate,* meaning very last.

The PENULTIMATE player chosen in the National Football League draft is truly most anonymous, for ironically the last one picked becomes "Mr. Irrelevant," and the subject of much attention.

penurious *(PEH-nyoo-ree-us) or (PEH-noo-ree-us), adjective*
Very poor, bordering on destitute; unable to pay for common necessities; or unwilling to spend money for indulgences; stingy; or barren or unfertile; not productive; can be used literally to describe land or figuratively to describe a mindset

In spite of America's overall wealth, there are still many PENURIOUS communities where whole neighborhoods and towns struggle simply to survive.

Her PENURIOUS ways had made her very wealthy but she had little to show for it besides a large bank account.

His PENURIOUS thought process was not up to the challenge of coming up with creative ways to solve the company's financial woes.

penury *(PEN-yeh-ree), noun*
Destitution; extreme poverty; financial want; or barrenness; having no resources or ability; infertile

Few tourists to resort islands ever see the PENURY in which most locals live their day-to-day lives.

In spite of the farmer's best efforts, the PENURY of the fields would simply not produce the crops he had hoped for.

per capita *(per KA-pih-tah), adjective*
Per person; pertaining to a single individual.

We find it satisfying to mull over the fact that the PER CAPITA income among our social contacts is greater than that of many countries.

perceptive *(PURR-sep-tuhv), adjective*
Quick to understand or discern things; showing an understanding of a person or situation. Related to perception or the capability of perceiving.

As the older sister of three siblings, Stephanie was very PERCEPTIVE of the needs of younger children, and she made a great babysitter.

percussive *(PURR-cuss-sihv), adjective*
Having the effect of an impact or blow. An instrument that requires beating to make music; a drum, cymbal, or triangle. A long drum solo has a percussive effect upon the eardrums and on the brain as well.

The PERCUSSIVE power of Justin's cross-check on the opposing player could actually be heard in the stands.

peregrination *(pehr-uh-gruh-NAY-shun), noun*
A trip taken by foot; a traveling or wandering, usually by foot

Instead of a whirlwind tour of Europe, the friends decided on a slower but more in-depth PEREGRINATION of the French countryside.

peremptory *(peh-REMP-toh-ree), adjective*
Refusing to allow debate, conversation, or refusal; requiring immediate attention and action without question; or urgent; characterized by being a command, not a request; or offensively arrogant and self-assured; bossy; self-important

Even more than his rank, the drill sergeant's PEREMPTORY tone and attitude made the new recruits fall in line.

Their boss was so laid-back that on the rare occasions she used a PEREMPTORY tone, no one even considered arguing with her.

His PEREMPTORY attitude had put off so many people that none of his coworkers felt sorry for him when he was publicly chastised for losing the account.

perennial *(per-EHN-ee-uhl), adjective or noun*
Lasting for a long period of time, perhaps even indefinitely; rejuvenating or reoccurring (adjective) or a plant that grows three or more seasons; or anything that reoccurs year after year (noun)

Eating properly and exercising are two known keys to PERENNIAL health and longevity.

She didn't have much time to garden so she planted PERENNIALS, knowing they would bloom year after year.

The Thanksgiving Day Parade is a trusted PERENNIAL and, for many families, signifies the start of the holiday season.

perfectionist *(PURR-fec-shuh-nist), noun*
Someone who is unaccepting of any fault, especially in his or her own actions.

Julie thought her teacher was a PERFECTIONIST, so she worked even harder on her essay.

perfervid *(per-FUR-vid), adjective*
Overly intense and passionate; overblown and dramatic.

We laughed at the distastefully PERFERVID love letters that Roland sent to Germaine.

perfidy *(PUR-fih-dee), noun*
Treason or treachery; a deliberate and intentional breach of trust; an act of betrayal

As Benedict Arnold learned, one act of PERFIDY is enough to erase years of loyalty and devotion to a cause.

perfunctory *(per-FUNK-tuh-ree), adjective*
Managed or handled without care or particular thought; done because it has to be done, not because it is cared about; phoned in; done with indifference

The bored clerk gave a PERFUNCTORY glance at the paperwork before automatically forwarding it on to the next department.

Know This Quote

"The tale is so contrived and PERFUNCTORY that many readers will be tempted to skip to the real story in the second half of the book." —Tim Parks, British novelist

periodic table *(peer-ee-AH-dick TAY-bull), noun*
The table that shows all known elements arranged according to their atomic numbers.

Many chemistry students are asked to memorize the PERIODIC TABLE.

peripatetic *(pehr-ih-peh-TET-ik), adjective*
Moving about; changing locations frequently; staying in place for short periods of time; traveling, traditionally by foot but common usage is more generalized

Growing up in a military family, his childhood was PERIPATETIC so he was often the new kid on the block.

peripheral *(peh-RIF-er-uhl), adjective*
On the edge; regarding the outer limits or boundaries; or being a secondary or less important concern; of less importance; not the main focus

The PERIPHERAL suburbs of the city were popular because rents were much lower but downtown was still easily accessible.

Many parents encourage their children to focus on grades and attendance instead of worrying about PERIPHERAL concerns while they are still in school.

periphery *(puh-RIFF-uh-ree), noun*
The outermost part or boundary; the outside edge.

Craig's plans are always on the PERIPHERY of what could charitably be called normal behavior.

permafrost *(PURR-muh-frost), noun*
Underlying soil or rock that is permanently frozen, found mainly in polar regions.

Digging a foundation during winter months in New Hampshire was like trying to hack through PERMAFROST.

permeate *(PER-mee-ayt), verb*
To fill a space; to spread throughout; to flow or pass through

The excitement leading up to graduation had PERMEATED the whole school, so that even the teachers seemed happier and more enthusiastic.

pernicious *(pur-NIH-shus), adjective*
Harmful in a slow, subtle way; dangerous and sly at the same time; causing damage in a slow, constant way; or deadly; highly destructive

The PERNICIOUS rumors about her, though false, managed to undermine her chances for promotion.

The doctors prescribed an aggressive course of treatment to counteract the PERNICIOUS disease.

perpetuate *(per-PEHT-yoo-ayt), verb*
To prolong or cause to continue; to keep something going, usually an attitude or belief

Glamour and fashion magazines risk PERPETUATING an ideal of feminine beauty that very few real women can ever hope to achieve.

perquisite *(PER-kwih-zit), noun*
A bonus that comes on top of the normal benefits of a job, as in a tip. Something considered to be an exclusive right or a consequence of holding a certain title, position, or job.

One of the PERQUISITES of working for a baseball team is being able to get free tickets whenever you want.

persecute *(PURR-suh-kyoot), verb*
To systematically subject a particular person, race, or group to cruel or unfair treatment. To make someone the victim of continual pestering or harassment. Not to be confused with *prosecute,* which means to have someone tried in a court of law for civil or criminal offenses.

Prosecutors may want to, but they are never allowed to PERSECUTE criminals.

persiflage *(PUR-suh-flahgz), noun*
Pleasant, joking chatter; gentle and good-natured teasing; lighthearted mockery; or a lighthearted, easy way of discussing even serious matters

The man was so well-respected that the jokes and stories told at his retirement ceremony never crossed beyond PERSIFLAGE.

The same PERSIFLAGE that made the reporter so good with human interest stories prevented him from ever making anchor and tackling hard-hitting news stories.

perspicacious *(per-spih-KAY-shuss), adjective*
Penetratingly discerning, perceptive, or astute; able to understand easily or discern.

While quite PERSPICACIOUS, Lauren still made too many grammatical errors for her essay to earn an A.

pert *(PURT), adjective*
Bold and lively in a pleasant and amusing way. Jaunty and stylish in design. Small, well-shaped, and pretty.

PERT was the only way to describe members of the women's gymnastics team.

perturb *(purr-TURB), verb*
To disturb, trouble, or worry someone. To create a state of confusion or disorder.

The baby's constant crying PERTURBED the neighbors, but the parents hoped they would understand.

perturbation *(pur-tur-BAY-shun), noun*
Anxiety; the state of being worried or disturbed; uneasiness

The young dancer often wondered if the PERTURBATION caused by auditions was worth the chance to land a Broadway role.

Know This Quote

"O polished PERTURBATION! golden care! / That keep'st the ports of slumber open wide / To many a watchful night."
—William Shakespeare

perusal *(puh-ROOZ-uhl), noun*
This word has two contradictory meanings. It can mean a detailed examination, as of a book or list of facts. It can also mean a casual, leisurely examination, as of items on the sale rack at your favorite department store. Look at the context to determine which meaning is appropriate.

The editor's quick PERUSAL of the manuscript led him to exclaim, "This is going to be a bestseller!"

pervade *(per-VAYD), verb*
To exist throughout; to spread completely

A sense of panic began to PERVADE the freshman dorms as the students got closer and closer to their first set of finals.

pessimism *(PES-ih-mih-zim), noun*
A gloomy mindset; the habit of seeing only the negative aspects of things; an attitude that the worst will always come of every situation

Although her friends tried to be understanding, her constant PESSIMISM made her difficult and depressing to be around for very long.

pestiferous *(pes-TIF-uh-rus), adjective*
Troublesome or annoying; breeding or spreading evil, corruption, or infectious disease.

Mosquitoes are the most PESTIFEROUS of insects, in all definitions of the word.

petrified (*PEHT-trih-fiyd), adjective*
Frightened or scared to the point of being unable to move, function, or think; or to turn an organic matter, such as wood, into a stonelike substance, generally caused by great lengths of time and pressure

Ever since she had been a child, the very thought of, let alone the presence of, spiders had PETRIFIED her.

The stone in her mother's necklace was actually PETRIFIED wood, polished to a high shine.

petroglyph *(PEH-troh-glif), noun*
A prehistoric drawing done on rock. Literally means "rock drawing."

The archeologists were ecstatic to find a PETROGLYPH with animal figures.

petulant *(PEH-choo-lunt), adjective*
Petty, childish, and sullen; demandingly pouty

The spoiled little boy grew up to be a PETULANT man who couldn't take no for an answer and always expected to get his way.

phalanx *(FAY-lanks), noun*
A large division or group of soldiers grouped closely together in an orderly fashion for marching or fighting.

Philip of Macedon armed each man with a long spear so the PHALANX bristled like a porcupine.

Pharisee *(FAH-ree-see), noun*
A person who is self-righteous and hypocritical.

The state Attorney General was a PHARISEE who prosecuted others for the same crimes he was secretly committing himself.

phenom *(FEE-nohm), noun*
An outstanding or unusual person or thing; someone or something phenomenal, remarkable, or impressively good or great. Not to be confused with *phantom,* which is something insubstantial and unreal.

Tiger Woods was recognized as a golf PHENOM when he was very young.

phenomena *(fih-NOM-ih-nah), noun*
Unusual, extraordinary events or happenings; significant and remarkable occurrences; the plural of phenomenon; or any happenings, occurrences, or events that can be recognized by any of the five senses

The strange lights and colors that appeared over the town during the week were PHENOMENA that no scientist could ever truly explain.

After his ear surgery, he was struck by the PHENOMENA of sounds as he heard them for the first time in his life.

Which Word?
Some plurals aren't as simple as adding an s or es to the end of a word. A phenomenon (fih-NOM-ih-non) is one extraordinary event. But two or more extraordinary events are phenomena (fih-NOM-ih-nah). Therefore, a single UFO is a phenomenon. Three sightings of UFOs are phenomena. The first means there is only one, while the second indicates more than one.

philanthropic *(fih-lun-THRAH-pick), noun*
Showing kindness, charitable concern, and generosity toward others; demonstrating benevolence toward mankind. Devoted to helping through charitable giving, bestowing wealth on public institutions or those in need.

The PHILANTHROPIC efforts of alumni donors sometimes go unrecognized, but it is never unappreciated.

philanthropist *(fih-LAN-throh-pist), noun*
A person who donates money, time, and resources to improve the overall welfare of humanity

He became a PHILANTHROPIST after making his first million as a way to give back to the world that had given him so much.

phlegmatic *(fleg-MA-tik), adjective*
Having an even, level temperament; unemotional; calm and difficult to fluster

Her PHLEGMATIC nature made her an excellent police officer because she kept her head no matter what the crisis.

phobic *(FOH-bik), adjective*
Showing or having an intense fear and dislike of something, often to an irrational degree. Affected with or arising out of a phobia.

When he closed his eyes and tensed his body as the elevator reached the highest floor, his PHOBIC nature became apparent.

phoenix *(FEE-niks), noun*
A mythical bird about the size of an eagle, but with brilliantly colored plumage, that dies by fire and then is reborn from the ashes.

One day the PHOENIX appeared in the forests of France, and legend has it that all the other birds become instantly jealous.

phonetic *(fuh-NEH-tik), adjective*
Belonging to or associated with sounds of human speech. Representing sounds of human speech in writing, often with special symbols or special spelling.

PHONETIC spellings are included in each entry in this book, so readers will know how to pronounce the words as they learn them.

photosynthesis *(FOH-toh-SIN-thuh-sys), noun*
The process green plants and other organisms use to convert light into an energy source. Happily for most other life forms, the byproduct of photosynthesis is oxygen, which means plants are responsible for the air we breathe.

When studying high school biology, we learned of the amazing biochemical process that is PHOTOSYNTHESIS.

physiognomy *(fiz-ee-OG-noh-mee), noun*
The facial features, generally used when using the facial features to tell a person's character or ethnic background; or the skill of reading or judging a person by his or her facial features; or the overall features, character, and look of any particular subject, living or nonliving

Subtle differences exist in the PHYSIOGNOMY of the various races and ethnicities found throughout the world.

Skilled in PHYSIOGNOMY after years of listening to students' excuses and rationales, most teachers can tell when someone is lying.

The PHYSIOGNOMY of the American Southwest is usually exactly what tourists hope it will be: warm, wide open, and full of friendly, welcoming people.

piazza *(pee-AH-zah), noun*

A large open square, this Italian word describes a common feature of most Italian cities, where churches and cafes can often be found. A covered passage with arches on one or both sides, usually attached to a building. A veranda or porch attached to a house. Not to be misused or confused with *pizza,* which also has Italian origins.

The Billings family was inspired by a recent trip to Italy, so they built a PIAZZA on the side of their home.

picayune *(pih-KEYE-yoon), adjective*

Of very little importance. Trivial, not worth much. The famous New Orleans newspaper is called the *Times-Picayune*—perhaps a reflection of how party people in that fun-loving city feel about serious events of the day? Or, as you will soon learn, was that the price of the paper?

The bride felt her soon to be mother-in-law's requests for the wedding were PICAYUNE and not worthy of consideration.

Where'd That Word Come From?

Picayune—In early eighteenth-century Louisiana, a French copper coin and the Spanish half-real coin were called picayunes. *Picayune* itself most likely derives from the Spanish *pequeña*, "little," and the coin of little size and value influenced the term *picayune* coming to mean anything small, insignificant, and of little importance.

pictograph *(PIK-toh-graff), noun*

A graphic symbol or picture representing a word or idea. A chart or diagram that uses symbols or pictures to represent values. Petroglyphs are drawn in pictograms.

Thank goodness the PICTOGRAPH for the women's bathroom is universally understood.

pied-a-terre *(Pyed-ah-TARE), noun*

A second home or apartment, usually small, used as a place to stay for short trips to the location in lieu of renting a hotel room.

We were amazed that Alison and her family could survive in a PIED-A-TERRE containing just 2,500 square feet.

piercing *(PEER-sing), adjective, noun*
A sharp, unpleasantly intense quality, often describing sounds that make you want to cover your ears. Also refers to powers of perceptions that are unusually acute.

The scream Susie's mother made when she saw Susie's navel PIERCING was indeed PIERCING.

piety *(PIY-eh-tee), noun*
The state of being religious, faithful, and devout

The priest's PIETY was balanced by his sense of humor and willingness to listen.

Know This Quote
"The path of true PIETY is so plain as to require but little political direction." —George Washington

pilfer *(PIL-fur), verb*
To steal small items of little value, especially on a habitual basis.

Even those teens who PILFER candy from the corner store should be prosecuted to learn right from wrong.

PIN *(PIHN), acronym*
Acronym for "personal identification number," a secret code that gives an individual access to things like bank or computer accounts and other web-based systems. People often refer to their "PIN number," which is rather redundant, if you think about it.

Too many make their PINs easy to guess, so they are not safe from identity theft.

pinnacle *(PIN-uh-kul), noun*
The highest or topmost point, as in a mountain or roller coaster. A natural peak. A pointed ornament on top of a buttress or parapet of a castle.

Robert reached the PINNACLE of his athletic career when he was named All-American after his senior season.

pious *(PIY-us), adjective*
Having extreme religious devotion and faith; marked by a strict moral code, usually based on religious belief; or marked by false faith or hypocritical devotion; falsely devout; or commendable, admirable, and honorable; praiseworthy

The woman's PIOUS nature led her to consider becoming a nun.

His PIOUS anger toward the hate crime managed to insult the people who truly followed the faith.

The man's PIOUS efforts to quit drinking finally paid off when he celebrated his one-year anniversary of not drinking alcohol.

pique *(PEEK), verb or noun*
To make someone feel irritated or put out; to wound someone's pride; or to create, stir up, or arouse; or to pride oneself on (verb) or a feeling of irritation or being put out, caused by a perceived slight or insult (noun)

She unintentionally PIQUED her neighbors when she didn't invite them to her annual Halloween party.
The staff's interest was PIQUED by the arrival of a dozen red roses for the young woman who worked in the mailroom.
He PIQUED himself on his ability to get along with anyone and fit into any crowd.
Her PIQUE at not being elected homecoming queen quickly dissolved when the young man she was interested in asked her to dance.

Know This Quote
"I want to kiss God on His nose and watch Him sneeze / and so do you. / Not out of disrespect. / Out of PIQUE. / Out of a man-to-man thing." —Anne Sexton, American poet and author

pitfall *(PIT-fal), noun*
An unrecognized or hidden source of trouble, difficulty, or danger; or a covered hole in the ground acting as a trap

It was his job to be on the lookout for any PITFALL that could delay the completion of the project.
The tiger ran straight into the PITFALL the hunters had dug when they realized it was on the hunt in the area.

pith *(PIHTH), noun*
The white, spongy lining inside the rind of many citrus fruits; or the soft center of the stem of a plant; or the heart of the matter; the essence or core of a thought, concept, or idea; the important part

Although the flesh of an orange is sweet, many people find the PITH to be a bitter distraction.
The cat had chewed the plants down to their PITH before anyone noticed it was happening.
The PITH of the speech was hidden among flowery language and fawning compliments.

pithy *(PIH-thee), adjective*
Brief yet forceful and to the point, often with a touch of wit.

The PITHY speech of the captain served to inspire the entire team to victory.

pittance *(PIT-tense), noun*
Very small amount of something, especially money, allowance, or salary.

The workers were considering a strike for they believed they were being paid a PITTANCE, much less than they deserved.

pixel *(PIK-sul), noun*
An individual tiny dot of light or color. Together, a number of pixels form the images on a computer, television screen, digital camera, or printed image. Not to be confused with *pixie,* a tiny supernatural creature known for its nasty tricks.

It's simple. The more PIXELS, the better quality the picture.

placate *(PLAY-kate), verb*
To make someone less angry, upset, or hostile, usually by saying or doing something to please. To appease someone, or act in a way to avoid another's anger.

It seemed to be our mom's job to PLACATE the rest of the family whenever we were upset.

plagiarism *(PLAY-juh-rih-zum), noun*
The act of presenting someone else's work or idea as your own. Something copied or someone else's idea presented as your own.

PLAGIARISM is the most egregious of all academic offenses.

plaintiff *(PLANE-tuff), noun*
Someone who brings suit in a civil court. Not to be misused or confused with *plaintive,* which means expressing sadness or sounding sad. However, a plaintiff will probably appear plaintive if she loses her case.

The PLAINTIFF in the case seemed as motivated by the potential financial award as she was by the determination of right or wrong.

platitude *(PLA-tih-tood), noun*
A statement that has been used so often it has lost any meaning or significance; a cliché; an unoriginal, obvious remark or observation, often made as if it were original or meaningful

The grieving widow had to fight to keep her patience when insensitive people offered her PLATITUDES instead of sincerity.

Often the introductions read by award presenters are filled with PLATITUDES, and they are not sincere or well delivered

platonic *(pluh-TON-ik), adjective*
Friendly, as opposed to romantic or sexual. Usually describes relationships between people who might be expected to be attracted to each other. Perfect in form, but not found in reality. The good thing about many high school relationships.

While teenage girls often seem okay with PLATONIC relationships, for some reason they are less acceptable to teenage boys.

plaudit *(PLAW-dit), noun*
An expression of praise, gratitude, or approval. Applause is a public form of plaudit, especially when delivered in an auditorium.

Something laudable, like graduating cum laude, is definitely worthy of applause and a PLAUDIT.

plausible *(PLAH-suh-bul), adjective*
Appearing believable; likely to be true, at least in a superficial sense. Persuasive in speech or writing. Pleasing but deceptive.

Justin's explanation for the auto accident seemed PLAUSIBLE to his parents, so he was not punished.

plenary *(PLEH-neh-ree), adjective or noun*
Entire and complete; full; without reservation; or attended by all members and qualified participants (adjective) or a meeting attended by all members, who would otherwise meet in smaller committees on a more regular basis (noun)

The United States government is a three-branch system with checks and balances built in so not even the President has PLENARY powers.

It was difficult to find a time to hold the PLENARY meeting because so many people's schedules had to be considered.

She enjoyed attending the PLENARY because it gave her a chance to see other people involved in the organization who were not on her committee.

plethora *(PLETH-uh-rah), noun*
Excess; overabundance; an embarrassing amount

The house manager rolled his eyes at the PLETHORA of demands made by the diva performing later in the week.

plumb *(PLUM), verb, noun, adjective, or adverb*
To figure out the depth or vertical alignment using a specific piece of metal; or to make straight; or to explore or experience completely; or to be employed or perform the work of a plumber (verb) or a metal weight at the end of a line used to measure water depth or vertical alignment (noun) or perfectly upright; vertical; straight up and down; or complete, absolute, and unquestionable; used only in very informal conversation (adjective) or perfectly; directly; squarely; used only in very informal conversation; or completely; absolutely; entirely; used only in very informal conversation (adverb)

The sailors had to PLUMB the waters to make sure the ship would not run aground in the shallows.

It was a struggle for the architect to get the weight-bearing wall PLUMB given the size and shape of the room.

Looking back on her past, she realized she had PLUMBED the depths and the heights of emotion and had lived a full life.

Since it was midnight and he didn't want to pay an extra fee, he tried to PLUMB the leaking pipe himself.

The PLUMB was lost when the line snagged on an underwater rock and snapped.

Even though they were, the walls of the haunted house didn't appear PLUMB due to the angles and intentionally misleading paint job.

Instead of impressing his date, his antics just made him appear a PLUMB idiot.

She squealed when his arrow flew PLUMB in the center of the bull's-eye.

He knew he was so tired after the all-nighter that his granny would have said he was "PLUMB worn out."

pluralism *(PLOOR-al-iz-im), noun*
The understanding and tolerance of a diversity of differing cultures and views within a single society.

As long as someone comes from a family of high-standing, we wholeheartedly embrace PLURALISM.

plutocracy *(ploo-TAH-kruh-see), noun*
Rule of society by the richest people; also, a society ruled by its wealthiest members. The overall influence of the wealthy, who control or influence the government or society.

Some argue that almost all societies are in some way a PLUTOCRACY, for the richest people do have a great deal of power.

poignant *(POYN-yunt), adjective*
Causing a sharp sense of sadness, pity, or regret. Appealing to the emotions. Acutely painful or affecting.

The film's final scene is meant to be POIGNANT, but I found it cloying and overly sentimental.

polemic *(puh-LEH-mik), noun*
A passionate, strongly worded, and often controversial argument for or against something or someone. Someone who engages in a dispute or argues strongly or passionately. The art of argument.

Attorneys are said to be professionals in the art of the POLEMIC, and sometimes we think passionate politicians are as well.

politic *(PAH-luh-tick), adjective*
Possessing or displaying tact, shrewdness, or cunning. You can see the connection between this word, *politician,* and *politics.*

When called POLITIC by his opponent, Peter thought it a compliment, until he learned otherwise.

polity *(PAH-lih-tee), noun*
A particular form of government; a system of government. The aspect of society oriented toward politics and government. A state, society, or institution thought of as a political entity.

The POLITY created by those who crafted the U.S. Constitution proved a model that many other countries adapted.

pollutant *(puh-LOO-tuhnt), noun*
Something that pollutes with the introduction of products that contaminate the air, soil, or water.

Few realized disposable diapers would be identified as a POLLUTANT because of their plastic composition and not their content.

polyglot *(PAH-lee-glot), adjective or noun*
Made up of or containing more than one language; or being able to communicate fluently in many different languages (adjective) or a person who can communicate and is comfortable with several different languages (noun)

The POLYGLOT text was helpful to students studying several languages.

The POLYGLOT travelers always managed to communicate with someone, regardless of what country they were visiting.

The embassy was hiring extra POLYGLOTS as additional staff during the particularly heavy tourist season.

polymath *(POHL-ee-math), noun*
A person with a wide range of intellectual interests or a broad base of knowledge in many different disciplines.

Stephen had so many academic degrees that his brother considered him a POLYMATH.

Know This Quote
"I had a terrible vision: I saw an encyclopedia walk up to a POLYMATH and open him up." —Karl Kraus, Austrian writer

ponderous *(PON-duhr-us), adjective*
Clumsy and slow, often due to great weight; laborious; or unnecessarily solemn and serious; boring; emotionally tiring and weighty

The rancher's usually graceful horse was slowed under the PONDEROUS burden of two extra riders.

By the end of the PONDEROUS speech, even the most attentive listeners were beginning to doze and lose interest.

pontificate *(pon-TIH-fuh-kate), verb*
To speak about something in a knowing and self-important way, often without qualification. To make a decree with self-righteous pomposity. To officiate when celebrating Mass, or making a church decree

While she was well respected as an English teacher, students tuned out when Ms. Horner PONTIFICATED on the virtues of art and dance.

portend *(pour-TEND), verb*
To indicate that something, especially something unpleasant, is imminent, going to happen; to suggest or foretell. Not to be confused with *pretend,* which means to make believe or to make others believe something untrue is true.

The anxiety in Hugh's voice PORTENDED for his parents what to expect of his behavior that day.

portent *(POR-tent), noun*
A sign or omen; an indication that something unusual or important, although often evil or bad luck, is about to occur

The mother of the bride refused to believe that rain on the wedding day was a PORTENT of what was to come in the marriage.

posit *(PAU-zit), verb*
To present or stipulate something for consideration; an assumption, suggestion, or fact.

The detective POSITED circumstances that would explain the forensics of the crime scene.

potable *(POH-tuh-bull), adjective*
Suitable for drinking, not containing harmful elements. While potable water is portable, they are not the same words.

The presence of POTABLE water was the one factor that would determine whether the castaways would survive.

potentate *(POH-ten-tayt), noun*
A powerful dictator, king, leader, or ruler.

A much-feared POTENTATE, Victor Von Doom, ruled Latvia with an iron fist.

pragmatic *(prag-MA-tik), adjective*
Handling things in a straightforward, logical manner; concerned only with facts; practical

He learned being PRAGMATIC rather than becoming emotionally involved was the best way to handle business dealings.

pragmatism *(PRAG-muh-tiz-um), noun*
The belief that one's actions should be guided primarily based on knowledge or opinion of what is likely to work best in a given situation; the imperative to always do what is practical and effective.

Our families have succeeded in amassing great wealth over many generations because we are all, at heart, practitioners of PRAGMATISM.

prattle *(PRAT-tuhl), verb or noun*
To chatter mindlessly; pointless, superficial talk (verb) or small talk; light, unimportant conversation (noun)

The examiner let the students PRATTLE on before the test because it seemed to calm their nerves.

Her daughter's PRATTLE was a pleasing background for her while she cleaned up after dinner.

precarious *(pree-CAYR-ee-uhs), adjective*
Dangerously unstable; likely to fall, slip, or collapse; hazardous; or dependent on unknown qualities; uncertain; shaky or questionable; or based on questionable, unproven theories or concepts

The walk down the steep slope was made more PRECARIOUS by the rain that had loosened the rocks.

The cyclist's lead in the race was PRECARIOUS with 100 more miles to ride and his closest competitor only two minutes behind him.

Her boss was hesitant to follow her advice due to the PRECARIOUS nature of the polls that had been conducted.

Know This Quote

"Existence is no more than the PRECARIOUS attainment of relevance in an intensely mobile flux of past, present, and future."
—Susan Sontag, American literary theorist, philosopher, and political activist

precedent *(PRES-ih-dent), noun*
A previous event that can be used as a guide for handling a current, similar event; earlier actions that can be used to justify taking similar actions in a similar situation

The office manager was concerned about the PRECEDENT she might be setting if she continued to let her assistant come into work late and leave on time.

precipitate *(pree-SIP-ih-tayt), verb or (pree-SIP-ih-tiht), adjective*
To fall or be thrown from a great height; or to happen quickly, usually unexpectedly and often without thought or planning; or to pour from clouds, to rain, snow, sleet, or hail (verb) or characterized by speeding ahead without caution; rushing headlong without thought or concern; or marked by acting with unnecessary and unwise haste; reckless; or unexpected, sudden, and without plan (adjective)

When the landslide hit, several houses on the coast were PRECIPITATED down the cliff and into the ocean.

The police feared a "not guilty" verdict in the latest hate crime case would PRECIPITATE a riot among the protesters.

The rain in February annoyed her because if it was going to PRECIPITATE in winter, she wanted it to snow.

The teens' PRECIPITATE race down the mountain could have ended very badly if another car had come along in the opposite direction.

The young couple realized their decision to move in together after only knowing each other a month had been PRECIPITATE.

The PRECIPITATE arrival of the king sent the household into a mad dash to prepare food and lodging for him and his retainers.

precipitous (*preh-SIH-pih-tus), adjective*
Done too quickly, without enough thought. On the verge of a dangerous course of action. Very high and steep.

Being an entrepreneur is a lofty goal, yet it can be a PRECIPITOUS position, requiring many risky decisions and much stress.

preclude *(PREE-klood), verb*
To take an action that makes something impossible; to actively prevent; or to be impossible due to a pre-existing condition

The club refused to PRECLUDE any child from joining because of inability to pay the fees.

Her susceptibility to migraines PRECLUDED her from drinking red wine.

precocious *(PREE-coh-shus), adjective*

Showing an early maturity; marked by earlier than usual mental development

The PRECOCIOUS little boy found it easier to relate to adults than to children his own age.

preconceive *(pree-con-SEEVE), verb*

To form an opinion or idea before information or experience is available to make an educated or fair judgment. Prejudice is almost always preconceived.

Teachers sometimes have PRECONCEIVED notions that boys are better at mathematics than girls.

precursor *(PREE-cur-ser), noun*

An event or concept that indicates what is to follow; or one that comes before; a forerunner

His mother secretly hoped that his earring and long black coat were not PRECURSORS to a rebellious, goth stage.

The PRECURSORS to today's sleek cell phones were large and unwieldy and had very little range.

Which Word?

Many words have virtually identical definitions. However, they cannot always be used in exactly the same way. Precursor (PREE-cur-ser) and predecessor (PREHD-ih-ses-ohr) are two of these words. The word precursor describes the forerunner or early model of a thing currently in use. It implies that the current model is better, more modern, or more effective than the original. Predecessor, however, is any person or thing that was previously used in the same capacity. It does not imply any evolution or growth.

predator *(PREHD-ah-tehr), noun*

A creature that hunts and feeds on other beings for its own survival; or one who destroys, hunts, hurts, or injures another, especially for selfish purposes

The big cats are some of the best known and fiercest PREDATORS on the planet.

As a businessman, he was a PREDATOR, but as a father, husband, and friend, he was gentle, loyal, and trustworthy.

predecessor *(PREHD-ih-ses-ohr), noun*

One who comes before another; the person who held the office or position before the person now in the role; or anything that has come before the current item

She hadn't been on the job long when she realized that her PREDECESSOR had left behind many unfinished projects that needed to be addressed quickly.

The new arena is more comfortable but it doesn't have the character of its PREDECESSOR.

predestination *(pree-dess-tih-NAY-shun), noun*
The belief that we do not have free will, and that our lives and destinies are preordained and beyond our control.

The problem with PREDESTINATION is that whatever happens, you can say that it was meant to be, and no one can prove you wrong.

predilection *(preh-dih-LEHK-shun) or (pree-dih-LEHK-shun), noun*
A preference; an established liking or fondness for something

Her small frame made it hard to believe she had a PREDILECTION for ice cream sundaes with extra hot fudge.

preen *(PREEN), verb*
To primp; to take extra care with grooming and appearance; or to clean fur or feathers, referring to an animal's bathing; or to boast, brag, or be otherwise self-congratulatory

The women's bathroom was full of girls taking a break from the dance floor to PREEN and generally freshen up.

The cat sat in the warm sunlight PREENING its thick, golden fur.

Everyone forgave his PREENING because they were as excited as he was about his recent promotion.

prejudice *(PREH-juh-dis), noun*
A preformed opinion, usually an unfavorable one, based on insufficient knowledge, irrational feelings, or inaccurate stereotypes. Holding opinions that are formed beforehand on the basis of insufficient knowledge. An unfounded mistrust, dislike, hatred, or fear of a person or group, specifically one of a particular religion, ethnicity, nationality, or status. Prejudicial people prejudge others.

PREJUDICE is an acquired characteristic that can be eliminated through education.

prelate *(PREH-lut), noun*
A high-ranking member of the clergy, including a bishop, abbot, or cardinal.

The pope is the highest PRELATE of the Roman Catholic Church.

premonitory *(PREH-mahn-ih-tor-ee), adjective*
Strongly indicative of or intuiting that something is going to happen.

The Harrisons sold their stock in that company because they had a PREMONITORY vision that the company would soon go bankrupt.

preposition *(pre-POH-sih-shun), noun*
The part of speech that shows the relation of nouns to each other and to the other parts of a clause. Examples include: at, about, and above. Not to be confused with *proposition,* which is an idea, offer, or plan put forward for consideration, or a sexual invitation.

A prepositional phrase begins with a PREPOSITION and ends with a noun or pronoun.

presage *(PREHS-ihj), noun or (PREES-ayj), verb*
A warning or foretelling that something bad is going to occur; an omen (noun) or to warn or predict something bad is going to occur (verb)

Medieval knights considered storm clouds on the night before a battle to be a PRESAGE of failure and possibly death.

She was concerned that her father's ailing health as he got older PRESAGED an unpleasant future.

prescience *(PREH-shehns), noun*
Knowledge of actions or events before they take place; foreknowledge.

Parents hope to have enough PRESCIENCE to protect their children from future harm.

prestidigitation *(PRESS-tih-dih-ji-TAY-shun), noun*
The performance of sleight-of-hand magic tricks.

The New Year's Eve gala at the Worthingtons included sumptuous meals, a full orchestra, and even a practitioner of PRESTIDIGITATION who amazed the children with her performance.

pretense *(PREE-tence), noun*
Behaving in a way that is not genuine, but meant to deceive others. A claim, especially one that has few facts to support it. To falsely act or claim to be surprised. Make-believe or imagined. An instance of pretending.

Many of Shakespeare's plays are crafted around ironic PRETENSE, when men played the parts of women who were pretending to be men.

pretentious *(PREE-ten-shus), adjective*
Showy in a way that tries to impress; characterized by attempting to appear grander, more important, or worthy of more esteem than is actually merited

The elaborately remodeled house looked PRETENTIOUS instead of elegant surrounded by the more modest homes in the neighborhood.

preternatural *(pree-tuhr-NATCH-uhr-uhl) or (pree-tuhr-NATCH-ruhl), adjective*
Extreme or extraordinary; far above and beyond what is normal

The characters' PRETERNATURAL happiness and friendliness appealed to young children and reminded adults of an earlier, simpler time.

prevalent *(PREH-veh-lent), adjective*
Widespread and accepted; commonly occurring, especially at a specific time and place

The PREVALENT attitude throughout Hollywood was that the movie released by the young, new director was going to break box office records and send him straight to the top.

prevaricate *(prih-VAYR-ih-kayt), verb*
To beat around the bush; to act or speak in a manner that avoids the truth

The congressman was able to PREVARICATE so well that the journalists didn't realize he hadn't answered their questions until after the press conference was over.

prima facie *(pree-ma FAY-shuh), adjective, adverb*
Something accepted upon the face of the evidence until further examination proves or disproved it.

We have PRIMA FACIE evidence that it was Evelyn who fed those lies to the society page gossip columnists.

primordial *(pry-MORE-dee-ul), adjective*
Relating to the beginning of time or the early periods of Earth's developments.

The Summerfelds' fortune has been in the family for so long that many of us joke that it has PRIMORDIAL origins.

pristine *(prih-STEEN), adjective*
So clean as to look new, unspoiled, not altered by human encroachment. In an original state; uncorrupted by later influence.

For many teenage boys the PRISTINE look and smell of a new car is intoxicating.

pro bono *(pro BOH-noh), adjective*
Done or undertaken for the public good without any payment or compensation, most often in reference to legal services.

Jay received the greatest financial reward from his corporate legal clients, but he got the most personal satisfaction from his PRO BONO work.

pro forma *(pro FOR-mah), adverb, adjective, noun*
Standard; following a commonly accepted format or process.

"Don't worry about reading the fine print," the manager told the young singer as he shoved the contract in front of him and put a pen in his hand. "It's just PRO FORMA."

probity *(PROH-bih-tee), noun*
Absolute integrity; the state of having strong principles and living by them; honor and honesty

History has painted many past leaders as men of PROBITY, forgetting that they were also human with human flaws and failings.

proclivity *(proh-KILHV-ih-tee), noun*
A tendency to behave or act in a certain way

She had a PROCLIVITY toward humor that made her invaluable at the office when tensions started to run high.

procrastination *(proh-cras-tih-NAY-shun), noun*
The habit of putting something off until the very last minute; the act of putting off or delaying until later

She was grateful the professor gave her an incomplete in the class rather than failing her due to her PROCRASTINATION in completing the final project.

proctor *(PROHK-ter), noun*
One who manages or supervises another person's activities and affairs.

A life of luxury would be so exhausting if it weren't for the many PROCTORS who take care of our mundane activities.

procure *(pro-KYORE), verb*
To seek and eventually gain ownership of something.

My book dealer recently PROCURED, at considerable expense, a first edition of Great Expectations *for our library.*

prodigal *(PRAH-dih-guhl), adjective or noun*
Extravagant in spending habits; financially irresponsible and wasteful; or giving an impressive, generous amount; withholding nothing (adjective) or a person who spends large amounts of money frivolously and irresponsibly (noun)

The young graduate built up nearly insurmountable credit card debt with his PRODIGAL spending habits before he realized what a mistake he was making.

Even her critics showered the mayor with PRODIGAL praise after her handling of the threatened union strike.

Even after she had moved out on her own, the young woman continued to be such a PRODIGAL that her father often slipped her extra cash.

prodigious *(preh-DIHJ-uhs), adjective*
Enormous; much larger in scope than usual; or impressive; awe-inspiring; extraordinary

He had a PRODIGIOUS thirst for knowledge, so reading in the library was his favorite way to spend his spare time.

His PRODIGIOUS talent brought audiences to their feet at the end of every performance.

prodigy *(PRAW-dih-gee), noun*
Someone who shows an exceptional natural talent for something at an early age. Something very impressive or amazing; a wonder, or marvelous example.

Anyone who can play in a symphony as a violin soloist at the age of nine is definitely a remarkable musical PRODIGY.

profane *(proh-FAYN), adjective or verb*
Marked by cursing, inappropriate, and offensive words; or nonreligious; secular; or characterized by being insulting to religions or faith (adjective) or to treat religion or faith in an insulting and disrespectful manner (verb)

His PROFANE humor that made him so popular in school didn't win him many friends in the business world.

The gospel singer had many religious CDs but also had a wide selection of PROFANE music as well.

Although she was an atheist, she tried very hard not to be PROFANE about her friends' religions and beliefs.

The young rebel had no problem spray painting the bridge but drew the line when his friends wanted to PROFANE the church.

profligacy *(PRUHF-lih-guh-see), noun*
Indulgence; the tendency to spend money unwisely, generally on luxury or unnecessary items, and without regard to budget concerns

The sisters enjoyed living a life of PROFLIGACY while growing up but their parents made it clear the girls would have to make their own way once they were adults.

profligate *(PRAH-flih-gut), adjective*
Extremely extravagant, wasteful, or shamelessly immoral. Extravagantly or recklessly wasteful.

Many rock stars take on PROFLIGATE lifestyles after making it big, but some settle down in time.

profuse *(proh-FYOOS), adjective*
Given in large amounts; handed out freely, with little reservation

The paper was so PROFUSE in its compliments of even mediocre achievements that praise from the editors didn't mean much.

prognosticate *(prog-NAH-stih-kate), verb*
To predict or foretell the future. To be an indication of likely future events.

Those television experts who try to PROGNOSTICATE elections are often wrong.

proletariat *(pro-leh-TARE-ee-uht), noun*
A class of society whose members earn their living solely by the exchange of their labor for money.

Your average dentist thinks he is upper class, but in reality, he is just another member of the PROLETARIAT.

proliferation *(proh-LIHF-eh-ray-shun), noun*
Rapid growth or increase in numbers, parts, or aspects

The PROLIFERATION of the earth's population has long been a concern of both scientists and environmentalists.

prolific *(proh-LIHF-ik), adjective*
Creating large numbers of works or results; or reproducing in large quantities

The PROLIFIC author could write up to three novels in a single year.

It was the gardener's hope that his plants would be PROLIFIC so the entire area would be green within just a few seasons.

prolix *(PROH-liks) or (proh-LIKS), adjective*
Excessively long or wordy, used when describing writings or a speech

The challenge of writing a study guide is to make it long enough to be useful but not PROLIX.

prolixity *(pro-LICK-sih-tee), noun*
Refers to a speech or piece of writing that is deliberately wordy and long-winded due to an ornate or formal style.

Ryan had trouble finding work as a speechwriter due to his penchant for PROLIXITY.

Know This Quote

"The writer who loses his self-doubt, who gives way as he grows old to a sudden euphoria, to PROLIXITY, should stop writing immediately: the time has come for him to lay aside his pen."
—Colette, French novelist

promulgate *(PRAH-mul-gate), verb*
To proclaim or declare something officially, especially to publicize formally that a law or decree is in effect. To put forward publicly or announce in an official capacity.

News of President Kennedy's assassination was quickly PROMULGATED throughout the school, even though no one but the principal's secretary had a radio.

propensity *(proh-PEN-sih-tee), noun*
Having a natural tendency to behave in a certain way

He had a PROPENSITY toward messiness that he knew he would have to get over.

propinquity *(pruh-PlN-kwih-tee), noun*
Nearness in space, time, or relationship.

The PROPINQUITY of the two families, who were neighbors for over twenty years, led to some close friendships as well as a few disagreements.

propitiate *(pro-PISH-ee-ate), verb*
To win over; to gain the approval and admiration of.

Bethany tried hard to PROPITIATE Suzanne, but was unsuccessful.

Know This Quote

"The life that went on in [many of the street's houses] seemed to me made up of evasions and negations; shifts to save cooking, to save washing and cleaning, devices to PROPITIATE the tongue of gossip." —Willa Cather, American author

propitious *(proh-PIH-shus), adjective*
Presenting a strong chance of success; favorable; appearing to be lucky

The man found it PROPITIOUS that on the day he had finally gotten up his nerve to ask the woman out, she was sitting in the break room by herself.

prosaic *(proh-ZAY-ik), adjective*
Plain, straightforward, and easy to understand; not flowery or poetic; or dull, boring, and unimaginative

The professor encouraged his students to be PROSAIC in their papers because he knew that having a clear writing style would serve them well in later life.

The actor's PROSAIC interpretation of one of the most emotionally moving monologues ever written made the casting agents cringe.

proscribe *(proh-SRIYB), verb*
To prohibit, ban, or forbid; or to declare illegal or immoral; to openly condemn

The director of the children's program decided to PROSCRIBE smoking anywhere on the grounds so the staff wouldn't give the kids a bad impression.

Many nations joined together to PROSCRIBE the crimes the rebels had committed during the civil war in their country.

proselytize *(PRAH-suh-luh-tize), verb*
To try to convert someone to a religious faith or political doctrine. To attempt to convert to one's religious faith.

Many are suspicious that born-again Christians all seek to PROSELYTIZE others.

prosperity *(pruh-SPAR-ih-tee), noun*
The state of being financially well-off; financially successful and comfortable

Many people leave their homelands and come to the United States hoping to find PROSPERITY and a better life.

protagonist *(proh-TA-guh-nist), noun*
The most important character in a novel, story, play, or literary work. The main participant in a contest or dispute. An important or influential supporter or advocate of a cause or issue.

Holden Caulfield, the PROTAGONIST of the famous coming-of-age novel, is a character that many teens can relate to.

protégé *(PRO-tuh-zhay), noun*
A young person who receives help, guidance, training, and support from someone older with more experience or influence. Someone protected, encouraged, or helped by another of superior status or rank.

Historically, it seems that each vice president was the PROTÉGÉ of the president, but that is not the case.

protocol *(PRO-tuh-call), noun*
Rules of correct behavior on official or ceremonial occasions; formal etiquette, as practiced in diplomatic circles. Formal agreement between states or nations, or preliminary draft of a treaty or agreement. In technical terms, the rules that govern how computers transmit and use information.

Official PROTOCOL requires that the American flag never be hung lower than that of another nation.

prototype *(PROH-tuh-type), noun*
The original model; experimental or trial version of a system or invention.

The PROTOTYPE of the first personal computer is now in a museum.

protuberant *(proh-TOO-buh-rant) or (proh-TYOO-buh-rant) or (preh-TOO-buh-rant), adjective*
Sticking out; bulging; swollen out

The carnival mirror gave his nose a large, PROTUBERANT look.

proverb *(PRAH-verb), noun*
A short, well-known saying that expresses an obvious truth and often offers advice; an adage. A popular saying, story, or maxim.

The tale of the tortoise and the hare is a PROVERB that teaches lessons about life as well as sport.

provident *(PRAH-vih-dent), adjective*
Making financial arrangements for the future; planning for and thinking about the future

Her grandfather was PROVIDENT enough to set up a savings account on her first birthday to pay for her college education.

provincial *(proh-VIN-shul), adjective*
Unsophisticated; not terribly educated; unworldly; may imply narrow mindedness or a certain degree of naivety

After living in the city for a year, she came to realize how PROVINCIAL some of her attitudes had always been.

provocative *(preh-VAHK-ah-tihv), adjective*
Marked by an ability to excite, intrigue, or cause a reaction, usually intentionally; or intended to arouse sexually

The PROVOCATIVE editorial calling for the resignation of the chief of police caused outrage among his supporters.

The PROVOCATIVE blouse really wasn't her style but her friends had assured her it was still appropriate.

proximity *(prok-SIM-ih-tee), noun*
Closeness or nearness, either in time or actual distance; next to

Even though the young man was usually quite composed, he always became clumsy and flustered whenever the young woman was in close PROXIMITY to him.

proxy *(PRAHK-see), noun*
The authority, typically in writing, to represent someone else or manage their affairs; a person authorized to act on the behalf of others.

While his mother was ill, Larry acted as her PROXY and made hospitalization decisions on her behalf.

prudence *(PROO-dens), noun*
The act of showing care and being concerned for the future; discretion; the ability to act in a way to avoid embarrassment, discomfort, or awkward situations

She suspected she would go into politics one day so she acted with PRUDENCE even when her friends were throwing caution to the wind.

prudent *(PROO-dunt), adjective*
Characteristic of good sense, care in managing practical matters, and a tendency to evaluate situations carefully so as to avoid risk. Careful management of resources.

Purchasing automobile insurance is always a PRUDENT act, and one required by the laws of most states.

prurient *(PROO-ree-yent), adjective*
Having or intending to arouse an unwholesome interest in sexual matters. Lewd, focusing excessively on sex.

The U.S. Supreme Court has reviewed cases to clarify obscenity issues and clarify whether a book is PRURIENT.

psychosomatic *(sy-ko-suh-MAH-tik), adjective*
Caused by mental factors, as in illness. Describes disorders with emotional or mental rather than evident physical causes.

When doctors could not identify any physical causes for her illness, they began to look for PSYCHOSOMATIC origins.

puerile *(PYOO-rul), adjective*
Silly in a childish way; juvenile. Immature; related to or characteristic of childhood. From the Latin for "boyish."

While Jack and Elaine were clearly in love, many thought his PUERILE actions around her inappropriate for a thirty-year-old.

pugnacious *(pug-NAY-shuss), adjective*
Inclined to fight or be aggressive. Prone to quarrels or fights; given to conflict or dispute.

On occasion, the coaches thought Kathy's PUGNACIOUS attitude was detrimental to her play on the soccer field.

punctilious *(punk-TIL-ee-uhs), adjective*
Very aware of the rules of conduct or etiquette; knowledgeable of every small detail.

His grandmother was PUNCTILIOUS and had insisted upon perfect table manners, even when he and his brother had been children.

pungent *(PUHN-jent), adjective*
Marked by a sharp, strong, or even bitter taste or smell; or penetrating; nearly viciously to the point; sharp

The neighbors were first alerted to the fire when the PUNGENT smell of smoke drifted from one apartment into the next.

Although she could be gracious and warm, she also had a reputation for making PUNGENT remarks if anyone took advantage of her kindness.

purport *(per-PORT), verb*
Claiming to be something you are not; pretending to do something you aren't in fact doing.

May wanted to PURPORT that she was the sister of Mick Jagger, but she thought no one would believe her.

purported *(purr-POR-tid), adjective*
Supposed or claimed to be true, but without evidence or proof. Represented as the real thing.

The PURPORTED sister of Queen Elizabeth was the star of the cruise, though no one could prove her relationship to the royal.

Know This Quote

"Doris Lessing PURPORTS to remember in the most minute detail the moth-eaten party dresses she pulled, at age thirteen, from her mother's trunk."
—Tim Parks, British novelist

purveyance *(purr-VAY-yunts), noun*
The act of supplying something, especially food. The task of providing, collecting, or requisitioning supplies for a king, queen, or army.

The PURVEYANCE of materials for the wedding cost more than had been allotted in the budget.

pusillanimous *(pyoo-sih-LAN-ih-mus), adjective*
Cowardly; lacking courage; fearful or spineless

The students' PUSILLANIMOUS whining when told they would be handling live reptiles annoyed the teacher even though she expected it.

putrefy *(PYOO-trih-fiy), verb*
To rot and produce a foul odor; to decay and smell bad

The family froze the chicken bones left over from dinner so they wouldn't PUTREFY before the trash went out later in the week.

pyre *(PIYR), noun*
A pile of wood, twigs, and other flammable material, usually used to burn a corpse as part of a funeral ritual

Even the guys choked up during the scene in the movie in which the hero lit the PYRE for the heroine's funeral.

pyrrhic *(PIR-ick), adjective*
A prize or victory won at the cost of an effort that exceeds its value.

Spending $20 at the carnival game to win his child a stuffed animal worth $5 was a PYRRHIC victory at best.

Q

quaff *(KWAHF), verb*
To drink deeply with great gusto and enjoyment, usually an alcoholic beverage

Oktoberfest is a traditional time to find friends laughing and QUAFFING ale while toasting each other's health.

Know This Quote
"We QUAFF the cup of life with eager haste without draining it, instead of which it only overflows the brim." —William Hazlitt, English literary critic and philosopher

quagmire *(KWAG-mire), noun*
An awkward, complicated, or dangerous situation from which it is difficult to escape; entanglement that offers no ready solution. Literally, a soft marshy area or boggy patch of ground that gives way when walked on. For some, descriptive of many teenage relationships: awkward, complicated, dangerous, and difficult to escape.

While building a new home at first seemed a wonderful idea, the project quickly became a financial and logistical QUAGMIRE.

quaint *(KWAYNT), adjective*
Charming in an old-fashioned way. Strange or unusual in a pleasing or interesting manner.

The students always thought it QUAINT that the alumni returned for the homecoming game.

qualitative *(KWAL-ih-TAY-tuhv), adjective*
Having to do with the quality or character of a thing, often as opposed to its size or quantity.

Dr. Burton would often criticize the research of his students as being too QUALITATIVE and not numerically driven.

qualm *(KWALM), noun*
A feeling of uneasiness; a feeling of doubt, worry, or concern

The woman's adventurous spirit allowed her to take great risks without the slightest QUALM.

quandary *(KWAHN-duh-ree) or (KWAHN-dree), noun*
A state of confusion or uncertainty about how to handle a difficult situation; a dilemma

He found himself in a QUANDARY when offered a job with a new company and a promotion from his current employer.

Elizabeth was in a QUANDARY about what courses to take in the first semester of her freshman year.

quantitative *(KWAN-tih-tate-uhv), adjective*
Able to be communicated in terms of quantity. Based on the amount or number of something; capable of being measured in specific numerical terms.

Accountants certainly need to keep an accurate QUANTITATIVE measure of their clients' interests.

quant jock *(KWAHNT johk), noun*
A phrase for someone who enjoys quantitative analysis; that is, applying numerical and statistical measurements to problems. Literally one who "rides the numbers," or is a "numbers cruncher."

The graduate students thought being termed a "QUANT JOCK" to be a compliment.

quantum leap *(KWAN-tuhm LEEP), noun*
A sudden, dramatic, and significant change or advance in thought. Derived from the behavior of subatomic particles, which quantum physics has revealed are able to travel great distances in almost no time at all.

Crick and Watson's QUANTUM LEAP from scientific research to creative thought revealed that DNA was a double helix.

quarantine *(KWAR-uhn-teen), noun*
Enforced isolation to those exposed to a contagious or infectious disease. The period of time during which people or animals are isolated.

The Mitchells thought it odd that even their goldfish had to be placed in QUARANTINE when they moved to Europe.

quark *(KWORK), noun*
An elementary particle; the smallest known quantity of matter.

It's amazing how something as small as a QUARK can generate so much enthusiasm and interest in physics researchers.

quarrelsome *(KWAH-rull-sohm), adjective*
Having a tendency to argue with people; tending to pick fights or angry disputes with others.

You are not the only person she has gotten into a fight with; she is QUARRELSOME with nearly everyone.

quasar *(KWAY-sar), noun*
A compact, extremely distant, ancient object in space whose energy output is equal to or greater than that of an entire galaxy.

QUASARS were once theoretical, then only observable as vague electrical impulses, but they are now observable as clear images through the Hubble Space Telescope.

quash *(KWAHSH), verb*
To repress or subdue completely.

She quickly QUASHED the rebellion of the other members of the PTO by reminding them of the superiority of her social contacts.

quaver *(KWAY-ver), verb*
To tremble and shake from fear, excitement, etc.

Eloise positively QUAVERED as she made her debut at her coming out party.

quean *(KWEEN), noun*
A disreputable woman; a prostitute.

Esmerelda can act like such a QUEAN when her boyfriends do not automatically give her the luxury items she requires.

queasy *(KWEE-zee), adjective*
Feeling ill in the stomach, as if on the verge of vomiting; easily nauseated. Causing a feeling of uneasiness or nausea. Again, like most teenage boys and girls before a date, or high school students before a test.

Driving a long distance on the bumpy road made almost everyone on the team bus feel QUEASY.

quell *(KWEL), verb*
To put an end to, often by the use of or threat of force; to force to stop; or to silence or subdue; or to ease; to calm; to make quiet

The military was able to QUELL the rebels before the resistance could gain a foothold and become bloody.

One look from the headmaster was enough to QUELL any thoughts the students might have had about making excuses or trying to get out of being punished.

If a child has been traumatized in some way, it becomes harder to QUELL even their irrational fears.

Know This Quote

"O the orator's joys! / To inflate the chest, to roll the thunder of the voice out from the ribs and throat, / To make the people rage, weep, hate, desire, with yourself, / To lead America—to QUELL America with a great tongue." —Walt Whitman, American poet and humanist

quench *(KWENSH), verb*
To satisfy a thirst by drinking. To put out a fire or light. To subdue a feeling, especially enthusiasm or desire. To cool hot metal by plunging it into cold water or other liquid.

Diligent students sometimes state that reading and writing is the only way to QUENCH their thirst for knowledge.

querulous *(KWER-uh-luss), adjective*
Inclined to complain or find fault. Whining or complaining. Describing someone who makes peevish complaints.

The QUERULOUS two-year-old felt better and stopped whining after his nap.

query *(KWIHR-ee), noun or verb*
A question or inquiry, generally used in formal situations (noun) or to ask a question, especially when expressing a doubt or concern; to request a clarification (verb)

The press corps had to present their QUERIES about the new policy in advance to the prime minister's staff.

The thesis review board QUERIED the candidate on many of the more unconventional and challenging aspects of the theories presented in her paper.

quibble *(KWIH-bul), noun or verb*
A minor objection or criticism, especially over a trivial matter (noun) or to find fault through nitpicking (verb)

The few QUIBBLES brought up by the pickiest judge were not enough to drop the skater's score in the competition.

The coupled QUIBBLED over many things but they were really deeply in love and both knew it.

quicksilver *(KWIK-sill-vuhr), adjective*
Tending to change rapidly and unpredictably. Literally "mercurial," like Mercury, the god who is also called Quick Silver.

The QUICKSILVER emotional transformations of manic-depressive individuals frustrate family members and psychologists.

quid pro quo *(KWID pro kwo), noun*
A fair exchange of assets or services; a favor given in return for something of equal value.

In a QUID PRO QUO, Stephen helped Alex with his math homework, while Alex did Stephen's chores.

quiescent *(kwee-EH-sehnt), adjective*
Marked by inactivity; being in a period of rest, usually temporary

The lab would seem QUIESCENT for months at a time then there would be a flurry of activity as a new breakthrough was discovered.

quietus *(kwy-EET-uhs), noun*
Something that ends or settles a situation.

A QUIETUS was ordered by a judge when Lucy and her neighbor Sue couldn't solve the problem on their own.

Know This Quote

"For who would bare the whips and scorns of time, / Th'oppressor's wrong, the proud man's contumely, / The pangs of disprized love, the law's delay, / The insolence of office, and the spurns / That patient merit of th'unworthy takes, / When he himself might his QUIETUS make / With a bare bodkin?" —William Shakespeare

quintessence *(kwin-TEH-sunts), noun*
The pure, essential form of a thing, in its most perfect form. Something that is the most typical example, as "the quintessence of greed." In ancient medieval philosophy, the fifth element after earth, air, fire, and water.

The announcer commented that those who competed in the triathlon were the QUINTESSENCE of speed, strength, and endurance.

quirk *(KWIHRK), noun*
A peculiarity of one's personality or manner.

One of the most omnipresent QUIRKS of the nouveau riche is that they still ask the price of a luxury item, rather than simply offering to purchase it.

quisling *(KWIZ-lehng), noun*
A traitor, especially someone who collaborates with an occupying force. Quiz yourself twice on this one—it's a word that means nothing like what it sounds.

Once the village was liberated, many of the leading citizens were now regarded as QUISLINGS.

Where'd That Word Come From?

Quisling—This word for someone who is disloyal at best, and an actual traitor at worst, derives from a Norwegian politician named Vidkun Quisling, who collaborated with the occupying Nazis during World War II.

quiver *(KWIH-vur), verb*
To shake rapidly with small movements.

It was hard to tell whether it was the cold or her nerves that was causing Jennifer to QUIVER so much.

quixotic *(kwik-SOT-ik), adjective*
Tending to take a romanticized view of life; motivated by idealism to the neglect of the practical. Hopelessly and impractically idealistic. Derived from the name of literary character Don Quixote.

Susan's QUIXOTIC search for "Mr. Right" inspired her to take many singles cruises, but all she got was seasick.

quizzical *(KWIHZ-ih-kuhl), adjective*
Unusual or comical; or, puzzled.

The QUIZZICAL look on Amanda's face, when David trailed a marriage-proposal banner behind his private plane, was absolutely priceless.

quondam *(KWAHN-dumm), adjective*
Former; at-one-time.

You should not hire the Wilkersons' QUONDAM servant because she has been known to break many objets d'art.

quotidian *(kwoh-TIH-dee-ahn), adjective*
Everyday, ordinary, or commonplace

After having been away from home for so long, she found pleasure in even the most QUOTIDIAN activities of daily life.

R

raconteur *(rak-uhn-TUHR), noun*
An excellent storyteller; one who tells amusing and interesting stories

He was such a gifted RACONTEUR he managed to make even the most ordinary events sound lively and interesting.

raillery *(RAIL-err-ee), noun*
Good-natured teasing.

"RAILLERY," said Montesquieu, "is a way of speaking in favor of one's wit at the expense of one's better nature."

raiment *(RAY-muhnt), noun*
Clothing or apparel of the finest quality.

When Priscilla entered the room attired in RAIMENT of pure gold, her guests gasped and more than one glass of wine was overturned on silken tablecloths.

raison d'être *(RAY-sohn DETT), noun*
Something that gives meaning or purpose to someone's life, or the justification for something's existence. From the French for "reason for being."

After teaching her first special education class, she knew her RAISON D'ÊTRE.

rakish *(RAY-kush), adjective*
Stylish in a dashing or sporty way. Having a streamlined look that suggests rapid movement through the water.

The juniors all looked very RAKISH in their white dinner jackets, formal trousers, and athletic footwear.

rambunctious *(ram-BUHNGK-shuhss), adjective*
Difficult to handle; wild and boisterous.

The teacher's aide was overwhelmed by the RAMBUNCTIOUS students.

> **Know This Quote**
> The golden age, when RAMBUNCTIOUS spirits were regarded as the source of evil." —Friedrich Nietzsche, nineteenth-century German philosopher

ramification *(ra-mih-fih-KAY-shun), noun*
The unintended consequence of an action, often one that complicates a situation or makes it harder to achieve the intended results. The process of branching out; offshoot or outgrowth, as in either ideas or actual branches on a tree or plant.

Too many teens fail to fully understand the RAMIFICATIONS of their actions.

ramify *(RAM-ih-fiy), verb*
To have or cause complications; to cause further difficulties to develop

The steps the group first took to repair the problem only seemed to RAMIFY the situation further.

ramshackle *(RAM-shakl) adjective*

Poorly maintained or constructed and likely to fall down, fall apart, or collapse. Shacks are ramshackle structures, ready to blow down at the first hard wind.

Tourists were shocked and saddened to see the RAMSHACKLE huts where the poorer residents of the island lived.

Where'd That Word Come From?

Ramshackle—What language did English borrow this word from? Greek? Latin? Nope—try Icelandic. *Ramskakkr,* "very twisted," is the possible Icelandic source for this word, meaning "loosely made or held together, rickety, shaky." Other possible origins include *ranshacle,* "to wreck or destroy by plundering"—which would make something *ramshackled* "wrecked or destroyed by plundering."

rancor *(rang-KOR), noun*

Long-standing anger; bitterness, especially when held and nurtured over time

None of her friends understood why she still spoke with such RANCOR about an event that had happened when they were all still in school.

randy *(RAN-dee), adjective*

Having a strong desire for sex. Again, like most teenage boys.

Adolescent boys are, by nature, RANDY, but they seem to get worse over the summer at the beach.

rankle *(RANG-kul), verb*

To cause persistent feelings of anger, irritation, or festering resentment. To feel slighted or annoyed because of a perceived slight, oversight, or criticism.

The criticism of parents does RANKLE children after a while, but sometimes it is important to listen to.

rapacious *(ruh-PAY-shus), adjective*

Greedy in an aggressive way; wanting more than one's fair share

In his will, the old man left everything to his servants and a few close friends because he was too aware of the RAPACIOUS nature of his family.

rapacity *(ruh-PAH-sih-tee), noun*

Greed for wealth, power, fame, and success, even at the expense of others.

An unquenchable desire for the finer things in life is not RAPACITY, as some have suggested. It is, instead, a mark of good taste.

rapprochement *(rah-PROWCH-ment), noun*
Re-establishment of friendly relations between nations following a period of hostility.

Lydia spoke at length about how RAPPROCHEMENT between the United States and some former Soviet nations has been a real boon to her family's prestige and wealth.

rapport *(ruh-PORE), noun*
A positive bond or friendly relationship based on friendship, trust, and a sense of shared concerns. Also, an established pattern of communication.

The substitute teacher developed a good RAPPORT with the students to ensure his own survival.

rapturous *(RAP-chur-us), adjective*
Expressing or causing great enthusiasm, happiness, ecstatic feeling, or pleasure.

Those who have the opportunity to see the Grand Canyon are often RAPTUROUS at the mere memory.

rarefied *(RARE-uh-fied), adjective*
Seeming distinct or remote from ordinary reality and common people; lofty or exalted. Showing very high quality, character, or style: refined. In a scientific sense, having a low density, especially owing to a low oxygen content.

When visiting the Oval Office, one is truly in a RAREFIED environment.

rarefy or rarify *(RAER-eh-fiy), verb*
To become thin; to make less dense; to weaken; or to have less oxygen than the norm, generally used to describe air at high altitudes

Women should be sure to take calcium as they age so that their bones do not RAREFY and become brittle.

As the mountaineers climbed higher, the air began to RAREFY, making it more difficult to breathe.

Which Word?

Most words have one spelling. However, every rule has exceptions. Rarefy is one of those exceptions. While the most common spelling is r-a-r-e-f-y, it is sometimes spelled r-a-r-i-f-y. They are both pronounced (RAER-eh-fiy.) Use the most common spelling should you choose to write the word. Just know that, if you see it spelled with an i, it is the same word and still spelled correctly.

ratiocinate *(ray-shee-OSS-inn-ate), verb*
To work toward the solution of a problem through logical thinking and reason.

Since the dawn of humanity, our best minds have failed to RATIOCINATE a method of proving God's existence.

raucous *(RAW-kuhs), adjective*
Loud and unruly; rowdy; disruptive and noisy

The neighbors were generally patient with the RAUCOUS parties thrown by the fraternity but sometimes called the police when things got too out of hand.

ravenous *(RA-vuh-nuss), adjective*
Extremely hungry or greedy for something; predatory. Intensely eager to be satisfied, to gratify desires.

RAVENOUS as they were, the team could hardly wait through the introductory banquet speeches before starting their meal.

ravishing *(RA-vih-shing), adjective*
Extremely beautiful, delightful, and pleasing to the eye.

As you would expect, the bride was RAVISHING as she walked down the chapel aisle.

raze *(RAYZ), verb*
To flatten; to completely destroy; to tear down to the ground

The town council decided to RAZE the run-down city hall and build a modern one on the same site.

reactionary *(ree-AK-shun-ayr-ee), adjective or noun*
Marked by opposing liberal political and social views; characterized by being against reform (adjective) or a person who holds very conservative views and beliefs (noun)

Most news talk show hosts are either so liberal or so REACTIONARY that the programs turn into nothing more than shouting matches.

She enjoyed her reputation as the only REACTIONARY on a campus of bleeding heart liberals.

rebuff *(ree-BUF), noun or verb*
A deliberately cold and abrupt rejection or refusal (noun) or to reject in a particularly cold or unfeeling way; or to push back; to repel (verb)

Although he hadn't expected to be granted an interview, he didn't think the secretary should have given him such a harsh REBUFF.

She tried to be subtle but eventually had to REBUFF his advances.

The defense managed to REBUFF the opposing team's final effort to make a score-tying goal.

rebuttal *(rih-BUHT-tuhl), noun*
A statement or speech given to contradict or answer a statement or speech that has come before it

The State of the Union Address is always immediately followed by a short REBUTTAL made by a ranking member of the minority party.

recalcitrant *(rih-KAL-sih-trunt), adjective*
Stubbornly resistant to the control or authority of others. Difficult to deal with, work with, or supervise.

The high school principal's office was like a second home for some RECALCITRANT students.

recant *(ree-KANT), verb*
To take back a statement; to vow one no longer believes a specific opinion or idea previously believed, generally made under pressure

In the 1600s and 1700s, many scientists whose discoveries challenged the Church were forced to RECANT their findings or else face death.

Know This Quote
"I cannot and will not RECANT anything, for to go against conscience is neither right nor safe."
—Martin Luther, the father of Protestantism

recapitulate *(re-kuh-PIH-choo-late), verb*
To summarize in concise form; to briefly retell the essential points of a story. In terms of biology, describes what a fetus does as it repeats the stages of the evolution of the species during its development.

Great public speakers are known for their abilities to RECAPITULATE and gesticulate.

recession *(ree-SESH-in), noun*
A troubled economy characterized by a decline in gross domestic product for two consecutive quarters; a period during which unemployment is on the rise, inflation is increasing, and consumer confidence and spending power is eroded.

The looming RECESSION has even hurt some of our families, who have had to let go of second yachts and one or two homes.

reciprocal *(ree-sih-PROH-cul), adjective*
Given in return; exchanged; felt or performed by each side

Although the generals were on opposing sides of the war, they had developed a RECIPROCAL admiration for the other's skill.

reciprocity *(res-ih-PRAH-sih-tee), noun*
The practice of exchanging goods, services, or ideals with another for mutual benefit; an exchange in which both parties gain

The couple said the reason they had stayed together for so long was they had a marriage of RECIPROCITY, love, and respect.

reclamation *(reh-cluh-MAY-shun), noun*
The conversion of unusable land into land suitable for farming or other uses. The extraction of useful substances from refuse. The claiming back of something once taken or given away.

The RECLAMATION of the inner city was deemed miraculous by those who lived there.

reclusive *(rih-KLOO-siv), adjective*
Withdrawn from the rest of the world; solitary and hermitlike. Shut off from the influences of the world or others.

After her husband died, Mrs. Hilton lived a RECLUSIVE life, rarely coming out of her house or speaking to anyone.

recompense *(REH-kum-pents), verb*
To pay someone for work or services. To give compensation for suffering, loss, or injury.

To RECOMPENSE Mrs. Williams for all her suffering would be impossible.

Know This Quote

"To be remembered after we are dead, is but poor RECOMPENSE for being treated with contempt while we are living." —William Hazlitt, English literary critic and philosopher

recondite *(reh-KON-diyt) or (rih-KON-diyt), adjective*
Difficult to understand; outside of common knowledge; or hidden; out of view; concealed

The New York Times *crossword puzzle is recognized as one of the most challenging and RECONDITE of any word puzzles.*

She hoped her dissertation would address some RECONDITE, undiscovered aspect of her field that would bring her acclaim.

reconnoiter *(reh-kuh-NOY-ter), verb*
To explore an area in order to gather information, especially about the position and strength of the enemy. To engage in reconnaissance. From the French, meaning "to explore."

The overly zealous coach, who was prone to military metaphors, said he would "RECONNOITER" rather than scout the opposing team.

recoup *(ree-COOP), verb*
To regain something lost; to make up for something lost. To make up for something that has been lost.

Habitual gamblers think they will RECOUP their losses if they just continue their risky behaviors.

recriminate *(rih-KRIM-uh-nayt), verb*
To bring up accusations against someone who has accused you.

After Natasha was snubbed by us for blabbing to the gossip pages, she RECRIMINATED by pointing out that some of us had leaked gossip ourselves.

recrimination *(ree-crih-muh-NAY-shun), noun*
An accusation made by someone who has been accused of a crime, usually against the original accuser. Recrimination is often a very effective form of retaliation.

The press was shocked when the RECRIMINATION of one of his aides involved the President in the Watergate cover-up.

recrudescent *(ree-KROO-dih-sent), adjective*
To start up again; to reoccur after a period of being dormant; to come out of remission

The brief truce hadn't made the RECRUDESCENT hostilities any less violent.

rectify *(REK-tih-fiy), verb*
To set straight or make right; to make amends by correcting the situation

He knew he had hurt his sister badly enough that a simple apology was not going to RECTIFY the matter.

As people get older, they are often inspired to RECTIFY past mistakes, particularly those associated with family and friends.

rectitude *(REHK-ti-tood), noun*
Moral virtue; rightness.

Susanna was appalled when the shopkeeper accused her of stealing; she thought everyone believed in her RECTITUDE.

Know This Quote
"The mind that's conscious of its RECTITUDE, / Laughs at the lies of rumor." —Ovid, Roman poet

recumbent *(rih-KUHM-bent), adjective*
Inactive, idle; lying down.

During our Italian cruise, we spent most of our time RECUMBENT on the bow of the yacht, soaking up the sun's rays.

recursive *(ree-KURSS-iv), adjective*
Pertaining to a process in which each step makes use of the results of the earlier steps.

The study of mathematics is a RECURSIVE learning experience.

recuse *(ree-KYOOZ), verb*
To disqualify someone from judging or participating in something because of bias or personal interest. To withdraw oneself from judging or participating in something for personal reasons.

Seeking a balanced jury, the defense attorney RECUSED many potential jurors until he approved of them all.

redact *(re-DAKT), verb*
To edit a comment, thought, or written document before going public with it.

"You may want to REDACT your opinion on your opponent's health care policies," his campaign manager warned him.

redolent *(RED-oh-lent), adjective*
An object possessing a rich scent or alluring aroma, or a situation with a hint or promise of rich possibilities.

Her rose garden was REDOLENT with the perfume of a thousand flowers.

redoubtable *(rih-DOW-tuh-bul), adjective*
Instilling fear or respect; causing awe; or worthy of respect and recognition

He used his REDOUBTABLE reputation in the military to gain a political appointment in civilian life.

Thomas Jefferson's REDOUBTABLE words declaring independence from Britain still have the power to move people the first time they read them.

redress *(rih-DREHS), verb or noun*
To remedy or make right; to make amends for or to (verb) or compensation; a remedy for a wrong done (noun)

The company promised to REDRESS the customer's complaints.

The jury was able to give the man financial REDRESS but it could never restore the emotional peace he had lost to the crime.

redundancy *(rih-DUN-dunt-see), noun*
A duplication, as in computer backup systems, created to reduce the risk of error or failure. Use of a word or phrase whose meaning is already conveyed elsewhere in a document or passage. Fulfilling the role of something already in place and functional; superfluous, no longer needed or wanted.

Many functions of the spacecraft were designed as REDUNDANCIES, that is, backup systems in case primary ones failed.

referendum *(REH-fuh-ren-dum), noun*
A vote by the whole of an electorate on a specific question. Also, the questions placed before this group by a government or governing body.

The results of the national REFERENDUM would not be binding, but it would tell leaders what the public desired.

reflexive *(reh-FLEK-siv), adjective*
Something that happens through reflex rather than deliberate choice or effort.

We don't mean to act imperiously toward the nouveau riche; it's just a REFLEXIVE and conditioned response.

refractory *(rih-FRAK-tih-ree), adjective*
Openly and stubbornly resistant to authority or control; or resistant to heat or other stimulus; or difficult to treat, referring to a medical condition

In the 1960s and 1970s, any time large groups formed to listen to a passionate speaker, there was always the concern the situation would change from peaceful gathering to REFRACTORY mob.

REFRACTORY glass is ideal for use in cooking because it will not break when exposed to high temperatures.

Her acne proved REFRACTORY enough she finally went to a dermatologist.

refuge *(REF-yooj), noun*
A sheltered or protected place that is safe from harm or threat. Protection or safe shelter from something or someone.

Many Cubans seek REFUGE in America and risk their lives to do so.

refulgent *(rih-FUHL-jent) or (rih-FOOL-jent), adjective*
Shining brightly; as if lit by the sun

The young mother had a REFULGENT glow that lasted throughout her pregnancy.

refurbish *(re-FUR-bish), verb*
To renovate or repair. To restore to a state of attractive completion.

Volunteers REFURBISHED the abandoned apartments in record time.

refute *(ree-FYOOT), verb*
To prove false or incorrect; to present opposing facts

The adventures he claimed to have always took place when he was alone so, as unbelievable as they seemed, no one could ever REFUTE them.

regicide *(REH-jih-siyd), noun*
The intentional killing of a king; murder or assassination of a king

Historically, REGICIDE was a risky if effective way for a pretender to the throne to take over the monarchy.

regress *(ree-GRES), verb*
To return or revert to an earlier, less advanced, and generally worse state. To move backwards. To cause someone to reenact an earlier emotional state or related behavior.

After she worked hard to raise her grades, a sudden illness caused Mary to REGRESS in her study habits.

regurgitate *(ree-GUR-jih-tate), verb*
To bring undigested or partially digested food from stomach to mouth. To repeat or reproduce what has been heard, read, or taught in a purely mechanical way without evidence of thought or understanding. Teens may prefer to say "hurl," "spew," or "toss cookies."

For some courses, all that is necessary to receive good grades is to memorize and then REGURGITATE facts, figures, or definitions.

reiterate *(ree-IH-tuhr-ayt), verb*
To repeat something, usually for clarification or emphasis

The professor's policy was never to REITERATE instructions.

rejoinder *(rih-JOIN-der), noun*
A clever or witty reply to a question or comment.

Lydia's often catty REJOINDERS quickly made her the bane of our group.

relegate *(rehl-uh-GAYT), verb*
To refer to another; to pass off responsibility for; or to demote; to lower in rank or responsibility; or to banish or expel; to put in an obscure or out of the way place

One of the joys of being CEO was that she could RELEGATE the minor tasks she hated.

The police officer was RELEGATED to desk work until he completely healed from the fall he took on the ice.

The ugly sculpture from her aunt was RELEGATED to the dusty top of a bookshelf.

relinquish *(ri-LIN-kwish), verb*
To give up or surrender. To give something up or put it aside, emotionally or physically.

When he took ill, Tim's father RELINQUISHED many of the more physical household chores.

remedial *(ruh-MEE-dyuhl), adjective*
Acting as a remedy or solution to a problem. Designed to help those with learning difficulties, or to improve skills or knowledge. Intended to cure or relieve symptoms of someone who is ill or challenged.

While some students are too embarrassed to track them down, REMEDIAL services available for those in need are often powerful and effective.

reminisce *(REH-muh-NISS), verb*
To talk, write, or think about events remembered from the past.

It seems odd to parents to hear teens REMINISCING about their elementary school years.

remiss *(rih-miss), adjective*
Negligent or careless.

Our servants know that if they ever are REMISS in their duties, then we will quickly fire them.

remittance *(ree-MIH-tunce), noun*
The sending of money to pay for a service or merchandise. Money sent as payment.

Credit cards seem to some as magic money, until you have to send a REMITTANCE to their issuer every month.

remonstrate *(ree-MON-strayt) or (reh-MUHN-strayt), verb*
To forcefully protest; to argue against

Although she was the only person to REMONSTRATE the action, several people in the meeting voted against it.

remorse *(rih-MORS), noun*
Deep regret or guilt for actions taken in the past

The jury gave the young man the lightest sentence possible because he showed such obvious and sincere REMORSE for his behavior.

remunerate *(rih-MYOO-nuh-rate), verb*
To pay money for goods or services, or compensate someone for losses or inconvenience.

After the accident, the insurance company REMUNERATED her for damages within twenty-four hours, so Martha got her car fixed quickly.

renaissance *(REH-nuh-sans), noun*
A rebirth or revival, as of something forgotten or that was once less known or popular. Capitalized, refers to the period of European history from the fourteenth through the sixteenth centuries, regarded as marking the end of the Middle Ages and the rebirth or beginning of major cultural and artistic changes.

The university's RENAISSANCE pleased its alumni, who were happy to see it return to its former educational excellence.

renege *(rih-NIHG) or (rih-NEHG), verb*
To go back on a promise; to fail to keep a commitment

The director was left in a bind when his financial backers RENEGED on their contract to fund the shoot.

renounce *(RIH-nowns) or (REE-nowns), verb*
To formally give up on a claim, title, or position; or to refuse to support any further; to deny or refuse to obey any longer

The prince shocked the world when he RENOUNCED his claim to the throne in order to enter the priesthood.

The Civil War began when the southern states RENOUNCED the authority the United States had over them and seceded from the nation.

renunciation *(re-nun-see-AY-shun), noun*
A denial or rejection of something, often for moral or religious reasons. An official declaration giving up a title, office, claim, or privilege.

Tim's RENUNCIATION of alcohol and drugs had such great consequences that he made others wish to follow his example.

Know This Quote
"With RENUNCIATION life begins." —Amelia E. Barr, British novelist

reparations *(reh-par-AYE-shins), noun*
Payments made by nations defeated in war to the victors, who impose these payments to recover from some of the costs of battle.

After World War I, REPARATIONS of 132 billion gold marks were imposed on Germany by the French.

repartee *(reh-pur-TEE), noun*
Conversation consisting of witty remarks, or a witty remark or reply. Also, skill in making witty conversation.

It was amusing to watch the girls practice their REPARTEE, hoping not to be embarrassed on their first dates.

repast *(rih-PAST), noun*
A meal

The poor man's REPAST may have been small but it was made with love and shared willingly.

repertoire *(REH-per-tware), noun*
A library of works that a group knows and regularly performs.

The philharmonic's REPERTOIRE includes most of the classical standards from Bach, Beethoven, Brahms, and Mozart.

repine *(rih-PIYN), verb*
To complain; to be discontented; to express dissatisfaction; or to long for; to miss

The woman seemed determine to REPINE about everything at the resort from the food to the weather in spite of the fact that everyone else was enjoying it.

Usually she enjoyed living in California but in autumn she REPINED for her childhood home in New England.

replete *(rih-PLEET), adjective*
Amply and completely supplied with something.
Having eaten enough.

Grandma's famous Sunday dinners were REPLETE with every tasty dish one could imagine.

Know This Quote
"The highway is REPLETE with culinary land mines disguised as quaint local restaurants that carry such reassuring names as Millie's, Pop's and Capt'n Dick's."
—Bryan Miller, American food critic

repose *(rih-POHZ), noun*
To be in a position or state of rest.

Carolyn put her baby in his crib and sighed at how peaceful he looked in REPOSE.

reprehensible *(rep-rhee-HENS-ih-bul), adjective*
Truly disgusting or deplorable; deserving of scorn

Some people believe the death penalty is a REPREHENSIBLE abuse of power while others believe it deters crime and provides the victims some justice.

reprobate *(REH-pruh-bate), noun*
Disreputable, unprincipled, or immoral person. Someone whose soul is said to be damned.

Being called a REPROBATE was shocking to Blake, who thought his behavior normal for a teenager.

reprove *(rih-PROOV), verb*
To reprimand or scold; to express displeasure

The principal REPROVED the students he caught under the stairwell cutting classes.

repudiate *(rih-PYOO-dee-ayt), verb*

To claim as invalid; to reject as being valid; or to vigorously deny as having any truth; to state something is completely false

Since the couple was married by a justice of the peace, the bride's mother REPUDIATED the union until it had been blessed by a priest.

He REPUDIATED the accusations against him long before the investigation proved he was not involved in the situation.

Which Word?

Many words have similar meanings but are used in different contexts. This is the case for renounce (RIH-nowns) or (REE-nowns) and repudiate (rih-PYOO-dee-ayt). To renounce something is to state it no longer has power or control, meaning it once did. On the other hand, to repudiate something is to claim it is and always has been false. To renounce is to reject as false now. To repudiate is to reject as false always.

requisite *(REH-kwih-zit), adjective or noun*

Necessary; required; vital (adjective) or that which is required; something essential (noun)

In order to lose weight, a person must take the REQUISITE steps of eating well and exercising.

The REQUISITES for the job included phone skills, a basic understanding of data entry, and attention to detail.

Which Word?

Words that are spelled similarly can cause confusion if you read too quickly. Requisite (REH-kwih-zit) and requite (rih- KWIYT) are close but not the same. A requisite is something that is required or vital, but to requite means to return feelings or pay back.

requite *(rih-KWIYT), verb*

To repay, as a debt; or to return an emotion; to feel the same way

The candidate knew she could never completely REQUITE all the debts she owed the people who had helped get her nominated.

His heart leapt when he realized the young woman did indeed REQUITE his feelings for her.

rescind *(rih-SIHND), verb*

To take back; to make void; to negate

The man's driver's license was RESCINDED after he was convicted.

resilient *(rih-ZIHL-yehnt), adjective*
Able to bounce back after a problem or difficulty; unbroken emotionally and spiritually; or springy; able to reshape after being squeezed or misshapen

Her friends were not too concerned about her when she lost the job because they knew how RESILIENT she had always been.

The toy was RESILIENT enough to withstand even a toddler's attention.

resolute *(reh-zuh-LOOT), adjective*
Possessing determination; motivated by or displaying determination and purposefulness.

Americans seemed even more RESOLUTE to fight terrorism after the horrendous events of September 11, 2001.

resolution *(rehz-uh-LOO-shun), noun*
Firm, unwavering determination; or a decision to do something; or the clarity or detail that can be seen in an electronically produced image; or the part of a book, movie, or story in which the plot is wrapped up; or an act or official suggestion presented to an official, voting body

Her RESOLUTION to be the first in her family to attend college drove her to study harder and more often than most of her peers.

Most people make at least one RESOLUTION at the beginning of every new year.

The RESOLUTION to the book was unsatisfying considering how much the readers had come to care about the characters.

The board could not vote on the RESOLUTION before it until a majority of the members were in attendance.

resonance *(REHZ-eh-nehns), noun*
The quality of being resounding or having great meaning; or deep, rich tones

The RESONANCE of President Roosevelt's words during World War II uplifted an entire nation and helped the world stay strong during a dark, frightening time.

The RESONANCE of the church bells rang out over the city.

resonate *(REH-zuh-nate), verb*
To echo; to make something else vibrate or produce a similar sound. To have an effect or impact beyond what is apparent. To produce a sympathetic response; "get on the same wavelength" with someone else.

The crying of any infant RESONATES with those who are parents, as they are sensitive to these sounds and the feelings they inspire.

respite *(REH-spit), noun*
Brief period of rest and recovery between periods of exertion or after something disagreeable; a temporary delay or stay of execution.

The coach felt the girls had earned a RESPITE from wind sprints because they were working so hard during practice.

resplendent *(reh-SPLEND-ehnt), adjective*
Unusually beautiful and dazzling; decorated in a breathtaking way

The cathedral was impressive at any time but when lit by the sunset it was RESPLENDENT and awe-inspiring.

restitution *(res-ti-TOO-shun), noun*
The return of something to its rightful owner. Compensation for a loss, damage, or injury. Return of something to the condition it was before it was changed. Attempt to repair damage caused by a wrongful act.

A bill authorizing RESTITUTION to the citizens interned in the camps recently cleared Congress.

restive *(RES-tive), adjective*
Stubborn and unwilling to accept rules or control; impatient with delay. Having little patience; unwilling to tolerate annoyances.

The RESTIVE players gathered around the coach, eager to get the game underway.

restrained *(rhih-STRAYND), adjective or verb*
Marked by emotional control or a cool manner; dispassionate (adjective) or held in place; physically controlled; kept from freedom of movement (verb)

His RESTRAINED manner made him appear indifferent, but he was simply very professional and knew when to control his emotions.

The dog was RESTRAINED by his leash and the tall fence but the mail carrier still didn't like the look of its teeth.

reticent *(REH-tuh-sunt), adjective*
Unwilling to communicate very much, talk a great deal, or reveal all facts.

On the first day of high school even the most outgoing students seem a bit RETICENT.

retinue *(RHEH-tih-noo), noun*
The group of employees accompanying an important person

The singer required rooms for herself and her entire RETINUE.

retort *(rih-TORT), verb, noun*
To reply in a sharp, retaliatory manner.

Carl had to bite back a sharp RETORT when Sallee criticized the couture gown his mother wore to the soiree.

retract *(rih-TRAKT), verb*
To draw back in; to pull back; or to take back a statement

Once the puppy left her alone, the cat relaxed, RETRACTED its claws, and went to sleep in the sun.

When he saw the shock on the young woman's face, he wished he could RETRACT the invitation but was grateful he hadn't when she accepted.

retroactive *(reh-troh-AK-tiv), adjective*
Reaching back into the past; effective as of an earlier date, especially in terms of contracts or agreements. Relating to or applying to things that have happened in the past as well as the present.

The reimbursement eligibility for those who paid the higher parking fee was made RETROACTIVE as of September 1.

retrograde *(REH-trow-grayed), adjective*
Reverting to an earlier state, condition, or style; harkening to an earlier time and place.

My favorite diner is decorated in a RETROGRADE art deco style.

retrospective *(reh-truh-SPEK-tuv), noun*
Something based on memory of past events, containing examples of work from many periods of an artist's life, or applying to things past as well as present. From the Latin for "backward vision."

The Warhol RETROSPECTIVE at the museum was amazing and so large that you couldn't see all of the exhibit in one visit.

revelry *(REV-uhl-ree), noun*
Boisterous festivity and merrymaking.

Christmas had always been a time of REVELRY for Ken's family; the whole clan got together and celebrated the season.

Know This Quote
"Midnight shout and REVELRY, / Tipsy dance and jollity." —John Milton, English poet

reverence *(REH-ver-uhns), noun*
A deep, loving respect or awe; great admiration combined with love; or an act that shows respect, often a bow or curtsy

The REVERENCE shown the old king was testament to what a fair and benevolent ruler he had always been.

The visitors kissed the cardinal's ring in REVERENCE as they entered the room before getting on with the interview.

reverent *(REHV-er-ehnt), adjective*
Characterized by showing respect; worthy of admiration

It is appropriate to maintain a REVERENT silence in all places of worship, regardless of your own beliefs.

revile *(rih-VILE), verb*
To make a fierce or abusive verbal attack; to curse or abuse in harsh language. To use insulting or abusive language; to denounce using harsh language. Something you may have done, but didn't know what to call it. Not to be confused with *revelry,* which means lively enjoyment or celebration.

For some time Nixon was REVILED by his critics, but after time he was respected and honored by many.

rhetoric *(REH-tore-ik), noun*
Artful use of language to get other people to see your point of view; making a persuasive case more through persuasive speech or writing than with actual facts and evidence.

Plato called RHETORIC "the art of ruling the minds of men."

rhetorical *(ruh-TOH-rih-kul), adjective*
Asked with no expectation of response; often describes sarcastic questions, or those the questioner knows cannot be answered. Persuasive and skillful, as in argumentation.

The dean's RHETORICAL skills were much needed as he explained the new alcohol policy to the entire student body.

ribald *(RIH-buld), adjective*
Humorous in a rude and vulgar way. Amusingly coarse, lewd, and off-color; often used to describe a joke about sex.

The football team became infamous for RIBALD behavior, and on occasion they were disciplined for it.

rife *(RIFE), adjective*
Prevalent, abundant, abounding.

The hotel was RIFE with tourists, so we quickly went upstairs to the penthouse.

rigmarole *(RIG-muh-roll), noun*
Absurdly complicated procedures and instructions; a bunch of unnecessary baloney.

The club had some value to him in business, but he quickly grew tired of all the RIGMAROLE at meetings.

rigor *(RHIH-gehr), noun*
Something hard to live through or manage; difficulty; difficult to endure; or strictness; extreme hardship

Many southerners who move north soon discover they are not cut out for the RIGOR of even one winter in Montana.

The RIGORS of boot camp are meant to weed out people who cannot handle the trials of combat.

riposte *(rih-POST), noun*
A quick, often witty or cutting, response to a comment or question.

Eileen was unable to offer one of her usual RIPOSTES when we descried her decision to eschew the season's fashion.

risible *(RIZ-uh-bul), adjective*
Funny or amusing; worthy of laughter

The RISIBLE antics of him as a baby with the puppy made him wish his mother had never gotten a video camera.

robust *(ROH-bust) or (roh-BUST), adjective*
Healthy, vigorous; well-built; able to withstand stress; or characterized by fullness and depth; hearty

The trainer's ROBUST health made her an inspiration to everyone in the gym, not just her own clients.

The ROBUST wrestler was willing to take on all challengers who thought they could go three minutes with him.

The ROBUST laughter coming from the basement assured her the men were having a good time shooting pool and watching the game.

roguish *(ROH-gish), adjective*
Mischievous, often in an unscrupulous or dishonest way. Like a rogue; known to have low morals and bad habits. Playful.

ROGUISH behavior is not to be appreciated or imitated, no matter the reputation of the rogue.

roisterers *(ROY-stir-ers), noun*
Partiers, celebrators, or an individual or group having a good time in a loud and boisterous manner.

The ROISTERERS' enjoyment of the party was so infectious, their neighbors joined them instead of complaining about the noise.

rotund *(roh-TUND), adjective*

Plump or chubby; curvy; referring to a person; or round; shaped as a sphere or orb; referring to an item or structure

His full beard, jolly laugh and ROTUND tummy made him a perfect man to play Santa Claus in the parade.

The cook stacked the pots in the cupboard because they were too ROTUND to fit on the shelves.

roué *(roo-AY), noun*

A dissolute man in fashionable society; a rake.

Margie's mother warned her against dating that ROUÉ.

Know This Quote

"A pretty wife is something for the fastidious vanity of a ROUÉ to retire upon." —Thomas Moore, Irish poet and songwriter

rubric *(ROO-brick), noun*

A class, category, title, or heading.

We decided to place Natasha's ball gown under the RUBRIC of "failed fashion choices."

rue *(ROO), verb*

To repent of and regret bitterly.

Elliott knew he would RUE the day that he decided to sell his Maserati, but he did so at his father's urging.

ruffian *(RUF-ee-uhn) or (RUF-yuhn), noun*

A person who is tough and disorderly, particularly one who commits a crime

The store owner knew the teens were just bored kids, not RUFFIANS, so he let them hang out in the parking lot after school.

ruminate *(ROO-muh-nate), verb*

To think carefully and at length about something; to ponder or review mentally, over and over in one's mind. The Latin roots of this word (literally, "chewing the cud") describes the action of cows, who stand for hours on end chewing the same grass over and over again.

Once they were admitted, the guidance counselor wanted every student to RUMINATE on which college admissions offer to accept.

rumination *(ROO-muh-nay-shun), noun*

The act of thinking about something in great detail, weighing the pros and cons over and over in your mind.

For busy people under stress, RUMINATION after going to bed is a frequent contributor to insomnia.

ruritanian *(roor-ih-TAYNE-ee-in), adjective*

Anything related to a romantic adventure or its environment.

The two lovers found Barbados to be a RURITANIAN paradise.

S

doctrinaire abstemious levity hubris panacea veracity cerebellum labyrinth criterion nonagenarian meticulous zither

erbiage quondam colloquial vok palpable paginatio incipient salutary evity redact fervent beleaguered yawnful elixir beneficent amoose pragmatism

sacrilegious *(sack-reh-LIIH-juss), adjective*
Openly insulting or disrespectful to the beliefs, religion, ideas, and practices of others—especially the ones they hold most sacred.

Bryson's insistence that Miró is more collectable that Warhol is positively SACRILEGIOUS.

sacrosanct *(SACK-roh-sankt), adjective*
Beyond criticism because it is considered sacred.

Carl was afraid to comment on Betty's cooking as she thought she was a great chef and considered her food SACROSANCT.

Know This Quote

"If men could get pregnant, maternity benefits would be as SACROSANCT as the G.I. Bill." —Letty Cottin Pogrebin, American editor and writer

sagacious *(suh-GAY-shuss), adjective*
Possessing excellent judgment and powers of discernment; that is, able to make wise decisions. Keen and farsighted, in terms of perception. Call a teacher sagacious, and you'll be very pleased to see how they react.

Professor Blake's SAGACIOUS reputation made him one of the university's most popular lecturers and advisors.

sage *(SAYJ), noun or adjective*
A wise person, usually implies wisdom gained from age (noun) or characterized by a sense of calm and great wisdom (adjective)

The old woman was considered a SAGE within the small community.

As a teenager, he had always rebelled against his grandparents' SAGE advice but longed for it once he was an adult.

Which Word?

Sometimes you may know only the most common definition of a word. Sage (SAYJ) may be one of those words. You know that sage is a shade of green. If you cook, you may know that sage is also a spice. However, if you double-check the listing in the book, you'll discover it is also a very wise person or an adjective indicating the presence of great wisdom.

salacious *(suh-LAY-shus), adjective*
Having to do with lust or sexual desire; bawdy; dealing with sexual matters in an indecent way

She preferred to work out at home so she didn't have to deal with the SALACIOUS looks that followed her when she was at the gym.

salience *(SAY-lee-uns), noun*
The quality of being important or striking. A particularly important or striking feature or relevant point of discussion.

Teachers grade student essays on the SALIENCE of their thesis statements, supporting paragraphs, and conclusions.

salient *(SAY-lee-ehnt) or (SAY-lyent), adjective*
The most important or striking aspect; the part that demands the most attention

Part of the attorney's job was to keep the jurors from being distracted away from the SALIENT points of the case.

saline *(SAY-leen), adjective*
Salty; describes a solution of salt and distilled water, especially one having the same concentration of body fluids.

Judy was so dehydrated that the doctor had to give her an intravenous SALINE solution.

salubrious *(sa-LOO-bree-uhs), adjective*
Promoting or encouraging health and well-being

The couple realized that the occasional weekend away from the demands of their jobs and children had a SALUBRIOUS effect on their relationship.

salutary *(SAL-yeh-tayr-ree), adjective*
Intending to be helpful or to repair a situation; healing; having a good result

Taking a SALUTARY soak in the hot springs may not cure every physical condition as once believed, but it is very good for curing stress-related ones.

salutation *(SAL-yoo-tay-shun), noun*
A gesture or phrase used to greet, recognize, or welcome. The opening phrase of a letter or speech, addressing the recipient or audience.

Brook was unsure whether to use the SALUTATION "Dear" when writing to someone she had just met.

salutatorian *(suh-loo-tuh-TORE-ee-un), noun*
The student graduating second highest in academic ranking. Something to strive for and be proud of.

Being the SALUTATORIAN, rather than the valedictorian, is nothing to be ashamed of.

sanctimonious *(sank-tih-MOAN-ee-us), adjective*
Overbearingly self-righteous and smug in the (perhaps mistaken) belief that one's opinion is correct, and possessing an air of moral superiority about one's opinion.

Gwen did not care for her sister's boyfriend; she found him to be incredibly SANCTIMONIOUS.

Know This Quote

"Not but I've every reason not to care / What happens to him if it only takes / Some of the SANCTIMONIOUS conceit / Out of one of those pious scalawags."
—Robert Frost, American poet

sanction *(SANG-shun), verb*
To give formal or official approval; or to punish with the intent of changing a behavior, generally on a national or international level

The family of the great actor convinced him to SANCTION a biography while he could still be interviewed directly.

The United Nations will SANCTION countries that don't abide by international treaties or law.

sanctum *(SANK-tuhm), noun*
A sacred place inside a church, mosque, or temple. A quiet and private place free of interference or interruption.

Many teens feel as if their rooms are SANCTUMS, and they forbid anyone to enter without permission.

sangfroid *(san-FWAH), noun*
The attitude or state of possessing a cool head and steadfast composure in the face of danger, adversity, or stressful situations.

The car crash shook him, but within seconds he recovered his SANGFROID and went to check on his driver.

sanguine *(SAN-gwinn), adjective*
Cheerfully optimistic; displaying a positive attitude. Also describes something blood-red in color, or flushed with a healthy rosy color.

After the accident, Ken remained SANGUINE, speeding his recovery and inspiring the nurses and doctors who treated him.

sapient *(SAY-pee-ent), adjective*
Wise.

The judge made a SAPIENT ruling in splitting custody between the two parents.

sardonic *(sar-DON-ik), adjective*
Cynically ironic; bitterly humorous

Her SARDONIC smile didn't quite hide her disappointment at being the last one cut from the competition.

sartorial *(Sar-TOR-ee-al), adjective*

Anything related to the way a person dresses, typically used to describe a man who wears finely tailored clothing.

Jonathan's personal tailor always makes sure that Jonathan radiates SARTORIAL splendor.

satchel *(SA-chul), noun*

A small bag, often with a shoulder strap, used for carrying books and personal belongings.

When the laptop computer became popular, everyone seemed to purchase and carry SATCHELS.

satiate *(SAY-shee-ayt), verb*

To satisfy completely; to want or need no more of a longing or appetite

The enormous library held enough books to SATIATE even the most enthusiastic reader.

satiety *(suh-TIE-ih-tee), noun*

The sensation or feeling of being full or having eaten too much.

Although we knew we would be struck by SATIETY, we could not resist the gustatory delights offered at the Whittingtons' New Year's gala.

saturate *(saht-CHUR-ayt), verb*

To drench with a liquid until no more can be held; to soak completely; to totally fill

The trick to growing basil from a seed is to SATURATE the soil when the seed is first planted and then keep it very moist thereafter.

saturnine *(SAT-ur-neen), adjective*

Gloomy, moody, and morose. Describes things under the influence of the planet Saturn, which in astrology is known for its cold and surly nature.

Oddly, after the death of his father, Harry became hopeful and optimistic rather than SATURNINE.

satyr *(SAY-ter) or (SAH-ter) noun*

A character from Greek mythology with the torso and head of a man but the ears, legs, and horns of a goat, known for enjoying self-indulgent celebrations

Pan, a Greek character who loved mischief and troublemaking, is often drawn or sculpted to appear as a SATYR.

savant *(SUH-vont), noun*
A wise or scholarly person, especially one with great knowledge in a very specialized field or area. Remember *Rainman*?

In an irony of nature, some autistic persons who cannot communicate normally possess intellectual powers that can only be described as those of a SAVANT.

savoir faire *(SAV-wah FAIR), noun*
The ability to act appropriately and adroitly in any situation. An obvious sense of confidence and proficiency. From the French for "knowing how to do (it)."

Amazing to his friends, Ron the quarterback demonstrated SAVOIR FARE during the debate competition.

savor *(SAY-vor), verb*
To enjoy completely; to appreciate with great gusto; often referring to the flavor of food

The historian was determined to SAVOR every moment, sight, and sound during her first visit to Washington, D.C.

savory *(SAY-vuh-ree), adjective*
A spicy, rather than sweet, flavoring; or morally pure; uncorrupted

The SAVORY meat pie was delicious and complemented the creamy sweet potatoes perfectly on a cold winter night.

When the judge's less-than-SAVORY past became public, he withdrew from the nomination process to save himself and the President further embarrassment.

Which Word?

It seems obvious that sweet and sweetly are related words. But look out for words that look related but really aren't. Savor and savory appear to be different forms of the same word, but they really are not. Savor (SAY-vor) means to appreciate greatly. Savory (SAY-vuh-ree) means either a spicy flavoring or pure and innocent.

scabbard *(SKA-burd), noun*
The sheath or holder for a knife or sword, usually made of steel or leather

The pirate withdrew his sword from its SCABBARD with an ease that indicated great experience in dueling.

scanty *(SKAN-tee), adjective*
Small to the point of being barely useful; less than is needed; barely adequate

Her SCANTY paycheck was barely enough to cover her monthly expenses, but it was worth it to live in the city she loved.

scapegoat *(SKAPE-goat), noun*
Someone who is made to take the blame for others. Someone who is unjustly blamed for causing upset or distress. Derives from an ancient Jewish practice of selecting a goat to accept the sins of a community.

Students become livid when they think they are being made the SCAPEGOAT for the actions of others.

scarify *(SKARE-ih-fie), verb*
To wound with harsh criticism.

We deemed it necessary to SCARIFY Eileen for having the nerve to criticize our fashion sense.

scarlet letter *(SKAR-lut LEH-tuhr), noun*
Reference to the novel of the same name by Nathaniel Hawthorne, in which an adulterous woman was made to wear a scarlet "A" to mark her as a sinner. Now, a metaphorical reference to a sign that adultery or other sin has been committed.

When word of her affair became public, it was as if she wore a SCARLET LETTER on her clothing, for she was shunned by those who were once her friends.

scathing *(SKAY-thing), adjective*
Severely critical and scornful, often referring to speech or writing about someone's conduct or performance.

The SCATHING review of the movie had no impact on its popularity or profitability.

scenario *(sih-NAH-ree-yoh), noun*
Outline of a play or dramatic plot, scene by scene. A screenplay. An imagined sequence of events that could become possible. Oh, a scene-by-scene story reveals a scenario.

Golfers have to think about all possible SCENARIOS when they choose clubs for each shot.

schism *(SKIH-zum), noun*
Division of a group into mutually antagonistic and disagreeing factions. One faction formed after a disagreement. A division in a religion, or a breaking away from the religion.

Presidential elections recently have created SCHISMS and anger among voters, rather than unified and motivated groups.

schmaltz *(SHMALTS), noun*
Exaggerated, histrionic speech or behavior meant to generate sympathy. From the Yiddish for melted chicken fat used for cooking and flavoring.

Planners often try to minimize the SCHMALTZ when organizing fundraising events for fighting serious diseases.

schmooze *(SHMOOZ), verb*
To chat socially and agreeably. To talk persuasively to somebody, often to gain personal advantage. What high school students often do to get a better grade from a teacher.

Steve has been SCHMOOZING his parents nonstop, a sure sign he wants something big.

scintilla *(sin-TIHL-lah), noun*
A tiny amount or a trace; a quick flash

The SCINTILLA of fear that shuddered through her when the power appeared to be out disappeared when the lights came on and her friends yelled, "Surprise!"

The castaways preserved a SCINTILLA of hope, along with a SCINTILLA of potable water.

Know This Quote
"The air twittered with bright SCINTILLAS of fading light." — Harlan Ellison, American author

scintillate *(SIN-tul-ate), verb*
To give off or reflect light as sparks or sudden flashes. To dazzle in a lively, clever, or witty way. To excite, set off a sudden reaction among others.

News about the new film has been hard to come by, but a few SCINTILLATING details have leaked out.

scion *(SIGH-uhn), noun*
A descendant or heir.

Bill watched on proudly as his SCION hit a home run to win his Little League game.

scofflaw *(SKAWF-lauw), noun*
Someone who ignores, or scoffs at, the law.

Eventually the SCOFFLAW will pay for his actions, if not for his parking tickets.

scrimshaw *(SKRIM-shauw), noun*
The teeth or bones of whales and walruses, engraved with detailed drawings, usually sea related.

Collectors of SCRIMSHAW understand how this art contributed to endangering whale populations, but they continue to cherish their prize possessions.

scrip *(SKRIP), noun*
Paper currency or coupons issued for emergency use. A list, receipt, or short piece of writing. A doctor's prescription.

During World War II, SCRIP was used to purchase gas and other commodities that were being rationed.

scrupulous *(SKROO-pyoo-lus), adjective*
Having great attention to detail; thorough and attentive; or highly moral; concerned with behaving well

The students took SCRUPULOUS notes knowing they could learn as much from the guest lecturer as they could any of their full-time professors.

Even when their relationship was rocky, he was too SCRUPULOUS to even think about having an affair.

seclusion *(seh-KLOO-shun), noun*
The state of being away from other people; being in an exceedingly private place

The writer found it helpful to go into SECLUSION the last month before an approaching deadline with her publisher.

sedentary *(SEHD-ehn-tayr-ee), adjective*
Inactive; characterized by sitting often and not getting much exercise

He discovered he was gaining weight once he took a SEDENTARY job after being a camp counselor for so long.

sedition *(seh-DIH-shun), noun*
Actions or words that encourage rebellion against a government; the act of trying to motivate people to overthrow the government

While complaining about the government is protected by the right of free speech, actual SEDITION is not protected.

sedulous *(SED-jel-lus), adjective*
Characterized by constant and diligent care and concern

She was willing to relax her SEDULOUS attempts to lose weight while they were on the cruise because she knew she would be diligent again at the end of the week.

semantics *(suh-MAN-tiks), noun*
The study of how language conveys meaning. An excessive focus on the way something is phrased, rather than what it says.

The coach's urging to "play aggressive" rather than "hurt the opponents" was a matter of SEMANTICS, and its interpretation depended upon which team you wanted to win.

semblance *(SEM-blunts), noun*
Outward appearance or show, usually not true. A representation, copy, or likeness.

When the principal entered the classroom being taught by a substitute, there appeared to be no SEMBLANCE of order.

seminal *(SEM-ih-nul), adjective*
Highly original and influential, as in ideas that inspire later developments. Relating to, containing, or carrying semen or seeds.

For many, the Ten Commandments are the SEMINAL expressions of laws, values, and societal norms.

sentient *(SEN-shunt), adjective*
Capable of feeling and perceptions; the quality of being conscious or aware. Capable of emotional response and of receiving impressions from the senses.

Any SENTIENT being should be able to notice the dreariness that comes with a cloudy day.

Know This Quote

"Many years ago, a particular creature was selected to develop into the dominant life form on this planet. It was given certain breaks and certain challenges, all of which, when utilized or overcome, marked it indelibly with particular traits as it moved along the road to a higher SENTIENCE." —Roger Zelazny, American science fiction writer

separatists *(SEP-prah-tists), noun*
Those who believe a particular region or group should be separated from a larger whole.

Some SEPARATIST Canadians want Quebec to be a separate nation from the rest of Canada.

sepulchral *(suh-PUHL-kruhl), adjective*
Hollow and deep; characteristic of a tomb; often used to describe certain voices.

Our butler's SEPULCHRAL voice instantly impresses our social contacts when they come to visit.

sequester *(si-KWES-ter), verb*
To isolate, cut off from everyday life and outside influences. To take legal possession of someone's property until a debt is paid or dispute resolved. To seize or demand the property of an enemy.

When the judge adjourned court for the day, he also SEQUESTERED the jury for the remainder of the trial.

serendipitous *(sare-un-DIH-pih-tuss), adjective*
Accidental in a happy and fortuitous way. Often describes useful discoveries made by accident, or important insights encountered as fortunate coincidences.

It was SERENDIPITOUS that Phil won new golf clubs a week before the club championship.

serendipity *(ser-en-DIP-it-ee), noun*
Attaining success, good fortune, or the object of your desire more through luck and random circumstance than deliberate effort.

What made him an Internet billionaire was SERENDIPITY more than brains or talent.

serene *(suh-REEN), adjective*
Clear and calm, without worry, disturbance, or stress. Bright without clouds.

Visiting the lake house always made her feel SERENE, so she went there before her wedding.

serpentine *(SUR-pen-teen), adjective*
Snake-like in shape or movement.

Donna thought Wanda looked positively SERPENTINE as her long tongue licked the ice cream cone.

Know This Quote

"For it is not possible to join SERPENTINE wisdom with columbine innocency, except men know exactly all the conditions of the serpent." —Francis Bacon, English philosopher, author, and statesman

servile *(SER-viyl), adjective*
Willing to serve others; most comfortable when serving another in a lesser or submissive role

The feminist movement grew from women wanting to be more than just SERVILE homemakers.

servitude *(SIR-vuh-tood), noun*
State of slavery, of being ruled or dominated. Work imposed as punishment.

Being forced to paint the house in order to earn his allowance felt like SERVITUDE to Burt.

sesquicentennial *(sess-kwa-sen-TEN-yuhl), noun*
A 150th anniversary, celebration of a 150th anniversary, or a 150-year period.

Historians reveal that the U.S. SESQUICENTENNIAL celebration in 1926 was much more reserved than the bicentennial of 1976.

severance *(SEHV-er-ans) or (SEHV-rans), noun*
The separation of parties or parts

The SEVERANCE of the smaller movie studio from its larger parent company was a shock to everyone who followed the film industry.

Unsure of whether they would receive any SEVERANCE, in the end they were happy to get three months' pay after the layoff.

shard *(SHARD), noun*
A piece of broken glass, pottery, metal, or other breakable material, usually having sharp edges

The SHARDS from the broken glass scattered across the kitchen floor, making it treacherous for anyone in bare feet.

simile *(SIH-muh-lee), noun*
A figure of speech that draws a comparison between two things, using "like" or "as," as in "teeth as white as pearls."

Robert Burns' famous poetic SIMILE, "Oh, my love is like a red, red rose," is oft quoted and more often felt.

sine qua non *(sie-nih kwah NON), noun*
An essential condition, feature, or prerequisite. Latin for "without which not."

Commitment is the SINE QUA NON for academic success.

sinecure *(SIYN-ih-kyoor) or (SIHN-ih-kyoor), noun*
A job that requires very little work but that offers a paycheck and other benefits

He needed a position that was basically a SINECURE so he would have time to study while he was at the office in order to keep his grades up.

sinuous *(SIN-yoo-uhs), adjective*
Curvy; characterized by having many turns and twists; or graceful and smooth

The SINUOUS road through the mountains was more dangerous than ever after the ice storm.

The cat's SINUOUS speed allowed it to outmaneuver the gangly puppy with ease.

siren *(SY-ren), noun*
A destructive, but seductively beautiful, beguiling woman; or, anything considered dangerously seductive.

Bob's friends thought he was crazy when he followed the SIREN's call and moved to Los Angeles to pursue an acting career.

Know This Quote

"It is natural to indulge in the illusions of hope. We are apt to shut our eyes to that SIREN until she 'allures' us to our death."
—Gertrude Stein, American author

skeptic *(SKEHP-tik), noun*
A person who automatically doubts the truth about ideas, concepts, or beliefs commonly accepted by others

She was such a SKEPTIC that she rarely believed in anything she couldn't see or touch, regardless of how strong an argument someone made in favor of the concept.

Which Word?

Think you know how to spell a word? Some words have multiple correct spellings. Skeptic is one of them. While the most common spelling is s-k-e-p-t-i-c, it is sometimes spelled s-c-e-p-t-i-c. They are both pronounced (SKEHP-tik). Use the most common spelling when you write the word. But know that if you see it spelled with a c, it is the same word and it is spelled correctly.

skiff *(SKIF), noun*
A certain kind of small boat propelled by oar, sail, or motor, usually with a flat bottom

> *A SKIFF WAS available during summer to take tourists from one side of the lake to the other.*

skullduggery *(skul-DUG-guh-ree), noun*
Practices carried out in a secretive way in order to trick people.

> *The SKULLDUGGERY of the Watergate burglars has become infamous, for it forced a President to resign.*

sluggard *(SLUH-gehrd), noun*
An overall lazy person, has negative connotations

> *He was so busy that his wife often reminded him that spending one afternoon relaxing would not turn him into a SLUGGARD.*

sluggish *(SLUH-gish), adjective*
Slow moving; slow to respond; having a lack of energy

> *The August day was so hot and lazy that even the river behind the house seemed SLUGGISH.*

sobriquet *(soh-brih-KAY), noun*
An unofficial name or nickname, especially a humorous one. Something almost every high school student has, although some just don't know what others call them behind their back.

> *How embarrassing that she would call him "Pookie," a private SOBRIQUET, in front of others.*

socialism *(SOH-shuh-lih-zum), noun*
A political theory that gives workers fair and equitable control over the goods and products they produce, as opposed to the free market principles and competition of capitalism.

> *Historically, SOCIALISM has proven to work in theory only, with little success in real-world application.*

Socratic method *(suh-CRA-tick METH-uhd), noun*
A process of teaching and learning, in which the teacher asks questions that force the students to think and arrive at their own logical conclusions.

Many of the best law professors use the SOCRATIC METHOD to teach students.

soi-disant *(soy-dih-SAHNT), adjective*
Self-styled.

A SOI-DISANT lady's man, Gary's focus was always on his next conquest.

sojourn *(SO-jern), noun*
A temporary visit or stay.

The Israelites' SOJOURN in the desert lasted for forty long years.

solace *(SOH-luhs), noun*
Comfort in difficult or trying times; ease from pain

After her grandfather died, she found SOLACE in the company of others who had loved him.

solicitous *(soh-LIHS-ih-tus), adjective*
Marked by being concerned; characterized by offering care and attention

She knew her friend was trying to be helpful while she was sick, but his SOLICITOUS nature was beginning to get on her nerves.

soliloquy *(suh-LIL-uh-kwee), noun*
The act of talking to yourself, from the Latin for "speak alone." In theatre, a monologue that lets a character express inner emotions that would be difficult to communicate in dialogue.

The SOLILOQUY is a dramatic device made famous by Shakespeare.

solipsism *(SAHL-ip-sihz-uhm), noun*
The notion that one's own experiences and thoughts are the only source of true knowledge.

The SOLIPSISM of some members of the leisure class is distasteful to those of us who, for example, know what our servants need even more than they do.

solstice *(SOUL-stis), noun*
A day of the year during which the sun is at its highest or lowest point in the sky, causing the shortest day of the year on December 21 (winter *solstice*) and the longest day of the year on June 21 (summer *solstice*).

Rachel always gets up to see the sunrise on the day of the summer SOLSTICE so she can say that she saw the sun rise and set on the longest day of the year.

solvent *(SAWL-vent), adjective*
Having enough money to meet all financial obligations; being able to pay one's debts

He worked very hard to pay off all his loans after college and planned to stay SOLVENT from then on out.

somnambulate *(som-NAH-byoo-late), verb*
To walk in your sleep.

Kenny shocked his teammates when he SOMNAMBULATED on their first road trip.

somniferous *(sahm-NIF-her-uhs), adjective*
Bringing on sleep or tiredness

Hot cocoa always had a SOMNIFEROUS effect on her, so it was her favorite late night drink when she couldn't sleep.

somnolent *(SAHM-nuh-lent), adjective*
Drowsy, sleepy, or lazy in a tired way

The baby fell asleep on her father's chest listening to the SOMNOLENT tones of his voice as he whispered to her.

Which Word?

Many words may seem synonymous, but subtle differences in meaning mean they cannot be used interchangeably. Somniferous (sahm-NIF-her-uhs) and somnolent (SAHM- nuh-lent) are two of these words. Something that is somniferous will bring on sleep or cause tiredness, whereas something that is somnolent is already sleepy and drowsy.

sonorous *(saw-NUH-rus) or (SAW-nuh-rus) or (SOH-nuh-rus), adjective*
Impressively deep, rich, and full, generally referring to a sound

His SONOROUS bass voice made him perfect to play the villain in the movie.

soothsayer *(SOOTH-say-ehr), noun*
Someone who predicts the future through magic, intuition, or other imaginative means.

Scientists are skeptical about anyone who claims to be a SOOTHSAYER, for they believe it impossible to foretell the future.

sophist *(SAHF-izm), adjective*
Sounding reasonable, yet patently false.

One can argue that what is learned in law school is largely the skill of making SOPHIST arguments that a jury can believe.

sophistry *(SOF-ih-stree), noun*
An intentionally misleading and false argument or claim used to misrepresent
Most people in the office were accustomed to his SOPHISTRY so it was more difficult for him to get the projects he wanted.

sophomoric *(sah-fuh-MOH-rick), adjective*
Showing a lack of judgment characteristic of immaturity. Also, relating to sophomores.
How strange and confusing it was to hear the principal call the junior class prank SOPHOMORIC.

soporific (*sah-POR-if-ik) or (soh-POR-if-ik), adjective or noun*
Tending to bring about sleep; sleepy (adjective) or a product or substance that brings about sleepiness (noun)
Riding in the car had a SOPORIFIC effect on the baby, so her parents drove her around the block when she wouldn't go to sleep.
The medicine was great for her headaches but it was also a SOPORIFIC, so she could only take it at night.

sordid *(SORE-did), adjective*
Demonstrating the worst aspects of human nature; immoral, tawdry, greedy. Undignified; dirty and depressing
Biographies are often profitable publications, especially those containing SORDID details about the lives of famous people.

specious *(SPEE-shus), adjective*
Reasonable at first glance but actually false; believable on the surface but not true; plausible but incorrect
Part of the professor's job was to point out the SPECIOUS logic in her students' arguments and help them find the truth of the situation.

speculative *(SPEH-kyoo-luh-tiv), adjective*
Based on conjecture or incomplete information. Describes opinions or conclusions not based on facts. Risky, in terms of an investment that is potentially profitable.
Even the most detailed statistical analyses of actuaries are only SPECULATIVE in nature.

spontaneity *(spon-tuh-NAY-uh-tee), noun*
Impulsive behavior that is not planned. Also, the source of such activity.
The SPONTANEITY of youth is looked back upon with great jealousy by elders.

spoonerism *(SPOON-er-iz-um), noun*

A phrase in which the syllables of neighboring words are accidentally interchanged.

A popular SPOONERISM states: "Cook a grilled cheese sandwich in lots of butter, let it get cold, and you have a chilled grease sandwich."

Sphinx *(SFINKS), noun*

A mythical creature with the head of a woman, the body of a lion, the wings of an eagle, and the tail of a serpent.

When Oedipus correctly answered the SPHINX'S riddle, the SPHINX leaped to its death in the valley below.

spurious *(SPYUR-ee-us), adjective*

False. Illegitimate, as in a child. True and believable but on the outside only. Forged.

Eric's belief that his bad grades were because teachers did not like him was SPURIOUS, for in truth, he was very well liked.

spurn *(SPERN), verb*

To reject in a cold and rude manner

She pretended to SPURN the girls getting ready for the dance but in reality she was just hurt because no one had asked her to go.

squalid *(SKWAH-lihd), adjective*

Disgustingly dirty; grimy and practically unlivable; or completely without morals or standards

The neighborhood had once been a SQUALID, dangerous part of town but the current residents had worked hard to make a decent place to live and raise a family.

The new CEO put an end to the SQUALID business practices his predecessor had developed and encouraged.

squalor *(SKWAH-lur), noun*

Shabbiness and dirtiness resulting from poverty or neglect. State of moral decay.

The investigation found that because the three children lived in SQUALOR, they would be better off in a foster home.

stagnation *(stag-NAY-shun), noun*

A period of time without growth; the state of not moving forward; often referring to an economic condition

The mountain village decided to turn itself into a tourist attraction to break the STAGNATION that had settled there since the last mine closed.

staid *(STAYD), adjective*
Fixed and settled; not distinctive; uninteresting.

Even though the Sandersons are an important family, we could hardly last the requisite hour at the family's STAID winter ball.

stalwart *(STAHL-wert), adjective*
Dependable, loyal, strong, sturdy, and courageous.

The STALWART support of his colleagues was what drove Dan to further achievements.

stately *(STAYT-lee), adjective*
Impressive, dignified, and graceful in manner. Grand and imposing in appearance.

First-time visitors to the White House are always impressed by its STATELY interior and impressive grounds.

stereotype *(STAY-ree-yo-type), noun*
An oversimplified opinion, usually based on prejudice or poor judgment, held by a group of people, usually about people or ideas foreign to them.

Bill Bradley, a Princeton graduate, professional basketball player, Rhodes Scholar, and U.S. senator lived a life counter to the STEREOTYPE of the dumb jock.

stigma *(STIG-mah), noun*
A mark of shame or embarrassment; something considered appropriate to hide

There is still such a STIGMA associated with counseling and therapy that many people are not getting the care they need because they don't want to be seen as crazy.

Where'd That Word Come From?
Stigma—From the Greek for "tattoo," this word for something that permanently stains someone's reputation comes from the ancient Greek practice of physically marking someone with a tattoo to distinguish him as belonging to a lower class.

stipulate *(STIH-pyoo-late), verb*
To specify a certain condition in an agreement or offer. To promise something formally or legally. In legal terms, to confess, admit, or agree to a fact, rather than require the opposition to prove the fact.

The will does STIPULATE that you must wait until you are thirty years old to receive the money.

stoic *(STOH-ik), adjective or noun*
Showing no expression; apparently immune to pain, hurt, or other emotion (adjective) or a person who shows little or no emotion regardless of the situation (noun)

She was so STOIC at the funeral that even her sister thought she was unaffected by their grandmother's death.

Although strangers thought he was a STOIC, his friends knew he was actually quite warm and open once he was comfortable in a situation.

stolid *(STAH-luhd), adjective*
Exceedingly calm; rarely emotionally out of control; dependable and unexcitable

Her STOLID presence was a blessing for the children who were confused by the other adults' reaction to the crisis.

strident *(STRIY-dent), adjective*
Obnoxiously and often unnecessarily loud

His STRIDENT objections to the plane's delay tried the gate attendant's patience.

stringent *(STRIHN-juhnt), adjective*
Rigorous, strict, severe.

"I hate your STRINGENT rules," screamed Louise after her father told her she couldn't stay out past midnight.

Know This Quote

"No laws, however STRINGENT, can make the idle industrious, the thriftless provident, or the drunken sober." —Samuel Smiles, Scottish author and reformer

strophe *(STROF), noun*
A stanza containing lines that do not conform to the type, style, or form of the poem in which they appear.

Those not wearing haute couture stick out at our gatherings like STROPHES stick out in short poems.

stultify *(STUHL-tuh-fie), verb*
To cause to appear foolish or ridiculous.

The out-of-date chapeau absolutely STULTIFIED Heather's otherwise immaculate couture.

stupefy *(STOO-pih-fiy), verb*
To make a person unable to think clearly; to stun; to dull the senses; or to amaze, shock, and astonish

The teacher's lectures were so boring they managed to STUPEFY all but the most attentive students.

His parents were STUPEFIED by his decision to take a year traveling around Europe instead of accepting the scholarship offered him by the university.

stymie *(STIY-mee), verb*
To confuse to the point of being unable to figure out the situation; to stop or halt progress

The construction of the bookshelf was STYMIED when he accidentally dropped the screws behind the couch.

subjugate *(SUB-jih-gate), verb*
To put someone, a group, or a nation under control. To cause to become subservient. To make another person perform your will.

Throughout history, dictators' attempts to SUBJUGATE other countries have failed in the end.

sublimate *(SUB-lih-mate), verb*
To bury and conceal the energy of an impulse or desire, usually one having to do with sex, in a pursuit considered more proper. To redirect an urge to a wholesome purpose.

An artist who can SUBLIMATE his feelings might find them transformed into great works.

sublime *(suh-BLIME), adjective*
Awe-inspiring beauty that seems heavenly. Of the highest moral or spiritual value; lofty, splendid, or complete.

The climbers were rewarded at the top of the mountain by a SUBLIME view of the valley.

subliminal *(sub-LIM-inn-uhl), adjective*
Operating below the threshold of consciousness, but still having an affect on the mind.

SUBLIMINAL advertising was a big fad in advertising in the 1970s.

Know This Quote

"The SUBLIME and the ridiculous are often so nearly related, that it is difficult to class them separately. One step above the SUBLIME makes the ridiculous, and one step above the ridiculous makes the SUBLIME again."
—Thomas Paine, English revolutionary and intellectual

subordinate *(suh-BOR-dih-nuht), adjective or noun or (sub-BOR-dih-nayt), verb*
Considered less important; secondary; lower in the hierarchy (adjective) or a person who is below another in rank or position (noun) or to make something or someone lower in importance than something or someone else (verb)

He was unwilling to take a position that was SUBORDINATE to the one he had previously held.

She was well-liked as a supervisor because she treated her SUBORDINATES professionally and with respect.

In modern relationships, the women do not need to SUBORDINATE their desires to men's.

Which Word?

Many words can be used as a noun, an adjective, or a verb. Subordinate is one of them. When used as a noun or an adjective, it is pronounced suh-BOR-dih-nuht. The noun subordinate is a person of lower rank or standing than someone else. The adjective subordinate indicates a lower rank or standing. When used as a verb, it is pronounced sub-BOR-dih-nayt. The verb to subordinate means to make something or someone less important than something else. Ready for a fun sentence? The president's immediate subordinate was only subordinate to the president, so his wishes were rarely subordinated to anyone else's wishes. Read closely so you don't confuse the parts of speech!

subpoena *(suh-PEE-nah), noun or verb*

An order requiring a person to appear in court to testify (noun) or to order a person to appear in court to testify (verb)

After witnessing the accident, she received a SUBPOENA to give her version of events.

The lawyer didn't want to SUBPOENA the child if there was any way to avoid it.

subrogation *(suh-bro-GAY-shin), noun*

The substitution of one person for another with respect to a lawful claim or right.

The SUBROGATION clause in the lease says that if the landlord cannot collect rent from the tenant, she has the right to collect from the co-signer of the leasing agreement.

subservient *(sub-SER-vee-unt), adjective*

Eager to follow wishes or orders. Bending to the will of another; servile.

In spite of how sexist it sounded, Ken thought that wives should be SUBSERVIENT to their husbands.

subside *(suhb-SIYD), verb*

To lower to normal or almost normal levels; to decrease; to ease off

The doctors told her she could not work out until two weeks after the pain in her broken foot had SUBSIDED.

subsistence *(SUB-sis-tense), noun*

The minimum—of food, water, clothing, shelter, and money—a person or family needs to survive.

All we need for SUBSISTENCE is the basics: the finest of everything.

substantiate *(suhb-STAN-shee-ayt), verb*

To confirm; to give proof of presented or presumed facts

The students had to SUBSTANTIATE every claim they made in their research papers.

subterfuge *(SUB-tehr-fyooj), noun*
A plan or strategy developed to mislead or trick

It took an elaborate SUBTERFUGE and the assistance of several of her friends to pull off the surprise birthday party.

subversive *(sub-VER-suv), adjective*
Intended to undermine a government or other institution, usually by secret actions performed from the inside; undermining.

Antiwar protesters of the 1960s were thought by many to be SUBVERSIVE and by others to be patriots who personified the value of freedom of speech.

succinct *(suk-SINKT), adjective*
Compact and clear, expressed without unnecessary words.

Thomas's acceptance speech was SUCCINCT, lasting only one minute and composed of fewer than a hundred words.

suffix *(SUH-fiks), noun*
A letter or group of letters added at the end of a word or part to form another word. An example: adding "-ly" to "quick" yields *quickly*.

The SUFFIX "ly" is the one commonly used for creating adverbs from adjectives.

sultry *(SUL-tree), adjective*
In terms of weather, hot and humid, with little or no breeze. In terms of human behavior, suggestive of passion or smoldering sexuality.

That morning, Marcia put on a sundress and flipflops to prepare for the SULTRY day the weatherman predicted.

Know This Quote

"Bare-headed in the SULTRY sun, Ahab stood on the bowsprit."
—Herman Melville, American author

sumptuous *(sum-CHYOO-uhs), adjective*
Large and elegant enough to indicate great time or expense; splendid

The reception included a SUMPTUOUS spread of delicacies and fine wines.

supersede *(Sue-per-SEED), verb*
When one thing takes the place of another or renders the former obsolete.

Running late, Carla decided that preparing dinner for her guests SUPERSEDED her desire to get the laundry folded.

supercilious *(soo-per-SIL-ee-uhs), adjective*
Acting as if one is better than others; snobby

The SUPERCILIOUS girl ended up feeling foolish when she realized the young woman she had ignored was the daughter of a famous rock star.

Where'd That Word Come From?

Supercilious—Dr. Franz Joseph Gall, the founder of the "science" of phrenology, claimed that people with big foreheads and higher brows have more brains. This led to the expression *highbrow,* which described an intellectual. *Supercilious,* meaning "disdainful," is related to the brow, too. It derives from the Latin for "raised eyebrow," which comes from the image of someone lifting an eyebrow slightly in disdain. Think Jack Nicholson here (though most people probably don't think of him as a highbrow).

superficial *(soo-per-FIH-shul), adjective*
Having to do only with the surface; skin deep. Concerned with or stating only the obvious, with little significance or substance. Not thorough.

The wound was SUPERFICIAL, requiring only cleaning and bandaging and no sutures.

superfluous *(soo-PER-floo-us), adjective*
Unnecessary; extra; more than enough

Since her walls were already covered in posters, buying another one seemed SUPERFLUOUS.

superlative *(sue-PURR-lah-tiv), adjective*
The quality of something's being the best in its class or quality.

Our family's show horses are SUPERLATIVE to the rest of the horses one can find in the county.

supernumerary *(soo-per-NOO-muh-ruh-ree) or (soo-per-NYOO-muh-ruh-ree), adjective*
Extra and not necessary; more than the usual amount; excessive

The coach was always grateful when he had a SUPERNUMERARY number of hopefuls try out because it meant he could be picky about his team and not have to settle for poor players.

supersede *(soo-pehr-SEED), verb*
Take the place of; replace; or to override or overrule

The SUV has SUPERSEDED the minivan as the choice for large families who need a roomy vehicle.

The boss' ideas SUPERSEDED all other suggestions, regardless of how valid they were.

supine *(soo-PIYN) or (SOO-piyn), adjective*
Having one's face up; lying on the back, face up; or showing lack of care, concern, or resistance in the face of injustice or wrongdoing

After her knee surgery, she could only lay SUPINE until the doctors took her out of traction.

The field workers found the residents of the neighborhood frustratingly SUPINE considering the crime rates in the area.

supplant *(suh-PLANT), verb*
To replace; to take the place of and perform the same function of another

The United Nations' goal was to SUPPLANT the dictatorship with a democratic government on the small island.

Know This Quote

"If we would SUPPLANT the opinions and policy of our fathers in any case, we should do so upon evidence so conclusive, and arguments so clear, that even their great authority fairly considered and weighted, cannot stand." —Abraham Lincoln

supplicate *(SUP-lih-cayt), verb*
To ask humbly for something; to plead with great earnestness

The people at the vigil took a moment of silence to SUPPLICATE God for the health and safety of the men and women serving in the military.

surcharge *(SUHR-charj), noun*
An additional charge above and beyond the price or original amount

He was going to get cash from the ATM but decided the $2 SURCHARGE was too much to pay just to have some extra money in his pocket.

surfeit *(SUHR-fit), adjective*
An extra amount; more than is necessary

Although she knew she would have a SURFEIT of food at the party, she thought it was better to have leftovers than have people leave hungry.

surreal *(suh-REEL), adjective*
Possessing a quality that makes something seem unreal; strange; bizarre; almost other-worldly.

The light coming from outside her window late at night seemed somewhat SURREAL.

surreptitious *(suh-rup-TISH-uss), adjective*
Secret or sneaky, especially in terms of actions and acquisitions. Stealthy.

Intelligence gathering is a SURREPTITIOUS activity, accomplished covertly.

susurration *(soo-suh-RAY-shun), noun*
A soft sound such as the murmuring from a hushed conversation in the next room or the rain gently falling on the roof.

He bought a device to help him sleep: an electronic synthesizer that mimics the SUSURRATION of a drizzle or a rainstorm.

suzerainty *(Suh-ZER-ant-tee), noun*
Paramount, unquestioned authority.

Although Robin disagreed, she was reluctant to challenge her boss's SUZERAINTY.

sybarite *(SIY-ber-iyt), noun*
A person devoted to luxury; one who is self-indulgent when it comes to pleasure and living well

Having grown up without any money at all, the wealthy actress quickly developed a reputation for being a SYBARITE.

sybaritic *(sih-bar-IT-ik), adjective*
Relating to self-indulgent sensuous luxury and pleasure.

Selena rubbed the suntan lotion over her tanned middle slowly, and the whole thing had an erotic, SYBARITIC quality that made the men's eyes pop out of their heads.

sycophant (*SIH-kuh-fant), noun*
Someone who flatters a powerful person for personal gain; an ambitious flatterer who tries to improve his status by fawning over those in authority.

Presidents and world leaders should not surround themselves with SYCOPHANTS, for they need to hear critical and realistic views regarding critical issues.

symbiosis *(sim-bee-OSE-sis), noun*
A mutually beneficial relationship among different species. A cooperative, mutually beneficial relationship between people, groups, or things.

The two top students found that a SYMBIOSIS was much better than a competitive relationship, so they studied together.

symmetrical *(SIH-met-trih-kuhl), adjective*
Balanced in proportion. Usually describes the even or balanced halves of a whole. Able to be divided equally in half.

Whenever Mom redecorated, she first looked for SYMMETRICAL relationships between pieces of furniture, and then made me and Dad do the lifting.

symposium *(sim-POH-zee-uhm), noun*
A gathering, for the purpose of discussing a particular subject and where learned people make presentations. A published collection of opinions or writing on a subject. Its plural is *symposia.*

The SYMPOSIUM on how to teach high school students was very well attended by teachers and administrators.

Where'd That Word Come From?

Sycophant—The old story, unproven but widely accepted, is that this word for an apple-polisher (basically, someone who sucks up to their superiors) originated in ancient Greece from the Greek *sukophantes* (*sukon*, "fig," and *phainen*, "to show"). This word referred to an informer on those who exported figs. At one time it was supposedly against the law to export figs from Athens, and *sukophantes*, later *sychophants*, often turned in violators of the law for their own selfish gain.

synchronicity *(sin-kruh-NIH-suh-tee), noun*
Coincidental events, especially thoughts or dreams, that seem related even though they are not obviously caused by each other. The great psychoanalyst Carl Jung used this term to describe an underlying connection of all parts of our lives, even those that we consider accidental.

You have experienced SYNCHRONICITY if you have ever been thinking of an old friend only to turn the corner and run right into her.

synchronous *(SIN-kro-nus), adjective*
Two events or processes that take place at the same time.

The Smythingtons and the Lyttons caused quite a stir among their social contacts after they scheduled SYNCHRONOUS galas.

syncopation *(sin-ko-PAY-shun), noun*
Music in which the beats are reversed: the normally loud beats are softer, and the beats normally subdued are emphasized.

The weird SYNCOPATION in the score made the music very difficult for the percussionists to follow.

syncretistic *(sin-kre-TIH-stik), adjective*
A set of beliefs obtained by combining elements of multiple cultures, religions, societies, or schools of thought.

Pauline's SYNCRETISTIC worldview comes from the fact that her family has traveled extensively across the globe.

synecdoche *(sih-NECK-duh-kee), noun*
A type of shorthand speech in which a partial description is understood by the reader or listener to represent the whole; e.g., saying "New York" in a discussion of baseball when you mean "the New York Yankees."

Marla could not stop using a SYNECDOCHE after she returned from her trip to England at which she met the royal family, saying repeatedly that she had met and socialized with "the crown."

synonym *(SYN-uh-nim), noun*
One or numerous expressions or words that have exactly or very nearly the same meaning. A word that means the same, or almost the same as another word; equivalent in meaning to another word.

If you are looking for a SYNONYM, a thesaurus is a good place to start.

synoptic *(sin-OP-tik), adjective*
Forming or involving a synopsis or summary.

The close of a presentation should be SYNOPTIC in nature.

synopsis *(sih-NOP-sis), noun*
A condensed version of a text; an outline or summary of principal points.

Those small paperback books that contain a SYNOPSIS of the novels that high school students read are quite popular, and some are well written, but they should never take the place of actually reading the assigned work.

synthesis *(SIN-thih-sihs), noun*
The combining of two or more individual parts to create a new whole

The SYNTHESIS of his charm and her intelligence made them an almost unbeatable debate team.

systemic *(sih-STEM-ik), adjective*
Relating to a system as a whole and not just its component parts.

The discarding of couture clothing that is less than a year old has become SYSTEMIC among our group.

syzygy *(SIZE-ih-gee), noun*
In astronomy, *syzygy* takes place when the Earth, sun, and moon all line up along a straight path.

Astronomers predict an eclipse for the next SYZYGY.

T

tableau *(ta-BLOW), noun*
A clear, descriptive representation of something; a picture. An artistic grouping of varied elements.

The prehistoric TABLEAUS in New York's Museum of Natural History are so lifelike that they scare young children.

taboo *(ta-BOO), adjective*
Forbidden from use in ordinary context; reserved for special or sacred functions. Also, forbidden on the grounds of bad taste or immorality.

At one time having a child out of wedlock was considered TABOO, but now it seems quite acceptable.

Where'd That Word Come From?

Taboo—The Friendly Islands (now Tonga) were visited by the English explorer Captain James Cook in 1777. It is in Cook's journals that we document the first use of *taboo* for something banned or prohibited. Cook had altered the spelling a little, from the Tongan *tabu*, which meant the same thing.

tabula rasa *(TAB-you-lah RAW-zah), noun*
Literally, a clean slate. In psychological terms, the mind before it takes on any impressions from society or experience. Also something that is pristine and new, without any preconceptions or existing features.

Teaching kindergarten is so rewarding, for each child's mind is in many ways like a TABULA RASA.

tacit *(TA-sit), adjective*
Understood or implied without being stated; not spoken.

Each juror's TACIT assumption must be that the defendant is innocent until proven guilty.

taciturn *(TAS-ih-tern), adjective*
Quiet or uncommunicative; not given to talking or making conversation

Her TACITURN uncle was embarrassed but flattered when asked to make a toast at the wedding.

Kenny was concerned that Emily's father's TACITURN nature indicated that he disapproved of their dating.

tactful *(TAKT-ful), adjective*
Able to say the proper things in order to keep good relationships with others. A tactful person is actually one who knows what not to say in order to avoid making others angry or upset.

How TACTFUL of her to decline his invitation by saying such nice things.

tactile *(TAK-tull), adjective*
Able to be felt or perceived by the sense of touch. Also, related to the sense of touch.

Velvet is pretty to look at, but it provides a mostly TACTILE pleasure.

talisman *(TAH-lus-mun), noun*
An object believed to give magical powers to those who carry or wear it. Anything believed to have magical powers.

Many indigenous people wear a TALISMAN to ward off evil.

tandem *(TAN-dum), adjective*
Two-seated, as in a bicycle. An arrangement of two or more items in which one is placed behind the other; single file. Also, acting in conjunction.

The team's warm-up featured a TANDEM lay-up drill that intimidated opponents and inspired the crowd.

tangential *(tan-JENT-shul), adjective*
Veering off from the main or current subject; departing from the plotted course. Peripheral. In math, relating to or involving a tangent.

Please stop; your TANGENTIAL information is only serving to confuse our decision making.

Know This Quote

"New York is full of people . . . with a feeling for the TANGENTIAL adventure, the risky adventure, the interlude that's not likely to end in any double-ring ceremony." —Joan Didion, American journalist

tangible *(TAN-juh-bull), adjective*
Able to be perceived with any sense, but especially via the sense of touch. Able to be understood and evaluated with the mind. Things that are tactile are also tangible, though the reverse is not always true.

Sometimes TANGIBLE rewards of teaching, like salary, are not what truly matter, for the intangibles also pay off.

tantalizing *(TAN-tuh-lie-zing), adjective*
Attractive and tempting, often due to unavailability or unattainability. In Aesop's fable, the fox found the grapes tantalizing in part because he could not reach them.

College is a TANTALIZING goal for many students, but low SAT scores and poor grades make this dream impractical for some.

Where'd That Word Come From?

Tantalize—Tantalus, a son of Zeus in Greek mythology, divulged the secrets of the gods to the humans. He was sent to Hades and punished with eternal thirst and hunger. The pool of water he stood in dried up whenever he tried to drink from it, and the tree branches above his head pulled out of reach whenever he reached for their fruit. This punishment gives us the word *tantalize.*

tantamount *(TANT-uh-mownt), adjective*
Being equal to in importance or seriousness; being as good as

> *For the young actor, the award nomination was TANTAMOUNT to a declaration that he had succeeded in achieving his life's dream.*

Tao *(DOW), noun*
Literally, "the way." An Eastern philosophy founded by Lao-tzu and described in the *Tao Te Ching.* Basically, an expression of the ultimate reality, the universal energy that makes and maintains everything. The order and wisdom of life and harmony with the universe.

> *She was reading a book with a more philosophical look at relationships called* The TAO of Dating.

tautology *(tow-TAH-luh-gee), noun*
A redundant repetition of meaning in a sentence or idea using different words. Unnecessary repetition—in different words—of an idea already stated.

> *Stating that you know a foreigner from another nation is a TAUTOLOGY, because all foreigners are from other countries.*

tawdry *(TAW-dree), adjective*
Gaudy, showy, and cheap, as clothes; or, base and mean, as motives.

> *Paul said he loved the dress his girlfriend wore to the dance, but secretly thought it was a bit TAWDRY.*

Know This Quote

"Far from being the basis of the good society, the family, with its narrow privacy and TAWDRY secrets, is the source of all our discontents." —Sir Edmund Leach, British author

taxonomy *(tak-SAH-nuh-mee), noun*
A logical system that describes the interrelationships of different things. In biology, the classification that assigns every organism a Latin name according to its genus and species, thus identifying its relation to other similar beings and its place in the system overall.

> *Prior to creating a lesson plan, each teacher must develop a TAXONOMY of learning objectives.*

technocrat *(tek-NUH-krat), noun*
A bureaucrat with training in engineering, economics, or some form of technology. Someone who believes that technicians, or the people who know how things actually work, should be the ones involved in government.

Stereotypically, TECHNOCRATS think less about emotional issues and how decisions impact people.

tectonic *(tek-TAH-nik) adjective*
Having to do with the geological structure of the earth, particularly the earth's crust. The study of *tectonics* investigates the way a planet's crust works, forming mountains and causing earthquakes.

TECTONIC plates are geologic features that some believe will cause a major earthquake with an epicenter in California.

teem *(TEEM), verb*
To abound or swarm.

As we walked into the nightclub, the paparazzi TEEMED around us like so many manic worker bees.

telekinesis *(tel-uh-kuh-NEE-siss), noun*
The supposed psychic power to move objects with the mind. From the Greek roots for "from a distance" and "movement."

Some comic book characters are known for their powers of TELEKINESIS.

teleological *(tee-lee-uh-LOJ-ik-uhl), adjective*
The notion that things exist for a purpose.

The fact that we have unsurpassable wealth and taste, while others who are less important endure hardship, is surely proof that we live in a TELEOLOGICAL universe.

temblor *(TEM-blor), noun*
An earthquake. From the Spanish verb meaning "to quake." Not a *trembler,* as some think, but in the same vein as *tremor,* which is a shaking or vibration before or after an earthquake.

Since the last earthquake all new construction was required to be built to withstand large TEMBLORS.

temerity *(tuh-MEHR-ih-tee), noun*
Fearless self-confidence; bravery and courage

Her TEMERITY allowed her to march into the dean's office and hand him her application in person.

temper *(TEHM-per), verb*
To moderate or lessen the impact of.

She tried to TEMPER the damage her loose tongue had caused her friends.

Know This Quote
"Yet I shall TEMPER so / Justice with mercy." —John Milton, English poet

temperance *(TEM-puh-rense), noun*
Self-restraint in the face of temptation; moderation.
Abstinence from drinking alcohol. What every parent hopes their high school student practices.

The new coaching staff demanded TEMPERANCE of the football team during the season.

tempest *(TEM-pust), noun*
A severe storm with high winds, rain, hail, or snow. A severe commotion or disturbance, especially with emotional upheaval. Turbulent, giving rise to many violent emotions or stormy actions.

The TEMPEST of Jim and Stephanie's argument was embarrassing to those who witnessed it.

tempestuous *(tem-PESS-chew-us), adjective*
Tumultuous and turbulent, as a personality.

Claire's TEMPESTUOUS personality is most likely linked to the fact that her father has married and remarried an excessive amount.

template *(TEM-plut), noun*
A master pattern from which other identical copies can be made; a pattern.

I've heard the secret to woodworking is to make a detailed TEMPLATE of each part before it is cut or carved.

temporal *(TEM-puh-rul), adjective*
Connected with life in the world, rather than spiritual life. Lasting only a short time. Related to or existing in time, as opposed to space.

The TEMPORAL issues associated with manned spaceflight to Mars are as complicated as the mechanical.

temporize *(TEHM-puh-rize), verb*
To gain time by being evasive or indecisive.

When an officious socialite tries to get too close to us, we do not feel the need to TEMPORIZE with our response; we simply remind her of her place.

tenable *(TEH-nuh-bull), adjective*
Justified in a fair or rational way; defensible based on sufficient evidence. Able to be maintained, held, or defended against attack.

Investors determined that further support of the company's owners was no longer TENABLE, so they approved a takeover.

tenacity *(tuh-NA-suh-tee), noun*
The quality of being unyielding; stubborn. The ability or tendency to stick firmly to a decision or opinion, without doubt or potential to change. The strength with which something sticks, holds together, or clings, particularly to a surface.

Marybeth's TENACITY was evident when she played the entire second half with a broken arm.

Know This Quote

"Women are TENACIOUS, and all of them should be TENACIOUS of respect; without esteem they cannot exist; esteem is the first demand that they make of love."
—Honoré de Balzac, French novelist and playwright

tenacious *(tuh-NAY-shuss), adjective*
Persistent, stubborn, obstinate.

Elizabeth was TENACIOUS and finally manged to get her novel published.

tendentious *(ten-DEN-she-us), adjective*
Describes statements or actions designed to promote one's beliefs or point of view.

Laura is TENDENTIOUS in her efforts to prove that she believes that a plentitude of fine jewelry is the key to happiness.

tenebrous *(TEN-uh-bruss), adjective*
Dark and gloomy.

Eloise and Marcus spent the day exploring the TENEBROUS forest that surrounded their family's Maine compound.

tenet *(TEH-nut), noun*
A set of established and fundamental beliefs, especially related to religion or politics; a principle. A fundamental belief held essential by a society, group, or organization. Not a *tenant,* who is someone who rents a property.

The TENET that "All politics is local" is one that few candidates forget.

tentative *(TENT-ah-tive), adjective*
Not completely set or agreed upon; still subject to change; or shy; timid; hesitant

She was not sure what time the meeting would end, so they made TENTATIVE plans to meet at eight o'clock.

The baby's first, TENTATIVE steps made his parents cheer so loudly she got scared and lost her balance.

tenuous *(TEN-yoo-uhs), adjective*

Weak, slight, and liable to break

The loose button on her coat was being held by one last TENUOUS thread so she knew she needed to repair it or risk losing the button.

The couple's relationship seemed TENUOUS at best, but their families hoped they could reconcile and stay married.

tenure *(TEN-yur), noun*

The holding of an official position, or the length of time that position is held.

Raises are based on performance rather than TENURE, so some who have been here a while might not be compensated as well as newcomers.

tepid *(TEHP-id), adjective*

Characterized by a lack of enthusiasm.

We greeted the new opera, with its mawkish plot and poor acting, with TEPID applause.

terminus *(TUR-mih-nus), noun*

The end points of a fixed transportation route, such as the beginning and end of a railroad or bus line. A point where something stops or reaches its end.

When developers learned that Maplewood would become the TERMINUS for the new rail system to New York City, they began buying up properties quickly.

terra cotta *(TARE-uh KAH-tuh), noun*

Pottery of a distinctive reddish-brown, usually unglazed at least in part. The earthenware clay used to make such pieces. The brownish-red color itself.

Native American pottery made of TERRA COTTA has become very popular among collectors of late.

terra firma *(TARE-uh FER-muh), noun*

Solid ground; not water or air. From the Latin for "firm ground."

After the harrowing airline flight, the passengers were so grateful to be on TERRA FIRMA that they kissed the ground.

terrestrial *(tehr-RES-tree-uhl), adjective*

Having to do with the earth or land

Although polar bears are mostly TERRESTRIAL, they are also very comfortable in the water.

terse *(TERS), adjective*

Short and to the point; abrupt; brief, may imply an unwillingness to speak

When he was angry, his answers to questions became TERSE and sarcastic.

tertiary *(TUR-shee-are-ee), adjective*
Third in order, place, importance, or succession. Third in a list, sequence, or progression.

Because the first two did not work, the TERTIARY option, using military action, was being discussed by leaders in private.

testament *(TESS-tuh-mint), noun*
Proof that something else exists or is true. A tribute. Also, a formal statement or speech outlining beliefs. The act of determining how property will be divided after death; a will.

The success of his son was a TESTAMENT to his parenting skills and love.

testimonial *(TESS-tuh-moh-nee-yul), noun*
A favorable report supporting the existence of a thing's qualities and virtues. A statement backing a claim or supporting facts. Something done or given in honor or gratitude for someone.

At the honors ceremony, Jane offered a TESTIMONIAL to all the teachers who had done so much to help her achieve all that she had.

tête-à-tête *(TET ah TET), noun*
A private conversation between two people; a face-to-face meeting. French for "head-to-head."

Soon after the wedding, the mother of the bride and mother of the groom had a lively and necessary TÊTE-À-TÊTE to address issues of the marriage.

thaumaturge *(THAW-mah-turj), noun*
A person who works miracles.

If you were ever to see Hannah early in the morning, just after she has awoken, then you would know Hannah's personal make-up artist is the epitome of a THAUMATURGE.

theism *(THEE-ih-zum), noun*
Belief in the divine, in the form of one or many gods. Usually, the belief that one god created the world and is still evident in the works of creation. It is important to note that theism is part of many different religions, not just those that follow the Bible.

As early civilizations progressed, THEISM became prominent and the worshiping of idols largely disappeared.

theocracy *(thee-AH-krah-see), noun*
A system of government in which priests rule in the name of God.

The Vatican is the ultimate THEOCRACY.

theorem *(THEE-uh-rum), noun*
A proposition or formula in mathematics or logic that can be proved from a set of basic assumptions. An idea that is accepted or proposed as true.

The Pythagorean THEOREM is memorized by all students and is used as a foundation for many mathematical proofs.

thesaurus *(thuh-SOH-rus), noun*
A book that lists words related to each other in meaning, usually presenting synonyms and antonyms.

Today, word-processing software usually includes a dictionary, a THESAURUS, and a spell checker.

thespian *(THESS-pee-un), noun*
An actor, especially a person who performs onstage in a play.

THESPIAN is an old-fashioned term for an actor, but it is one that some performers prefer.

think tank *(THINK tahnk), noun*
A group of experts that researches certain subjects, comes up with solutions to complex problems, and gives advice, most often to the government.

After graduation, many students of Political Science sought positions with THINK TANKS, so they could continue their research.

Third World *(THERD werld), noun*
In general, developing nations with minor economies. The bigger capitalist industrialized nations are called the First World, and the industrialized communist nations were known as the Second World.

The debt of THIRD WORLD nations was so large it had to be excused, for if payment were demanded countries would be bankrupt.

thoracic *(thoh-RA-sick), adjective*
Involving or located in the chest.

The family feared what the THORACIC surgeon had to say about the procedure.

throng *(THRONG), noun*
A large crowd of persons or objects. Definitely not to be used or confused with *thong,* a very brief type of underwear or swimsuit bottom.

Let's wait here for fifteen minutes to avoid the THRONG of people trying to get to their cars in the parking lot.

thwart *(THWORT), verb*
To oppose, confuse, or defeat. To keep someone from achieving their goals or plans.

Steve's plan to surprise his parents was THWARTED when his little sister left their present out in the open.

timorous *(TIM-er-us), adjective*
Nervous and hesitant; showing a lack of confidence or courage

The young singer's voice was TIMOROUS in front of the audience until she relaxed and got into the song.

tincture *(TINK-cherr), noun*
A trace amount or slight tinge.

The tragic opera was leavened with a TINCTURE of comic relief.

tirade *(TIE-raid), noun*
A long, overblown, angry speech, most often a criticism or denunciation; an extended outburst of harsh talk.

Sadly, Frank had come to fear his wife's TIRADES so much that he avoided coming home.

titillate *(TIH-tuh-late), verb*
To excite or stimulate someone in a pleasurable way.

Stories about rock star romances seem always to TITILLATE, no matter how old the listeners.

titular *(TITCH-uh-luhr), adjective*
A person who is a leader by title only, but lacks any real power.

The Queen is the TITULAR head of the British empire.

tombolo *(TOM-bo-low), noun*
A split that joins an offshore island to the mainland.

Until they decide to build a bridge, the single-lane road on the TOMBOLO is the only way onto and off of the island.

tome *(TOAM), noun*
A thick or heavy book on a serious subject.
A scholarly book on an academic subject.

Aren't you lucky you're reading a book on words, rather than a TOME on the history of the English language?

Know This Quote

"She carries a book but it is not / the TOME of the ancient wisdom, / the pages, I imagine, are the blank pages / of the unwritten volume of the new." —Hilda Doolittle, American poet and memoirist

toothsome *(TOOTH-suhm), adjective*
Voluptuous and sexually alluring.

Dorienne is TOOTHSOME thanks mainly to her plastic surgeon and her family's attractive fortune.

topical *(TOP-ih-kuhl), adjective*
Having to do with issues of current or local interest.

All the debutantes at the ball wasted our time with inane attempts at TOPICAL conversation about politics and other distasteful matters.

topography *(tuh-POG-ruh-fee), noun*
The arrangement of the physical features of a place, area, or physical object; the "lay of the land."

After her return from Europe, Lauren spent most of her time talking about the dazzling alpine TOPOGRAPHY of Switzerland.

torpid *(TOR-pid), adjective*
Slow, lacking energy or enthusiasm; inactive and lazy

The oppressive heat made even the dogs TORPID, lying in the shade, tongues lolling.

torpor *(TOR-pur), noun*
The state of being tired, lazy, or inactive; apathy or indifference

The TORPOR that settled over the offices when the candidate appeared to be losing couldn't be shaken even by a slight rise in the polls.

Know This Quote

"A multitude of causes unknown to former times are now acting with a combined force to blunt the discriminating powers of the mind, and unfitting it for all voluntary exertion to reduce it to a state of almost savage TORPOR."
—William Wordsworth, British Romantic poet

tortuous *(TORE-chew-us), adjective*
Intricate and indirect; not straightforward.

Even though her roommate found going to the gym invigorating, Penny found it to be TORTUOUS.

torque *(TORK), verb*
To twist; to apply pressure causing a turn or rotation

The football player TORQUED his knee badly enough that he left the game, but not badly enough to cause serious damage to the ligaments.

torrid *(TOR-ihd), adjective*
Scorching hot; overheated; parched; or passionate and fiery; or energetic to the point of frenzy

Traveling through the TORRID desert sands takes care and preparation or it can be a dangerous journey.

Their TORRID love affair evolved into a marriage that lasted over fifty years.
The TORRID activity at the hotel before the arrival of the prime minister was well masked by a calm and professional lobby staff.

tort *(TOART), noun*
In legal terms, a wrongful act for which damages can be sought by an injured party. Not to be confused with *torte,* a rich cake of many layers sandwiched together with cream filling.

Law students find classes on TORTS to be the most interesting and, ultimately, when they practice law, the most practical.

totalitarian *(toh-TA-luh-tare-yun), adjective*
Centralized, in terms of official government power. Describes a form of government in which control is concentrated in the hands of one ruler or party, with no opposition permitted. Adolf Hitler and Joseph Stalin both led totalitarian regimes, even though they came from opposite ends of the political spectrum.

The TOTALITARIAN state of the Soviet Union ultimately fell, decades after it was founded.

totem *(TOH-tuhm), noun*
Anything that serves as a venerated symbol.

Our various formal and informal gardens are TOTEMS to our emphasis on the importance of the natural world.

tout *(TOUT), verb*
To praise highly, usually hoping to convince of worth or even to sell

She TOUTED the benefits of yoga for overall health so often that her friends finally tried it in spite of being skeptical.

tractable *(TRAKT-ah-bul), adjective*
Controlled or managed easily, referring to a being or a situation

The puppy became far more TRACTABLE after six weeks of obedience school.

tractate *(TRAK-tayt), noun*
A treatise.

Amanda's mother delivered a TRACTATE to her daughter about socializing with the right people after she learned that Amanda had been spending time with middle class families.

traduce *(tra-DOOCE), verb*
To lie and create false impressions in order to make something or someone seem shameful or bad. It's easy to deduce when one does traduce, just by listening to the mean things being said.

Angry over one thing or another, Page TRADUCED her sister so frequently that her parents had to intervene.

trajectory *(truh-JEK-tuh-ree), noun*
The path a projectile makes in space under the action of forces including thrust, wind, and gravity. The course a flying object takes after takeoff.

The TRAJECTORY of all flights was being monitored and guided by the air traffic controllers.

tranquil *(TRAN-kwill), adjective*
Calm, quiet. Free of disturbance or commotion. Unagitated, with no signs of anxiety or agitation.

After years of looking for the best vacation location, the Burtons found their lake home to be the most TRANQUIL place.

transfiguration *(tranz-FIG-yoor-ay-shun), noun*
A dramatic change in appearance, especially one that glorifies or exalts someone.

The popular make-over shows bring about physical and emotional TRANSFIGURATIONS for their participants.

transfix *(tranz-FICKS), verb*
To make someone temporarily unable to move; to hold motionless. To pierce someone or something through with a weapon or sharp object.

The deer stood TRANSFIXED, paralyzed by the headlights of the car.

transgress *(tranz-GRESS), verb*
To cross a line and do something wrong, often disobeying a command, guideline, moral code, or law. To go beyond a limit, usually in a bad way.

David TRANSGRESSED by crossing into Mr. Peterson's yard to play ball.

Know This Quote

"Unjust laws exist; shall we be content to obey them, or shall we endeavor to amend them, and obey them until we have succeeded, or shall we TRANSGRESS them at once?" —Henry David Thoreau, American author and transcendentalist

transient *(TRAN-zee-ent), adjective or noun*
Fleeting or temporary; passing with time; or staying in one place for a short period of time before moving on (adjective) or a person who moves from place to place (noun)

She was grateful for her friends' encouragement and reminders that the depression caused by the breakup was only TRANSIENT and she would feel happier soon.

Few civilians understand the TRANSIENT nature of the military and how often soldiers move from one post to the next.

He was skilled enough to get work wherever he went so he chose to be a TRANSIENT in order to see the country.

transitory *(TRAN-zih-tor-ee), adjective*
Temporary and short-lived

The TRANSITORY stress of meeting her deadlines was worth the joy she found in her job on a day-to-day basis.

transliterate *(tranz-LIT-uh-rate), verb*
Literally, "to write across." To write words from other languages in a familiar alphabet. Even if the meaning of the foreign word is unknown, through transliteration it can at least be properly pronounced.

Thank goodness the prayer book was TRANSLITERATED, for they did not know how to read the Hebrew alphabet.

transmogrify *(trans-MOG-ruh-fie), verb*
To change appearance in a disturbing way.

We cannot abide that particular interior decorator because he always manages to TRANSMOGRIFY tasteful displays of luxury into pompous tableaus of arrogant wealth.

transpire *(tranz-PIRE), verb*
To give off water vapor, especially through the surfaces of plant leaves. To be exposed; to come to light and become known. To occur.

As they recalled, the events of the accident seemed to TRANSPIRE in slow motion.

transubstantiation *(tran-sub-STAN-she-aye-shun), noun*
The notion of endowing something with symbolic value beyond its physical construct.

TRANSUBSTANTIATION is used as a technique in marketing, transforming shabby and gauche items into supposed examples of tasteful luxury.

travail *(truh-VALE), verb*
To work hard, especially over a long period of time, at a physically demanding job. Sometimes used to describe the labor of childbirth.

Harriet TRAVAILED all the way through her chemotherapy, which some say is as painful as the illness.

travesty *(TRAV-ehs-tee), noun*
An over-the-top, exaggerated, or twisted take on the truth of something; a distorted version

The sound of her singing was a TRAVESTY until after the surgery when her voice was returned to its former range.

treachery *(TREH-chuh-ree), noun*
An act of betrayal or deceit; treason. A severe violation of trust.

Benedict Arnold's name has become synonymous with the words TREACHERY and traitor.

treacle *(TREE-kuhl), noun*
Contrived or mawkish sentimentality.

That writer's work is suffering in quality, as we could hardly sit through the TREACLE of her recently opened opera.

treatise *(TREE-tiss), noun*
A scholarly, formal written work that deals extensively with a given subject. A systematic essay or written argument on a particular subject. What you will be able to write once you incorporate these words into your vocabulary.

Freud's TREATISE on psychoanalysis and causes of mental illness was controversial for its time.

tremulous *(TREHM-yuh-luss), adjective*
Timid and fearful.

With TREMULOUS mien, Anthony asked Gwendolyn if she would consent to a joining of their families.

trenchant *(TREHN-chent), adjective*
Forceful, meaningful, and emotionally heated

Their politics were different enough that they often engaged in TRENCHANT debates but neither took them personally.

trepidation *(tre-pih-DAY-shun), noun*
Fear about the future or a particular future event. Involuntary trembling.

A look of TREPIDATION was visible on his mother's face when Justin went for his first driving lesson.

triage *(TREE-ahj), noun*
The process of prioritizing sick or injured people for treatment, according to severity and condition.

It was amazing to see how calmly TRIAGE was completed at the site of the train crash.

tribunal *(trie-BYOO-nul), noun*
A defense, usually unofficial, of the rights of an individual. Also a court or other forum where justice is meted out. If you've ever wondered why so many newspapers are called the *Tribune,* the first definition of this word should be your answer.

The military TRIBUNAL was formed to judge those suspected of terrorist activities.

trifling *(TRIY-fling), adjective*
Unimportant; not worth dealing with; insignificant, referring to an amount or the importance of a thing

She saved the TRIFLING paperwork for the end of the day so she could handle the major issues when she was most alert earlier in the day.

triptych *(TRIP-tick), noun*
A picture or carving on three panels, or a set of three associated paintings or other works of art.

Scott wanted to buy just the center painting, but the gallery owner refused to break up the TRIPTYCH.

trite *(TRYTE), adjective*
Overused; lacking in interest or originality. Something you don't want someone to say about your writing or speech, so read and use this book!

Oh, how TRITE every interview with a political candidate sounds.

Triton *(TRY-ton), noun*
A mythical creature, similar to a mermaid, with a human torso and arms, gills under the ears, and a tail like a dolphin.

TRITONS served Neptune as his attendants.

troglodyte *(TRAHG-lah-dyte), noun*
A person considered to be primitive, out of date, coarse, uncouth, ill-mannered, or brutish.

Sick and tired of going out with TROGLODYTES, Janet told her friends she was through with blind dates.

tropism *(TROH-piz-uhm), noun*
A natural inclination or propensity to react in a given way to a certain stimulus. Comedians hope that laughter is a tropism that characterizes their act.

All of the plants in the room leaned toward the window as a result of their TROPISM toward light.

truckle *(TRUHK-uhl), verb*
To submit obsequiously to a command.
We have trained our servants to TRUCKLE to our every whim.

truculence *(TRUK-yoo-lens), noun*
The state of being eager and ready to fight over petty issues
The TRUCULENCE that he had been known for throughout high school mellowed while he was in college to the point his friends from home barely recognized him.

truculent *(TRUK-yoo-lehnt), adjective*
Easily angered; having a chip on one's shoulder; defiant and aggressive
The young woman spent a good deal of time in detention because of her TRUCULENT attitude in the classroom.

trumpery *(TRUHM-puh-ree), noun*
Something without value; a trifle.
The TRUMPERY that the Smythingtons collect and call "art" is, clearly, distasteful dreck.

truncate *(TRUNG-kayt), verb*
To shorten by cutting off an end, used figuratively and literally
The dance was unexpectedly TRUNCATED when the fire alarm went off, triggering the sprinklers.

tryst *(TRIST), noun*
A prearranged meeting, especially one made privately or secretly between lovers. Originally meant "to make an arrangement with."
Both were nervous planning their TRYST, for they feared their affair would somehow be revealed.

tumescent *(too-MESS-ent), adjective*
Becoming or already engorged, full, swollen, or rigid.
After the hurricane, our Florida compound was flooded by the TUMESCENT intra-coastal waterway.

tumid *(TOO-mid), adjective*
Pompous and swollen with pride.
We cannot stand it when Katherine wins arguments about couture and art collecting because the TUMID expression that crosses her face after a conversational victory is so loathsome.

tumult *(tuh-MULT), noun*
A violent, chaotic, or noisy commotion; an uproar. A psychological or emotional upheaval or agitation. Major mudslides cause tumult.

The TUMULT of having twenty-two-year-olds in the house for a birthday party was too much for Lisa's mother to handle.

turbid *(TUR-bid), adjective*
Muddy and unclear; stirred up, can be used literally or figuratively

She knew she would never find the ring she had dropped in the TURBID river.

turgescent *(tur-JESS-ent), adjective*
Becoming or appearing swollen or distended.

His abs were so neglected, his stomach became TURGESCENT after a big meal.

turgid *(TER-jid), adjective*
Swollen due to fluid; or excessively fancy and flowery, used to describe a way of speaking or writing; pompous

The TURGID fruit practically exploded when the children bit into the flesh, dripping juices down their chins.

He meant his TURGID speech to sound impressive but it only sounded as if he was putting on airs.

turmoil *(TER-moyl), noun*
A state of great confusion or agitation; frightening uncertainty

The country was thrown into TURMOIL after the assassination of the prime minister.

turpitude *(TER-pih-tood) or (TER-pih-tyood), noun*
Wicked, immoral behavior; evilness; obscene and vulgar actions

He lived a life of TURPITUDE before cleaning up his act.

tutelage (*TOOT-uh-lidj) or (TYOOT-uh-lidj), noun*
Protection or guardianship; or the acts of a teacher or mentor; instruction

While the great works of art toured the country, they fell under the TUTELAGE of the museums hosting them, so security was increased at each site.

She learned more about the business world in six weeks under her supervisor's TUTELAGE than she had throughout her entire college career.

tyro *(TIY-roh), noun*
A beginner; someone new to a field of study or business

The firefighters respected each TYRO more and more the longer they were willing to put up with the gentle hazing every new guy was put through.

doctrinaire
abstemious
levity hubris panacea
veracity cerebellum
labyrinth
criterion
nonagenarian
meticulous
quondam
colloquial
wok palpable
incipient salutary
redact fervent
beleaguered yawnful
elixir beneficent

ubiquitous *(yoo-BIK-wi-tuss), adjective*
Seemingly present everywhere at once. So common as to appear to be all places.

Some think the Mercedes has become a UBIQUITOUS symbol of wealth, while others consider it one of conspicuous consumption.

ulterior *(uhl-TEER-ree-ohr), adjective*
Hidden; beyond what is acknowledged or admitted to

Since he didn't feel he deserved the promotion, the young man wondered if his boss had ULTERIOR motives for giving it to him.

Know This Quote

"When one has extensively pondered about men, as a career or as a vocation, one sometimes feels nostalgic for primates. At least they do not have ULTERIOR motives." —Albert Camus, Algerian-born French author and philosopher

ultimatum *(ul-tih-MAY-tum), noun*
An expression that includes a demand along with the consequences, usually negative, of failing to meet the demand. A set of terms that cannot be compromised, without predetermined consequences occurring.

Either pay the rent by midnight on the thirty-first, or be thrown out in the street: that was Simon's ULTIMATUM.

umbra *(UM-brah), noun*
A planet's shadow, especially the shadow of the Earth upon the moon.

A solar eclipse is caused by the Earth passing through the moon's UMBRA upon the sun.

umbrage *(UM-brij), noun*
Resentment or annoyance arising from an offense; something or someone causing intense irritation.

Principal Michaels took UMBRAGE at the suggestion that he was only concerned with test scores, and not with students.

unassuming *(uhn-uh-SOOM-ing), adjective*
Modest and unpretentious.

The Binghamtons just bought a lovely, UNASSUMING 5,000 square-foot chalet in the Rockies.

unbridled *(un-BRY-duld), adjective*
Without limitations or boundaries; uncontrolled and unrestrained.

The customer's UNBRIDLED fury at being denied a refund was a sight to behold.

unceremonious *(un-sair-uh-MOAN-ee-us), adjective*
Discourteously abrupt, hasty, rude.

The maître d's UNCEREMONIOUS manner only made us love the new French restaurant all the more.

uncharted *(UHN-chart-uhd), adjective*
Not surveyed or recorded on a map. Not previously encountered, experienced, or investigated. Often confused with *unchartered,* meaning not officially authorized or permitted by a governing body.

Boldly but stupidly, the group decided to embark on UNCHARTED waters in their small boat.

unctuous *(UNK-chew-us), adjective*
Possessing an untrustworthy or dubious nature; characterized by an insincere manner.

Local car dealers doing their own TV commercials often communicate in an UNCTUOUS, almost laughable manner.

unctuous *(UNG-chwuhs), adjective*
Slippery and greasy; oily. Smug and obsequious in an attempt to charm or convince. Describes a texture that is soft and smooth, like an oil or ointment. Containing or composed of oil or fat.

Mud baths may not be healing, but they can be soothing, and they are most definitely UNCTUOUS.

undaunted *(un-DAHN-tud), adjective*
Not put off or deterred by the prospect or even the likelihood of failure, loss, or defeat.

UNDAUNTED, the underdog football team faced the state champions and almost won.

underhanded *(un-dur-HAN-dud), adjective*
Secret and dishonest, with intention to deceive or cheat. Most underhanded people seek to get the upper hand any way they can.

His attempts to discredit his opponent with rumors and lies were definitely UNDERHANDED.

Where'd That Word Come From?

Underhanded—Card sharks are proficient at palming cards, holding extra cards under their hands. The word *underhanded,* "in a secret or stealthy manner," eventually came to refer to anyone who steals from or takes advantage of another in a sneaky and crafty way.

underling *(UN-dur-ling), noun*
A servant or subordinate, especially one regarded with contempt or as of little importance.

Robin was not Batman's UNDERLING; he was his crime-fighting partner.

underwrite *(UN-dur-wryt), verb*
To insure someone or something by accepting liability for losses. To guarantee the sale of an issue of securities at a predetermined price. To agree to provide funds or cover any losses.

The fledgling filmmakers asked parents and friends to UNDERWRITE their first feature film.

undulate *(UN-jeh-layt) or (UN-dyeh-layt), verb*
To move in a smooth, steady motion; to sway; to swing

The motion of the sea caused the ship to UNDULATE in a soothing way, practically rocking the passengers to sleep.

unequivocal *(uhn-ih-KWIV-uh-kull), adjective*
Possessing a clear meaning or answer.

When Peter asked Meaghan to go on a date, her UNEQUIVOCAL answer was "no."

unflinching *(un-FLIHN-ching), adjective*
Strong and unhesitating, especially in the face of difficulty. Courageous.

Mary's UNFLINCHING dedication to her children was evidenced by her holding two jobs.

Know This Quote

"A gentleman doesn't pounce . . . he glides. If a woman sits on a piece of furniture which permits your sitting beside her, you are free to regard this as an invitation, though not an UNEQUIVOCAL one."
—Quentin Crisp, British writer, actor, and model

ungainly *(un-GAIN-lee), adjective*
Awkward and clumsy.

One of the hallmarks of this year's fashionable shoes is that they make one seem UNGAINLY on anything other than marble flooring.

uniformitarianism *(you-ni-form-ih-TARE-ee-uhn-izm), noun*
The belief that change on Earth takes place slowly, gradually, and at a uniform rate rather than through short, sudden, catastrophic events.

The fact that the families of our servants have been with us for many, many generations would seem to be proof of UNIFORMITARIANISM.

unilateral *(yoo-nih-LA-tuh-rul), adjective*
Undertaken independently, as in decisions made by only one of many political parties. One-sided. Also, responsibility born by or imposed upon one party or individual.

The allies resolved that no member country would take any UNILATERAL action that might threaten mutual security.

unimpeachable *(un-ihm-PEE-chuh-bull), adjective*
Above reproach; impossible to discredit or slander.

We promoted Carla to upstairs maid because her job performance has been UNIMPEACHABLE.

unorthodox *(un-OR-thuh-docks), adjective*
Not following conventional or traditional beliefs or practices. Not practicing or conforming to or accepting traditional religious practices.

Her teaching methods may be UNORTHODOX, but they clearly get results, as all of her students passed the state exam.

unpalatable *(un-puh-LA-tuh-bull), adjective*
Having an unpleasant taste or effect; disagreeable and undesirable. Not pleasant, acceptable, or agreeable.

I am surprised that you didn't understand that the consequences for your bad behavior would be UNPALATABLE.

unrefined *(un-ree-FIND), adjective*
In a natural state; not processed, with all impurities still intact. Displaying poor social graces; unschooled in approved tastes and behaviors.

Snobs at the country club shunned those they thought UNREFINED.

unrenumerative *(un-re-NEW-mer-ah-tiv), adjective*
A job, investment, business venture, or other activity that pays little or no financial return.

She found her job at the coffee shop to be an UNRENUMERATIVE effort.

unsavory *(un-SAY-voh-ree), adjective*
Tasteless, bland; unappetizing. Morally unacceptable or distasteful. Similar to *unseemly,* which means contrary to accepted standards of good taste or acceptable behavior, or occurring at an inconvenient time or place.

How scared were you when we went into that twenty-four-hour diner full of UNSAVORY characters?

Know This Quote

"Our future is inextricably linked to what happens in Washington DC, and we know that is a very UNSAVORY reality." —Don Libey, direct marketing advisor

untenable *(uhn-TEN-ah-bul), adjective*
Unjustifiable; impossible to defend or maintain an argument for

The entire group found his comments on a woman's role in the workplace to be UNTENABLE and sexist.

untoward *(un-TOHRD), adjective*
Inappropriate; socially unacceptable and uncomfortable; improper

Everyone at the party tried to ignore his UNTOWARD behavior as the man got drunker and drunker.

unwarranted *(un-WAR-rehn-ted), adjective*
Having no justification or basis in fact

Enough of her friends were at the dance that she quickly decided her fears of being bored and alone all night had been UNWARRANTED.

unwieldy *(un-WEEL-dee), adjective*
Not easy to handle or to manage.

The stack of magazines Monica was carrying were UNWIELDLY and she dropped them on the floor.

upbraid *(up-BRAYD), verb*
To scold; to criticize

The boys looked so miserable and their plans had failed so terribly that their mother couldn't bring herself to UPBRAID them for going against her wishes and trying to launch the raft into the river.

Know This Quote

"Now mark me how I will undo myself. / I give this heavy weight from off my head, / And this UNWIELDY sceptre from my hand, / The pride of kingly sway from out my heart." —William Shakespeare

uproarious *(up-ROAR-ee-yus), adjective*
Defined by noisy confusion; loud and boisterous. Extremely funny and causing people to laugh aloud.

I hear the new headliner at the comedy club has an UPROARIOUS routine.

urban myth *(UR-bun mith), noun*
A bizarre story in wide circulation, presented as though the events actually happened. Characterized by the fact that the person telling the story never experienced the events herself but always knows a friend or aunt or other third party who can vouch for their truthfulness.

One of the most often repeated URBAN MYTHS has to do with alligators living in the sewers of Manhattan.

urbane *(urr-BAYN), adjective*
Sophisticated, refined, or courteous. Well versed in the social graces. Not to be confused with *urban,* which means related to a city. Some urban dwellers are urbane, though not all.

> *Jordan could not stop talking about how URBANE everyone was on her cruise to England.*

urbanization *(ur-ban-ih-ZAY-shun), noun*
The growth of cities brought about by a population shift from rural areas and small communities to larger ones.

> *URBANIZATION, which began in the United States in the late 1800s, was in part triggered by the shift from an agricultural economy to an industrial one.*

usurp *(YOO-surp)* or *(YOO-zurp), verb*
To take the place or power of another illegally

> *In the past, it was vital for a king to have a legitimate heir or else risk others trying to USURP the throne.*

usury *(USE-err-ee), noun*
To charge illegally high or excessive interest rates on a loan.

> *Loan sharks lend money at USURIOUS rates, and break your legs if you don't make back the principal with interest on time.*

usurper *(you-SIR-per), noun*
A person who seizes a position of power through illegal means, force, or deception.

> *Julia called Liz a USURPER when Liz unexpectedly won the school election.*

Know That Quote

"A USURPER in the guise of a benefactor is the enemy that we are now to encounter and overcome." —William Leggett, American poet and fiction writer

utilitarian *(yoo-tih-lih-TARE-ee-un), adjective*
Designed for practical use rather than beauty; pragmatic. Characterized by a concern for the practical or useful.

> *In selecting a car to buy, Hank took a UTILITARIAN approach, rather than choosing the one that was flashiest or most likely to impress.*

utopia *(you-TOE-pee-uh), noun*
A perfect or ideal society.

> *Many of us who are accustomed to wealth have learned to accept that we must make our own UTOPIAS, rather than to rely on the actions of outside forces or agencies.*

utopian *(yoo-TOH-pee-yun), adjective*
Typical of an ideal world, a perfect state or place. Related to admirable but impractical ideas or ideals.

The UTOPIAN dreams described in literature of the early twentieth century did not translate into realities.

Where'd That Word Come From?
Utopian—In his 1516 book *Utopia,* Sir Thomas More invented the word "utopia" for a fictional island where everything is perfect, using the Greek for "nowhere" (*ou,* "not," and *topos,* "a place"). Eventually, this word came to mean any ideal, visionary place, and the adjective *utopian* came to describe anything that is ideal, but impractical.

utterance *(UH-ter-runts), noun*
Something uttered or vocalized; a word or sound spoken aloud. A style of speaking.

How proud they were that the baby's first UTTERANCES sounded like "Daddy."

uxorious *(uhk-SAWR-ee-us), adjective*
Doting on one's wife to an excessive degree.

Some called Peter an extremely devoted husband, but others called him UXORIOUS.

Know This Quote
"The same things change their names at such a rate; / For instance—passion in a lover's glorious, / But in a husband is pronounced UXORIOUS." —Lord Byron, British Romantic poet

V

vacillate *(VA-suh-late), verb*
To be indecisive; waver between options. To sway from side to side.

Wishing not to VACILLATE on the issue, the mayor stood firm on his position not to raise the sales tax.

Know This Quote
"But modern character is inconstant, divided, VACILLATING, lacking the stone-like certitude of archaic man. . . ." —Saul Bellow, American author

vacuous *(VA-kyoo-uss), adjective*
Lacking in ideas. Having no content; empty-headed. That which is empty is vacuous.

Some politicians are VACUOUS, telling constituents what polls reveal are the most popular positions on particular issues.

vagary *(VAY-guh-ree), noun*
An unexpected, unpredictable change; a sudden change that cannot be explained

Her mother was constantly amazed by the VAGARIES of teenage fashion and style.

vainglorious *(vayne-GLOR-ee-us), adjective*
Conceited; boastful; prone to showing off and bragging.

Although the scion of a well-established family, Gordon is so VAINGLORIOUS that you'd think him a parvenu!

vainglory *(VAYN-glohr-ee), noun*
Excessive and undeserved arrogance in oneself; extreme, undeserved arrogance

The young light designer's VAINGLORY only made him look foolish in front of the older, more experienced stage hands.

valorous *(VAH-ler-us), adjective*
Marked by extreme bravery; daringly courageous

The VALOROUS teen saved his little sisters from the fire after a candle tipped over in their room.

valuation *(val-you-AYE-shun), noun*
The calculated worth or value of an asset, based on a rigorous appraisal.

One of the accounting firm's services is business VALUATION, where you can pay to have an accurate appraisal of what your business would sell for if acquired.

vanguard *(VAN-gard), noun*
That which is at the forefront or the leading edge; the most advanced group.

Robert is among the VANGUARD of area oenophiles.

vanity *(VA-nuh-tee), noun*
Excessive pride, especially in one's appearance. Something considered futile, worthless, or empty of significance. Vanessa's vanity required her to have several mirrors in her van.

Her VANITY was legendary, as she could not pass a mirror without gazing into it and admiring herself.

vapid *(VA-pid), adjective*
Uninteresting and unchallenging

His parents knew he was maturing when he brought home an intelligent and witty young woman instead of the VAPID girls he usually dated.

variance *(VAY-ree-unts), noun*
A difference or variation. A difference of opinion or attitude. In legal terms, the difference between two statements, documents, or steps.

The VARIANCE between the positions of management and labor was so strong that a strike was inevitable.

variegated *(VAYR-ih-gay-ted)* or *(VAYR-ee-gay-ted), adjective*
Having different colored streaks or spots; marked by having variety, can be used literally or figuratively

The VARIEGATED leaves in early September were the first signs that autumn was coming and the leaves would soon be changing fully.

vehement *(VEE-uh-ment), adjective*
Intense; forceful; marked by strong feelings or emotions

The old woman was VEHEMENT in her insistence that her grandson go to college, even if she had to pay for it herself.

In the 1960s, many expressed VEHEMENT dissatisfaction with the administration policy regarding the Vietnam conflict.

venal *(VEE-nuhl), adjective*
Corrupt; willing to take bribes; able to be paid off

The new warden fired every guard who had a VENAL reputation in order to restore order to the prison.

Know This Quote

"Give me but the liberty of the press, and I will give to the minister a VENAL House of Commons." —Richard Brinsley Sheridan, Irish playwright and statesman

vendetta *(ven-DEHD-dah), noun*
A long, drawn out feud between two parties or families, usually implies a desire on at least one side to seriously damage the other side

Conservatives claim liberals have a VENDETTA against them while the liberals tend to claim just the opposite.

veneer *(VIN-eer), noun*
A false front or false face; a superficial and phony attitude

She emitted a VENEER of happiness for the party but was actually very stressed over the deadline she faced at work the next day.

venerable *(VEN-her-ah-bul), adjective*
Due great respect, usually because of age, character, or wisdom

The VENERABLE rabbi was sought for advice not only by his own synagogue but by other leaders in the community.

The VENERABLE professor amazes everyone with his wisdom, sensitivity, and concern for students who are now sixty years younger than he.

venial *(VEE-nyul)* or *(VEE-nee-uhl), adjective*
Slight and easy to forgive; minor, used to describe actions that aren't quite acceptable

The police took the girl home and made her tell her parents about her VENIAL act of vandalism for spray painting the bridge rather than charge her with a crime because she had never done anything like it before.

veracious *(ver-AY-shus), adjective*
Consistently honest and truthful; accurate most of the time

The VERACIOUS newspaper frequently received praise on the national level for being unbiased and straightforward.

veracity *(ver-ASS-ih-tea), noun*
The characteristic or habit of being truthful and conforming to accepted standards of behavior.

Roger pled his case with such VERACITY that the judge let him off without a fine.

Know this Quote

"The world is upheld by the VERACITY of good men: they make the earth wholesome."
—Ralph Waldo Emerson, American poet, essayist, and transcendentalist

verbiage *(VER-bee-idj)* or *(VER-bidj), noun*
Speech or writing that is wordy; the use of too many words

The editor's job was to take the author's VERBIAGE and make it easier for the average reader to understand clearly.

Good teachers inspire students to eliminate VERBIAGE from their writing and express themselves succinctly.

verbose *(ver-BOHS), adjective*
Using or having more words than necessary; using such flowery or technical language that the meaning is obscured

The professor was known to be so VERBOSE that his students often had a hard time recognizing what was important and what could be ignored.

I really wanted to vote for him, because he appears intelligent, but I find his speeches are almost always VERBOSE.

verdant *(VER-duhnt), adjective*
Lush and green, such as grass or other plants

The VERDANT park was the perfect and most romantic place he could think of to propose.

veritable *(VEHR-ih-tuh-bul), adjective*
Real or actual, often used to intensify a metaphor; synonymous with *verifiable.*

He was so good at trivia games that they teased him that he was a VERITABLE encyclopedia of trivial information.

Granny's attic is a VERITABLE museum of 1950s clothing, records, and memorabilia.

vernacular *(ver-NAK-yoo-lur), noun*
The everyday language of people as spoken in a particular country or region, in contrast to an official or formal language. The common spoken language of a group, as compared to formal written or literary language.

The VERNACULAR of rap musicians is full of expletives and is becoming more commonly used in public places.

vernal *(VER-nul), adjective*
Related to spring.

Lucas's favorite seasonal ritual is watching the VERNAL flowers bloom.

Know This Quote

"One impulse from a VERNAL wood / May teach you more of man, / Of moral evil and of good, / Than all the sages can." —William Wordsworth, British Romantic poet

vers libre *(VERSS LEE-breh), noun*
Free verse, a style of poetry requiring no rhyme or meter.

H. L. Mencken observed that VERS LIBRE is "a device for making poetry easier to write and harder to read."

vertiginous *(ver-TIJ-uh-nuss), adjective*
Causing vertigo, imbalance, dizziness, or stumbling.

Mallory and Michael enjoyed their weekend getaway to Paris, spending many moments staring at the Parisian skyline from the VERTIGINOUS heights of the Eiffel Tower.

vestige *(VEST-idj), noun*
A small amount; a trace; a tiny indication that something exists

The last VESTIGES of anxiety about owning her own home disappeared the first time she walked in the door after signing the paperwork.

vestigial *(VESS-tih-jee-ul), adjective*
Describes a remaining sample or trace of something that is disappearing or has already all but disappeared.

Some babies are born with a VESTIGIAL tail at the base of the spine.

vex *(VECKS), verb*
To cause irritation. That which aggravates causes vexation.

The constant demands of her two-year-old vexed Mary to the point of tears.

vexation *(VEKS-ay-shun), noun*
Being annoyed or frustrated; or that which causes someone to be annoyed or frustrated

He tried to hide his VEXATION with the young woman who was holding up the line when he was already late for a meeting.

Although the VEXATIONS of high school seem important at the time, they become less so as time passes and people mature.

vicarious *(vi-KARE-ee-uss), adjective*
Experienced through another person, via sympathy or imagination. To gain pleasure from actions not one's own.

Parents often live VICARIOUS lives through their children, and they do so with great pride.

vicariously *(vye-KARE-ee-uss-lee), adverb*
To enjoy imagined feelings and experiences largely by observing or hearing about another person's life and adventures.

Married for over twenty-five years, Roger often told his single friends that he lived VICARIOUSLY through them.

vicissitude *(vis-SIHS-ah-tood)* or *(vis-SIHS-ah-tyood), noun*
Regular and methodical changes and variations taking place over a very long time, usually pluralized; or unforeseen or unexpected changes, often leading one to another, usually pluralized

The two women, now old and gray, had known each other since childhood and had seen each other through all the VICISSITUDES of life.

Know This Quote

"VICISSITUDES of fortune, which spares neither man nor the proudest of his works, which buries empires and cities in a common grave." —Edward Gibbon, British historian

Looking back at the diner where she had gotten her first job, the actress was amazed at the VICISSITUDES that had brought her to the awards podium.

vigilant *(VIJ-eh-lent), adjective*
Watchful; aware and attentive

The baby's aunt was even more VIGILANT than his parents because she was so nervous about something happening while she was babysitting.

The family retriever was ever VIGILANT and barked whenever a stranger came near the house.

vignette *(vin-YET), noun*
A brief story, incident, or episode, usually told to illustrate some point.

Adding a VIGNETTE or two to a speech can help make abstract ideas clearer.

vilify *(VIL-ih-fiy), verb*
To speak or write harshly and often incorrectly about something or someone; to insult cruelly

She took the high road and refused, in spite of embarrassing questions, to VILIFY her ex-husband in the press.

Even before the trial began, the accused murderer was VILIFIED in the press, so the defense attorney asked for a change in venue.

vindicate *(VIN-dih-kayt), verb or adjective*
To clear of charges or prove innocent; or to prove justified; to be proven right or correct

The testimony of the eye witness VINDICATED the wrongly accused man.

In spite of herself, the young mother felt VINDICATED when her husband had a hard time getting the baby bathed and dressed after he'd criticized her for how long it took.

Which Word?

Many words can be used as either a verb or an adjective. Vindicate (VIN-dih-kayt) is one of them. The verb to vindicate means to prove innocent. The adjective vindicate is the way someone feels when they have been proven innocent or their stance has been justified. When used as an adjective, the word is often vindicated. So it could be said that a wrongly accused man will feel vindicated once the evidence vindicates him.

vindication *(VIN-dih-KAY-shun), noun*
The act of clearing someone or something from blame, guilt, suspicion, or doubt. Evidence or argument used to prove someone innocent of false charges.

Graduating cum laude from the school that had once rejected him was VINDICATION for Robert.

virago *(vuh-RAY-goh)* or *(vuh-RAH-goh), noun*
An extraordinary woman of uncommon strength, courage, and vigor; or a woman considered noisy, violent, and demanding

Nearly every man who helped settle the American West had a VIRAGO by his side, willing to take every risk right along with him.

The president's secretary was such a VIRAGO that everyone from the customers to the president himself were just a little afraid of her.

virtu *(vihr-TOO), noun*
An appreciation for and love of art or the arts; or a grouping of fine art pieces taken or considered together

Few people expected a police officer to have such VIRTU that he quite happily spent his days off at the museum.

The VIRTU of boxes displayed at the museum were all that survived from the larger collection owned by the queen prior to the revolution.

virtuoso *(vihr-choo-OH-soh) or (vihr-choo-OH-zoh), noun or adjective*
A master in the field of study, usually the arts (noun) or showing mastery of the skills required for a specific field of study, usually the arts (adjective)

The university prided itself on hiring only VIRTUOSOS to teach even the most basic freshman classes.

The critics called the singer's VIRTUOSO performance the best ever heard in the opera house.

virulence *(VEER-yoo-lunts), noun*
Rapid, extreme, and malicious, as in quick and fatal diseases. Malicious, bitter, or hostile. Not to be confused with *violence,* which means the use of physical force to injure or damage.

The VIRULENCE of AIDS was shocking to physicians who did not know what was causing so many unexplained deaths.

visage *(VIZ-idj), noun*
The face; facial features or expressions; or the outward appearance

Regardless of the situation, he maintained a calm VISAGE that didn't even hint at worry or concern.

The rocky VISAGE of the cliff became more intimidating as the climbers got closer and could see it clearly.

vis-à-vis *(VIZ-ah-vee), preposition*
Opposite from, or face to face with. In relation to, or in comparison to. Often misused to mean "about" or "concerning."

I would like you to discuss your raise VIS-À-VIS all your supervisors and peers.

visceral *(VIH-suh-rul), adjective*
Instinctive, rather than based on reasoned thinking. Deeply felt; showing basic emotions. Literally "from the viscera," or bodily interior.

Not fearing any injury to herself, her VISCERAL response was to lash out at those who threatened her children.

Know This Quote
"[Multiculturalism's] passions are political; its assumptions empirical; its conception of identities VISCERAL." —Joyce Appleby, American historian

viscous *(VIHS-kuhs), adjective*
Having a thick, gooey texture that does not flow easily

The students knew the lab experiment had gone wrong when the liquid, which was supposed to pour easily, turned into VISCOUS ooze instead.

vitiate *(VISH-ee-ayt), verb*
To decrease the value; to make less worthy or worthwhile

The counselors were afraid the rules that were put in place to protect the program would actually VITIATE it and hamper the children's success.

vitriol *(VIH-tree-ahl), noun*
Extreme bitterness and hatred. Writing or speech that expresses this feeling in caustic or harsh writing or speech.

How sad it is that the VITRIOL of all parties in the Middle Eastern conflict could not be transformed into hope.

vituperate *(vih-TOO-per-ayt) or (vih-TYOO-per-ayt), verb*
To use harsh, blaming, and vicious language, especially against another person

The senator was known to VITUPERATE against whichever group or organization had most recently spoken out against her pet projects, so no one paid her any attention.

vituperative *(vih-TOO-per-ah-tiv) or (vih-TYOO-per-ah-tiv), adjective*
Abusive; unnecessarily harsh

She was shocked by the VITUPERATIVE message her sister left on the answering machine after their recent quarrel.

vivacious *(vy-VAY-shuss), adjective*
Joyful; happy, spirited; possessing a positive attitude about and enthusiasm for life; a person who lives life to the fullest.

Even after her family maintained some steep revenue losses, Sandra retained her VIVACIOUS character.

vivify *(VIV-ih-fiy), verb*
To make more interesting or lively; to make come alive

A good teacher can VIVIFY even the dullest of subjects for a class.

Which Word?

Don't get confused by words that look or sound almost identical. Vilify (VIL-ih-fiy) and vivify (VIV-ih-fiy) can easily be confused. To vilify is to spread lies and say nasty things about another person. To vivify is to energize or bring something to life. Just remember to read carefully!

vociferate *(voh-SIH-fuh-rate), verb*
To shout something out loudly; to make a noisy exclamation, demanding attention.

Susie VOCIFERATED her strong objection to her parents' insistence that she babysit for her two younger sisters.

vociferous *(voh-SIHF-er-us), adjective*
Loud and noisy; unrestrained and boisterous; generally referring to protests or cheers

The Red Sox were met with VOCIFEROUS cheers and rowdy celebrations after winning the World Series for the first time in over eighty years.

Know This Quote

"Let the singing singers / With vocal voices, most VOCIFEROUS, / In sweet vociferation out-vociferize / Even sound itself."
—Henry Carey, English poet

volitional *(voe-LISH-uhn-uhl), adjective*
Describes an action performed or thought achieved through deliberate and conscious effort.

Our servants' persistent and VOLITIONAL attention to detail makes them absolutely indispensable to us.

voluble *(VOL-yuh-bul), adjective*
Characterized by talking a great deal, usually implies speaking well and intelligently

The candidate's VOLUBLE style was effective because she could sound like an intellectual or a small-town girl, depending on which was appropriate.

voluptuous *(vuh-LUP-chew-us), adjective*
Anything arising from or giving extreme sensory or sensual pleasure.

A VOLUPTUOUS banquet was the highlight of the Masterlys' Thanksgiving gala.

voracious *(voh-RAY-shuss), adjective*
Ravenously hungry. Desiring or consuming things in great quantities. Eager or enthusiastic about an activity.

"It is hoped that after you finish this English literature course you will become a VORACIOUS reader of Shakespeare," the professor said.

vortex *(VOR-teks), noun*
Liquid or gas swirling in a spiral that sucks everything in or near it toward its center; a problem or situation that draws in everyone around it.

The permanent whirlpool where the river goes underground is a dark VORTEX sucking in everything in its current.

vox populi *(VOKS-pop-you-LYE), noun*
Expression of the prevailing mood, concerns, and opinions in a country.

In response to an environmentally friendly VOX POPULI, more and more corporations are "going green."

doctrinaire
abstemious
levity hubris panacea
veracity cerebellum
labyrinth
criterion
nonagenarian
meticulous zither
W
erbiage quondam
colloquial
wok palpable paginatio
incipient salutary
evity redact fervent
beleaguered yawnful
elixir beneficent
amoose pragmatism

waft *(WAFT), verb*
To carry lightly, as if caught in a breeze.

She was awakened by the smell of coffee WAFTING into her bedroom.

Know This Quote
"This quiet sail is as a noiseless wing / To WAFT me from distraction." —Lord Byron, British Romantic poet

waggish *(WAG-ish), adjective*
Joking, witty, and mischievous.

Some thought Peter was a troublemaker, but he really was just WAGGISH.

waif *(WAFE), noun*
A stray person or animal.

The occasional nouveau riche WAIF may float into our circle, but she rarely lasts long.

wan *(WAHN), adjective*
Showing or suggesting ill health or unhappiness.

William looked a little WAN after his girlfriend broke up with him.

wanderlust *(WON-dehr-lust), noun*
A strong and innate desire to travel far from home.

Monique's WANDERLUST often took her far away from her family.

Know This Quote
"In our WANDERLUST, we are lovers looking for consummation." —Anatole Broyard, literary critic for the *New York Times*

wane *(WAYN), verb*
To gradually decrease; to fade away; to become diminished.

Once she finally received the Cartier watch from her father, Karen's interest in the timepiece quickly WANED.

wangle *(WANG-guhl), verb*
To accomplish by underhanded methods.

Jennifer managed to WANGLE an invitation to the Clarksons' party, even though she is the gauchest of the area's parvenus.

wanton *(WON-tun), adjective*
Without restraint or inhibition, especially in sexual behavior. Without reason or provocation. Completely unrestrained or lacking discipline. Certainly not to be confused with *won ton,* a small Chinese dumpling.

Such WANTON disrespect for the law could not be ignored or excused.

warrant *(WAR-unt), verb*
To authorize or guarantee. To serve as a justifiable reason to do, believe, or think something. Also, to guarantee something as the truth or dependability of something or someone.

The child's minor accident did not really WARRANT the temper tantrum that followed it.

wary *(WAHR-ee), adjective*
Cautious; alert and on guard

A smart woman is WARY but not afraid when she is out on her own after dark.

waspish *(WOS-pish), adjective*
Irascible and petulant; given to resentment.

Rebecca can be WASPISH, but we forgive her because she gives the best galas.

wassail *(WAH-sull), noun*
A salute or toast given when drinking to someone's health, well-being, or success.

We lost count of the mugs of beer consumed with the numerous WASSAILS to our teacher wishing him a happy retirement.

watershed *(WAH-ter-shed), noun*
An important event, period, time, or factor that serves to distinguish two separate phases. Literally, a ridge that diverts water in a new direction.

High school commencement is a true WATERSHED event in a young person's life.

watermark *(WAW-terr-mark), noun*
A faint design, graphic, or lettering pressed into paper while it is still in pulp form.

The CEO's classy letterhead bears a WATERMARK of the company logo.

wayfaring *(WAY-fair-ing), adjective*
Traveling on foot.

We spent many WAYFARING weekends during our month-long jaunt in France last year.

wayward *(WAY-word), adjective*
Willfully disobedient. Behaving in an erratic, perverse, or unpredictable manner.

Your WAYWARD actions will someday cause you much pain, so please try to change your ways.

weal *(WEEL), noun*
Prosperous well-being; vitality.

Jordan is convinced that expensive jewelry is necessary for one's WEAL and welfare.

wean *(WEEN), verb*
To ease someone off of something they have become dependent on

The doctors noted it was time to WEAN him off the pain medication he'd been given after the surgery so he wouldn't become addicted.

wearisome *(WE-ree-sum), adjective*
Physically or mentally tiring or tedious. Not to be misused or confused with *worrisome*, which means causing anxiety or distress, or having a tendency to worry.

Of course I found the 10K run WEARISOME, wouldn't you?

weir *(WEERE), noun*
A low dam or barrier built across a river either to control water levels or catch fish.

When the water level in the Passaic River lowered during a drought, a stone WEIR built by Indians for catching fish became visible.

weltschmerz *(VELT-schmayrtz), noun*
A lingering sorrow that some believe is a given in life.

When we snubbed Margaret for buying so many fashion knockoffs, her WELTSCHMERZ lasted until we forgave her.

wend *(WEND), verb*
To go; to proceed.

The funeral procession WENDED its way down the curving boulevard.

Know This Quote

"As they WEND away / A voice is heard singing / Of Kitty, or Katy, / As if the name meant once / All love, all beauty." —Philip Larkin, British poet, novelist, and jazz critic

Westernize *(WES-tur-nize), verb*
To adopt customs or beliefs common to Europe or North or South America. To impose such customs on other peoples.

Not having visited the country in ten years, Gary was surprised at how much more it had become WESTERNIZED.

wherewithal *(WAIR-with-all), noun*
Means or resources; money.

We certainly have the WHEREWITHAL to visit that restaurant, but we will not because the maître d' does not know his place.

whimsical *(WHIM-sihk-uhl), adjective*
Characterized by acting playfully or amusingly erratic; lighthearted; or dependent on chance; unpredictable

Although he had been dreading taking his sister and her friends to the fair, the children's WHIMSICAL enjoyment of the day turned out to be contagious and he enjoyed himself after all.

The weather in Scotland seemed WHIMSICAL throughout their vacation, bringing rain and fog one day and bright, warm sunshine the next.

whimsy *(WIMM-zee), noun*
The quality of being quaint, odd, and playfully humorous in an endearing way. An idea that has no obvious reason to exist.

The idea of winning the lottery is for many simple WHIMSY, yet they buy a ticket each week.

wistful *(WIHST-full), adjective*
Yearning, pensive; having an unfulfilled desire.

The rich businessman knew his secretary was WISTFUL about not finishing college, so he paid for her courses.

Know This Quote

"How truly does this journal contain my real and undisguised thoughts—I always write it according to the humour I am in, and if a stranger was to think it worth reading, how capricious—insolent & WHIMSICAL I must appear!" —Frances Burney, British novelist, diarist, and playwright

whitewash *(WITE-wash), verb*
To paint with whitewash. Also, an attempt to conceal unpleasant facts by covering them over as though they did not exist.

How absurd his stories became whenever Brian attempted to WHITEWASH his guilt.

whodunit *(hoo-DUH-nit), noun*
A novel, movie, or play focusing on solving a crime, usually a murder.

Agatha Christie's works are some of the best WHODUNITS I've ever read.

wily *(WHY-lee), adjective*
Skilled at using clever tricks to deceive people. The roadrunner's perpetual enemy, after all, is Wile E. Coyote.

You shouldn't confuse "WILY" with "intelligent," for deceiving others isn't really a smart thing to do.

winnow *(WIH-noh), verb*
To separate grain from chaff by tossing it in the air or blowing air through it. To examine closely in order to separate the good from the bad, unusable, or undesirable components.

Investigators WINNOWED through thousands of pieces to reconstruct the plan and determine factors that caused the crash.

winsome *(WIN-suhm), adjective*
Winning and engaging; charming.

Lydia looked quite WINSOME throughout her coming out party.

witticism *(WIT-ih-sihz-em), noun*
A pun, joke, or funny remark

Her WITTICISM was the perfect remedy for the tension that had been building in the staff meeting.

wizened *(WIZ-uhnd), adjective*
Withered; shriveled; dried up

Moira spent so much time out in the sun during her Mediterranean trip that she came back positively WIZENED.

woebegone *(WOE-buh-gone), adjective*
Feeling or looking distressed or sorrowful.

"Please, Coach, go talk to the team, for they look so WOEBEGONE after the loss," the shortstop's Mother urged.

wreak *(REEK), verb*
To inflict something violent, especially punishment or revenge. Not to be misused or confused with *reek,* which means to stink.

It's shocking to see how much havoc a two-year-old can WREAK in just a few minutes.

wrest *(REST), verb*
To pull away; to take something by force or threat.

Polly scolded her child when he WRESTED a toy away from his cousin.

writhe *(RYTHE), verb*
To make a violent twisting and rolling movement, often as a result of severe pain. To squirm with intensity.

The running back WRITHED in agony as he waited for the trainer to arrive.

wunderkind *(VUN-dur-kund), noun*
Someone who is extremely successful at a young age; prodigy. Literally, German for "wonder child."

Little Joey was thought to be a WUNDERKIND because he sang so beautifully at such an early age.

X / Y / Z

Xanadu *(ZAN-uh-dyoo), noun*
A place of perfect, idyllic beauty.

She considered her garden her own, personal XANADU.

xanthic *(ZAN-thick), adjective*
Of a yellowish tint or color.

After Laura wore a XANTHIC dress to the spring ball, the area's nouveau riche followed her example at subsequent galas.

Know This Quote

"In XANADU did Kubla Khan / A stately pleasure-dome decree: / Where Alph, the sacred river, ran / Through caverns measureless to man / Down to a sunless sea" —Samuel Taylor Coleridge, English poet

Xanthippe *(zan-TIP-ee), noun*
An ill-tempered, shrewish woman.

Felicia is far from a XANTHIPPE simply because she interacts only with certain members of the household staff.

xebec *(ZEE-beck), noun*
A small, three-masted ship used in the Mediterranean for commerce that once was a favorite vessel of the leisure class.

All of the amassed XEBECS ruined the otherwise spectacular views from our villa during the month we spent on the Greek Isles.

xenocurrency *(zen-uh-KURR-uhn-see), noun*
Money that is circulated or traded in money markets outside its country of issue.

The Wallaces stopped speculating in XENOCURRENCY once rumors of a worldwide recession began circulating.

xenogamy *(zih-NAHG-uh-me), noun*
Cross-pollination among plant species.

The secret of our award-winning formal gardens is the careful use of XENOGAMY.

xenophile *(ZEN-uh-file), noun*
Someone who is attracted to foreign styles, customs, manners, etc.

All of us are XENOPHILES because American customs and cultural products are so gauche.

xenophobe *(ZEE-nuh-fobe), noun*
Someone with an unreasonable fear or dislike of foreign people or foreign things.

Those who express concerns about the country's liberal immigration and open border policies are regularly called XENOPHOBES by those who oppose their views.

xenophobia *(zeh-neh-FOH-bee-yah) or (zee-noh-FOH-bee-yah), noun*
The irrational fear of anything or anyone from another country or foreign country
Although international travel tends to be an excellent cure for XENOPHOBIA, the people who suffer from it the most are usually the least likely to go overseas.

xenoplastic *(ZEN-uh-plass-tick), adjective*
Of, or occurring between, distantly related individuals.
We always have the senders of cards and letter carefully screened because some of us have been involved in XENOPLASTIC schemes by which total strangers suggested they belong to our family.

xerochilia *(ZEER-uh-kile-ee-uh), noun*
Dryness of the lips.
Kyle may be cute, but the way he treats his chronic XEROCHILIA with common lip balm is nothing short of distasteful.

xerophyte *(zihr-ih-FIYT), noun*
Any plant that requires very little water in order to grow and thrive
Many gardeners will actually drown cacti not realizing they are XEROPHYTES and therefore grow better without being watered on a weekly basis.

xerosis *(zih-ROH-sis), noun*
The typical hardening of aging skin and tissue.
Ophelia constantly visits European spas to slow the onset of XEROSIS.

xiphoid *(ZIE-foid), adjective*
Shaped like a sword.
We can always spot Carlson's private plane because it is covered with the same XIPHOID shapes that adorn his family's crest.

xylography *(ziy-LOG-raf-ee), noun*
The act of making art or print using woodprints and blocks to transfer ink, generally refers to a primitive technique
Although it was eventually replaced by typesetting, originally, XYLOGRAPHY was considered a fast and efficient way to illustrate and print documents.

xylophagous *(ziy-LOF-ih-gus), adjective*
Feeding on, living on, or burrowing into wood, as an insect
Termites can cause nearly irreparable damage to wood structures because they are XYLOPHAGOUS by nature.

yahoo *(YA-hoo), noun*
Not just an Internet portal—this words refers to an offensive, crude, or brutish person, a bumpkin.

You shouldn't let yourself get upset by the cruel comments of YAHOOS like those guys.

Where'd That Word Come From?

Yahoo—Yahoos, in Jonathan Swift's satire *Gulliver's Travels,* were hateful beasts in human form who prefer "nastiness and dirt." This may have been a pun by Swift on a Greek word sounding like *yahoo* that meant sleepy, or "dopey."

yammer *(YAM-uhr), verb*
To whine or complain loudly and at length.

The way Roland YAMMERS about being thrown out of Yale, you'd think he hadn't begged his father to make the expulsion happen!

yantra *(YAHN-truh), noun*
A geometric diagram used to help one meditate.

During Eloise's foray into Buddhism, she kept forgetting her mantra, so her teacher gave her a YANTRA that she could affix to the wall in front of her meditation cushion.

yardarm *(YAHRD-arm), noun*
Either of the outer portions of a square sail.

During the regatta, the yachts sailed YARDARM to YARDARM, appearing as though they may collide at any moment.

yare *(YAR), adjective*
Easily moved, steered or maneuverable, generally used when describing sailing vessels

The small boat was YARE in a way the captain of the large yacht wasn't expecting, so he had to adjust his style to match the boat's responsiveness.

yaw *(YAW), verb*
An erratic, side-to-side motion; or, to swerve.

A fast-moving cold front caused Sasha's Learjet 60 to YAW dangerously for several minutes.

yawnful *(YAWN-full), adjective*
Arousing tedium or boredom.

Eleanor's YAWNFUL story about her month doing volunteer work made many of us bolt for the doors.

yawp *(YAWP), noun, verb*
A raucous, clamorous noise; or, to make such a noise.

Carla regretted her offer to watch her friend's puppy after listening to the loud YAWPING all night long.

Know This Quote
"I sound my barbaric YAWP over the roofs of the world." —Walt Whitman, American poet and humanist

yearling *(YEER-ling), noun or adjective*
A creature that is one year old (noun)
One year old (adjective)

The YEARLINGS in the petting zoo were popular attractions with the children who were afraid of the older, larger animals.

The entire world watched the YEARLING government to see if the country would settle into a democracy or if civil war would break out again.

yen *(YEN), noun*
A longing; an urge or desire; craving

The young man had always had a YEN to travel to Ireland and see the town where his grandfather had grown up.

yenta *(YEN-tuh), noun*
A woman considered a busybody or gossip.

Spreading rumors amongst ourselves is one thing, but Rebecca has gained a reputation as a YENTA because she also blabs to the help.

yeoman *(YOE-mun) noun*
An attendant, servant, or lesser official in a royal or noble household. A petty officer performing chiefly clerical duties in the U.S. Navy. An assistant or other subordinate. A loyal, dependable worker.

All organizations need some who perform the roles of a YEOMAN, completing administrative tasks.

yeti *(YEH-tee), noun*
A large, hairy creature, rumored to live in the mountains

The locals' stories about the YETI that roamed the mountainside were no longer humorous now that the hikers were isolated and alone at their campsite.

yew *(YOO), noun*
A particular type of evergreen tree, surrounded by myth and legend because of its extremely long life span

It was once believed that witches would gather under the boughs of the YEW trees on the night of the full moon in order to cast spells and work magic.

yob *(YAHB), noun*
A cruel and loutish young man; a bully.

Jerry was bullied by a hulking YOB named Bull throughout elementary school.

Know This Quote

"Mick Jagger, alternately slurring YOB and lisping lordling, is classlessness apotheosised."
—Phillip Norman, British author

young Turk *(yung terk), noun*
A young person, especially one of a group, who attempts to wrest control of an organization from older, established, more conservative individuals. Historically, a member of a liberal pro-democratic Turkish nationalist movement in 1908.

How amazing it is that each of those YOUNG TURKS is now worth over a million dollars after the initial public offering.

younker *(YAHN-kuhr), noun*
A young man or child.

Alex has been a fine horseman since he was a mere YOUNKER, playing with his family's thoroughbreds.

yuppie *(YUH-pee), noun*
A young, educated city-dwelling professional, usually regarded as materialistic and self-focused.

Do you remember when being called "YUPPIE" was a compliment?

Where'd That Word Come From?

Yuppie—This slang term came from the acronym YUP (for "young urban professional"). In 1983, syndicated columnist Bob Greene wrote how this word for materialistic professionals was related to an earlier word for young radicals from the 1960s: "While [Gerry Rubin] and Abbie Hoffman once led the Yippies—the Youth International Party—one social commentator has ventured that Rubin is now attempting to become the leader of the Yuppies—Young Urban Professionals."

zabaglione *(zah-buhl-YOH-knee), noun*
An Italian dessert delicacy featuring a foamy, custard-like mix of egg yolks, sugar, and wine.

Even though the café has been discovered by the general public, we still go to the café for its delectable ZABAGLIONE.

za-zen *(ZAH-ZEN), noun*
Meditation in a cross-legged posture.

Christopher has taken to practicing ZA-ZEN, but at heart, we know his goal is still acquisition of wealth and power, not personal enlightenment.

zealot *(ZEL-eht), noun*
A person who believes so strongly in an idea, political party, or religion that it becomes more important than just about anything else

Even though there are ZEALOTS at either end of the political spectrum in the United States, most people consider something other than politics their top priority.

Know This Quote

"What a noble aim is that of the ZEALOT who tortures himself like a madman in order to desire nothing, love nothing, feel nothing, and who, if he succeeded, would end up a complete monster!" —Denis Diderot, French philosopher

zealous *(ZEH-lus), adjective*
Actively and unreservedly enthusiastic; fervent or fanatical.

At first those students named to the hall patrol seemed overly ZEALOUS, giving summonses to almost everyone.

zeitgeist *(ZIHT-giyst), noun*
The defining spirit of a time; the overall mood of an era

The free-spirited ZEITGEIST of the 1920s was too quickly replaced by the despair of the Depression in the 1930s.

zenith *(ZEH-nith), noun*
The highest point or climax of a thing or event. The peak or apex.

It's hard to predict the ZENITH of an athlete's career, but it is easy to identify it in hindsight.

zero tolerance *(ZEE-roe TAH-luh-runts), noun*
Unwavering enforcement of a rule, regulation, or law, especially regarding antisocial behavior.

After the quarterback was caught drinking, the entire team was told that the attitude toward any future drinking would be ZERO TOLERANCE.

zelig *(ZEH-lig), noun*
A chameleonlike person who seems omnipresent.

The parvenus try so hard to be ZELIGS, blending in seamlessly at our functions, but we can always spot them for the intruders they are.

zen *(ZEHN), verb*
Generally speaking, to figure out the answer to a difficult problem with a flash of sudden insight.

After days of indecision regarding which gala to attend on a particular night, Danielle managed to ZEN the answer and make her choice.

Zionism *(ZYE-on-iz-um), noun*
The modern political movement to establish a Jewish homeland in Palestine.

The Wassersteins give charitably not only to the community, but also in support of ZIONISM because the family has many relatives living in Palestine.

zonifugal *(zoh-niff-YOU-gull), adjective*
Passing out of, or away from, a region.

Our multinational European jaunt contained many ZONIFUGAL changes that, often, caused us to feel disoriented.

zonk *(ZAWNK), verb*
To stun or stupefy.

We were positively ZONKED by Marie's choice of couture for the very important Sanderson gala.

zoomorphic *(zoe-uh-MORE-fihk), adjective*
Having the form of an animal.

The Rossingtons' formal garden is peppered with delightfully ZOOMORPHIC topiaries that seem to mix flora and fauna in equal measure.

zymurgy *(ZIMM-ur-jee) noun*
The scientific study of the brewing and distilling fermentation process. Very often the last word in any alphabetical list!

No, I won't accept your excuse for drinking beer as a ZYMURGY experiment!

APPENDIX A

Common Mistakes

Beware to All Who Enter Here!

The English language is a complex one, and we, as a society, tend to be lazy when it comes to language. This is not necessarily a bad thing. This way of speaking gives our language color and flavor. However, laziness and colloquialisms (look it up if you need to; it's in the main body of the text!) have no place in formal essays. If you are writing for the SAT or the GRE, the testers expect you to be able to write the way the language is supposed to be used, not the way it is used in everyday conversation.

This appendix addresses some of the more common mistakes made with both words and grammar. Perhaps these are not the mistakes you make. You should still be aware of them and let them be a guide to help you figure out what mistakes you might make.

Already/All ready

It is easy to interchange these two because, after all, they are the same word, right? Only they aren't the same word and actually have very different meanings. *Already* means something has already occurred or been accomplished, as in *She had already studied for the test so she was able to go to the movies with her friends.* This is very different from *all ready,* which means *prepared,* as in *The room was all ready for the party.* You can always use a synonym if you can't remember but it's best to learn the different definitions so you can use these words, as well their synonyms, properly.

Appendix/Appendices

An appendix is a section at the back of the book that adds necessary information that just didn't fit in the main text. This is an appendix—the main purpose of the book is to teach vocabulary, so grammar tips weren't particularly appropriate for the main text. However, the vocabulary is geared to people studying for the SAT or the GRE. In light of that, it seemed appropriate to have grammar tips in here somewhere. Thus, they were added to the appendices. Notice that change? That change is the point of this piece of information. When there is one additional section at the end of a book, it is an *appendix (uh-PEN-diks).* Currently, there is a debate over how to pluralize the word "appendix." Some dictionaries and sources state "appendices" *(uh-PEN-dih-seez)* is the only truly correct way to do so. Others state "appendixes" *(uh-PEN-diks-es)* is as correct as "appendices." However, as with the GRE, I recommend you deal with the *best* answer. "Appendices" has been recognized as correct for longer, therefore your safest, smartest bet is to use "appendices." Remember, one appendix, several appendices.

Between/Among

These two words are often confused. They seem interchangeable. However, they are not. *Between* is used to indicate two things or people—and *only* two. *Among* is used to indicate three or more. Here's an example: *The teacher shared the crayons between the students.* Implicitly, the teacher only has two students. If he has more than two students, to be correct the sentence must read: *The teacher shared the crayons among the students.*

Bring/Take

Here's a question—do you bring something to a party or do you take something to a party? It's a dilemma. Before you can choose between *bring* and *take*, you must first establish where the speaker is or will be, even if it means playing with the sentence a little bit.

In order for the correct choice to be *bring*, the object in question must be going to or along with the speaker. Here's an example:

You and your best friend have been invited to a potluck dinner. Since you obviously don't want to arrive with the same dish, you ask her *What are you going to bring to the party?* In this case, *bring* is the correct choice because you, the speaker, are going to be at the party as well.

Assume, however, that you wake up on the day of the party too sick to attend. You are in charge of dessert, and no dinner party is complete without dessert. So you call your best friend and ask her *Will you take the dessert with you tonight?* In this case, she is *taking* the dessert because the dessert is going away from you, the speaker. If she is a good friend, she will also *bring* you, the speaker, aspirin for your headache and hot tea for your throat.

Remember, bring along with or to the speaker and take away from the speaker.

Could Of/Would Of/ Should Of

This is one example of ways people can be lazy with their speech. Nearly everyone has used one of the above phrases at some point in time. They are, however, all incorrect. Instead of writing *could of*, write *could have*. It was using the contraction "could've" and slurring the "have" at the end of the full phrase "could have" that developed the incorrect one in the first place. Therefore, instead of writing *She would of agreed to babysit if she hadn't had to study that night*, be sure to write *She would have agreed to babysit if she hadn't had to study that night.* "Should have" is perfectly acceptable. "Should of" is perfectly wrong.

Except/Accept

Since these two words are pronounced so similarly, it is often hard to tell them apart when they are spoken. This has led to confusion around which word is used at which time. *Except* means to exclude or excluding. *Everyone went to the party except John, who had to work that night.* On the other hand, *accept* means to respond favorably to something or to understand something is common or normal. *John's roommate accepted the invitation in John's place. This happened so often that it was an accepted practice for the roommates to attend parties in each other's stead.* They're easy to confuse.

Flammable/Inflammable

This one seems easy. The prefix *in* tends to mean "not." There's correct and incorrect, frequent and infrequent, separable and inseparable. So what's the problem? You have heard the saying, "There's an exception to every rule." *Flammable* and *inflammable* are the exception to the "in means not" rule. Flammable means quick to burn or flame. Inflammable means quick to burn or flame. Instead of being antonyms as they would appear to be, they are actually synonyms. Feel free to interchange these two all you wish.

Hung/Hanged

You were probably taught that "hanged" is incorrect. That the past tense of hang is hung. That is true except under one condition. When discussing the old-time style of execution, the criminal is hanged. *The little girl hung her brother over the railing* is correct. *The cattle rustler was hanged at dawn* is also correct.

Irregardless/Regardless

Irregardless is not actually a word. Yes, it is in common use. And yes, it has become so commonly used that it is now in the dictionary. It is however generally marked as informal or slang. When people say "irregardless," what they mean is "regardless." Since *regardless* means in spite of everything or anyway, just use *regardless*. That's the word you really want. As for *irregardless*, just don't use it. Ever.

Lose/Loose

Somewhere along the line, these two words became confused in many people's writings. But their meanings are very different. They are even pronounced differently so this confusion cannot be explained away by the way they sound when they are spoken as is the case with some of the other examples. *Lose* means to misplace. *Loose* means not tight.

Prefix/Prefixes

I want to draw attention to this particular question because of the appendix/appendices note above. Remember in the opening statement of this appendix, it was noted that the English language is a complex one? Here is an excellent example of that. It would seem logical that if there is debate over the plural of *appendix* then there would be debate over the plural of *prefix*. However, there is not. The plural of *prefix* is, in fact, *prefixes*.

Stationary/Stationery

In the case of these two words, it isn't so much that people get them confused as it is many people simply do not know the second word even exists. They see *stationery* and think it is a misspelling of *stationary*. However, that is not the case. *Stationary* means staying still, not moving. *Stationery,* though, is the word that describes the paper on which letters are written.

Their/There/They're

All of us at some point in our lives have had to stop and think about this combination of words. Unfortunately, there is no magic trick to remembering which is which. You just have to memorize and remember. If something belongs to more than one person, it is *theirs. Whose car is it? It's their car.* When indicating placement, the word you want is *there. Where is the car? The car is over there.* The last one is the only one that can be played with a little because it is a contraction. If the phrase "they are" is appropriate, then you know *they're* is the correct choice. *Who is driving the car? They're driving the car.* Go slowly if this is one of your trouble spots.

Who/Whom

Many students get trapped into thinking that if they want to sound formal and educated, using *whom* is an easy way to succeed. Unfortunately, using *whom* incorrectly is also an easy way to look as if you don't quite know what you're talking about. The best trick to have up your sleeve when it comes to *who* and *whom* is to rework the sentence just a bit. Would it make sense to rephrase the sentence with a *to* in front of the word in question? If the question is *Who gave you the sweater?*, rewrite it as *To who gave you the sweater?* That just sounds silly. In this case, the correct word is *who.* However, if the question is *Who are you giving the sweater to?*, the rewrite would be *To whom are you giving the sweater?* That makes more sense. In this case, the correct word is *whom.* If the word *to* can logically be placed in front of the word, choose *whom.* Otherwise, stick with *who.*

Y'all

If you are from the northern half of the country, you may not even know this phrase. However, if you are from the southern half of the country, you are probably very familiar with it. *Y'all* (the contraction for *you all*) is used frequently in the southern states as a plural for you. It is, however, inappropriate in formal communication. Leave it out. Use *you* as the singular and *all* as the plural instead.

Four More Common Mistakes

If you understand words and grammar—and the SAT and GRE testers do!—certain common mistakes can be the bane of your existence. Here we'll briefly touch on four of the most common ones: apostrophes, the word *at*, double negatives, and quotation marks. Avoiding these mistakes will increase your essay scores and endear you to the testers.

Apostrophes

First and foremost, making a singular into a plural does not require using an apostrophe. Apostrophes are used only to indicate possession or in a contraction. For example, you may see a sign in a store that reads: *Checks accepted with proper identification.* This is correct. They accept checks. They accept lots of checks, so long as everyone has proper ID. And nothing belongs to the checks. There is no possession in the sentence, therefore there should be no apostrophe. Here's another example: *The dog's leg was cut.* This is also correct. In the sentence, there is one dog and the leg belonging—possessed by—the dog is cut.

When writing about two or more people or things that possess something, the apostrophe is placed *after* the *s*. Therefore, the sentence would read: *The dogs' leashes were tangled.* There are two dogs. They each have a leash and those leashes were entwined.

You can often tell how many items are involved by where the apostrophe is placed. Take this sentence: *The fire hydrants' spray soaked the entire street.* According to this sentence, there is more than one fire hydrant spraying water. How can you tell that? Because the apostrophe is placed *after* the *s* at the end of the word. If the sentence read: *The fire hydrant's spray soaked the entire street,* you would know there was only one fire hydrant.

While these rules may seem intimidating at first, they don't need to be. Just remember to ask yourself if the word is plural or possessive. If it is only plural, leave out the apostrophe. If it is possessive, add an apostrophe.

A quick word about *its* and *it's*: deciding whether or not to add an apostrophe to the word *it* seems to be one of the most difficult decisions for writers to make. When *it* becomes possessive, *do not use an apostrophe.* No possessive pronouns contain apostrophes—hers, his, theirs . . . its.

An apostrophe is only used for the contraction of *it is.* An easy reminder for test taking and other formal writing purposes is that you should never use an apostrophe with the word *it.* Either, *it* is possessive and thus has no apostrophe, or *it's* is a contraction of *it is* and thus you should spell it out. Avoid using contractions when writing a formal essay or document. Spell out both words.

At

When used correctly, the word *at* is a perfectly acceptable addition to a sentence. *The couple waited at the bar until their table was ready.* However, when used incorrectly, the word *at* will make testers—and anyone else who cares about grammar—cringe. Avoid using the word *at* at the end of a sentence at all costs. If you have lost a book and are asking about its location, the question is *Where is it?* The question is *not Where's it at?* It really is that easy.

Double Negatives

A double negative is a situation where *not* or another negative word is put in front of a word that already carries a negative connotation, such as "not inappropriate" or "can't hardly." This automatically creates a positive connotation but also creates confusion. While this may have its place in informal or stylized writing, it is inappropriate in formal writing. In the above examples, you would use "appropriate" and "hardly" instead. Both are more concise and far clearer to your reader.

Quotation Marks

Everyone knows to use quotation marks when citing a source or quoting a person directly. Quotation marks can also be used around a single word, but they should not be used for emphasis. It has become common practice to put quotation marks around *any* word that needs emphasis. This is incorrect. To stress a word, italicize or underline it.

Quotation marks used around a single word or phrase indicate this word is being used to indicate a different definition than the word usually carries. Consider it the "wink, wink," inside joke indicator of punctuation. Let's take a sentence and break it down.

Did you meet her friend, Brandon, at the party?

Written like that, it is straightforward. The woman in question has a friend named Brandon, and Brandon was at a party.

However, add strategic quotation marks and the sentence takes on a whole new meaning:

Did you meet her "friend" Brandon at the party?

The quotation marks indicate that the speaker means something other than the standard definition of the word *friend,* and the meaning of the question changes slightly. Perhaps everyone knows or suspects the woman and Brandon are dating but she continues to try to hide it, introducing him only as her friend. Perhaps Brandon is actually her biggest rival at work and she only invited him hoping to get some dirt on him. Whatever the situation, the quotation marks indicate Brandon is something other than a friend.

APPENDIX B

Frequently Misused Words

Many, many words in the English language are misused on a daily basis. Using key words correctly, however, can make you stand out in college interviews, job interviews, and any other time you want to prove you are well educated. Here are four of the most commonly misused words, their correct definitions, and an explanation of how to avoid misusing them again.

Aggravate

In casual conversation, using "aggravate" synonymously as "annoy" is perfectly acceptable. In formal situations, they should not be used interchangeably. Use "aggravate" when you mean to make an already bad situation worse. Use "annoy" if you mean to irritate. So, if you are having a really bad day to begin with, the obnoxiously loud person on the subway does indeed aggravate the situation. However, if you are having a delightful day, the same person behaving the same way is annoying, not aggravating. Scratching may aggravate a rash by spreading it and making it worse. A mosquito is annoying. Generally speaking in formal writing and speech, situations become aggravated. A person becomes annoyed.

Ambivalent

A surprising number of people do not understand what *ambivalent* truly means. Yes, it is difficult to make a decision when one is ambivalent. However, most people believe it is difficult to make that decision because the person is indifferent or doesn't care one way or another about the outcome. In reality, the exact opposite is true. To be ambivalent is to care deeply about two options or outcomes that are at odds with one another. A woman who wants to marry the man she loves but does not want the responsibility of entwining her life with another's is ambivalent. A man who has been offered a dream job 5,000 miles away from his elderly parents who need his care is ambivalent. Thus, ambivalence occurs when both options carry very high stakes and the person cares deeply about both. It is never used as a synonym for indifference.

Ironic

Interestingly enough, *ironic* and its different forms are used correctly as often as they are used incorrectly. Something is ironic when it is poignantly unexpected, highlights human inconsistencies, or teaches a lesson about human nature. And what in the world does that mean? What it means is that a coincidence, even a poignant one, is just a coincidence. An ironic situation is one that moves us deeply by the unexpected and often unfair result.

Something to watch for—if there is no expectation or lesson involved, there is no irony. If a man meets a woman randomly and then discovers she is married, it is not ironic because there was no reason to expect her to be single. If, on the other hand, the same man goes out and meets a woman for the purpose of a one-night hookup, falls in love with her, and then discovers she is married and leaving town at the end of the week—that's irony. First, he had reason to expect her to be single. Second, there was a lesson about human nature: All he was looking for was a hookup and instead he found a love he couldn't have.

Irony is a tough concept to grasp. Your quick fix is to ask yourself *Was there an expectation? Was there a lesson in human nature?* If the answer to either of those questions is yes, go with irony. If not, stick with coincidence.

Peruse

Peruse has come to be used the same way the phrases *to skim* or *to glance at briefly* are used. These, however, are incorrect definitions. Peruse is actually defined exactly oppositely. If you peruse something, you read it carefully, cover to cover. You may skim a menu but you probably won't peruse it, regardless of what your server says. Perusing contracts before signing them is, on the other hand, a very good idea. When writing or speaking, be sure to use the correct definition, not the common one.

APPENDIX C

Using Roots and Prefixes to Decipher the Words You Don't Know

We have to admit something here. Even after reading this great book, you will still find unfamiliar words in books, magazines, newspapers, and tests.

One great way to learn new words is to break them down into smaller parts. Understanding these parts can help you make better educated guesses when trying to determine word meaning and usage. The following lists should be of value in uncovering the meaning of some of the new words that you will encounter in school and beyond.

Positive or Intensifying Roots

- **am, amic (love, friend):** As in *amity* (friendship) or *amicable* (friendly).
- **ben, bon (well, good):** As in *benefactor* (person who does good), *bonus* (added rewards), or *benign* (harmless).
- **fid (faith, trust):** As in *affidavit* (written oath).
- **pac (peace):** As in *pacify* (to soothe), or *pacifist* (person opposing war).
- **sacr, sanct (sacred, holy):** As in *sanctify* (make holy), *sacrosanct* (holy, most sacred), or *desecrate* (profane something sacred).
- **soph (wise, wisdom):** As in *philosophy* (search for wisdom of life).
- **vit, viv (life, lively):** As in *vitality* (animation and liveliness) or *vivacious* (spirited and lively).

Negative Roots

- **bel, bell (war):** As in *belligerent* (looking for a fight) or *bellicose* (having a hostile fighting nature).
- **err (wander, mistake):** As in *errant* (wandering, truant) or *erroneous* (full of mistakes).
- **fall, fals (untrue, false):** As in *falsify* (lie) or *infallible* (without fault).
- **mal (bad):** As in *malignant* (virulent), *malcontent* (someone discontented or dissatisfied), or *dismal* (gloomy, depressing).
- **mor, mort (death, die):** As in *mortal* (something causing death), *moribund* (dying), or *morbid* (gloomy).

Other Roots

- **agri (field, land, farm):** As in *agrarian* (having to do with farming).
- **anim (mind, spirit, soul):** As in *animated* (full of life).
- **annu, enni (year):** As in *annuity* (yearly pay) or *annual* (each year).
- **anthrop (man, mankind):** As in *anthropology* (study of humans) or *misanthrope* (one who hates people).
- **aud, audit (hear, listen to):** As in *auditory* (having to do with hearing).
- **auto (self):** As in *automatic* (self-acting) or *automobile* (self-propelled vehicle).
- **brev (short, brief):** As in *brevity* (briefness) or *abbreviation* (shortened word).
- **cap, capt, cepte, cip (take):** As in *captive* (someone taken).
- **ced, cede, cess (yield, go):** As in *concede* (to yield) or *recess* (go out).
- **chrom (color):** As in *monochromatic* (of one color).
- **chrono (time):** As in *chronology* (order in time).
- **corp (body):** As in *corpulent* (fat).
- **dem (people):** As in *democracy* (rule by the people).
- **gen (kind, birth, origin, race):** As in *engender* (found or begin) or *generic* (universal, general characteristics).
- **hem (blood):** As in *hematology* (study of blood).
- **hom, homo (man):** As in *homage* (honor a man) or *homogenous* (of the same kind).
- **man (hand):** As in *manuscript* (by hand, original) or *manipulate* (move by hand).
- **mob, mot, mov (move):** As in *mobility* (able to move) or *remote* (far removed).
- **ora (speak, pray):** As in *oral* (referring to speech) or *oracle* (prophet).
- **phon (sound):** As in *phonograph* (record player).
- **psych (mind):** As in *psychology* (study of the mind) or *psychosomatic* (between body and mind).
- **quer, quir, quis (ask, seek):** As in *query* (question) and *inquire* (ask about).
- **sci (know):** As in *conscious* (aware, knowing).
- **script (write):** As in *transcript* (written copy).
- **urb (city):** As in *urban* (of the city) or *urbane* (sophisticated and citified).
- **vert, vers (turn):** As in *avert* (turn away), or *convert* (turn from one to another).

Positive or Intensifying Prefixes

- **arch (chief):** As in *archbishop* (a bishop of the highest rank) or *architect* (designer of buildings or the chief builder).
- **bene (good, well):** As in *benefactor* (one who does good) or *benevolent* (wishing well).
- **eu (good, well, beautiful):** As in *eulogize* (speak well of someone) or *euphemism* (pleasant way of saying something unpleasant).
- **extra (beyond, outside):** As in *extraordinary* (unusual, exceptional) or *extracurricular* (outside course of studies).
- **hyper (above, excessively):** As in *hyperbole* (overstatement).
- **pro (for, before, in front of):** As in *proponent* (supporter) or *progress* (going forward or further).
- **super (over, above):** As in *supernatural* (beyond the normal) and *superintendent* (one who watches over).
- **ultra (excessively):** As in *ultraconservative* (overly conservative).

Negative Prefixes

- **an, a (without):** As in *anarchy* (without government).
- **anti (against, opposite):** As in *antidote* (remedy for poison) or *antipathy* (dislike, aversion).
- **contra (against):** As in *contradict* (disagree) or *controversy* (dispute, argument).
- **de (down, away from):** As in *debase* (lower in value) or *decant* (pour off).
- **dis, di, dif (not, apart):** As in *discord* (lack of harmony) or *diverge* (go in different directions).
- **ex, e, ef (out, off, from):** As in *exhale* (breathe out) or *eject* (throw out).
- **in, ig, il, im, ir (not):** As in *incorrect* (wrong), *illegal* (against the law), or *immature* (not fully grown).
- **mal, male (bad, badly):** As in *malediction* (curse) or *malefactor* (evildoer).
- **mis (wrong, ill, not):** As in *misbehave* (act badly) or *misfortune* (bad luck).
- **non (not):** As in *nonsense* (something absurd).
- **ob, oc, of, op (against):** As in *object* (give reasons against) or *oppose* (stand against).
- **sub, suc, suf, sug (under):** As in *subjugate* (bring under control).
- **un (not):** As in *untrue* (false).

Other Prefixes

- **ab, abs (from, away from):** As in *abduct* (lead away) or *abnormal* (away from the usual).
- **ad, ac, af, ag, an, ap, ar, as, at (to, forward):** As in *advance* (go forward) or *aggravate* (make worse).
- **ambi (both):** As in *ambivalent* (having both emotions).
- **ante (before):** As in *antebellum* (before the Civil War).
- **auto (self):** As in *automobile* (vehicle moving by itself).
- **bi (two):** As in *biennial* (every two years).
- **cata (down):** As in *cataclysm* (upheaval) or *catastrophe* (calamity).
- **circum (around):** As in *circumspect* (cautious, looking around).
- **com, co, con (with, together):** As in *combine* (merge with).
- **di (two):** As in *dichotomy* (division into parts) or *dilemma* (choice between two poor alternatives).
- **en, em (in, into):** As in *emphasize* (put stress into).
- **in, il, im, ir (in, into):** As in *invade* (go in like an enemy).
- **inter (between, among):** As in *intervene* (come between).
- **intra, intro (within):** As in *introvert* (person within himself).
- **meta (involving change):** As in *metamorphosis* (change of shape).
- **mono (one):** As in *monolithic* (uniform) or *monotony* (boring sameness).
- **multi (many):** As in *multiplicity* (numerousness).
- **neo (new):** As in *neophyte* (beginner).
- **pan (all, every):** As in *panorama* (comprehensive view) and *panacea* (cure-all).
- **per (through):** As in *perforate* (make holes through).
- **peri (around, near):** As in *perimeter* (outer boundary) and *peripheral* (marginal, outer).
- **pre (before):** As in *precede* (go before).
- **re (back, again):** As in *respond* (answer).
- **se (apart):** As in *segregate* (set apart).
- **syl, sym, syn, sys (with, together):** As in *symmetry* (congruity) or *synchronous* (at the same time with).
- **trans (across, beyond, through):** As in *transparent* (letting light through).
- **vice (in place of):** As in *vicarious* (acting as a substitute).

APPENDIX D

Words of Wisdom from a High School Student, a College Admissions Officer, and a College Student

You've almost finished this book. You should now understand the power of words and why enhancing vocabulary and cultural literacy can have a positive impact on your academic, social, and personal success. You've reviewed the definitions of more than 2,000 words, and you've learned where a number of them originated.

In the sections that follow, we offer words to consider when seeking success in high school, during the college admissions process, while at college, and throughout the rest of your life.

Six Words to Know for High School

realization *(REE-uh-lie-zay-shun), noun*
The act of bringing something into existence. Something that has been understood or accepted.

I have come to the ***REALIZATION*** *that high school is an important time, upon which I will build my future.*

Junior year is important. You realize that you are not far from college and what adults call "the rest of your life." It's not easy to look ahead when you are a teenager, because you don't want to seem too thoughtful. Realizing that you must think ahead is a bit scary, but it's something you know you have to do. Now, you also realize that a good vocabulary will lead to better grades, better SAT scores, better college essays, and, if you think about it, a better future.

preparation *(preh-puh-RAY-shun), noun*
The work or planning involved in making something or someone ready or involved in putting something together in advance.

High school really is ***PREPARATION*** *for college and more.*

Prepare yourself now for college. Start taking classes that interest you whenever possible, in addition to those you must take to meet requirements. Take elective classes that might have to do with possible college majors or careers. Even think about taking classes in the summer through special programs at local colleges or community colleges. Look at college Web sites, visit a few schools in person with your parents or friends, and talk to seniors about why they applied to certain schools or why they decided to attend specific schools. Don't wait until your senior year.

work ethic *(WERK EH-thick), noun*
A dedication to work, or a belief in the value of hard work.

Bad grades sometimes are a result of a poor ***WORK ETHIC****, not a lack of intelligence.*

High school students must start to develop, continue to build, and show others a good work ethic. Or, should I say a good *home*work ethic. Doing your homework at the same time, in the same place, and in the same way every night is a good habit to develop in high school. Good habits should never be broken; in fact, they can be strengthened when you get to college. By the time you are a junior, you should do homework because you want to, not just because your parents, teachers, or coaches say you have to. The work ethic you show on the field as an athlete, or as a club member or leader, or when you work on chores or special projects, should be as strong as your homework ethic.

confidence *(KON-fuh-dents), noun*
A belief or self-assurance in one's ability to succeed. A belief in someone or something to act in a trustworthy or reliable fashion.

It's hard to say which comes first, the chicken or the egg, or CONFIDENCE and good grades.

Be as confident as you can, because positive attitudes can lead to positive outcomes. Coaches teach that getting psyched up can influence how you play, and that visualizing success in your mind can lead to actual success on the field. It's easy to say "Be confident" and "Don't stress about the present or future," but if you can really turn these words into feelings, you can build unstoppable momentum. Each year in school has prepared you for the next, so you should feel more and more confident as you progress. By junior year your overall confidence should be strong. If it isn't, make it stronger by working harder and finding others who will say good things about your efforts.

self-knowledge *(self-NAH-ludge), noun*
An understanding of oneself, particularly one's abilities, character, and motives.

It has been said that the most important knowledge that you hope to gain is SELF-KNOWLEDGE.

By your junior year, you begin to learn who you are and what you want others to know about you. Do you like being known as a good student, an athlete, a good listener, a funny person, a good friend, or all of these? Do others know your true feelings, or are you afraid to share them? Know what you can and, when necessary, cannot do. Don't put yourself in positions to fail unless they can make you stronger. But do try to take risks if you can learn from them. Know who you are now and who you want to be in the future, and don't be afraid to let others know.

commencement *(kuh-MENTS-munt), noun*
The act of beginning or starting. Also, a ceremony for conferring degrees or granting diplomas at the end of an academic year.

*Your **COMMENCEMENT** ceremony marks both an end and a beginning.*

While some call it "graduation," others call it "commencement." It means the beginning of the rest of your life, not just the end of high school. Learn from the past, and look forward to the future. It is a little bit scary, but it is your future and it will be great.

Nine Words to Know in College

change *(CHAYNJ), noun*
Alteration, variation, or modification (important rhyming words) or the results of these. A variance from a routine or pattern, most often a welcomed one.

***CHANGE** is scary but necessary as one grows.*

College brings big change, and not just to your address. Your whole world changes, from academics to friends, food, sleep patterns, study habits, and social life. Realize from the beginning just how much change you will have to face. Welcome change as natural to diminish anxiety, and it will make the transition easier. Change is good!

advisor *(ad-VIE-zur), noun*
Someone who gives advice. Someone who advises students on academic issues, including course selection.

*College **ADVISORS** are always crucial, yet the best ones are not always those officially assigned the job.*

When you walk into a class, don't just consider whether a professor or subject matter will be interesting. Think about whether this person would make a good formal or informal advisor. In college, your advisor is your strongest advocate, your source of advice, and your friend—or can be, if you choose well. At some schools, you have a general advisor or a group of general advisors available until you declare your major. After that, you are either assigned or you select someone from within your chosen academic department to serve as your "major advisor." But please, don't limit those who serve as advisors to persons who hold specific titles. Everyone can and should be thought of as an advisor and advocate. The sooner you identify a faculty member, administrator, or older peer who can be an active listener and inspirational counselor, the sooner you can start building a relationship that can truly help your college career.

independence *(in-duh-PEN-dunts), noun*
Freedom from dependence on or control by another.

INDEPENDENCE at college is a blessing, a curse, and ultimately a gift to be used wisely.

College offers growth potential and independence like you have never had before. Embrace it and use it for good. Just because your parents aren't around doesn't mean you should go crazy. Well, it's almost as simple as that. Establish good habits on your own. Learning how to be independent, how to schedule time well, will only help you have more fun, less stress, and fonder memories as college progresses.

For me, independence means identifying daily and weekly to-do lists or goals and then scheduling time to complete them. Knowing what I have to do, and when, helps me stay on track and, frankly, independent. If assignments and readings take control of you because you have ignored them, then you are clearly not very independent. If you maintain control over them, then you are the master of your academic, social, athletic, and personal schedule. And you can get some sleep in as well.

choice *(CHOYSE), noun*
The power or chance to choose among different things; the decision to select one thing, person, or course of action over another.

*The **CHOICES** between one class and another, one teacher or another, or one major and another are just some of those that you can expect at college.*

Classes, professors, living arrangements, going to the game, dinner, sleep? Should I cram for that exam, or have I studied enough? What major and why? College offers so many, many choices. While at times you feel that you have to make these choices alone, in truth you always have someone to turn to if you need advice. So don't rush into important academic or life-altering decisions, but don't fret over them either. Seek feedback from friends, family, faculty, and professional advisors when needed. Don't sweat the small stuff, and always think about consequences, especially when you are deciding whether you've studied enough and if it is time for a little fun. Do take advantage of the great opportunities college has to offer. It is a once-in-a-lifetime scenario. Learn how and when to make serious choices and when to be spontaneous and intuitive.

add/drop *(ad-drop), adjective*
Referring to the practice of allowing one to change one's original selection of academic courses by adding or removing courses after the beginning of the semester.

During the ADD/DROP period you have the time to decide which courses are really right for you.

Thank goodness that many decisions, including those about course selection, are not permanent. That's one of the beauties of college. Don't be afraid to sign up for a class or two that may be out of the norm. In fact, when you want to carry a load of five classes, do sign up for six, or if you want to finally narrow down to four, you can start with five or six. Even as a first-semester freshman (although many don't realize it), you can shop for and try on classes to see if they fit. Attend classes for a week or two to see if they fit your schedule, your academic areas of interest, or your long-term goals. If you hate the class, or there are scheduling conflicts, or if you are not in the mood to write the five required papers, you can always drop it, as long as you do so before your school's add/drop deadline. In fact, these two words, or one "slashed word," may be among the most important and practical for you to know.

time management *(time MA-nidge-ment), noun*
The process of deciding how to divide the amount of time available among various tasks and activities.

Once you are living on your own, good TIME MANAGEMENT is an essential skill.

For most students there are no required or supervised study halls in college, and no teachers, coaches, or parents will hound you to do your homework or show up for practice or class. College in most circumstances offers the structure of scheduled classes, but few other chronological requirements are part of any given day. You need to make your own daily and weekly schedule and stick to it. Find ways to put your schedule on paper, in a spreadsheet, or a PDA. Keep your schedule handy, regularly update it, and reward yourself when you stay on target. Personal rewards, whether a latté, some TV, DVD, or CD time, or an IM to friends, reinforce positive time-management behaviors. The stuff that adults and other books tell you is true. Time management is the key to college success.

experience *(EK-spear-ee-uhns), noun*
Involvement in an activity, or exposure to events or people, leading to an increase in knowledge and skills. Knowledge of and skills gained by being involved in or exposed to something over time.

Do maximize the quantity and quality of ***EXPERIENCES*** *you have in college.*

Where else can you give blood at lunchtime, and then play inner-tube water polo; learn about the ocean floor before breakfast, then go back to bed; or, after a very busy day, go to a hockey game and party until tomorrow? College is a unique blend of eclectic experiences. Don't be afraid to try new things! And, as that old saying goes, "Learn from experience, for it is the best teacher."

home *(HOME), noun*
Where a person or family lives together. The place where a person finds refuge, security, and safety, where they can receive rest, nourishment, and shelter.

HOME *for some is thought to be where one's heart is, but for all it is where both one's head and heart are.*

College isn't just a place where you study. It is that proverbial home away from home. For approximately four years, it is where you sleep, socialize, dine on the finest cuisine (just kidding!), and learn by reading, listening, and questioning. The sooner you make college your home, the better. Once you feel secure in this setting, success follows in all areas of this new life. But never forget that you can have two or more homes; two places where the people you love share space, and where you can feel safe and nurtured. Yes, home is where your heart and head are. It's an attitude and not just a place. Look for it, and you will find it wherever you go.

fun *(PHUHN), noun*
A feeling or an activity that provides a time of enjoyment or amusement.

It's strange, but some think it's ***FUN*** *to be in the library when it closes.*

Don't forget to have fun! With the stress of the known, of midterms, papers, and finals, and the unknown, of the future, you can lose sight of the fact that college is fun! Well, it is! So go out and have some!

These are the words that I hope will help you realize what college is about. Build a strong foundation for the four years after high school (college), and beyond (life in the real world). The words that make up your written and verbal vocabulary are really the brick and mortar upon which the exciting edifices (a great word, that one) of your life will be constructed and constantly renovated. Words do create worlds—literary, social, academic, and career worlds. Use them to create the best places for you and those you love.